KT-481-973

Explorer Florida

Emma Stanford

Front cover
Top: *Art deco buildings along Ocean Drive, Miami (J. Davison)*
Centre (left to right): *(a): Palm tree (J. A. Tims); (b): Detail of a hamburger (J. A. Tims); (c): The killer whale, Lolita, at Seaquarium (J. Davison); (d): Symbol of the Sunshine State (P. Bennett); (e): Angel fish at Key West Aquarium (J. A. Tims)*
Back cover
Left: *Miami's South Beach (J. Davison);*
Right: *Duelling Dragos (Universal Orlando)*
Spine: *Flamingo Lagoon at SeaWorld*

Page 2: *number plates*
Page 3: *lifeguard's hut, Fort Lauderdale*
Page 4: *oak tree, Panhandle*
Page 5: *(a) American alligator*
Page 5: *(b) Bahia Mar yacht marina*
Page 6: *Gumbo Limbo Nature Trail*
Pages 6/7: *Fort Lauderdale beach*
Page 7: *boat at John Pennekamp Coral Reef State Park*
Page 8: *on the Anhinga Trail, Everglades National Park*
Page 9: *launch of the Space Shuttle* Columbia
Page 51: *South Beach*
Page 109: *detail of a shiny 'hog'*
Page 137: *'The Spirit of Ecstasy'*
Page 173: *colorful shells, Captiva Island*
Page 199: *palm tree*
Page 237: *water-bike on St. Pete Beach*

Written by Emma Stanford
Updated by Lindsay Bennett

Published by AA Publishing, a trading name of Automobile Association Developments Limited, whose registered office is Fanum House, Basing View, Basingstoke, Hampshire, RG21 4EA. Registered number 1878835.

ISBN-10: 0-7495-4751-0
ISBN-13: 978 07495 475 1

A CIP catalogue record for this book is available from the British Library.

Color separation by KDP, Kingsclere, UK
Printed and bound in Italy by Printer Trento Srl

Find out more about AA Publishing and the wide range of travel publications and services the AA provides by visiting our website at www.theAA.com/bookshop.

Revised fifth edition 2006
First published 1993

Titles in the Explorer series:
Australia • Boston & New England • Britain • Brittany
California • Canada • Caribbean • China • Costa Rica • Crete
Cuba • Cyprus • Egypt • Florence & Tuscany • Florida
France • Germany • Greek Islands • Hawaii • India • Ireland
Italy • Japan • London • Mallorca • Mexico • New York
New Zealand • Paris • Portugal • Provence • Rome
San Francisco • Scotland • South Africa • Spain • Thailand
Tunisia • Turkey • Venice • Vietnam

A02413

How to use this book

ORGANIZATION

Florida Is, Florida Was

Discusses aspects of life and culture in contemporary Florida and explores significant periods in its history.

A–Z

Breaks the state down into regional chapters, and covers places to visit, including walks and drives. Within this section fall the Focus On articles, which consider a variety of subjects in greater detail.

Travel Facts

Contains the practical information that is vital for a successful trip.

Accommodations and Restaurants

Lists places to stay and places to eat alphabetically by region. Entries are graded budget, moderate or expensive.
Hotels:
Expensive over $180
Moderate $120–180
Budget under $120
Restaurants:
Expensive over $40
Moderate $25–40
Budget under $25

ABOUT THE RATINGS

Most of the places described in this book have been given a separate rating. These are as follows:

►►► **Do not miss**

►► **Highly recommended**

► **Worth seeing**

Contents

TURTLE
CROSSING

TONS O' FUN
GLASS BOTTOM & SNORKEL TOURS

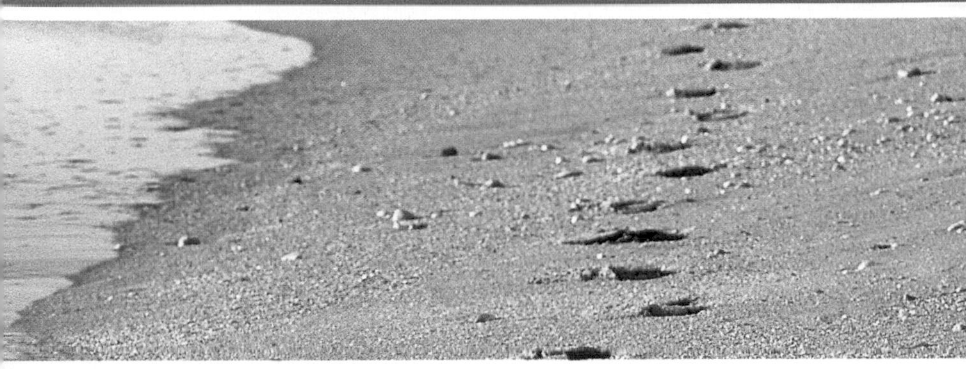

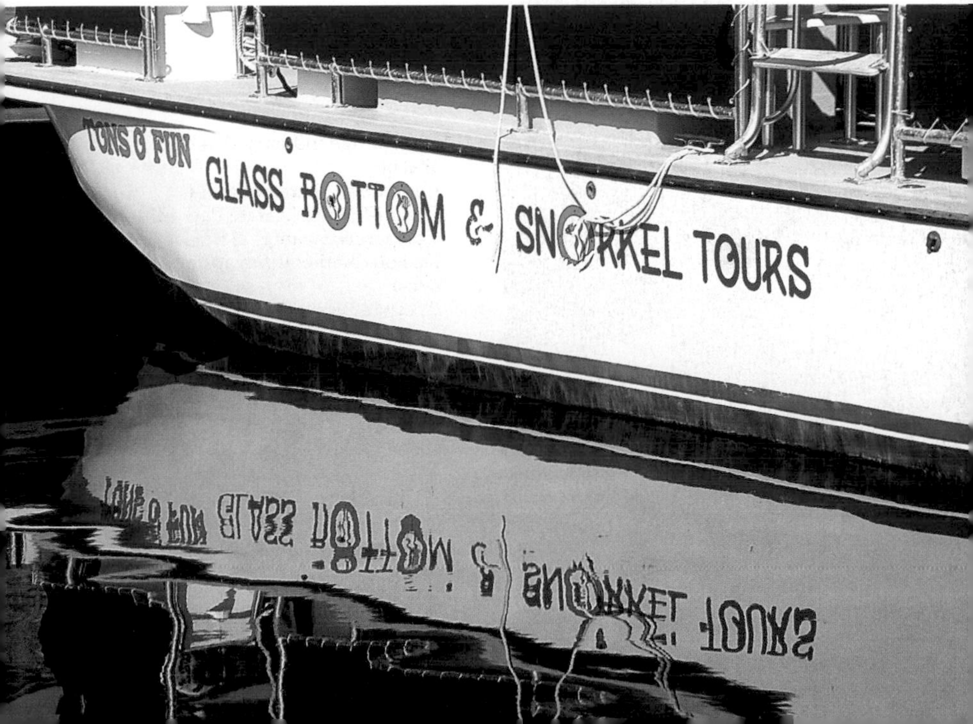

Emma Stanford has written, edited and contributed to a variety of books on California, Hawaii, the Caribbean, France and Spain, as well as Mediterranean port guides for the US Navy.

My Florida

The green heron sat with his back to me studiously ignoring my poised camera, and continued to survey the brackish water for signs of life—and lunch. A moorhen stepped gingerly from lilypad to lilypad; above, a pair of snowy egrets preened in an elaborate courtship ritual. I'd decided to pass on the alligator-wrestling and, instead, ended up transfixed by one of Florida's most appealing sideshows, the spectacular birdlife that had 19th-century naturalist John James Audubon falling off his perch with excitement as he toured the Florida Keys with a sketch-book in the 1830s.

Florida's main events—art deco in Miami Beach, Orlando's amazing theme parks, the subtropical Florida Keys, fabulous golfing, blinding white-sand beaches—are every bit as alluring as the brochures claim. But, for me, part of the fun is to venture beyond the hype and discover some of Florida's less well-publicized attractions.

The Great Outdoors, showcased by Florida's admirable network of well-maintained state parks, is one surprise. The peninsula may be flat for the most part, but it is far from featureless. Woodland trails and wildlife spotting, canoe runs and snorkeling or diving in freshwater springs make a grand change from foot-slogging around the theme parks. There is superb fishing from piers, jetties and bridges, or Hemingwayesque types can head for deeper waters on the trail of wahoo, tarpon and marlin.

On the cultural front, Florida offers several world-class art galleries, while there is a growing interest in the state's colorful past with restored historic houses, ancient Native American sites and local history museums offering a fascinating insight into early Florida lifestyles from the Native Americans encountered by 16th-century Spanish explorers to pirates, planters and pioneer farmers.

Florida is an ideal two-center vacation destination, so venture out beyond Miami and the theme park experience and explore another side of the Sunshine State.

Emma Stanford

Florida Is & Was

GEORGIA
ALABAMA
Crestview
Ponce de León
Marianna
L Seminole
Milton
Monticello
Chattahoochee
Maclay State Gardens
Fort Walton Beach
Quincy
Pensacola
Point Washington
Tallahassee
National Museum of Naval Aviation
Apalachicola
Wakulla Springs
Panama City
St Marks
Perry
Apalachee Bay
Port St Joe
Apalachicola
Cape San Blas
St George Island
0 50 100 150 200 km
0 50 100 miles

Movie set in Miami

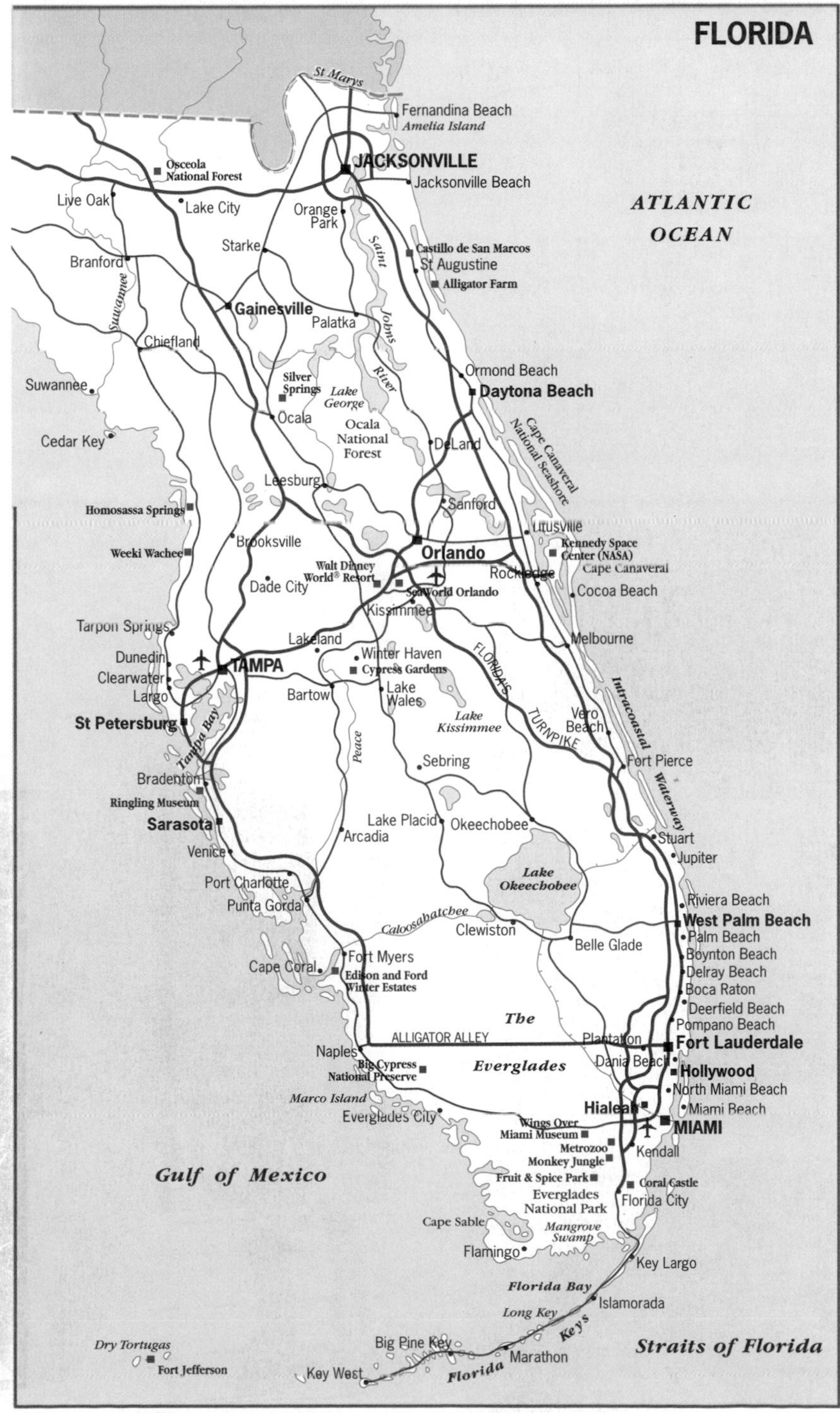
FLORIDA
ATLANTIC OCEAN
Gulf of Mexico
Straits of Florida
St Marys
Fernandina Beach
Amelia Island
JACKSONVILLE
Jacksonville Beach
Osceola National Forest
Live Oak
Lake City
Orange Park
Starke
Castillo de San Marcos
St Augustine
Alligator Farm
Branford
Suwannee
Gainesville
Palatka
Saint Johns River
Chiefland
Suwannee
Silver Springs
Lake George
Ormond Beach
Daytona Beach
Cedar Key
Ocala
Ocala National Forest
DeLand
Cape Canaveral National Seashore
Leesburg
Sanford
Homosassa Springs
Titusville
Kennedy Space Center (NASA)
Cape Canaveral
Brooksville
Orlando
Weeki Wachee
Walt Disney World® Resort
Rockledge
Dade City
SeaWorld Orlando
Cocoa Beach
Kissimmee
Tarpon Springs
Lakeland
Melbourne
Dunedin
TAMPA
Winter Haven
Cypress Gardens
Clearwater
Largo
Bartow
Lake Wales
Florida's Turnpike
St Petersburg
Tampa Bay
Lake Kissimmee
Vero Beach
Intracoastal Waterway
Peace
Sebring
Fort Pierce
Bradenton
Ringling Museum
Lake Placid
Okeechobee
Sarasota
Arcadia
Stuart
Venice
Jupiter
Lake Okeechobee
Port Charlotte
Punta Gorda
Riviera Beach
Caloosahatchee
West Palm Beach
Clewiston
Palm Beach
Belle Glade
Fort Myers
Boynton Beach
Cape Coral
Edison and Ford Winter Estates
Delray Beach
Boca Raton
Deerfield Beach
The Everglades
Pompano Beach
Alligator Alley
Plantation
Fort Lauderdale
Naples
Big Cypress National Preserve
Dania Beach
Hollywood
North Miami Beach
Marco Island
Hialeah
Miami Beach
Everglades City
Wings Over Miami Museum
MIAMI
Metrozoo
Monkey Jungle
Kendall
Fruit & Spice Park
Coral Castle
Everglades National Park
Florida City
Cape Sable
Mangrove Swamp
Flamingo
Key Largo
Florida Bay
Islamorada
Long Key
Florida Keys
Dry Tortugas
Big Pine Key
Fort Jefferson
Marathon
Key West

11

If you were to pick a tree to represent northern Florida it would be the stately live oak, while the symbol of the south would be the palm. In central Florida, the citrus family rules, and groves of glossy orange, lemon, grapefruit and lime trees bask in the famous Florida sunshine.

Florida and orange juice go hand-in-hand. As far as statistics go, the state is one of the world's largest citrus-growing regions and its groves produce around 25 percent of the orange juice and 50 percent of the grapefruit juice on the world market. Spanish explorers introduced oranges to Florida in the 16th century, and by the time the first grapefruit was planted in 1825, wild orange trees could be found all over the state. With the introduction of water and rail transportation in the 1880s, citrus multiplied in the central Florida region. The glossy-leaved groves spread southeast to Indian River, around Fort Pierce, then down to Miami after the frosts of 1894–95. The marvelously fragrant white orange blossom was adopted as Florida's official state flower in 1909; orange juice became the state beverage in 1967.

AN INFINITE VARIETY Florida's citrus fruits come in all shapes and sizes—hefty Duncan white and rosy-pink grapefruits, oranges, tangerines, tangelos (tangerine-grapefruits), Temple oranges (tangerine-oranges), lemons, limes and the nut-size kumquat. Marmalade, preserves, candies, orange-blossom honey and even citrus wine are a tribute to the ingenuity of local residents.

Most citrus fruits require at least 300 days of sunshine and take 12 months to mature. The citrus harvest begins in October with grapefruits and ends in July with oranges. Ripe fruits can be left on the tree for several months, so it is not unusual to see last year's crop surrounded by the new season's blossoms. A mature grapefruit tree can produce around 1,000 fruits each season.

A Florida citrus grove

KEY LIME PIE The Key lime is a small, round, yellowish-colored fruit that is a Florida specialty, and the essential ingredient of Key lime pie. This delicious tangy dessert is said to have been invented by a cook named Sarah at the Curry Mansion in Key West. However, the exact construction of Key lime pie—the consistency of the pie crust, and the choice between meringue (for purists) or whipped cream topping—remains a contentious issue in kitchens across the state (see suggested recipe).

Key lime pie filling
4 eggs
14 oz. can condensed milk
½ cup Key lime juice
1 tsp. lemon extract
8 tbs. sugar
Separate eggs. Beat together yolks, condensed milk and juice. Add one pinch salt. Beat whites to soft peaks; add lemon extract and beat in sugar. Fold one-third of egg-white mixture into lime filling and place in pie shell. Top with remaining egg white. Bake at 350°F/180°C for 20–25 minutes. Chill before serving.

Trucking the oranges

TASTE THEM FRESH! Roadside stalls piled high with fresh fruit and vegetables are a familiar sight throughout Florida. Beyond Greater Miami's city limits, Miami-Dade County is one of the top 100 citrus-producing counties in the United States. The winter "market basket" of Homestead is laden with avocados (once known as alligator pears), cucumbers, cantaloupes and watermelons, limes, strawberries and tomatoes. Buy them from farmers' markets or roadside stalls or stop by a U-pick for a real taste experience.

In the central region, look for glossy purple eggplants (aubergines), squashes and okra. There are apples, pears and pecans in the north.

BLACK GOLD The fertile drained Everglades region around Lake Okeechobee is another source of fruit and vegetables. It is also the land of black gold—not oil, in this case, but sugarcane. Its huge sugarcane crop makes Clewiston the sugar capital of the state. Half the nation's raw sugar consumption (around 1.5 million lbs/675,000kg) is hand-harvested here by machete-wielding laborers. Clewiston's other claim to fame is its cabbage-palm business, which supplies the fresh hearts of palm dished up in chic Florida restaurants.

The southern corner of the state yields an abundance of exotic tropical fruits. Home-grown bananas, carambolas (star fruit), figs, guavas and papayas can be found in local supermarkets. The origins of the mango crop can be traced back to a shipment of 35 mango trees delivered from Calcutta in 1888.

❑ Florida will use any excuse for a festival. For two fruit-inspired extravaganzas, check out the annual Plant City Strawberry Festival in February and June's Monticello Watermelon Festival, whose hotly contested melon seed-spittin' competition requires unusual skills. ❑

Anchored to the North American continent by Georgia and Alabama, the Florida peninsula is bordered on each side by salt water. The state can claim a tidal shoreline extending over 8,000 miles (12,880km) via hundreds of sandy beaches, wide bays, estuaries, lagoons and a host of offshore islands.

AROUND THE COAST Florida's east coast is protected from the Atlantic by a string of barrier islands. These islands taper off like stepping stones into the gentle curve of the Florida Keys to Key West, just 90 miles (145km) from Cuba. The rounded southern tip of the peninsula holds the Everglades, a vast swampland region that stretches over 10 million acres (4 million hectares) and crumbles into the waterways of the Ten Thousand Islands region off Florida's lower west coast. Sandbars and islands line the west coast and Gulf of Mexico, while the northern Gulf shore of the Panhandle offers some of the finest barrier-island beaches, created by blinding white quartz sand washed down from the Appalachian Mountains over thousands of years. Areas of these magnificent coastal dunes are protected as part of the **Gulf Islands National Seashore** (see page 245).

FLOWING WATER Inland northern Florida is a land of rolling hills and pine forests, criss-crossed by freshwater springs and swift tannin-stained rivers like the Apalachicola, Blackwater and Suwannee. Below Florida's thin soil, deep fissures in the limestone foundations release freshwater springs fed by subterranean watercourses.

Wakulla Springs, south of Tallahassee, claims to be one of the world's deepest springs, pouring forth gallons of water per minute. At **Florida Caverns State Park**, near Marianna, you can look below the earth's surface. This is the only place in the state where the water table drops sufficiently enough to reveal spectacular stalagmites and stalactites in limestone caverns.

STILL WATERS A low ridge extends from the north into the lakeland region of central Florida. Forests give way to prairie land and an estimated 30,000-plus lakes and ponds varying in depth from a few inches to around 30 feet (9m). **Lake Okeechobee** is the second largest body of fresh water wholly within the United States, some 750sq miles (1,943sq km) in total area, but only 14ft (4m) deep at its lowest point. This freshwater reservoir is the starting point of the Everglades, the primary source of a 50-mile-wide (80.5km) river of grass that extends across the state to the Gulf of Mexico. The 1.5-million acre (600,000ha) **Everglades National Park** covers only one-seventh of the true Everglades region, but acts as showcase for its diverse flora and fauna.

THE EVERGLADES Patches of brilliant green herald the presence of hardwood "hammocks," the local name for stands of trees that have found a slightly elevated limestone outcrop on which to take root above the swamp. Ranging in size from just a few feet to several acres, they are a refuge for bobcats, deer, hawks, owls and other wildlife. Pinelands and areas of cypress swamp (one of the finest for sightseeing purposes is **Corkscrew Swamp**) also provide useful animal habitats. Coastal mangrove forests flourish where the Everglades meet the Gulf. The nutrient-rich, brackish water trapped in the mangroves' complex root system creates an ideal habitat for numerous native animals and birds.

BAYS AND ISLANDS The mangrove-lined back bays of the west coast are a fascinating unofficial wildlife refuge teeming with fish and wading

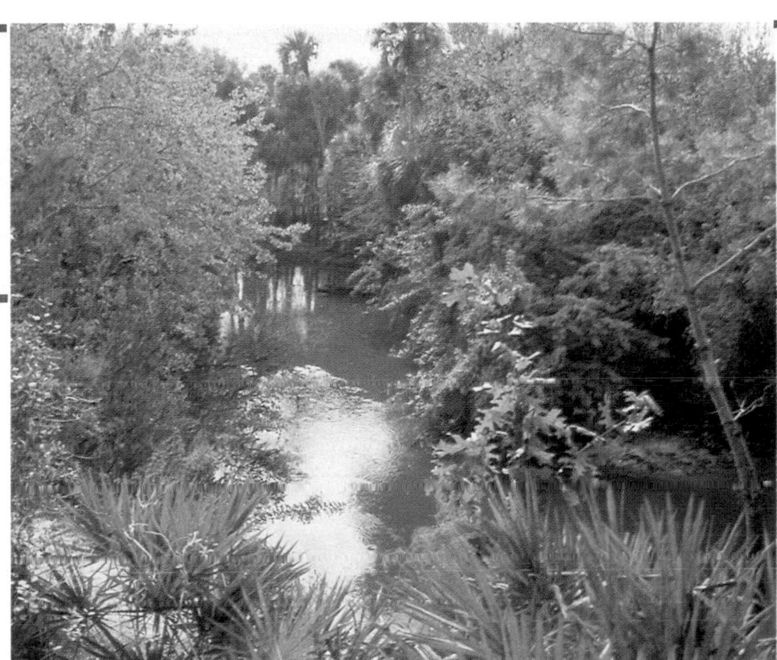

Florida's watery wildernesses provide refuge for a wide variety of creatures

birds. This is a favorite haunt of manatees, too. These gentle, endangered 3,000 lb (1350kg) sea cows enjoy a plentiful supply of river weed and water hyacinths in the warmer waters. On the Gulf, the islands of **Sanibel** and **Captiva** are renowned for their seashell beaches, as is **Cayo Costa State Park**, where sea turtles lay their eggs. **Pine Island Sound** is a favorite playground of the friendly bottlenose dolphin.

❏ Midway up the east coast, nature lovers should not miss two exceptional protected areas: the **Canaveral National Seashore** and **Merritt Island National Wildlife Refuge**. The latter harbors 21 endangered species in its freshwater lagoons, salt-water marshes and hammocks—all close to the Kennedy Space Center. In winter, the population is swelled by a magnificent roll call of migrating birds. ❏

THE FLORIDA KEYS are a 150-mile (241km) chain of fossilized coral-rock islands, short on beaches but fringed by reefs. Vegetation is sparse, with pockets of tropical hardwoods, slash pine, mangroves and prickly pears. The Gulf Stream flows in a northerly direction around the Florida Keys and the southern tip of the peninsula, warming the reef-strewn seas. This is a diver's paradise, well-served by aquatic parks like the **John Pennekamp Coral Reef State Park** off Key Largo and the vast **Biscayne National Park**, south of Miami. The Atlantic waters as far north as the Gold Coast are still warm enough for diving.

Dolphins haunt west coast bays

Florida's subtropical climate, with its distinct growing seasons, is augmented by extraordinarily diverse natural habitats that support a wealth of native and imported plant life. Brilliant hibiscus, oleander, colorful azaleas, scented gardenias and clouds of bougainvillea gladden the eye; palms, sea grapes and magnificent live oaks cast welcoming shadows in the heat.

EVERGLADES FLORA Botanists from around the world have marveled at the sheer variety of plant life that flourishes in Florida. No fewer than 2,000 plant species, both temperate and tropical, grow side by side in the Everglades. **Sawgrass**, a marsh plant edged with small sharp teeth and a menace to explorers, predominates in the region, accounting for nearly 8 million Everglades acres (3.2 million hectares).

Willows, **pines** and tropical hardwoods, such as **mahogany** and **live oak**, grow on outcrops of limestone creating shady hammocks. The **gumbo limbo**, affectionately known as the "tourist tree" for its peeling red bark, reminiscent of sunburned skin, is also found here. An unwelcome addition is the parasitic **strangler fig**. Its seed, carried on the wind or by birds, lodges in the host tree; as the strangler fig grows, it drops a tangled mass of aerial roots to the ground while wrapping itself around the host trunk, depriving it of light, water and nutrients.

Hammock woods are also festooned with air plants (epiphytes) such as **orchids** and **bromeliads**. Although attached to a host tree, these plants are nonparasitic, gathering water and nutrients that run down the bark. **Spanish moss**, which tumbles from live oaks and cypresses, is another epiphyte.

In addition to lovely orchids like the creamy vanilla orchid, mule-ears and fragant night-blooming epidendrum, there is a wealth of beautiful Everglades flowers. These include colorful pink gerardia, morning glory, spider lilies, purple pickerel weed and Glades lobelia, yellow carpets of splatterdock and water lilies.

An exotic hibiscus bloom

❏ For a gentle introduction into what plants to look for, visitors to Miami should head for the peaceful surroundings of Fairchild Tropical Botanic Garden, in South Miami. Other glorious gardens include A. B. Maclay State Gardens in Tallahassee; Cypress Gardens in Winter Haven; Harry P. Leu Gardens in Orlando; Marie Selby Botanical Gardens in Sarasota; and Washington Oaks State Gardens in Anastasia Island. The prize for the biggest banyan tree is captured by the Edison Winter Estate in Fort Myers. ❏

Native Keys palms

TREES OF THE SWAMPLANDS
Cypress trees can grow at depths of water in which most trees would drown. It is thought that their curious conelike "knees" help them to breathe. Dwarf **pond cypress** is the most common variety. Though few lofty **bald cypresses** survived the 1930s lumber era, you can see these formidable 600- to 700-year-old giants still in Big Cypress National Preserve and Corkscrew Swamp, north of Everglades National Park.

PINES AND PALMS On higher ground, **saw-palmetto** and **slash-pine** forests survive on next to no soil, finding purchase in hollows and potholes filled with a rich residue of peat and marl. The feathery, non-native **Australian pine**, found throughout Florida, is considered a pest. This tree is fast encroaching upon native species, and determined attempts are being made to eradicate it.

Palms are an essential ingredient of the Florida skyline. Of the hundreds of palms to be seen, 11 species are native to the state. **Cabbage palms**, **coconut palms**, **queen palms** and the elegant **royal palm** appear in hammocks and along the roads, as do the tall, thin **Washingtonia palm** and the fantail **traveler's palm**, while the squat **jelly palm** is common in northern parts of the state. In the Panhandle, glossy **magnolia** forests interrupt the endless march of pine, and the live oaks in this area are awe-inspiring.

PLANTS OF THE COAST Mangroves form probably the single most important plant system in Florida. They stabilize the shoreline, reduce storm damage, filter runoffs and feed and harbor a multitude of land, sea and air creatures. Their ability to obtain fresh water from salt water is unique. There are several types of mangroves, such as **red mangroves**, supported on arched prop roots, which grow closest to the water's edge. **Black mangroves** push up hundreds of pencil-thin root tips (pneumatophores) to help them breathe. **White** and **buttonwood mangroves** are found higher up the shore.

Coastal hammocks are **sea grape** territory, with their round, leathery leaves and bunches of fruit used to make jellies. Clumps of **sea oats** anchor the coastal dunes and are protected by law.

Florida's abundant bird life guarantees good birdwatching. On an early-morning stroll along the beach you'll almost certainly spot brown pelicans, gulls galore, terns, scurrying sanderlings and maybe a cormorant or two.

EARLY RECORDS Florida's birds have fascinated and enchanted visitors from the early days. One of the first records of native bird life, Catesby's *Natural History of Carolina, Florida and the Bahama Islands*, was published in London in 1731. A century later, renowned American ornithologist John James Audubon ventured down through Florida to Key West gathering material for his epic *Birds of America*. Audubon's detailed descriptions of the rare roseate spoonbill, flocks of flamingos and pristine white snowy egret "arrayed in more brilliant apparel than I have seen before" were translated into beautiful etchings. Yet less than a century ago these same birds were on the verge of extinction, slaughtered for their gorgeous plumage, a popular period-fashion accessory.

BIRDS OF THE WETLANDS
Everglades National Park is one of the most remarkable natural preserves in the world. Together with its northern neighbors, Big Cypress and Corkscrew swamps, it supports an extraordinary treasury of bird life. As well as providing sanctuary, they are a prime breeding and feeding ground for myriad species of wading birds. The **roseate spoonbill** has survived here, though it is still on the endangered list. A Florida native with rose-colored plumage, red eyes and a bald head, it has a distinctive spatulate beak that it sweeps from side to side to trap food.

The endangered **wood stork** nests in swampland cypress hammocks. Largely white, it has black-tipped wings with a span of more than 5ft (1.5m); it feeds for fish using its sensitive beak to feel beneath the water's surface. White clusters of apple-snail eggs cling to Everglades trees and plants from May through September. The adult snails are the sole diet of the few hundred remaining **Everglades kites**, with their curved bills designed for extracting the snails' bodies. The eggs are also an important food source for the jerky-legged **limpkin**, an ibis-like wading bird.

❑ One of the strangest birds is the anhinga, or snakebird, which swims through the water with only its thin, flexible neck above the surface. Anhingas dive to skewer fish on their pointed beaks, surface, flip their catch into the air and retrieve and swallow it with practiced aplomb. Despite its aquatic lifestyle, the anhinga's feathers are not waterproof, so it is common to see it drying its wings by the water's edge. ❑

HERONS, EGRETS AND PELICANS
The **great blue heron** and dainty **little blue heron** can be seen throughout the state. The Keys are the best place to spot the **great white heron**, which stands almost 5ft tall (1.5m). Its yellow-green legs distinguish it from the **great egret**, which stalks on spindly black legs.

The smaller **snowy egret** barely survived the plume hunters. Its beak and legs are black, but its large feet are gold-colored. **Cattle egrets** arrived from Africa in the 1950s. They feed off insects disturbed by cattle and can often be spotted perched on a cow's back.

The ubiquitous **brown pelican** is a familiar sight on the coast, perched on pilings, bobbing on the swell, or skimming low over the waves in search of food.

Purple gallinule

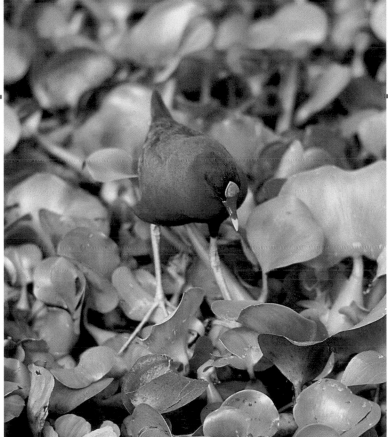

RAPTORS Birds of prey are a dramatic addition to Florida's wide blue skies. The handsome **red-shouldered hawk**, with its black-and-white back feathers and reddish breast, lives off frogs, lizards and snakes. It can often be seen perched on telegraph poles or fence posts near roadsides. **Ospreys** are also seen throughout the state, building nests close to water where they catch fish using their powerful talons.

Among other birds of prey are graceful **swallow-tailed kites**, **black** and **turkey vultures** and the endangered **Southern bald eagle**. Rangers in the Everglades and at Merritt Island, on the Atlantic coast, will point out the eagles' enormous nests, which can measure more than 6ft (1.8m) across.

BIRDS OF THE WOODLANDS In woods throughout the state, woodpeckers can be heard if not seen, drilling into dead wood for beetles and ants. The **pileated woodpecker** has a distinctive red crest that contrasts with the black plumage on its back. Another woodland resident, the **barred owl** is named for the distinctive brown stripes on its breast. Also look for minute **gnatcatchers** zipping around the bushes, or the crimson flash of a jaunty **red cardinal**.

The alligator is to Florida what the kangaroo is to Australia—part of the scenery and a favorite tourist attraction. The world's first alligator attraction, the St. Augustine Alligator Farm on Anastasia Island, was founded in 1893, leading the way for a host of imitators.

THE AMERICAN ALLIGATOR An adult male alligator can grow up to 16ft (4.8m) or more, though most are around 12ft (3.6m), and females are usually 8 to 9ft (2.4–2.7m) in length. These cold-blooded reptiles need to bask in the sun to warm up enough to function. During the winter dry season, they earn the sobriquet "Keeper of the Everglades," because they fulfill an important role by digging sizable "gator holes" in the ground. Water seeps up to fill these holes, providing life-sustaining oases for plants, birds, fish and other animals. Alligators mate in the spring, and the female lays 20–60 leathery eggs around June. If the temperature rises above 90°F (32°C), the hatchlings will be male; if it falls below 87°F (30.5°C) they will be female. Baby alligators feed themselves from the start, hunting crayfish, frogs, insects and snakes. Alligators will eat anything. They may appear slow and awkward, but they can move at frightening speeds, and their powerful jaws can snap shut with massive force. Do not attempt to feed them or you could end up on their lunch menu.

THE AMERICAN CROCODILE This shy reptile is a much rarer sight, found only in the saltwater Florida Bay area. A lighter greenish gray color, crocodiles have narrow tapering snouts, and the teeth of their upper and lower jaws are visible in profile (an alligator's lower set of teeth fits inside its upper jaw).

ON THE ENDANGERED LIST Florida's most visible endangered mammal is the **manatee** (see panel page 204), a huge and gentle sea cow that inhabits rivers and coastal areas. Here the slow-moving creature is particularly at risk from boat traffic (41 percent of manatee deaths are caused by watercraft collisions). The best time to see manatees is during the cool winter months (Nov–Mar) when they venture upstream to find warm spring waters. An endangered Everglades inhabitant is the beautiful tawny **Florida panther**. The 30–50 remaining big cats, 6ft (1.8m) long and weighing 60–130lbs (27–58kg), are seriously threatened by the

Young alligators are on their own as soon as they leave the egg

Gently smiling jaws

destruction of their natural habitat through (among other things) mercury poisoning in the food chain. Female panthers can give birth to two to four kittens every other year, while an adult male will range more than 500sq miles (1,295sq km) hunting for deer, raccoons, wild pigs and other prey.

The dainty **Key deer** is perhaps living on borrowed time as development eats away its limited habitat on Big Pine Key and the surrounding islands. The smallest subspecies of the white-tailed deer, Key deer grow to only around 24–28in (60cm) in height. Around 70 out of a population numbering around 800 deer are killed by drivers every year.

OTHER MAMMALS Raccoons and opossums share an often fatal attraction for highways. **Raccoons** that make it across can be seen along the water's edge searching for food, while **opossums**, along with **squirrels** and **wild turkeys**, root about in the woodlands, keeping a wary eye out for hungry short-tailed **bobcats**.

Armadillos arrived from Central America in the 19th century. They dig and burrow into timber for insects and fungi, scour the ground for fruit and rely on speed for protection. Their shells are made of tough plates covered and joined by leathery skin. Females give birth to four offspring, all of the same sex.

Cotton rats, **marsh rabbits**, **otters** and **spotted skunks** inhabit marshland regions throughout the state.

LIZARDS, SNAKES AND AMPHIBIANS Native **green lizards** and **skinks** are regulars to the woodland scene, while **Cuban lizards** (the male has a puff sack on his throat) can be spotted in urban areas. The largest and most poisonous Florida snake is the **water moccasin**, a relative of the rattlesnake; **pygmy rattlesnakes**, **black rat snakes** and **indigo** and **king snakes** are other reptiles to watch out for. **Walking catfish** are one of Florida's strangest sights.

❑ Turtle-watching is a fascinating Florida pastime. Leatherback turtles, which can grow up to 6ft (1.8m) long and weigh a ton (literally) and loggerhead, green, rare hawksbill and Kemp's Ridley turtles all swim in Florida waters and must leave the relative security of the ocean to lay their eggs on the beach during the nesting season (May 1–Oct 31). Federal laws have been introduced to protect the remaining nesting areas, and state laws prohibit bright lights on the beach at certain times because they may confuse hatchlings that are heading for the ocean. ❑

Writer and artist Frederic Remington, known chiefly for his portrayals of the Old West, complained that Florida's cow hunters sadly lacked "the bilious fierceness and rearing plunge which I had associated with my friends out West," though his artistic nature allowed that "they are picturesque in their unkempt, almost unearthly wildness." One of his subjects was folk hero Bone Mizell, who listed branding cattle with his teeth among his accomplishments.

LIFE ON THE PRAIRIE The Spanish introduced cattle and horses to Florida in the 16th century. Livestock thrived in the rolling green central prairie region south of Gainesville, now known as Paynes Prairie, a state preserve near Micanopy. When prospective settlers rejected the cattle and land that the Spanish offered them, the missions taught local Native Americans to herd the livestock instead, and they proved very adept in their new rôle.

White settlers arrived from the north in the 19th century, and brought their own techniques. For instance, Remington noted their use of cur dogs, rather than horses, which were saved for other purposes, to round up the herd, and remarked on the newcomers' practice of building strong log corrals approximately a day's march apart all through the woods of the vast ranch lands.

Cowboy boots—an essential item of Western gear, sold off the shelf

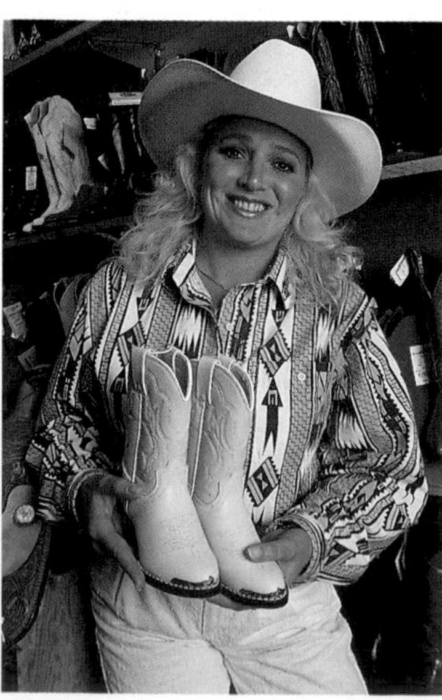

During the 1930s, Brahman cattle were introduced and crossbred with native species. Herds of these humpbacked beasts are a familiar sight in fields along the roads, often providing a comfortable perch for white cattle egrets. Among the inhabitants at the **Babcock Crescent B. Ranch**, outside Fort Myers, are Senepol cattle, quarter horses, named for the quarter-mile races they run, and a herd of bison. An adventurous swamp-buggy ride will take you to the 70-year-old commissary, once the company stores, where saddles still hang over the verandas and cowmen go swaggering by (see page 205).

CATTLE TOWNS Arcadia is a sleepy cattle town 20 miles (32km) north of the Babcock ranch. High noon in the restored main street looks like a scene from a Western movie. Though present-day cowmen are more likely to roll into town in a battered pickup than on horseback, the twice-yearly rodeo is as traditional as they come, and the local Western outfitters are equipped with the classic clothes—pearl-buttoned shirts, string ties and cowboy boots.

Kissimmee, just outside Orlando, is a curious combination of cattle town and theme park dormitory. The Kissimmee Sports Arena has a

popular Friday night rodeo, with authentic bronco-riding, calf-roping and barrel-racing and the town hosts the twice-yearly Silver Spurs Rodeo.

Another realistic cattle town is **Davie**, just outside Fort Lauderdale. Davie has hitching posts galore, cacti, swinging saloon doors on the town hall and even a "ride-through" service at the local McDonald's.

WHERE CHAMPIONS ARE BORN At the heart of the state, **Marion County** is the cornerstone of Florida's thoroughbred horse country. More than 27,000 Floridians are employed in the state's billion-dollar equine industry, and 400 of its 600 farms and training centers are in Marion County, ranged around the county seat of Ocala.

Florida competes heavily with California and Kentucky, also major equine centers. The Sunshine State enjoys similar advantages to Kentucky, with its famous bluegrass. Florida has its own limestone-enriched pastureland, which accounts for the strong, light bones of dynamic Kentucky Derby winners, such as the great Needles and, more recently, Unbridled.

Drive U.S. 301, or better still, minor roads like S.R. 200, for a beguiling vista of rolling green meadows and pristine white fencing, interspersed with galloping thoroughbred horses. Many of the farms you will find along these roads are open to the public.

For details: **Florida Thoroughbred Breeders' and Owners Association** (tel: 352/629-2160; www.ftboa.com).

Excitement at Davie's rodeo

❑ For a look at Florida's ranch culture, nothing beats a good rodeo. Fans head to Arcadia's **All Florida Championship Rodeo**, 124 Herd Street (March and October, tel: 863/494-2014; www.arcadiarodeo.com) and Kissimmee's **Silver Spurs Rodeo**, Silver Spurs Arena, U.S. 192 East (February and September/October, tel: 407/677-6336; www.silverspursrodeo.com). **Rodeos** take place on Friday at 8pm in the Kissimmee Sports Arena (tel: 407/933-0020); and Davie's Wednesday-night **Jackpot Rodeos** are at the Davie Rodeo Arena, 6591 S.W. 45th Street (tel: 954/475-9787; www.fivestarrodeo.com). ❑

It may sound like a cliché, but Florida really is a giant cultural melting pot. The state "where everyone is from somewhere else" welcomes around 1,000 new residents every day, and the diversity of Florida's demographic profile is probably only rivaled by that of another great magnet for immigrants, California.

Home-grown migrants from the northern states (and a healthy proportion of Canadians) account for the majority of the population growth. However, where once newcomers were largely retiree "snowbirds" flocking south to enjoy an ice-free winter and tax advantages, Florida's present-day migrants are much more likely to include large numbers of young professionals and families equally intent on the good life in the sun and the work opportunities offered by a burgeoning business sector. North Americans are not alone in recognizing Florida's possibilities. A relatively short hop to the south, Latin America and the Caribbean have provided another source of enthusiastic migration and, as the word spread about Florida's boom economy and increasingly attractive leisure profile in the 1990s, significant numbers of European migrants also jumped aboard the bandwagon bound for the Sunshine State.

Multicultural faces in the crowd

MULTICULTURAL MAKE-UP There is nothing new in Florida's multicultural make-up. From the initial influx of curious pioneers in the 18th century, the state has never attracted one stereotypical settler or any one nationality in particular. The original European occupants of the peninsula, the Spanish, were replaced by French noblemen, English adventurers, American planters and Creek Native Americans whose descendants, the Seminoles, are considered Florida natives even though they have inhabited the state for only 200 years. Over the following century or so, Caribbean islanders introduced Bahamanian architecture to the Keys, the Scots built golf courses in Dunedin, Cubans brought cigars to Tampa and Greek sponge-divers introduced bouzouki music and spinach pastries to Tarpon Springs.

Florida's multicultural diversity is one of the state's most appealing characteristics and locals like to celebrate it in every shape and form with a calendar of festivals, attractions and special events. For example, you could experience a Greek-style Epiphany Day (January 6) with Greek Orthodox religious processions, music, dancing and feasting in Tarpon Springs; or take part in the colorful Caribbean-style Goombay Festival (first weekend of June) in Miami's funky Coconut Grove district.

CULTURAL ATTRACTIONS In the southern part of the state, you will find several Seminole-owned and

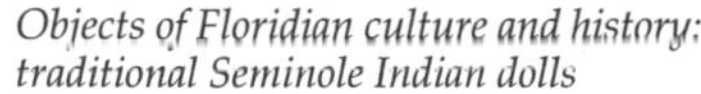
Objects of Floridian culture and history: traditional Seminole Indian dolls

operated attractions that offer a chance to learn a little more about Florida's Native Americans. Tourist villages on the Tamiami Trail (U.S. 41) west of Miami, and the Ah-Tah-Thi-Ki Museum outside Fort Lauderdale, demonstrate traditional Seminole crafts and culture. Rather less traditional but popular Everglades air-boat rides and alligator-wrestling are also available, and gambling presents a different type of entertainment, several casinos around the state on Seminole land with resorts at Miami, Tampa and Holllywood.

The significant role of Miami's Cuban community in shaping the modern city is reflected in the collections of Casa Bacardi at the University of Miami, a repository of archives, films and photos of pre- and post-revolution Cuban culture (www.casabacardi.iccas.miami.edu). For a dash of vintage Cuba in the heart of Miami, check out nightclubs devoted to the pre-Revolutionary Havana sound, catch sidewalk dominoes players click-clacking away at tables beneath the trees on Calle Ocho (S.W. 8th Street) in Little Havana, and make a reservation for pop-diva Gloria Estefan's traditional Cuban restaurant on Miami Beach.

Miami Beach itself celebrates more than 200 years of Jewish history in the state with the Sanford L. Ziff Jewish Museum of Florida (www.jewishmuseum.com), housed in a former South Beach synagogue. There is also an emotionally moving Holocaust Memorial. Heading north up to the Gold Coast, the Morikami Museum and Japanese Gardens in Delray Beach commemorate a colony of Japanese pineapple farmers with beautifully landscaped grounds, crafts displays and demonstrations of the traditional Japanese tea ceremony.

❑ Cracker culture has better press in Florida than most other southern states, where the word has been used disparagingly to describe the poor and disadvantaged. In Florida, a Cracker refers to anything that's native to Florida.

Cracker architecture can be seen in the wooden pioneer homes throughout the state. A good example would be the Cracker homestead on the Marjorie Kinnan Rawlings State Historic Site, south of Gainesville. Meanwhile, Cracker cooking is a byword for southern-style barbecue, grits (cracked corn breakfast porridge), catfish and hearty portion control. ❑

Florida is a magnet for sports lovers. Everything from golf and canoeing to greyhound racing and jai alai finds loyal supporters in this sports-crazy state, and millions of vacationers every year can also enjoy the excellent facilities.

In Palm Beach County alone there are more than 145 golf courses, 1,100 tennis courts and 47 miles (75.5km) of oceanfront beaches offering scuba diving, surfing, sailing and other watersports, plus sportfishing. Baseball, croquet, greyhound racing, jai alai and two polo clubs just about complete the sports picture in this one small area.

COURSES AND COURTS Florida's **golf** courses are glorious. The Sunshine State has developed into a top golfing destination, well supplied with challenging courses by the likes of Pete Dye and Tom Fazio, plus a tremendous choice of excellent public courses. This is the birthplace of Jack Nicklaus, after all. Naples, on the west coast, claims to be the "Golfing Capital of the World." Although golf is played all year round, winter is by far the busiest season.

Tennis aces can have a ball

Tennis resorts and training schools are another intrinsic feature of the Florida sporting scene, and the state is home to Nick Bolletieri's tennis camp, training ground for many tennis greats. Sports-oriented resorts are a popular alternative to regular hotels.

HEAD FOR THE WATER As the first rays of sun streak the Atlantic Ocean, **surfers** can be seen crouching over their boards waiting to catch the first wave of the day. **Waterskiers** and **jet skiers** carve trails through the water and **catamarans** zip to and fro. There is also **parasailing** for the adventurous or **pedal boats** for those less inclined to get wet.

Marinas are packed with charter boats offering **sportfishing** excursions for marlin, pompano, sailfish and shark. Islamorada in the Florida Keys claims to be the "Sportfishing Capital of the World"—Pompano on the Gold Coast and Destin in the Panhandle may beg to differ.

Meanwhile, **scuba divers** and **snorkelers** flock to the Gold Coast and Keys to explore the dazzling coral reefs and artificial dive sites warmed by the Gulf Stream.

One way of exploring Florida's inland water courses is by **canoe**. The Blackwater and Suwannee rivers in the Panhandle, the Myakka and Peace rivers near Arcadia, the southern tip of the Everglades and the Keys are a few prime locations. Saltwater and freshwater **fishermen** on the rivers and back bays should obtain a fishing license, available from tackle shops.

A SPORTS LOVERS' PARADISE Spectator sports such as basketball and football attract enthusiastic crowds. Baseball, in its season, does

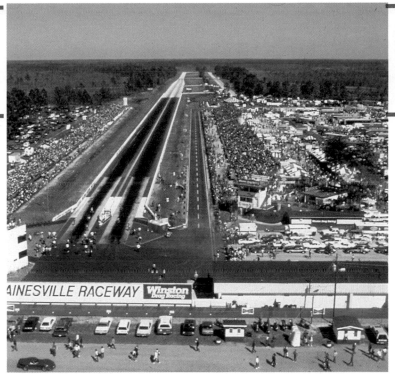

Sports are big in Gainesville

the same. February signals the arrival of major-league teams from around the country for the start of the six-week spring training program.

Central Florida welcomes the Houston Astros to Kissimmee, and the Atlanta Braves to Orlando's Walt Disney World.

On the west coast, the New York Yankees practice in Tampa, the Philadelphia Phillies in Clearwater, the Boston Red Sox and Minnesota Twins train in Fort Myers and the Toronto Blue Jays warm up in Dunedin.

Over on the east coast, the St. Louis Cardinals take up residence in Jupiter, while the Los Angeles Dodgers claim Vero Beach. Fans can turn up to watch the practice sessions, and the Grapefruit League games, which attract a million-plus fans each year. Attending these smaller games can be just as exciting as regular season play.

No auto racing fan should leave Florida without a visit to Daytona, the "Birthplace of Speed" and home of "the other 24-hour race." U.S. stock-car racing was virtually born here at the Daytona Speedway, and February's Race Weeks culminate in the world-famous Daytona 500. There are stock-car race tracks around the state from West Palm Beach to Tampa and Pensacola. Sebring's 12-hour endurance race is another classic, and downtown Miami hosts an annual springtime Grand Prix.

❑ Pari-mutuel betting was legalized in Florida in 1931. It opened the doors to a flood of sporting activities, including the now widely popular greyhound racing, horse-racing, which takes place on four courses in Miami alone, and the fast and furious ball game of jai alai, which is something of a Florida specialty. ❑

Mickey Mouse hit Florida in 1971, when Walt Disney's Magic Kingdom opened its doors outside Orlando. However, the state's love affair with tourist attractions was already well established.

Cypress Gardens, near Winter Haven, Florida's first and longest operated theme park, has been packing them in since the mid-1930s. Further encouraged by the success of Disney, themed attractions have sprung up around the state, and exotic animals and birds have come to roost in a wide variety of specially created "natural habitats" from the African plains of Tampa's Busch Gardens to Orlando's SeaWorld. There is fun on tap at water parks, zoos, adventure zones, miniature golf courses and arcades.

WALT DISNEY WORLD® RESORT Disney continues to draw crowds as one of the world's number one tourist destinations. The **Magic Kingdom®**, with its cast of Disney characters from Cinderella to Dumbo; science-with-a-smile and cultural exhibits at **Epcot®**; and **Disney-MGM Studios®** were joined in 1998 by **Disney's Animal Kingdom®**, which delivers exotic landscapes and close encounters with animals, together with dinosaurs, Disney characters and great rides. The Disney complex also includes two unique water parks, **Blizzard Beach** and **Typhoon Lagoon**, plus the sprawling **Downtown Disney** entertainment district, loaded with shopping and dining. The nightclubs of Downtown Disney's **Pleasure Island** offer plenty of after-dark entertainment.

UNIVERSAL CHALLENGE Nearby there is hot competition in the form of **Universal Studios Orlando**. At **Universal Studios**, Revenge of the Mummy–the Ride, TERMINATOR 2®: 3D BATTLE Across Time and MEN IN BLACK™–Alien Atttack™ (among others) are the theme for rides that are cute, stomach-churning and hair-raising, respectively. Universal's **Islands of Adventure** park, opened in 1999, breathes life into favorite cartoon characters, from Spider-Man and Popeye to Dr. Seuss, in dramatically themed areas with shows and rides to match. Between the entrance to both parks is **Universal Studios CityWalk** full of shopping, dining and entertainment. Also under Universal's wing, about a block from the parks, is a major water park, **Wet 'n' Wild**—the water playground of choice if you want to get wet in the International Drive area.

MORE AROUND ORLANDO Still in Orlando, **SeaWorld Orlando**, Florida's most popular marine park, features an all-star cast of whales, dolphins, sea lions and otters. You can also see Penguin Encounter; an eerie collection of eels, venomous fish and sharks in Terrors of the Deep; plus a nightly Polynesian dinner show. Don't miss **Discovery Cove,** SeaWorld's sister park, where interactive marine adventures are the specialty, along with bottlenose dolphin and stingray encounters.

In Kissimmee, the local splash zone is **Water Mania**. Both parks offer children's versions of the big slides, and dryer options such as sunbathing.

A half-hour drive away, **Cypress Gardens** combines spectacular floral displays with almost 40 rides, four roller coasters and ice-skating shows—the park's kitsch trademark—the hoopskirted Southern Belles, who pose in their antebellum-style gowns on the beautiful manicured lawns. The park hosts regular concerts year-round.

TAMPA ADVENTURES Some 90 minutes by car from Orlando is **Busch Gardens** in Tampa. Spreading out from a recreated Serengeti Plain, with its array of African wildlife, themed districts re-create sections of

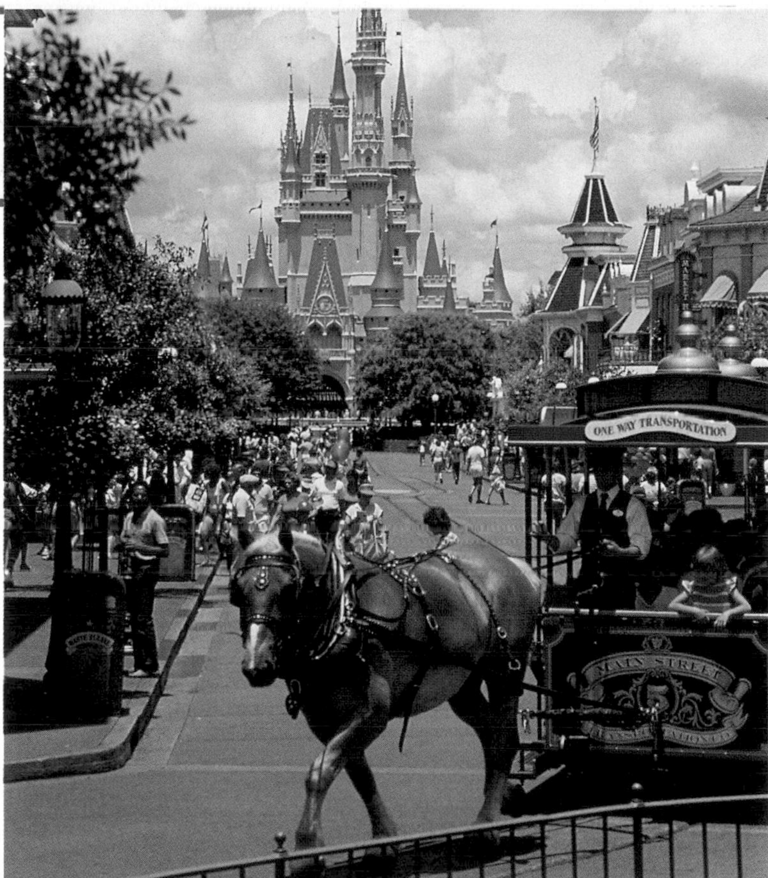

the African continent, from a Moroccan souk to a southern African village. A dolphin theater, an ice show, rides and children's play areas keep company with the wildlife—of which there is a lot. **Adventure Island**, 1 mile (1.6km) away, makes a splash with its Tampa Typhoon water slide, a leisurely ride through a simulated rain forest and more adventures.

EAST COAST DUO The East Coast plays host to **Adventure Landing Water Park** which has two venues close to Jacksonville, while Daytona visitors can cool down at the **Daytona Lagoon**.

Top: Main Street U.S.A., the centerpiece of Walt Disney World Resort's Magic Kingdom, with Cinderella Castle rising up at the end

❏ Best of the rest:
Miami: Miami Seaquarium.
Keys and Everglades: Theater of the Sea, Islamorada.
Central Florida: Wild Waters and Silver Springs, Ocala.
Gold Coast: Lion Country Safari, West Palm Beach.
East Coast: Adventure Landing, Jacksonville Beach.
West Coast: Weeki Wachee Spring, north of Tampa.
Panhandle: Gulfarium, Fort Walton Beach.
Panama City Beach: Shipwreck Island Water Park ❏

French science fiction writer Jules Verne predicted Florida's space age future in his novel, From Earth to the Moon, published in 1863. Verne described "Florida...shaken to its very depths" by the liftoff of a rocket named Columbiad. Was it coincidence or intent that named the 1980s Columbia Space Shuttle program? Was there a well-read scientist with a sense of humor at work?

INTO THE SPACE RACE The first scientific studies exploring the use of rocketry for space flight were published in the early 20th century. During the 1930s, German scientists made dramatic leaps forward in the development of rocket technology, culminating in the World War II V-2 guided missile. Later many of these scientists continued their work in peacetime for the United States and the Soviet Union. By the late 1950s, the space race was on. In October 1957, the Soviets launched *Sputnik 1* into Earth's orbit, followed in January 1958 by the Americans' *Explorer 1*. When the National Aeronautics and Space Administration (NASA) was set up later that year, it selected the missile-testing range at Florida's Cape Canaveral Air Force Station as its test base and inaugurated the *Mercury* manned space program. Once again the Soviets got there ahead with Yuri Gagarin's first manned space flight in *Vostok 1* on April 12, 1961. Less than a month later, on May 5, Alan Shepard became the first American in space, with a 15-minute suborbital flight in a *Mercury* capsule.

❑ Though plans for manned space flight are uncertain, unmanned exploration has been successfully expanded with the launches of probes to study Mars, the red planet, the rings and moons orbiting Jupiter, and the structure of meteors. ❑

GEMINI* AND *APOLLO Work on the giant Launch Complex 39 began in 1962 across the Banana River from Cape Canaveral. NASA's operations moved across the water to Merritt Island in 1964, the first year of the two-man *Gemini* missions and an estimated 400,000 visitors took the opportunity to tour the newly named Kennedy Space Center Complex.

After several unmanned launches, the first manned *Apollo* flight was accomplished in December 1968, with a three-man crew. On July 20, 1969, Neil Armstrong and Edwin "Buzz" Aldrin Jr.'s moonwalk from *Apollo 11* made them the first men on the moon.

THE SPACE SHUTTLE NASA's next target was to develop a reusable manned spacecraft, the Space Transportation System (S.T.S.), better known as the Space Shuttle. Three basic elements make up the Space Shuttle system: a 212ft (64m) Orbiter, shaped like an airplane; two solid-fuel booster rockets; and an external tank containing liquid hydrogen (fuel) and liquid oxygen (an oxidizer). These elements produce a degree of flexibility that permits the Orbiter to take off like a rocket, orbit like a spacecraft and return to Earth, landing on a runway like a glider or an airplane. The boosters are jettisoned after about two minutes and parachute to Earth, where they are retrieved and reused. The cargo bay can transport bulky cargoes, such as communications and scientific research satellites, into the Earth's orbit. Disabled spacecraft and hardware can be recovered and repaired

in the bay, and loads weighing as much as 32,000 lbs (14,400kg) can be returned to Earth.

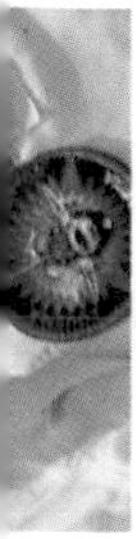

The Space Shuttle's maiden voyage on April 12, 1981, marked the real beginning of space travel. These reusable craft are designed for years of service, allowing for routine space flights that will service the space station programs of the 21st century. The Shuttle will form the backbone of the manned flight program and the transportation link to the International Space Station.

Unfortunately in the first decade of the new millennium, the Space Shuttle program faced serious criticism after the catastrophic break-up of Shuttle Columbia on re-entry on February 1, 2003. Design flaws and cost cutting were cited as possible contributory factors and though a successful mission blasted off from Kennedy in August 2005, the Space Shuttle fleet is to be retired in 2010, leaving the future of the International Space Station in doubt.

Kennedy Space Center, Rocket Garden

A new era of space exploration is about to begin.

WINDOW INTO SPACE Florida is the heart of America's pioneering space program, and there is no better place to see the story unfold than at Kennedy Space Center (see pages 192–193 and 196). The center's Visitor Complex is the gateway to an in-depth look at space travel, illustrated through dozens of displays, collections of memorabilia and space hardware, re-creations and actual film footage of mankind's exploration of space. There are bus tours to Launch Complex 39 and the historic Cape Canaveral Air Force Station launch sites, as well as IMAX movies and the Astronaut Memorial, a 42ft (12.5m) high, 50ft (15m) wide granite "space mirror" that tracks the sun throughout the day and commemorates U.S. astronauts who have died in the line of duty.

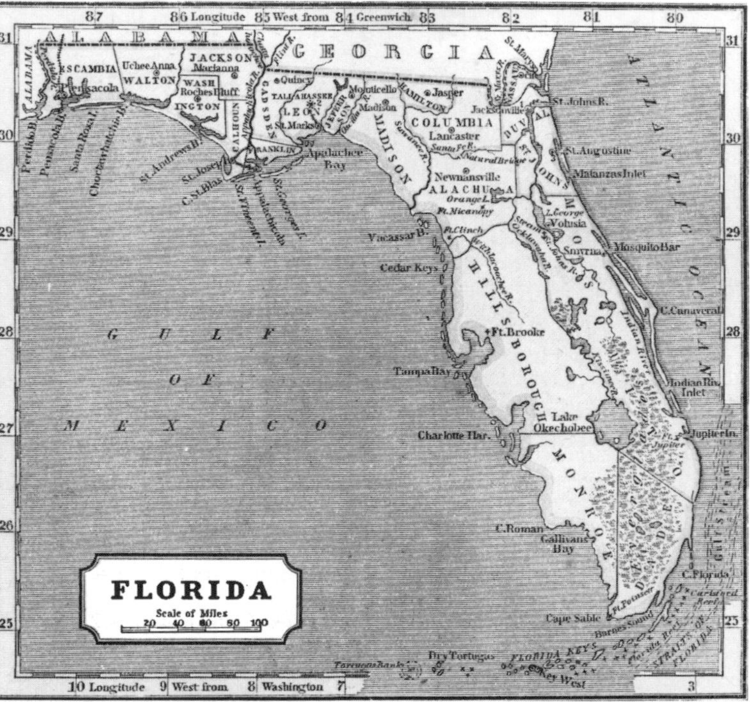

Cypress swamp, primeval-looking Florida landscape

Most of the Florida peninsula tacked onto the bottom right-hand corner of North America is just about as flat as a pancake. Its highest point, near the border with Georgia, is a mere 345ft (103.5m) above sea level. Thus, the story of its origins is something of a surprise.

FIRE AND WATER About 200 million years ago, when the ancient continent of Pangaea began to break apart, a chain of island volcanoes rose from the sea, curving south from the mainland toward Cuba and the Bahamas. As the sea level rose and fell during the period of the Pleistocene epoch, these volcanoes were gradually eroded. The deep sea-filled trenches formed gathered sediment to create massive limestone deposits reaching depths of 18,000ft (5,400m). Fossilized remains found in the north indicate that Florida was still under water while dinosaurs roamed the rest of the continent. Its warm waters were home to the prehistoric forerunners of turtles, sharks, whales and manatees (sea cows).

EMERGENCE OF DRY LAND Around 20 to 30 million years ago, Florida finally appeared as a flat, swampy plateau cemented to the mainland by millions of years worth of collected sediment, coated with a rich phosphorous residue from the waves. As the last Great Ice Age advanced from the north, gigantic glaciers devoured the sea, and Florida doubled in size as the waters receded. No glaciers reached very far south, so Florida became a safe haven for all kinds of creatures, from mammoths and saber-toothed tigers to tiny deer, wolves, bears and swamp-dwelling alligators. Their fossilized remains are frequently uncovered by phosphate-mining operations.

FROM ISLAND TO PENINSULA After the Ice Ages came the rains. The rains flooded the porous limestone, creating underground freshwater reservoirs, transformed sinkholes into springs and filled numerous rivers and thousands of lakes. The outline of the peninsula was still being shaped by the changing sea level, as can be seen from the graduated terraces sloping away from the center of the state into the Gulf of Mexico, but around 6,000 years ago the Florida of today was recognizable. Florida's 1,350-mile (2,187km) seashore, fringed with islands and coral reefs, enclosed a land rich in plant life, animal life and water—a land waiting for human habitation.

Fairchild Tropical Gardens, Miami

Columbus discovered the Americas when they blocked his passage westward in 1492. Convinced that India was just around the corner, he christened the offshore islands the "West Indies" and the native inhabitants "Indians."

THE FIRST-COMERS Some historians believe that the first Americans migrated from Asia across the Bering Strait after the last Ice Age, around 20,000 years ago. This extraordinary journey may have continued for 10,000 years, as different groups of migrants gradually spread out over the North and South American continents. There is no trace of any large native primate from which humans could have evolved, so it is possible that all "Americans," from the Inuit (Eskimos) of Alaska and Canada to the Araucanian people of Chile, are descended from the first Mongoloid migrants. However, there is a growing argument that supports the theory that certain South American groups developed separately and are unrelated.

Archeologists believe the first Floridians arrived in the northern Panhandle region about 10,000 to 12,000 years ago. The traditional view maintains that these first settlers arrived as part of the general migration south, but similarities between early Florida culture and the cultures of some of the tribes of Central and South America indicate a remigration north.

The first migrants were hunter-gatherers who arrived to a promised land of sunny skies and rich hunting, surrounded by a bountiful ocean. Armed with simple flint-tipped spears, they traveled the peninsula and subsisted on mammoth, bison, boar, deer, fish and shellfish, quail, duck and goose.

Native American totem pole

EARLY SETTLEMENT By 5000BC, groups of Native Americans had settled in villages along the St. Johns River. These semipermanent communities practiced the orderly disposal of garbage, and their refuse dumps, known as middens, have provided archeologists with precise clues to the habits and culture of the original settlers. Mounds of discarded shells indicate a healthy seafood diet; broken arrowheads and weapons chart the development from crude spears to more sophisticated hunting methods; and, from around 2000BC, a startling cultural advance is demonstrated by the presence of shards of pottery. This is a clear guide to the highly developed culture of these southern tribes, as the art of fashioning clay vessels and baking them was not discovered for another eight centuries in most of North America.

Cultivation of maize began around 1000BC, giving rise to the emergence of crude irrigation schemes particularly in the Lake Okeechobee area of central south Florida. Advances in the tribes' ability to feed themselves led to something of a population explosion, and settlements gradually

Remnants of a proud culture

appeared across the entire peninsula. Estimates of the aboriginal population around the time of the arrival of the Spanish vary enormously, with a median of about 100,000 spread throughout the state and divided into tribes. The peoples included the Timucuans in the central and northern areas and the Apalachee in the north and east Panhandle region. Tampa Bay was settled by the Tocobega, while Calusas hunted in the southwest coast, and Tequestas controlled the Everglades and southeastern shores.

A RICH CULTURE The apparent lack of a written language among Florida's original Native Americans has proved a major stumbling block in furthering our understanding of the everyday life of the peninsula's early inhabitants. Archeological investigations at important historical sites, such as Crystal River (see page 204), are still uncovering more questions than answers, though several significant cultural periods have been identified, such as the Deptford culture (500BC–AD300), the Weedon Island culture (AD300–900), and the Safety Harbor culture (AD900 up until contact with Europeans).

Jean Ribaut, a French mariner who helped colonize Florida, described the Native Americans in the mid-16th century as "of tawny color, hawk nosed and of a pleasant countenance." They wore light deerskin coverings and colored earrings made from inflated fish bladders, and organic body paint. Ribaut was impressed by the Native Americans' hunting methods—disguised in deerskins and horns, they could sneak up close to their prey for the kill.

Tribal government was administered by chieftains, who were advised by elders and priests. Animal sacrifices were made to appease the sun god, and firstborn children were sacrificed in a demonstration of respect for the tribal chief. Human bones up to 6,000 years old were discovered in burial sites. Reserved for important figures, these burial mounds increased in size and ingenuity until they became massive earthworks visible for miles around on complex road and canal systems that developed along similar lines to those of the ancient Aztec and Mayan civilizations of South and Central America.

THE BEGINNING OF THE END The arrival of the early explorers signaled trouble ahead for Florida's early inhabitants. The greatest dangers were neither weapons nor land disputes, but European ailments, such as measles and chicken pox, against which the Native Americans had no defense.

When Spanish explorer Juan Ponce de León sailed from his base in Puerto Rico on March 3, 1513, he was going in search of the lost island of Bimini and its legendary fountain of eternal youth. A month later, on Easter Sunday, he landed near present-day St. Augustine and named the new territory La Florida, *after the Spanish Eastertide Feast of Flowers,* Pascua Florida.

Ponce de León's explorations led him around the Keys (the Spanish for island is *cayo*)—which he named *Los Martires* because they reminded him of a chain of martyred men—and up the west coast of the peninsula to Charlotte Harbor, now known as Fort Myers. He was met by Native Americans shouting in Spanish. Whether the Spanish words had been learned from contacts with native South Americans or from foraying slave hunters is not known.

The first attempt to colonize Florida was a disaster. Ponce de León returned in 1521 with 200 settlers and missionaries, but their settlement was attacked before the foundations were complete, and the Spanish retired to Cuba, where Ponce de León died from an arrow wound.

Exploring the past

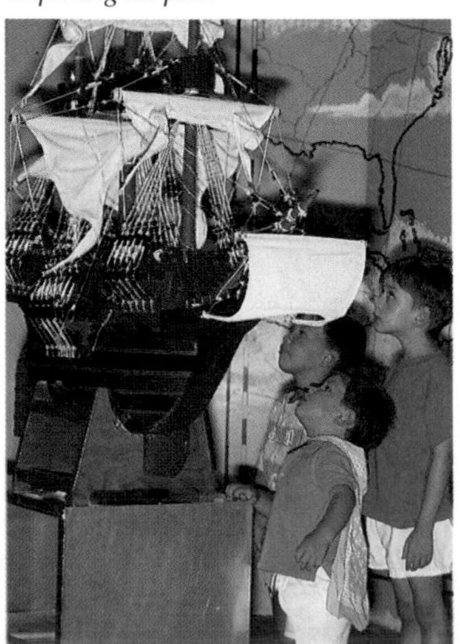

❑ Italian navigator and explorer John Cabot may have been the first European to see Florida when he sailed down the North American coast on a charting mission for King Henry VII of England. Although he never set foot ashore, 16th-century maps of Cabot's voyages appear to confirm that he spotted the Florida peninsula. ❑

DREAMS OF GOLD In 1528, Pánfilo de Narváez landed in Tampa Bay with a force of 400 men. They trailed north into the Panhandle in search of gold, leaving instructions for their ships to join them. Disease and tribal raids took their toll, the ships never turned up and the few remaining expeditioners set sail in makeshift boats from which there were only four survivors (who reappeared in Mexico some eight years later).

There were still dreams of undiscovered pots of gold when Hernando de Soto fielded a further expedition in 1539. Setting out from Tampa Bay in March of that year, de Soto led his 1,000 battle-hardened *conquistadores* and fortune-seekers deep into North America's interior. They ventured as far as North Carolina and Alabama, where de Soto died of a fever on the Mississippi River after three years of fruitless searching. By this time the promise of gold was beginning to wear a little thin. It is now believed that any gold the Native Americans possessed had probably been recovered from Spanish shipwrecks along the coast.

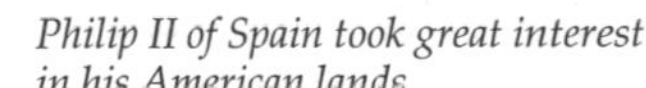
Philip II of Spain took great interest in his American lands

EUROPEAN INROADS Tristán de Luna y Arellano made the next attempt to establish a permanent Spanish settlement on the peninsula. This nobleman and veteran of several campaigns sailed into Pensacola Bay with a total of 1,500 soldiers, priests and craftsmen in 1559. Their luck was no better, and the combination of Luna's shortsighted management, crippling food shortages and a violent hurricane forced them to retreat in 1561.

By this time, although the Spanish had continually failed to establish a foothold in their vast new territory, their presence was being felt in a far more long-reaching and insidious fashion. European diseases were savagely depleting the Native American population, and raids by slave traders from strongholds in the West Indies were driving the Native Americans from their traditional homelands. Within 200 years, the original inhabitants of Florida would no longer exist.

For a record of these lost Floridians, we are indebted to the French. Spurred by Spain's failure to colonize, French explorer Jean Ribaut made several forays along the Florida coast. In 1564, a colony of Huguenots founded a settlement on the St. Johns River at Fort Caroline. Here, Ribaut and his cartographer Jacques le Moyne, compiled a fascinating account of the local tribes complete with detailed descriptions of the Native American dress, customs and practices.

This French Protestant enterprise proved too much for Spanish Catholic pride, and Philip II dispatched Pedro Menéndez de Avilés to dislodge the French. Menéndez landed south of the St. Johns River on August 28, 1565, on the feast of St. Augustine. Not long after this, the Huguenots were defeated.

❑ Menéndez was also commanded by Philip II to spread Catholicism throughout the New World; he set about his task with unprecedented patience and humanity. Jesuit priests were established at Tampa Bay and Charlotte Harbor, and by the 17th century the Native American Catholic reserves were formed. ❑

St. Augustine grew to become the oldest continuously inhabited European settlement in the United States—despite numerous attempts by hostile raiders, England's Sir Francis Drake included, to remove it from the face of the earth.

On learning of Menéndez's victory over the French colonists, Philip II of Spain declared it was a wholly justifiable "retribution...upon the Lutheran pirates," which would act as a lesson to all. However, Spain's problems with foreign fortune hunters, particularly those on the high seas, were only just beginning.

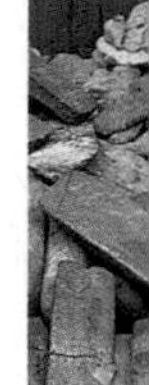

THE PLUNDERERS PLUNDERED Throughout the 16th and 17th centuries, Spanish treasure fleets, laden with gold, silver, copper and precious stones pillaged from Spain's West Indian and South American colonies, plowed slowly homeward around the southern tip of Florida. They attracted buccaneers like bees to honey. Attacking the lumbering galleons from smaller, swifter craft, pirates could easily escape with their booty and hide out in the impenetrable maze of coastal mangrove swamps and play hide-and-seek around the Florida Keys.

❏ Potential profits far outweighed the danger, as Francis Drake soon discovered. Drake returned from a successful foray to the New World with Spanish booty worth some $3 million, was knighted by Queen Elizabeth I on the docks at Deptford, and sent straight back to colonize North America—all the time continuing to deny that he harbored any hostility toward Spain. ❏

Booty from a treasure ship

DISASTER AT SEA The treasure ships had numerous natural hazards to face as well, including treacherous tides, knife-edged coral reefs concealed in the shallows and violent storms that descended with little warning. On September 4, 1622, a fleet of Spanish galleons, guarded by men-o'-war, upped anchor in Havana harbor and set sail for home. Among the vessels were the *Nuestra Señora de Atocha* and the *Santa Margarita*, both lying low in the water, weighed down by their priceless cargoes. The following evening, they and six other vessels lay at the bottom of the Florida Straits, victims of a violent hurricane that had also killed no fewer than 550 men.

It was some 350 years before a marine salvager and Florida legend named Mel Fisher located the site and its fabulous golden bounty, part of which is now on show at the **Mel Fisher Maritime Museum** in Key West (see pages 100 and 106).

BLACK CAESAR'S DOMAIN The Keys had long been a haven for smugglers and pirates ("wrecking" constituting a significant part of the economy), and there are more wrecks cluttering up the reefs here than anywhere else around the coast. Some ships, no doubt, fell prey to natural disasters, but many others are said to have been lured to their fate by false signals, the victims of legendary pirates such as the notorious Black Caesar. Reputed to be an escaped slave, Black Caesar distinguished himself by single-handedly capturing small vessels from his base just north of Key Largo. He then graduated to the post of trusted henchman to the infamous Edward Teach, alias Blackbeard.

Pirates sharing their spoils at the end of a day's work. From A Book of Pirates, *1905*

Caesar's lust for wealth and power, and his wanton cruelty, forced the authorities to act. In 1718, flying the *Jolly Roger* flag, Lieutenant Robert Maynard captured Teach's ship, the *Queen Anne's Revenge*. Teach was killed in the course of the battle, and Black Caesar was brought back in chains to Virginia, where he was hanged.

GASPARILLA The Treasure Coast area around Fort Pierce and Vero Beach is another fruitful spot for salvagers—11 vessels of the Spanish Plate Fleet sank here in 1715. On the Gulf Coast, gold coins have been washed ashore at Naples after heavy storms, and there was certainly plenty of shipping and pirate action around Tampa Bay and the Charlotte Harbor area, where legendary mutineer-turned-buccaneer, José Gaspar—also known as Gasparilla—carved his violent niche into the folklore of Florida.

Captiva Island is said to have been named after one of his more famous exploits—the abduction of the Spanish infanta and her escort of 11 Mexican maidens in 1801. Once he landed on the island, Gaspar handed the captive maidens over to his crew and claimed the Spanish princess for himself. When she refused to co-operate with him, he had her executed.

❑ According to local storytellers, José Gaspar was a high-ranking gentleman who staged a bloody mutiny on the Spanish galleon *Florida Blanca* in 1785. As Gasparilla, he terrorized passing sea traffic for 37 years, capturing or sinking some 36 ships between 1784 and 1795. ❑

Gaspar's seafaring days came to an end in 1822 when an American warship, masquerading as a British trader, attacked his pirate ship with a blast from a concealed gun battery. Realizing he was a goner, Gasparilla committed suicide by leaping overboard. The day of the big-time Florida pirates was almost over, though the Laffite brothers, French pirates, and the mysterious Tavernier, their associate, were still harrying American ships from south of the border well into the 19th century.

During the 17th century, British slave traders made frequent raids into Spanish territory to capture native Florida tribespeople. The cattle-herding skills of the Native Americans, acquired while living in segregated reserves under the Spanish, were highly prized and sought-after.

BRITISH OPPORTUNISTS Raids were becoming more prevalent by the beginning of the 18th century, and the British slave traders had formed an alliance with the Creeks, members of the Muskogeah Native American tribe from Alabama, Georgia, and the Carolinas. After the raids, many Creeks stayed on, occupying former Spanish farmlands and other Native American territory. Because they had deserted their own tribes in the north, they became known as *Seminoles*, from a Creek word meaning "runaways" or "wanderers."

When Spain and Britain ended the Seven Years War with the Treaty of Paris in 1763, Britain received Florida in exchange for Cuba. As the Spanish sailed away with the remnants of the aboriginal population, the British moved in with their Creek allies, and the two communities coexisted amicably enough.

Vast tracts of land were swiftly annexed and granted to settlers, together with financial inducements. Rice, sugarcane and indigo plantations were carved out of the fertile soil by African American slaves, many of whom were assimilated into Native American communities through servitude and marriage.

SPANISH REOCCUPATION Britain occupied Florida for only 20 years. With British reserves severely depleted by the American Revolution, Spain saw a golden opportunity to reclaim lost American territory. They landed a force at Pensacola, and captured west Florida in 1781. Four years later, the Second Treaty of Paris saw Florida back in Spanish hands—but it was to bring its old conqueror little joy.

The Seminoles largely ignored the Spanish jurisdiction and soon found their land claims being disputed by a steady flow of white settlers from the north. Native American migrants continued to move south, and escaped African American slaves from the Southern states sought refuge in Spanish territory, incurring the wrath of Georgia's powerful planters.

THE FIRST SEMINOLE WAR Tension built up along the border between Florida and Georgia, and relations between the Seminoles and the white settlers were worsening. General (later President) Andrew Jackson leaped upon the flimsiest pretext to thunder into Florida and attack the Seminoles by the Suwannee River. This was the First Seminole War of 1817–1818.

DESPERATE MEASURES In 1819, Spain canceled its $5 million debt to the United States and left Florida for good, opening the door to further white settlers. In 1823, an attempt was made to restrict the Seminoles to a 4-million-acre (over 1.5 million hectares) reservation in central west Florida. It failed. The Removal Act of 1830 sought an even more drastic solution—Seminoles were exiled to reservations in Arkansas, west of the Mississippi. Senior chieftains journeyed west to view the land in 1832, but after just one chief had agreed to sign away his tribal lands, the process was halted by the arrival of a man named Osceola.

THE SECOND SEMINOLE WAR Young, handsome and confident, Osceola was widely respected, and he succeeded in uniting the various tribes to fight the Second Seminole

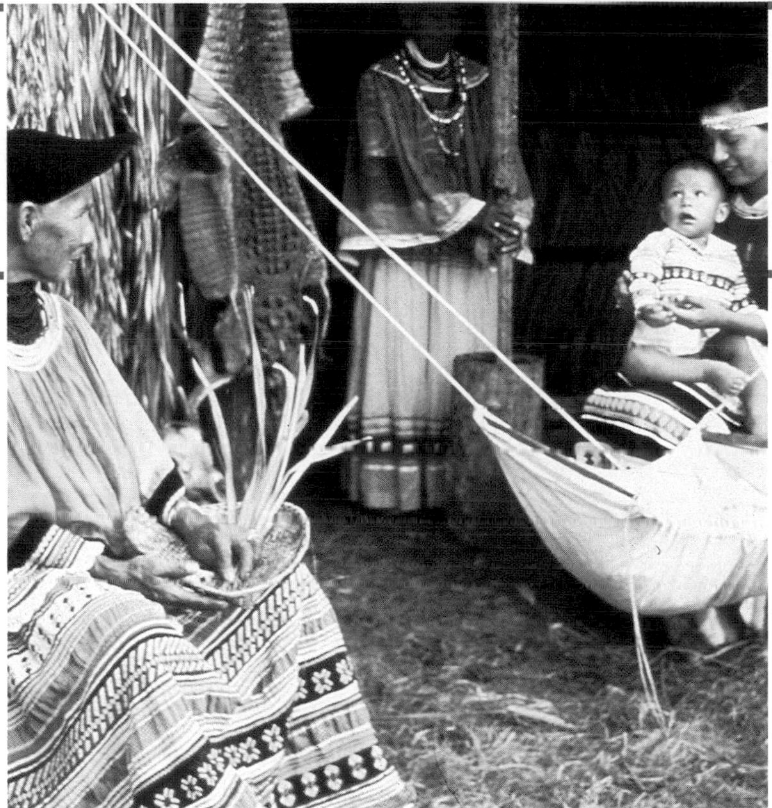

A Seminole family

War, which lasted seven long and bloody years (see also page 43). His capture, by trickery, while he was negotiating under a flag of truce in 1837, prompted a considerable public outcry. He died a year later, incarcerated in Fort Moultrie, South Carolina.

Osceola was succeeded by Chief Coacoochee (Wild Cat), but the spirit of the Seminoles had been broken, and they were no match for the United States' forces with their superior weaponry.

❑ Osceola, who was part European, had no shortage of grievances against the United States. One of the main ones, though, was against those who had kidnapped his wife Che-cho-ter (Morning Dew). This insult to his tribe and family he could never forgive. ❑

SURRENDER AND SURVIVAL Some 3,000 Seminoles traveled the so-called "Trail of Tears" across the Mississippi in 1842. A handful of renegades, led by Chief Billy Bowlegs, slipped into the Everglades and continued to pursue settlers and the army into the Third Seminole War of 1855. But the Seminoles were finally forced to surrender in 1858, and the chief was escorted west. An additional 300 Seminoles retreated deep into the Everglades, emerging only to trade alligator skins, deer-hides and small amounts of produce. It is their descendants who make up the present-day Seminole population and the smaller Miccosukee group. In 1911, the U.S. government allocated reservation lands to Florida's Native Americans.

When Spain canceled her debt to the United States by relinquishing control of the Florida peninsula in 1819, General Andrew Jackson was appointed the territory's first governor. Old Hickory, as he was known for his toughness, arrived to take up his post in 1821, but he remained only three months before heading for Washington, where he eventually became president in 1828.

A CENTRAL GOVERNMENT One of the most important questions facing Floridians was where to establish their state government. The two major settlements, Pensacola and St. Augustine, were a three weeks' journey apart at opposite sides of the peninsula. In 1832, two scouts were sent out on horseback, one from each of the principal towns, and they met midway between the two, in the rolling hills of northern Florida. It was here that the town of Tallahassee was built.

By 1824, Florida's early legislative councils were convening in three log cabins near the site of the present-day Capitol building in Tallahassee. These cabins were replaced by a two-story masonry structure in 1826, but as Florida moved toward statehood, a larger and more impressive building was thought to be appropriate. Congress found $20,000 and commissioned a capitol, which was completed just in time to welcome the new state government on March 3, 1845.

Union guns at Fort Brady during the Civil War

SETTLEMENT AND SLAVERY During the 1820s, land grants and financial inducements encouraged a steady stream of white settlers to northern Florida, where they planted cotton, rice, tobacco and sugarcane; stole Native American lands; and forced African Americans into slavery. The port of Jacksonville, founded in 1821, helped open up the interior. Pioneers ventured down the St. Johns River to set up their trading posts, and grew indigo and citrus fruits along the banks and into the interior.

Down in the Keys, Caribbean immigrants were introducing their own distinctive architecture and establishing plantations of fruits such as pineapples, bananas and mangoes.

One of Florida's early senators, David Levy Yulee, was Caribbean-born. His sugar plantation and mill near Homosassa, on the Gulf Coast, was operated by 1,000 slaves. As in other Southern states, the slavery system was the backbone of the plantation economy, and it is estimated that some 25,000 slaves labored under the yoke of King Cotton in Florida.

❑ The cotton industry turned little Apalachicola (now famous for its oysters) into the third largest port on the Gulf Coast during the 1830s. Another claim to fame is Dr. John Gorrie's ice-making machine, invented here in 1848. Eventually, it led to the development of air-conditioning and refrigeration. ❑

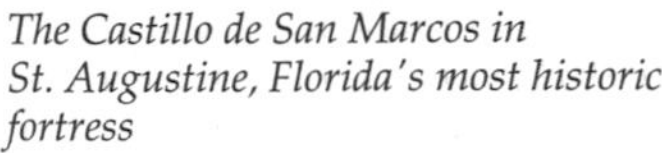

The Castillo de San Marcos in St. Augustine, Florida's most historic fortress

Florida's population almost doubled, from 34,370 to 66,500, between 1830 and 1845. Skirmishes between the Native Americans and white settlers became more frequent and bloody, and the government's efforts to deport the Native Americans by the Removal Act of 1830 resulted in the Second Seminole War (1835–1842). Fort Lauderdale, Fort Myers, and Fort Pierce were all founded in response to the war. The total cost ran to more than $40 million (see also pages 40–41).

THE CIVIL WAR During a brief respite, the first cross-state railroad was built between Fernandina and Cedar Key. It opened in 1861. But Florida had barely recovered from its internal conflicts when pressure from wealthy plantation owners ensured that the 16-year-old state secede from the Union on January 10, 1861. Allied to the Confederate states, Florida went to war against the Union—and, as history tells us, lost.

Florida's main task in the Civil War was to provide food for the Confederate army, though Key West, among other places, remained loyal to the North, and became a vital staging post for Union troops. The Confederates won a battle at Olustree, near Lake City, and Tallahassee became the only Confederate capital east of the Mississippi not to fall to Union forces, when a "cradle and grave" troop of old men and boys successfully repelled the Northerners at the Battle of Natural Bridge in March 1865.

Two months later, after General Robert E. Lee surrendered the Confederate cause at Appomattox, the Union flag was run up above the state capitol.

❑ Florida still takes pride in its Confederate history. After the war ended, many senior Confederate figures were forced to flee, among them Secretary of State Judah P. Benjamin. Benjamin took refuge with Major Robert Gamble on his plantation at Ellenton, near Tampa. Today, the house is immaculately restored as the J. P. Benjamin Memorial (see page 204). ❑

At the end of the Civil War, President Andrew Jackson appointed a provisional government to oversee the reconstruction of Florida. It was not for some 20 years, however, until the coming of the railroad, that the state finally flourished.

AFRICAN AMERICAN RIGHTS A constitutional convention met in October 1865, the secession order was annulled, and laws were introduced to safeguard African Americans' civil rights. But the changes were largely superficial, and although the state government eventually bowed to pressure to include the African American population in its political processes, the requirements for those seeking high office automatically disqualified most African American candidates.

There were some exceptions, however. When the vote was granted to all male citizens of Florida aged 21 and over (including African Americans) in 1868, Jonathan C. Gibbs, Florida's first African American cabinet member, was elected. Born of free parents in Philadelphia, Gibbs came to Florida after the Civil War to serve as a Presbyterian missionary. He was appointed secretary of state in 1869.

Meanwhile, nine-tenths of Florida's African Americans were working in the fields. In the 1870s, the Florida chapter of the Ku Klux Klan began to terrorize local African Americans. Despite these injustices, Harriet Beecher Stowe—whose antislavery epic *Uncle Tom's Cabin* had done so much to rally the abolitionists when it was published in 1852—did note that Florida's African Americans were better off than those in neighboring states.

❏ By the 1870s, even tourists were venturing into the interior of Florida—albeit from the comfortable confines of the luxury steamboats that plied the St. Johns River. ❏

OPENING UP THE STATE In spite of the threat of yellow fever and malaria, there were still plenty of settlers eager to make a go of it in Florida's open spaces. Citrus plantations boomed, and in 1881 the state sold 4 million acres (over 1.6 million hectares) to Hamilton Disston, who drained land in the Kissimmee and Caloosahatchee valleys to build settlements and for farming.

THE RAILROAD BARONS In the 1880s, two businessmen were to transform the state by building railroads. Henry B. Plant pioneered a cross-state railroad to Tampa on the Gulf Coast; Henry M. Flagler decked the Atlantic Coast with a necklace of luxurious resort hotels that stretched from Jacksonville to Key West, linked by his East Coast Railroad.

State land grants in exchange for development were a powerful incentive for the railroad builders. For every mile of track between Tampa and Kissimmee—a distance of 75 miles (121km)—Plant received 5,000 acres (2,000ha) of virgin territory. In 1884, with just 63 hours to spare on the contract he made it into Tampa and began work on the $3.5 million, 500-room Tampa Bay Hotel.

WIDER CONNECTIONS Plant also added to his growing transportation system a steamship service to Key West and Cuba. In 1885, Vincente Martinez Ybor moved his Cuban cigar-making industry from Key West to Tampa Bay. That same year inventor Thomas Alva Edison found a good spot beside the Caloosahatchee River at Fort Myers, down the coast from Tampa, to build himself a winter home.

Tampa's Cuban connection generated anti-Spanish propaganda, and in 1898 Teddy Roosevelt and his

Locomotives old and new

Rough Riders, the first Regiment of U.S. Cavalry Volunteers, rode into town en route to the Spanish–American War in Cuba. A young British journalist named Winston Churchill covered the news from the comfort of Plant's hotel.

EAST COAST SPLENDOR Though Plant was a prime mover in the development of Florida, the state's transition to a fashionable winter vacation area was largely due to the efforts of Henry M. Flagler. Honeymooning in St. Augustine in the early 1880s, Flagler was disappointed by the lack of facilities and determined to bring the resort up to standard. The magnificent Spanish-Moorish-Revival-style Ponce de León Hotel opened in 1888. The Hotel Ormond at Ormond Beach followed in 1890. The Royal Poinciana opened in Palm Beach in 1894.

During the winter of 1894–95, a terrible freeze destroyed citrus plantations as far south as Fort Lauderdale. In 1896, Miami pioneer Julia Tuttle persuaded Flagler to extend his East Coast Railroad line to Miami, where citrus trees still flourished, by sending him a bouquet of orange blossoms untouched by the freeze farther north. Flagler's railroad eventually reached Key West in 1912, a year before his death.

❑ Though the Ponce de León Hotel is now a college and the Hotel Ormond and Royal Poinciana have disappeared, there is one exceptional reminder of the days when Florida's Atlantic Coast was the premier winter playground of the Vanderbilts and Rockefellers. **The Breakers** at Palm Beach, originally a Flagler creation, was rebuilt in the 1920s after a fire, and its seven-story Italian Renaissance-style facade, lofty ceilings, and magnificent furnishings are still a sight to behold. ❑

In 1912, when Henry Flagler steamed into Key West aboard his famous "Railroad That Went to Sea," his dreams were finally realized. This was a romantic project from its inception, and it cost Flagler dearly.

The last 156-mile (251km) section of the East Coast Railroad system, extending from Homestead south of Miami down through the Keys, took seven years and several million dollars to complete. But somehow anything seemed possible in Florida at the beginning of the new century.

NEW FRONTIERS Entrepreneur Carl Fisher arrived in Miami as Flagler was celebrating. There he met New Jersey horticulturist John Collins who was struggling to transform a failed avocado plantation into a residential area on a strip of sand three miles out in Biscayne Bay. Fisher advanced Collins $50,000 to develop the land in exchange for a 200-acre (80ha) plot. They built a wooden bridge across to the mainland, the longest in the country at the time, and in 1915 Fisher started a dredging operation that would almost double the size of the island, now known as Miami Beach.

As the mangrove wilderness was tamed, elegant hotels, shopping malls, golf courses and tennis courts sprang up along the beach. Across the bay, industrialist millionaire James Deering built himself a magnificent mansion, Vizcaya; farther up the coast, self-taught architect Addison Mizner was enchanting the well-to-do with his Spanish-Mediterranean-inspired creations in Palm Beach. By the 1920s, Florida was definitely on the map, and everybody wanted a little piece of it.

REAL ESTATE MADNESS It was with a sense of adventure that the first "tin-can tourists" drove the length and breadth of the country in their shiny new Fords, Oldsmobiles and Packards. The shortage of hotels could not deter them. They set up tented cities on the beach and dined out of tin cans. And they were easy targets for the squadrons of smooth-talking salesmen who hurried south as rumors spread of the real estate mania. The Marx Brothers even made a film about it called *Coconuts*. These shark-like salesmen, the "binder boys," made fortunes overnight reselling options on undeveloped lots to the uninitiated. Elaborate advertising campaigns, involving huge sums of money, further fueled the dreams of those who raced south to invest in a little Florida sunshine.

THE ENTREPRENEURS George Merrick, founder of America's first planned community, spent $3 million in a single year advertising his Coral Gables development in Miami. This was one of the finest results of the land-boom era, and one of the most enduring. Its French, Dutch South African and Chinese neighborhoods are still regarded as some of the most desirable residential areas in Miami (see page 54).

Inspired by Carl Fisher's success in Miami Beach, Charlie Rodes tackled the swamps of Fort Lauderdale. By dredging a series of parallel channels, he raised a neat clutch of finger islands that lent the city a Venetian air—and earned Rodes a fortune.

Meanwhile, Addison Mizner was doing so well in Palm Beach that he and his brother, Winston, snapped up 16,000 acres (6,400ha) of land around the fishing hamlet of Boca Raton. In 1925, they launched a fulsome advertising campaign which incorporated the slogan "I'm the Greatest Resort in the World!" and sold $26 million worth of contracts before they had built a single Venetian-style bridge.

END OF A DREAM The land boom reached its height in 1925, and within a year Mizner's Boca Raton was already being decried as "Beaucoup Rotten." Disaster hit the resort when Miami was struck by a hurricane, and a couple of banks collapsed the following spring. Real estate investors realized they'd been duped when they took stock of their precious plots. Some plots were under water in swamps, while others were buried beneath mosquito-infested mangrove thickets. Things went from bad to worse. A drastic hurricane swept across the lower edge of the state in 1928, leaving more than 2,000 people dead and millions of dollars' worth of property destroyed. In the wake of this catastrophe came the stock market crash of 1929, which marked the beginning of the 1930s Depression years.

Florida's sunshine has drawn visitors to the state for more than 100 years

❑ The land boom also hit the Gulf Coast. Real estate guru Wilson Fuller wrote a book describing his experiences in St. Petersburg, where his creative practices allowed him to transform a single investment of $50,000 into $270,000 in a few simple moves. Just down the coast, in Sarasota, circus king John Ringling threw causeways across the bay to barrier-island Longboat Key, where he built an attractive shopping district to spare his wife and guests the trouble of journeying to Palm Beach. ❑

The collapse of the land boom and the ensuing Great Depression left a string of paper millionaires turned paupers—and an unpleasant taste in the mouths of many investors.

Florida suffered less than the rest of the United States. Here, while the rest of the country was locked in gloom, it was one of the few bright spots on the horizon: The promise of sunny skies and palm-fringed beaches still worked magic.

THE 1930s After a quiet start, the rest of the decade was actually a time of expansion for the state. Hardest hit by the crash, Miami was also the first to recover, and confident new building programs signaled that the city was on the road to recovery. Miami Beach blossomed with the construction of art deco hotels, and embraced the Moderne style a few years later.

Miami's high-rises

The Hialeah Park Race Track opened in 1931 to celebrate the legalization of pari-mutuel betting. This drew a large and enthusiastic crowd to the greyhound tracks, as well as to the jai alai *frontons* (as the venues for this pelota-like game are known). Legalized betting also attracted the attention of organized crime, and gangster Al Capone retired to a heavily guarded estate on Palm Island, where he died in 1947. With no state income tax or inheritance tax, and its inviting climate, Florida also welcomed less infamous retirees.

During the mid-1930s, the state benefited from a number of wide-ranging federal-aid programs. Land reclamation, public buildings and transportation were covered by the brief, as were cultural, educational and welfare projects.

When Flagler's former Overseas Railroad was destroyed by the Labor Day hurricane of 1935, federal relief workers picked over the ruins and built the Overseas Highway. Meanwhile, the Florida Emergency Relief Agency (F.E.R.A.) worked together with local residents to gentrify Key West, which rapidly attracted literary types.

TOURISTS AND ASTRONAUTS By the early 1940s, Florida's population of 2 million was outnumbered by tourists in winter. Between 1945 and 1954, to cope with the demand, more hotel rooms were built in Greater Miami alone than in all the rest of the United States. In 1959, the nation's first scheduled domestic jet air service commenced between New York and Miami, and brought a new generation of tourists.

Jet airliners were not the only hardware streaking across Florida's wide blue yonder. In 1958, the Cape Canaveral Air Force Station, halfway

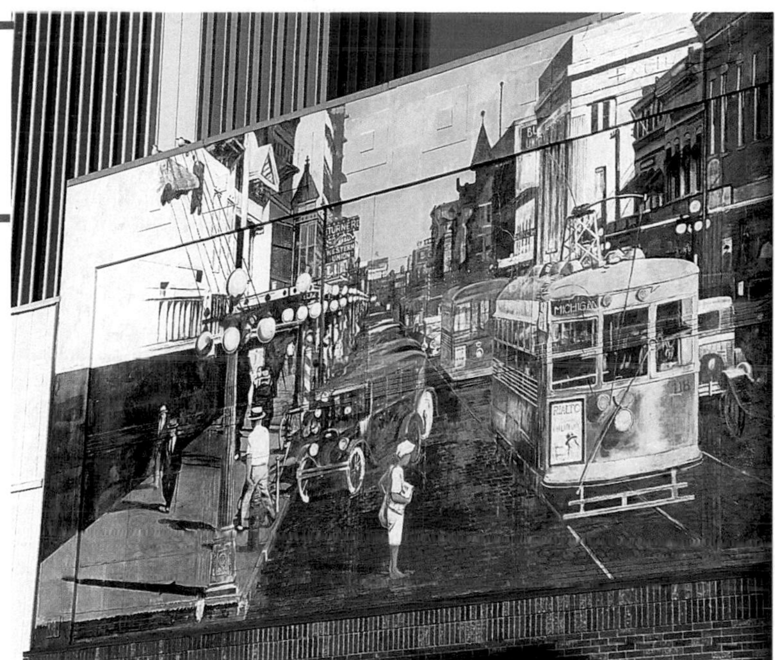

Mural in downtown Tampa

up Florida's Atlantic Coast, was chosen by the newly established National Aeronautics and Space Administration (NASA) as a testing ground for its early satellite and rocket programs. Later NASA built its own facility nearby. World attention was focused on the Kennedy Space Center's monitors for the historic *Apollo 11* moonwalk, when Neil Armstrong carried mankind one step farther into the future.

THE DISNEY PHENOMENON Mickey Mouse arrived in 1971. Preparations for the theme park began quietly in the early 1960s, when Walt Disney targeted the state—and specifically the area near Kissimmee and Orlando—as the ideal site for his new venture. Good communications and transportation, plus year-round sunshine were all factors in his choice, along with the availability of huge tracts of undeveloped land—possibly the greatest attraction.

Appalled by the commercial sprawl that had sprung up around his California Disneyland, Disney was determined to control the surroundings on this project. Executives were sworn to secrecy as agents began to buy land. By the time an announcement was made in 1965, Disney had amassed 28,000 acres (11,200ha), a site twice the size of Manhattan. The Magic Kingdom opened its doors in 1971, Epcot in 1983, Disney-MGM Studios in 1989 and Animal Kingdom in 1998. Together they make up the world's number-one tourist destination and have attracted more than 500 million visitors since 1971.

INTO THE FUTURE Florida continues to grow from strength to strength. Tourism, born in the 1880s, is now the backbone of the state's wealth as it moves into the 21st century. Florida's financial sector and high-tech industries are also booming, and attract an increasingly youthful quota of new residents. During the 1990s, attempts to address major ecological concerns such as pollution and damage to reefs and wetlands made some progress, but there is still much to do if Florida's precious wilderness areas and wildlife are to be preserved for the next generation.

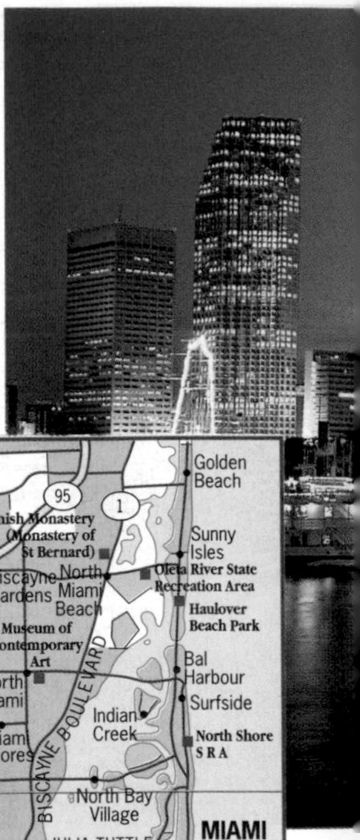

STRETCHED ALONG THE GLITTERING blue waterfront of Biscayne Bay, Miami is a palm-fringed beach resort, a financial powerhouse and a gateway to Latin America all rolled into one. Dynamic, exotic and forward-looking, the city's profile has never been higher. Not bad for a far-flung pioneer settlement that rose from the swamps little more than a century ago.

Today, Miami-Dade County covers an area of 1,946sq miles (5,040sq km) and has 2.25 million residents, but when pioneer settler Julia Tuttle arrived by mailboat in 1875, all she found were the remains of Fort Dallas, a Seminole trading post and a few scattered plantations around the bay.

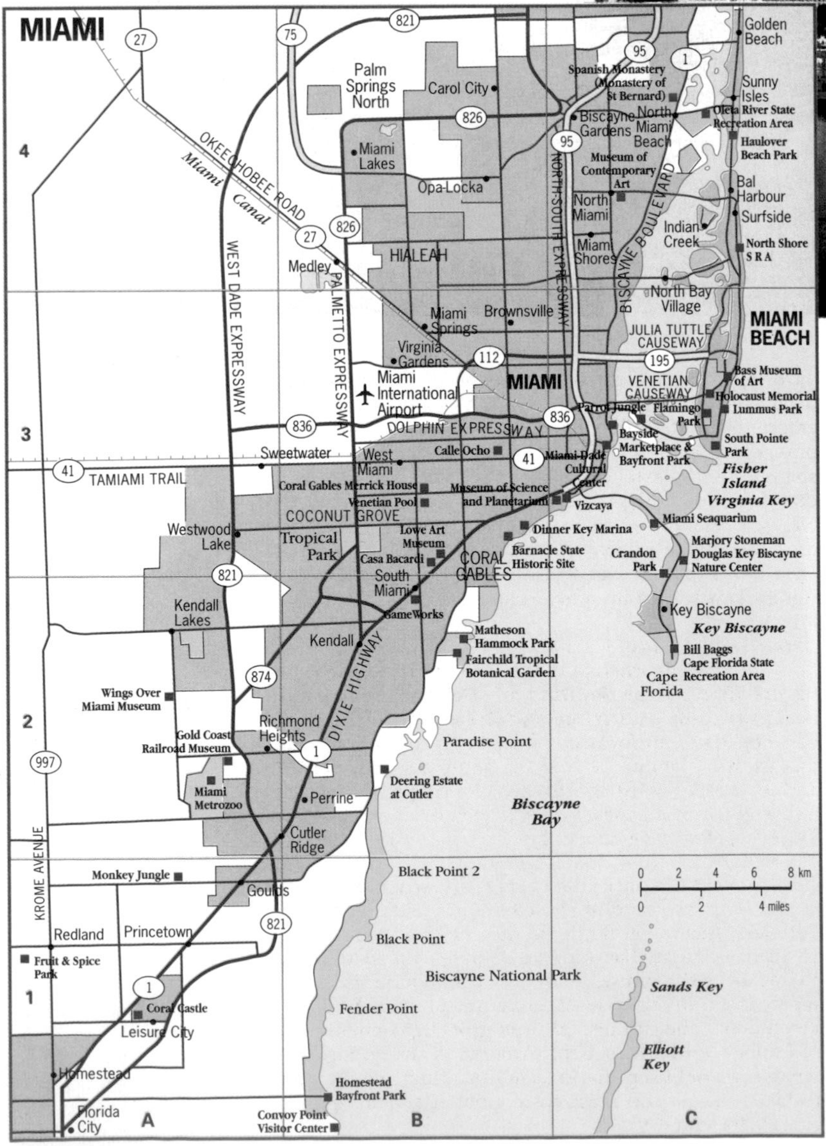

A–Z Miami

Left: The Downtown skyline rises dramatically behind the blazing lights of Bayside Marketplace

During the terrible winter frost of 1894–1895, which decimated citrus groves as far south as Palm Beach, the enterprising Mrs. Tuttle sent a bouquet of unfrosted orange blossoms to railroad baron Henry Flagler, persuading him to extend his tracks south to Miami. They duly arrived, hotly pursued by a stream of wealthy Northerners who built palatial winter retreats on the foreshore, while developers such as George Merrick created elegant **Coral Gables**, and Carl Fisher and John Collins landscaped an offshore avocado plantation into **Miami Beach**.

For all its vast size, Miami is very much a conglomeration of neighborhoods, each with a distinctive flavor—from the chic **Art Deco** and **SoBe** areas of Miami Beach to neo-Bohemian **Coconut Grove**. Downtown rejuvenation has transformed the formerly bleak financial district with landmark concrete-and-glass architecture and a state-of-the-art sports arena; an impressive $250-million Performing Arts Center opens its doors in 2006. The latest upcoming area is the Design District just north of downtown.

Bordering the financial district to the west, **Little Havana** is the spiritual home of the city's one million Cubans (although many of them no longer live there). The Hispanic influence has added a definite twist to Miami's character and culture, and the community is well-represented in both local government and financial institutions. The city also attracts growing communities of Caribbean islanders, Latin Americans and an increasing number of Europeans to its multicultural mix, and the result is one of the most cosmopolitan and intriguing cities in the country.

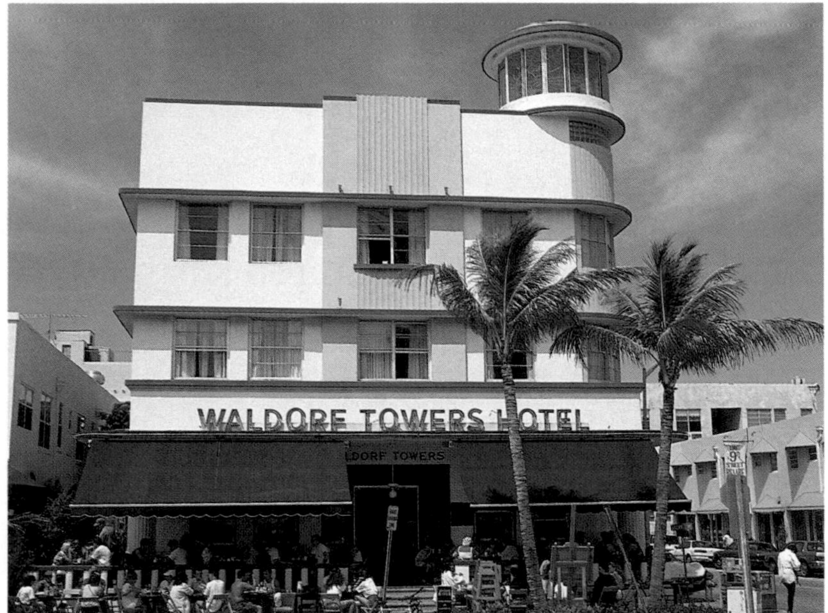

The 1930s has been brought back to life on Miami Beach's Ocean Drive

CITY HIGHLIGHTS

Miami's neighborhoods

ART DECO DISTRICT AND MIAMI BEACH Rocketed to worldwide fame as one of the most recognizable jet-set haunts of the 1990s, the stylish Art Deco District covers a mere 12-block portion of Miami Beach, which is actually a 7sq mile (18sq km) barrier island linked to the mainland by causeways across Biscayne Bay. But this historic district contains more than 800 art deco buildings listed on the National Register of Historic Places, and is the centerpiece of the ultra-chic area known as **SoBe** (South Beach), which occupies the southern tip of Miami Beach and out to around 28th Street.

Miami Beach's building boom began in earnest after World War I with a flourish of Mediterranean Revival architecture relying heavily on romantic styles from the Old World. The earliest art deco buildings date from the mid-1920s and are richly decorated with local images such as palm trees and flamingos, earning the soubriquet "tropical deco." The less whimsical Moderne style from the 1930s represented a new age of mass-production, with streamlined aerodynamic designs and vibrant materials including chrome, glass block and neon.

Today, SoBe's main drag is **Ocean Drive**, where strikingly restored art deco hotels overlook the green swathe of Lummus Park to the Atlantic a few steps away. Restaurants, cafés and other watering-holes squeeze up against the sidewalk, inviting you to sit back and watch the fascinating parade of pedestrians, dog walkers, in-line skaters and limos that regularly brings the traffic to a complete standstill (particularly at night, when SoBe is transformed into the nightlife capital of the city).

There is excellent shopping in designer stores on Collins Avenue and the attractive open-air Lincoln Road Mall, plus numerous good restaurants and dozens of hotels to suit all tastes and budgets, from surprisingly affordable hostels to elegant little boutique accommodations housed in art deco gems. Several of the biggest and grandest beach resort hotels are found just to the north of SoBe. Farther north are the quieter districts of Surfside, Bal Harbour (with a sophisticated shopping center) and Sunny Isles—a popular option for family holidays, with affordable accommodations, great beaches, fishing and watersports.

COCONUT GROVE When Doctor Horace P. Porter opened his Cocoanut (*sic*) Grove Post Office in 1873, there were only two coconut palms growing in the grove. However, the name caught on when the town of Coconut Grove was incorporated in 1919, and a plentiful supply of palm fronds cast their shadows on the shopfronts and outdoor cafés of this pleasant Mediterranean-style neighborhood. Bordering Biscayne Bay, Coconut Grove is a 10-minute drive south of downtown Miami. Its intimate village-like atmosphere has long attracted visiting artists and writers; veteran Everglades conservationist Marjorie Stoneman Douglas lived here for more than 70 years.

Coconut Grove was the product of a friendship between early settlers Charles and Isabella Peacock and Yankee visitor Ralph Middleton Munroe. Munroe encouraged the Peacocks to establish a small hotel in 1884, which prospered with the arrival of Henry Flagler's railroad 12 years later. Rustic camps began to spring up along the bayfront, and eventually Munroe built his own home, **The Barnacle**, now a state historic site (see page 57).

The Peacock Inn expanded and soon employed a number of Bahamian immigrants, who constructed their distinctive wood-frame "conch houses" along Charles Avenue. The city's Bahamian heritage is celebrated in style every June when the lively **Goombay Festival** takes

FESTIVAL TIMES
Festivals are big in the Grove. In January, there is the annual Taste of the Grove food festival; while the annual three-day Arts Festival in February includes demonstrations, lectures and live jazz. Autumn brings the Columbus Day Regatta, during which more than 65 vessels compete in 21 classes over a weekend. In December, there is the crazy King Mango Strut Parade, a good-natured spoof on the Orange Bowl Parade.

Milkshakes and bartop jukeboxes at a 1950s-style retro haunt in Coconut Grove

MIAMI DESIGN DISTRICT
Brainchild of leading South Beach developer Craig Robins, the Design District is Miami's latest happening neighborhood. Since 1995, almost $25 million has been plowed into the 18-block "village" north of downtown, and refurbished old buildings are filling up with exciting interior design and furniture showrooms, galleries and restaurants. Notable occupants of this "SoHo of the South" already include Holly Hunt and Waterworks and Robins has plundered his own extensive contemporary art collection to adorn public spaces.

place, complete with processions, "junkanoo" bands and street stalls. On the corner of Charles Avenue, the decorative 1920s **Coconut Grove Playhouse**, opened as a movie theater in 1926, is now home to one of south Florida's leading theater companies (see page 79).

At the heart of the Grove, boutiques, galleries and restaurants line Main Highway and Commodore Plaza; the upscale Streets of Mayfair and neon-lit CocoWalk complexes on Grand Avenue offer more of the same. Down on the waterfront, you'll find Dinner Key, named for a favorite picnic spot of the area's early residents. There is also David Kennedy Park with a bayshore fitness course, walking trails and children's playground. To the north, the **Vizcaya Museum and Gardens** and the **Museum of Science and Planetarium** are major attractions.

CORAL GABLES At the height of the 1920s land boom, developer George Merrick laid the foundations for America's first planned community, Coral Gables. Almost 70 years later, Merrick's exclusive estate remains one of the most prestigious neighborhoods in town. Between the broad main boulevards, quiet tree-lined streets wind past villas and walled compounds, fountains, plazas and green open spaces. Coral Gables House, on Coral Way, was Merrick's boyhood home.

The development of **The Villages** was Merrick's pet project. Although he never traveled, he gave these enclaves architectural styles ranging from French to colonial Dutch South African. The community was entered through gateways like the imposing **Puerto del Sol** at the intersection of Douglas Road and the Tamiami Trail. Among this neighborhood's highlights are the Spanish Mediterranean-style **City Hall** on Miracle Mile and Merrick's stunning **Biltmore Hotel**, on Anastasia Avenue, easily identified by its 16-story tower, a replica of Seville's Giralda Tower.

Coral Gables' main thoroughfare, **Miracle Mile**, is known for its good restaurants and shopping. To the

Colonnade Building, Coral Gables

south is the University of Miami, founded on land donated by Merrick. Here, the **Lowe Art Museum** exhibits the Kress Collection of Renaissance and baroque art. Farther south, on the bayshore, the **Fairchild Tropical Botanic Garden** is one of the largest such gardens in the Continental United States.

DOWNTOWN A mixture of gleaming skyscrapers, old-style office blocks, cultural centers and building sites, Miami's downtown district is now smartening up after several decades of neglect. Downtown Miami spans both sides of the Miami River, with its main thoroughfare, Flagler Street, running east–west from the bayfront.

Two important arts centers on Flagler Street are the 1920s **Gusman Center for the Performing Arts** (174 E. Flagler), which plays host to the highly regarded Florida Philharmonic Orchestra, as well as an annual film festival and the **Miami-Dade Cultural Center** (see page 62). Flagler Street has a variety of major stores and small shops, but **Bayside Marketplace** attracts more shoppers. Just next door is the new **American Airlines Arena** multipurpose sports and entertainment venue. Parking is a problem downtown, however, so use the cheap and efficient Metromover transportation system.

LITTLE HAVANA Since the 1960s, Cuban refugees and immigrants have been resettling in Miami. They have brought their language, customs and heroes to this 3.5-acre (1.5ha) district just west of downtown, and infused it with a distinctive Latin American flavor.

S.W. 8th Street, better known as **Calle Ocho**, is the commercial heart of the district and the place to find a good Cuban sandwich or a window full of votive statues, buy a handrolled cigar or an embroidered *guayabera* shirt or check out the action in **Domino Park**, on the corner of 15th Street. A night out in a Cuban restaurant is an experience, and the annual March fiesta is one of Miami's biggest and best street parties.

LUNCH IN LITTLE HAVANA

A meal in itself, a Cuban sandwich is constructed on a heroic scale. Locals gather on the sidewalk outside the sandwich shop windows sipping tiny cups of Cuban coffee while they wait for their sandwiches to be built. Long, crusty loaves of Cuban bread are split and piled high with ham, pork, Swiss cheese and pickles, then baked in a pizza oven and finished off with mild-to-hot peppery sauce.

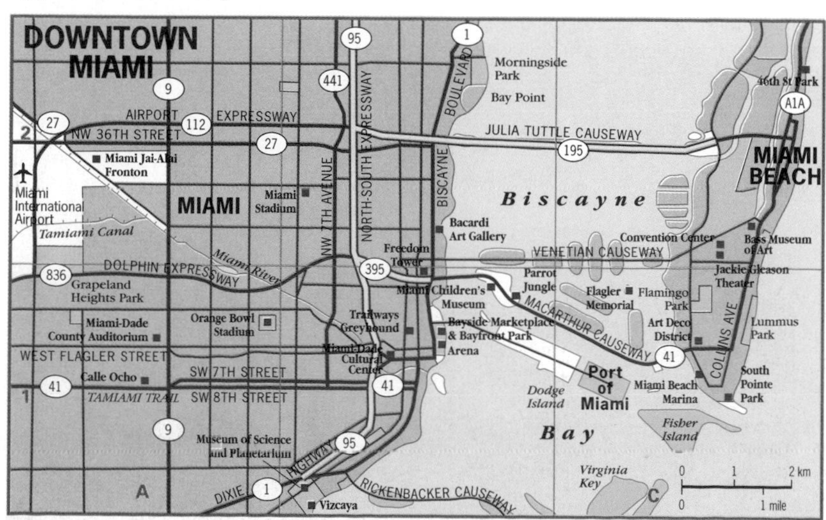

Walk

Through the Art Deco District

Start on Ocean Drive at 5th Street, and walk north.

Take the Lummus Park sidewalk for the best view of the outstanding art deco hotels en route to the **Art Deco Welcome Center**, 1001 Ocean Drive (*Open* Mon–Fri 11–6, Sat 10–10, Sun 11–10).

Turn left on 10th Street for two blocks.

Pass **Essex House** (1001 Collins Avenue) with its beautifully restored foyer adorned by a mural and an etched-glass flamingo window. Then check out the friezes on the former **Washington Storage Building** (1001 Washington Avenue), where snowbirds once stored their furnishings after the winter season. Today it houses the fascinating **Wolfsonian-F.I.U. Museum of Art and Design 1885–1945** (*Open* Mon, Tue, Sat, Sun noon–6, Thu–Fri noon–9 . *Admission: inexpensive*).

Turn right on Washington.

Along Washington, look for two art deco-era public buildings: the old **Miami Beach City Hall** (1130 Washington); and the **U.S. Post Office** (1300 Washington).

At **Espanola Way**, turn left.

This quaint Mediterranean-inspired side street is a great place to window shop or stop for a cold drink.

Turn right onto Pennsylvannia.

A couple of blocks north, the pedestrianized **Lincoln Road Mall** is a terrific shopping, dining and entertainment district.

To complete the circuit, head east on Lincoln Road, turn right on Collins, and left on 15th Street to rejoin Ocean Drive.

Pastel colors characterize the restored facades of Miami's Art Deco District

Coconut Grove

Start at the corner of Grand Avenue and Main Highway, at the heart of the Coconut Grove shopping district. Walk down Main Highway.

The first stop is the **Coconut Grove Playhouse** (3500 Main Highway), rebuilt in 1927 after a hurricane. Its Spanish rococo facade has elaborate stuccowork, parapets and twisted barley-sugar columns.

On the right, **Charles Avenue** was the home of the Grove's first black community, founded in the 1880s. Note the traditional Miami-Bahamian "conch" architecture.

Continue on Main Highway for five minutes to the corner of Devon Road on the right.

Ivy-clad **Plymouth Congregational Church** was erected in 1917, and resembles a Spanish mission building, constructed of hand-cut local coral rock. Palms flank the 400-year-old walnut and oak door (from a monastery in the Pyrenees), and there is a pretty garden cloister.

Return from Devon Road along Main Highway.

Hiding behind a tangled wall of trees, the secluded **Barnacle State Historic Site** (3845 Main Highway) is the oldest Miami home still on its original foundations. The cleverly restored 1891 pioneer residence includes many original furnishings and Coconut Grove resident and naval architect Ralph Midleton Munroe's wooden ketch, *Micco*, is on display in the boathouse (see page 58).

Continue to retrace your steps back along Main Highway to CocoWalk where you will find boutiques, outdoor cafés and restaurants galore.

The Barnacle State Historic Site is a gracious reminder of Coconut Grove's early days

The Barnacle, built by Ralph Midleton Munroe in 1981

Exotic foliage adorns the high-rise facade of the Bacardi Imports building

► Bacardi Art Gallery 55 B2

2100 Biscayne Boulevard; tel: 305/573-8511 ext. 366
Open: Mon–Fri 9–5

North of downtown, the eye-catching 1930s blue-and-white mosaic-tiled Bacardi Imports building makes an unusual local landmark. A small museum (*Admission free*) documents the Bacardi family history. Visit by appointment only.

►► Bal Harbour 50 C4

9700 Collins Avenue, Miami Beach; tel: 305/866-0311
Open: Mon–Sat 10–9, Sun noon–6

This is an exclusive, beautifully laid out shopping mall, with a handful of notable European designer boutiques joining the ranks of top American stores, including Saks Fifth Avenue and Neiman Marcus.

►► Barnacle State Historic Site 50 B3

3485 Main Highway, Coconut Grove; tel: 305/442-6866, www.floridastateparks.org
Open: Fri–Sun for tours at 10, 11.30, 1 and 2.30.
Admission: inexpensive

One of the oldest homes in Miami, the Barnacle was built by Coconut Grove pioneer and naval engineer Ralph Midleton Munroe in 1891. The historic two-story building has period furnishings, a steep hipped roof in the shape of a barnacle and views across the bay (see Walk, page 57).

►► Bass Museum of Art 55 C2

2121 Park Avenue, Miami Beach; tel: 305/673-7530, www.bassmuseum.org
Open: Tue–Sat, 10–5 (second Thu of month to 9), Sun 11–5.
Admission: moderate

Housed in an elegant 1930s Streamline former library, the Bass displays a notable collection of European Renaissance, baroque and rococo art, American, Asian and contemporary works, textiles, tapestries, as well as a section containing architectural plans and photographs detailing the development of Miami Beach. To contain all these elements, the museum has almost doubled in size with the opening of improved galleries, a café-terrace and stores in an $8-million expansion program designed by celebrated architect Arata Isozaki, and inaugurated in mid-2000. The Bass also hosts frequent historic and contemporary exhibitions of American and international art.

► Bayfront Park *55 B1*

100 Biscayne Boulevard

The 32-acre (13ha) Bayfront Park skirts the shoreline from Bayside Marketplace to the cruise ships in the port of Miami. Joggers pound past the palm trees incessantly, and there is an amphitheater that hosts popular open-air concerts. Plaques around the **John F. Kennedy Memorial Torch of Friendship** represent Miami's friendly ties with Latin America: The gap in the row of plaques is being saved for Cuba, which will be added when relations with the communist Castro regime change.

►►► Bayside Marketplace *55 B1*

401 N. Biscayne Boulevard; tel: 305/577-3344, www.baysidemarketplace.com

Open: Mon–Thu 10–10, Fri–Sun 10am–11pm

Right on the bay, fronting the downtown district, this is one of Miami's busiest attractions. There are more than 150 shops—ranging from wacky gift stores to popular clothing outlets, and a Warner Bro. Studio and Disney store. South American crafts stalls, sellers of cheap sunglasses and sports outfitters vie for attention, while entertainment is provided by street performers. There are plenty of restaurants, bars and coffee shops.

The dockside bustles with charter boats heading off on sightseeing trips around the bay. Live music brightens the atmosphere at night, and the restaurant scene, which includes the tastes of Mexico, China, Thailand and Italy, is sure to satisfy any craving.

► Casa Bacardi

1531 Brescia Avenue, Coral Gables; tel: 305/288-2822, www.casabacardi.iccas.miami.edu

Open: Mon–Fri 10–5 with extended hours throughout the year

With funds donated by the Bacardi family, the University of Miami has opened The Institute for Cuban and Cuban American Studies. The interactive repository of history and culture has exhibitions of photographs and testimonies of pre- and post-Communist Cubans, a Spanish-language cinema and an annual film festival.

► Coral Castle *50 A1*

28655 S. Dixie Highway, Homestead; tel: 305/248-6345, www.coralcastle.com

Open: daily 9–6. Admission: moderate

When Edward Leedskalnin, a 26-year-old Latvian immigrant, was left at the altar by his fiancée, he found solace in building this unique castle out of solid coral rock. Constructed between 1920 and 1940, the 3-acre (1.2ha) castle is one of south Florida's original tourist attractions (see panel on page 60). Coral Castle now offers a 30-minute state-of-the-art audio tour.

Entertainment on the Bayside

ROCK SOLID
In the course of constructing his coral testimonial to lost love, the 5ft-tall (1.5m) Leedskalnin shifted some 1,100 tons of rock single-handedly. He furnished the castle with stone tables and chairs, and a telescope pointed at the North Star. There's also a 9-ton swinging gate that can be opened with a gentle push.

Masts bristle in Dinner Key Marina

▶ Coral Gables Merrick House and Gardens *50B3*

907 Coral Way; tel: 305/460-5361
Open: Wed and Sun only, 1–4 (guided tours); gardens daily until dusk. Admission: inexpensive
The boyhood home of Coral Gables developer George Merrick, this modest house surrounded by attractive gardens was founded in 1903. This 3,000-acre (1,200ha) estate was the basis for his dream of a brand-new city. The house has been carefully restored in the style of the 1920s, and many of the furnishings are genuine family pieces, including portraits and Mrs. Merrick's grand piano.

▶ Deering Estate at Cutler *50 B2*

16701 S.W. 72nd Avenue; tel: 305/235-1668, www.deeringestate.com
Open: daily 10–5. House tours are at 10.30 and 2. Last ticket sold one hour before closing. Admission: moderate
Charles Deering's waterfront preserve (360 acres/144ha) on Biscayne Bay could not be more different from his brother James's manicured Vizcaya estate. It's now a park, with acres of mangroves, pinelands, palms and tropical hardwood hammocks. You can tour the grounds on foot or by bus, and a 3-hour guided canoe trip is offered twice daily. Deering's stone mansion and a timber-framed hotel, which was the original property on the estate, are both being restored and are open to visitors.

▶ Dinner Key Marina *50 B3*

3400 Pan American Drive, Coconut Grove
Start/finish point of the annual Columbus Day Regatta (October), this was where early Grove residents set out on boating and picnicking expeditions, hence the name. Today you can admire the art deco Miami City Hall, originally the Pan Am seaplane terminal, visit one of many waterfront bars, rent charter boats and go windsurfing.

▶▶▶ Fairchild Tropical Botanic Garden *50 B2*

10901 Old Cutler Road; tel: 305/667-1651, www.fairchildgarden.org
Open: daily 9.30–4.30. Admission: moderate
More than 80 acres (32ha) of spreading lawns, lakes and exotic species from around the globe comprise these wonderful botanical gardens. The "must-see" area is the McLamore Arboretum, 10 acres (4ha) of flowering trees and shrubs, a 187-yard (168m) pergola draped in exotic vines, and a collection of desert plants. The Palmetum Walk spotlights an extraordinary variety of palm trees. Then stop off at the Windows to the Tropics hothouse for displays of tender orchids, aroids and bromeliads before visiting the Tropical Fruit Pavilion with its collection from the Amazon and Southeast Asia.

▶ Freedom Tower *55 B1*

600 Biscayne Boulevard
The 1925 Spanish-Mediterranean-style Freedom Tower, modeled after the Giralda Tower in Seville, Spain, was built to house the *Miami News*. It earned its present name when it served as a refugee-processing center for more than 600,000 Cubans during the 1962 crisis. It is hoped to restore the tower to house a museum of the Cuban experience in Miami.

A cool vista in Fairchild Tropical Garden

▶ Fruit and Spice Park *50 A1*

24801 S.W. 187th Avenue, Redland; tel. 305/247-5727
Open: daily 10–5. Admission: inexpensive

More than 500 varieties of fruits, vegetables, herbs, nuts and spices, gathered from every corner of the earth, flourish at this unusual botanic park near Homestead. There are guided tours on weekends, as well as tours of the local historical districts. The shop sells a wide variety of gourmet food.

▶ GameWorks *50 B2*

The Shops at Sunset Place, 5701 Sunset Drive, South Miami; tel: 305/667-4263, www.gameworks.com
Open: Sun–Mon 11–11, Tue–Thu noon–11, Fri–Sat 11am–2am

Steven Spielberg helped design this chain of activity centers that will wow bored kids (and their parents) with a wide selection of state-of-the-art games played out in themed zones. If battling dinosaurs or aliens, or testing your coordination skills with simulated jet-ski, motorcycle or baseball action appeals, this should be fun.

▶ Gold Coast Railroad Museum *50 A2*

12450 S.W. 152nd Street; tel: 305/253-0063, www.goldcoastrailroad.org
Open: Mon–Fri 10–4, Sat–Sun 11–4. Admission: inexpensive

This collection of historic locomotives includes the *Ferdinand Magellan*, the only Pullman car designed specifically for U.S. presidents. Definitely a must for train buffs, with weekend train rides around the 68-acre (27ha) site.

▶▶ Haulover Beach Park *50 C4*

10800 Collins Avenue, Sunny Isles Beach; tel: 305/944-3040

This major recreational park offers the best of Florida's natural attractions, including a 2-mile (3km) stretch of hotel-free seashore, complete with golden sands, Atlantic surf, a nine-hole golf course, deep-sea fishing, picnic areas with barbecue facilities, boat rentals and walking trails.

▶▶▶ Key Biscayne see page 63. *50 C4*

HOLOCAUST MEMORIAL

Symbolically located at 1933–1945 Meridian Avenue in Miami Beach, this emotionally moving memorial's centerpiece is a 42ft (12.6m) bronze arm rising from the ground, with sculptured people climbing the arm seeking escape. A memorial wall with victims' names and a meditation garden complement the sculpture.

A sampling of more than 8,000 works of art at the Lowe Art Museum on the University of Miami campus

ENJOY A GOOD BOOK
The state-of-the-art Miami-Dade Regional Library (227 23rd Street), opened in October 2004, features a reading garden and coffee lounge, offering the perfect environment for cultural relaxation.

►►► Lowe Art Museum *50 B3*

1301 Stanford Drive, Coral Gables; tel: 305/284-3535
Open: Tue, Wed, Fri and Sat 10–5, Thu noon–7, Sun noon–5.
Admission: inexpensive
Excellent small museum on the University of Miami campus housing the fine Kress Collection of Renaissance and Baroque Art, plus American artworks, Native American, Western, Oriental and Pre-Columbian arts and crafts.

► Marjory Stoneman Douglas Biscayne Nature Center *50 C3*

6767 Crandon Road; tel: 305/361-6767, www.biscaynenaturecenter.org
This is the place to brush up on southeast Florida's fascinating natural history. Activities include marine life expeditions, walks through coastal hammocks, fossil rock reefs and on the beach, plus bike and canoe trips. All trips are led by a naturalist guide and are by reservation only.

► Miami Children's Museum *55 B1*

980 MacArthur Causeway, Watson Island; tel: 305/373-5437, www.miamichildrensmuseum.org
Open: daily 10–6
This facility was opened in 2003 and its mission is to allow kids to develop and learn through play. The 12 themed areas include child-size banks, a TV studio and a cruise ship. Other galleries offer instruction through play, including a wellness area with messages about diet and exercise. Ocean Odyssey introduces the undersea world.

►► Miami-Dade Cultural Center *55 B1*

101 W. Flagler Street
Art Museum: Tue–Fri 10–5, Sat–Sun 12–5; tel: 305/375-3000. Admission: inexpensive
Historical Museum: Mon–Sat 10–5 (Thu till 9), Sun 12–5; tel: 305/375-1492. Admission: inexpensive
One of downtown's celebrated architectural showpieces, Philip Johnson's complex houses the **Miami Art Museum**, which concentrates on artworks from the 1940s to the present, and hosts major touring exhibitions; the **Historical Museum of Southern Florida** offering an interesting glimpse into Florida's history, from prehistory to the present and the **Miami-Dade Public Library**.

This former coconut plantation in Biscayne Bay, once a haunt of wreckers and hunters, is a favorite weekend retreat for Miami's urbanites. It is linked to the mainland by the Rickenbacker Causeway, which forms an impressive curve across the bay.

Virginia Key Key Biscayne's sister island, Virginia Key is fringed by **Hobie Beach**, which offers plenty of parking for those who want to fish, swim and windsurf. Farther on, the golden domed **Miami Seaquarium** gives visitors a chance to get face to face with dolphins, sharks and whales (see page 64). Another major attraction is Virginia Key's **Miami Marine Stadium**, which stages "Pops by the Bay" summer concerts, international rowing regattas and powerboat racing.

Key Biscayne Bear Cut Bridge makes the short hop from Virginia Key to Key Biscayne. At the north end of the island, Bear Cut becomes Crandon Boulevard. The boulevard bisects the lush 500-acre (22ha) **Crandon Park**, where jogging paths and 2.5 miles (4km) of public beaches welcome outdoor enthusiasts and offer facilities for picnickers. The park's ocean side is lined with luxury hotels and condominiums, and facilities include one of the finest 18-hole golf courses in the US, plus a tennis complex that plays host to international tournaments. At the north end of the beach, the **Marjorie Stoneman Douglas Biscayne Nature Center** offers hands-on marine encounters and a program of walks and talks on Florida's natural world.

Away from it all The southern tip of the island is given over to the **Bill Baggs Cape Florida State Recreation Area**, originally named Cape Florida by early explorer Ponce de León in 1513. This 406-acre (162ha) preserve is the site of Florida's oldest lighthouse and the oldest surviving structure in South Florida. The **Cape Florida Lighthouse** was erected in 1825 to warn ships off the treacherous reefs along the coastline. A 122-step spiral staircase climbs up to an observation post with panoramic views of the bay. Below, there is a reconstructed New England-style keeper's cottage with period furnishings.

Near the beach area, edged by pines and sea grapes, a concession stand sells snacks and bait and rents tackle, snorkels, bicycles and gear for windsurfers. At the bayside sea wall, you can hook snook, bonefish or grouper. There are walking trails, good birdwatching and turtles nesting in season.

BRIDGE WITH A VIEW
The William M. Powell Bridge rises 75ft (22.5m) above the water to eliminate the need for a draw span. The Old Rickenbacker Causeway Bridge, which was replaced by the Powell Bridge, is now a fishing pier with good views of downtown Miami.

Cape Florida Lighthouse

Siesta-time for one of Miami Metrozoo's inhabitants

HURRICANE ALERT
Hurricanes are common in Florida between June and November, with August to October being the peak season for the storms. In 1992, Hurricane Andrew slammed into Florida's east coast just south of Miami, where it did an estimated $20 billion in damage, killed at least 22, and left thousands homeless.

►►► Miami Metrozoo *50 A2*

12400 S.W. 152nd Street, Kendall; tel: 305/251-0400, www.miamimetrozoo.com
Open: daily 9.30–5.30 (last tickets sold at 4).
Admission: moderate

Miami has a zoo to be proud of in this well-planned and thoughtfully executed, largely cageless zoo. Metrozoo's 290-acre (116ha) site features areas of simulated African jungle and veldt, and Asian and European forest, which are home to more than 800 animals representing 191 species. Unfettered by old-fashioned bars, animals roam on islands surrounded by moats in convincingly re-created habitats. Among the major attractions are the Tiger Temple, Wings of Asia, displaying 70 species of rare and exotic birds, and the African Plains exhibit, where giraffes, ostriches and zebras graze on a simulated plain. A 2-mile (3km) monorail circuit takes visitors around the zoo and its aviary, with stops along the way for the Wildlife Shows, the Children's Petting Zoo and the Ecology Theater, where alligator petting offers a real Florida experience. The koala exhibit is another highlight.

►► Miami Seaquarium *50C3*

4400 Rickenbacker Causeway; tel: 305/361-5705, www.miamiseaquarium.com
Open: daily 9.30–6. Admission: expensive

Founded in 1955, the Seaquarium shows its age. However, as a family attraction it is a reliable favorite and houses a huge variety of marine life, from dolphins and sea lions to rescued manatees and turtles. A wide choice of attractions includes live shows, touch tanks and a nesting area for giant turtles and several species of sea birds. But the Seaquarium's star crowd-pullers are Salty the sea lion, Lolita the killer whale (campaigners are working to see her released from her cramped quarters) and the most famous dolphin of them all, Flipper (the *Flipper* movies and TV show were filmed here). The Seaquarium also operates the Water And Dolphin Exploration program (WADE), a two-hour, hands-on dolphin experience (tel: 305/365-2501).

► Miccosukee Indian Village/Airboat Tours *86 B2*

30 miles (48.5km) west of Miami on Tamiami Trail (U.S. 41); tel: 305/223-8380, www.miccosukeeresort.com
Open: daily 9–5. Admission: inexpensive

This is a classic tourist attraction, but an enjoyable one nonetheless. There is alligator-wrestling, and airboat tours into the Everglades (the latter are an unforgettable experience). Traditional Miccosukee food and crafts are on sale at the cultural center.

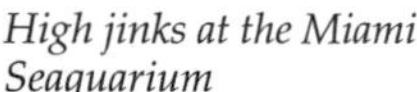

High jinks at the Miami Seaquarium

Although most families make a beeline for the theme parks, Miami also has plenty to offer the young and the young-at-heart. Beaches beckon, resort hotels run special programs for junior guests, restaurants welcome kids and there are many attractions designed specifically for families.

Fun is the name of the game at the **Museum of Science & Planetarium**, which also arranges family kayaking excursions in Florida Bay. There are games galore at the Spielberg-inspired **GameWorks** complex in South Miami, and little kids can have a ball at the new **Miami Children's Museum**.

Animal magic Southern Florida's sunny climate has given local zoological parks the edge over many of their cold-weather cousins. Top favorites are **Miami Metrozoo** and **Parrot Jungle**, where carefully recreated habitats provide a home away from home for hundreds of exotic species. In addition to the on-site playgrounds and children's petting areas, frequent animal shows aim to educate as well as to entertain.

Miami Seaquarium, across the Rickenbacker Causeway, is another must. Exhibits include rescued manatees and there are great shows which combine snippets of fascinating data with amazing feats. Visiting toddlers can be pushed around in the comfort of special dolphin-shaped strollers that are available at the park entrance.

Water, water everywhere Water babies are in luck on Miami's beaches. Gently sloping sandbars extend for several hundred yards before reaching deep water, so there is plenty of shallow swimming and paddling. Public beaches have concession stands, shaded picnic areas and sun umbrella and deck-chair rentals. The **Bill Baggs Cape Florida State Recreation Area**, on Key Biscayne, is an excellent spot for families, with a beach, picnic shelters, a café, playground, fishing piers, bait for sale and tackle for rent, plus bikes and trikes to ride on the woodland trails. A marina complex is planned; meanwhile visitors can rent kayaks and windsurfing gear to use for a spree on the ocean waves.

The **Biscayne National Park** (see page 89) offers great family snorkeling and scuba-diving excursions. Or take a dip in the historic **Venetian Pool** in Coral Gables, which is more sedate, but its calm waters, snack bar and changing facilities are ideal for young children.

Sports The Florida Marlins play baseball in town, and there is hot National Basketball Association action from home team, the Miami Heat. American football notables, the Miami Dolphins, pack the Pro-Player Stadium during football season, from September through December.

The Miami Jai Alai Fronton features this fast and furious Basque sport, and lots of local color.

WEEKEND ITINERARY

Day one: Head for Coconut Grove's Vizcaya Museum and Gardens and the Museum of Science & Planetarium. Lunch in Coconut Grove. Explore Coral Gables and seek out the Villages; or make for the Miami Seaquarium. Then it's Bayside Marketplace for shopping and sunset drinks. Dinner in Little Havana.

Day two: Taxi to Miami Beach. Stop for brunch in the Art Deco District, then return to Bayside for a Biscayne Bay cruise.

Older children may enjoy a few hours under sail on the bay

ORCHIDS IN BLOOM
Most subtropical orchids grow on trees, so you need to look up to see them. Their trailing aerial roots gather water and food released by tree bark after rain. Many orchids are scented, and they come in an amazing variety of colors.

► Monkey Jungle 50 A1

14805 S.W. 216th Street; tel: 305/235-1611, www.monkeyjungle.com
Open: daily 9.30–5. Admission: expensive

Set among the flower nurseries south of the city, Monkey Jungle is renowned for its free-ranging macaque colony, where the monkeys cavort high above the visitors enclosed in covered walkways below. However, other inhabitants such as gibbons, black spider monkeys, colobus and tamarins are secured behind the bars of conventional cages arranged in the shade of a hardwood hammock. A collection of parrots provides a splash of color. Three semi-educational shows rotate throughout the day. A gift shop sells kitsch monkey memorabilia.

► Museum of Contemporary Art (MoCA) 50 C4

770 N.E. 125th Street, North Miami; tel: 305/893-6211
Open: Tue–Sat 11–5, Sun noon–5; last Fri each month 7pm–10pm. Admission: inexpensive

Opened in 1994, the Museum of Contemporary Art is a slick 23,000sq ft (2,070sq m) gallery with a permanent collection of more than 400 works and an innovative and at times provocative attitude to the arts scene with eight to ten strong exhibitions annually. The permanent collection includes works by John Baldessari, Alex Katz, Julian Schnabel, Yoko Ono, Nam June Paik and Trenton Doyle Hancock.

►►► Museum of Science & Planetarium 55 B1

3280 S. Miami Avenue, Coconut Grove; tel: 305/854-4247
Open: daily 10–6. Admission: moderate

This museum, with more than 140 touchable exhibits and live demonstrations, sets out to win over children from the word go. Kids can have fun learning about science from the principles of physics to health issues. Traveling exhibitions in conjunction with the Smithsonian Institution are a regular feature and are beautifully

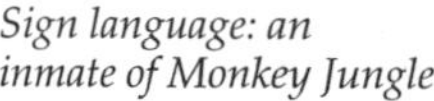

Sign language: an inmate of Monkey Jungle

presented. There are plans to develop a new $200 million Science Center of the Americas with the Smithsonian. There's also a Wildlife Center displaying reptiles such as a large albino Burmese python, iguana and tortoises and injured birds of prey that are rehabilitated before being released back into the wild where possible. The separate Planetarium (combination ticket), a tribute to the wonders of space travel, puts on fantastic multimedia laser and astronomy shows (tel: 305/854-2222).

▶▶▶ Parrot Jungle 55 B1

111 Parrot Jungle Trail, Watson Island; tel: 305/2-JUNGLE, www.parrotjungle.com
Open: daily 9–6. Admission: expensive
Set on an island betwen Miami and Miami Beach, parrot Jungle is part-zoo, part-animal theme park set in verdant tropical surroundings and offering over 1 mile (1.6km) of trails. The Parrot Bowl amphitheater plays host to some rather kitsch but renowned trained-bird shows and there are more animal antics including the drama of performing white tigers at the Jungle Theater. Lizard lovers should head for the Serpentarium or down to the Everglades Habitat, but the whole *raison d'être* of Parrot Jungle since it opened in 1936 are the birds—macaws, parakeets and parrots—whose aviaries are scattered around the island.

▶ South Pointe Park 55 C1

Washington Avenue at Biscayne Boulevard
On the southern tip of Miami Beach, this 17-acre (7ha) park is a popular recreational spot with a beach and fitness course. Fishermen are welcome, and there are a children's playground, picnic areas and barbecue grills. Concerts are staged at an amphitheater.

▶ Spanish Monastery 55 C4

16711 W. Dixie Highway, North Miami Beach; tel: 305/945-1462
Open: Mon–Sat 10–4, Sun noon–4. Admission: inexpensive
Founded in Segovia, Spain, in 1141, the former Monastery of St. Bernard was spotted by newspaper magnate William Randolph Hearst while he was on an art-buying trip to Europe in the 1920s. Hearst had the cloisters dismantled and shipped to his vast San Simeon estate in California, but when Florida customs officials replaced the blocks in the wrong cases, the project was abandoned. The painstaking five-year task of piecing it all together was finally undertaken 25 years later, and the delightful result is now an Episcopal church and wedding venue.

▶▶ Venetian Pool 50 B3

2701 DeSoto Boulevard, Coral Gables; tel: 305/460-5356, www.venetianpool.com
Closed: Mon in winter; call for schedules. Admission: inexpensive
In a moment of inspiration, George Merrick transformed an obsolete quarry into this delightful, Venetian-themed swimming hole landscaped with beaches and bridges, striped poles and quaint grottoes. The astonishingly blue lagoon must rate as one of the first themed waterparks. The Miami Opera performed here (in the drained pool) in 1926, and swimming stars Johnny Weissmuller and Esther Williams also made appearances.

WEEK'S ITINERARY

Day one and day two: As for the weekend itinerary (see page 65).

Day three: Biscayne Nature Center walk; or just relax on Key Biscayne.

Day four: Parrot Jungle; picnic in Matheson Hammock Park; Fairchild Tropical Garden.

Day five: Hialeah; Spanish Monastery; cool off on the Sunny Isles Beaches.

Day six: Everglades National Park, Main Visitor Center, near Homestead; return via Coral Castle.

Day seven: Metrozoo and Wings over Miami Museum.

Companionship in Parrot Jungle

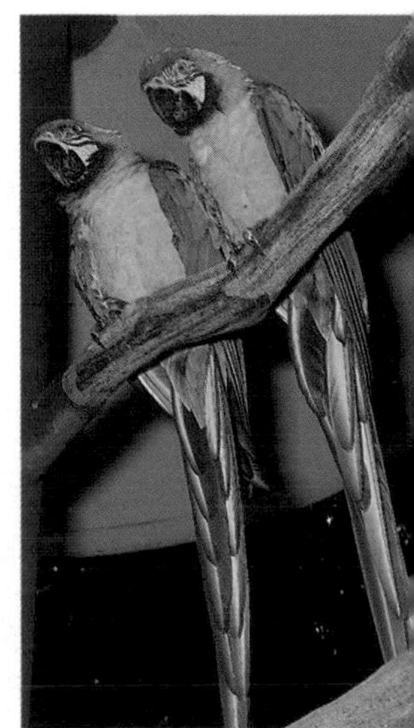

Vizcaya, a bit of Italy in America

SPANISH CONNECTIONS
James Deering named his Biscayne bayside estate for its Spanish connections. Vizcaya means "elevated place" in the Basque language of the northern Spanish region which lies on the Bay of Biscay (Biscayne is a corruption of Biscay). His chosen motif was a caravel sailing ship similar to the Spanish vessels that once put into Biscayne Bay to replenish their supplies of fresh water. A small bronze caravel decorates the entrance gate to Vizcaya on S. Miami Avenue.

►►► Vizcaya Museum and Gardens *55 B1*

3251 S. Miami Avenue, Coconut Grove; tel: 305/250-9133, www.vizcayamuseum.org
Open: daily 9.30–5; gardens until 5.30; ticket office closes at 4.40. Admission: moderate

On the northern boundary of Coconut Grove, this fabulous neo-Renaissance villa was built between 1914 and 1916 as a winter residence for industrialist James Deering. A great admirer of European architecture and style, Deering was an avid collector. When he began work on Vizcaya, Deering sent young designer Paul Calfin to Europe, and between them they furnished the house with carpets from Portugal, ceilings from Italy, chandeliers from France, Roman statuary and antique treasures from the finest periods of European design. The building itself is the work of F. Burrell Hoffman, who was a mere 29 years old at the time, and who created an elegant northern Italian-style villa arranged around a courtyard.

The house is now a museum. Each of the 34 rooms on display represents a particular style, such as the gracious 18th-century English Adams Library featuring a concealed door in the bookcase, the magnificent Rococo Salon and the Renaissance Hall. The extensive grounds were landscaped with a combination of Italian- and French-pattern formal gardens that lead down to Biscayne Bay and a Venetian water landing, while the entire estate is surrounded by a native hammock of mature tropical hardwoods.

Refreshments are available in a pleasant restaurant-café and there is a gift shop.

► Wings over Miami Museum *50 A2*

14710 S.W. 128th Street, Kendall; tel: 305/233-5197, www.wingsovermiami.com
Open: daily 10–5. Admission: moderate

This museum in Tamiami Airport is just the place to check out the history of flight. Dedicated to the preservation and restoration of historic planes it has a range of aircraft including Yaks, Stearman and a Saberjet.

Excursions

Boat tours, rental and charter

Club Nautico of Miami Beach, *Pier E, International Yacht Harbor, 300 Alton Road* (tel: 305/673-2502). Full-, half-day and hourly powerboat rental.

Heritage Schooner Cruises, *3145 Virginia Street, Coconut Grove*. One- and two-hour sightseeing cruises aboard *Heritage of Miami II* a twin-masted 85ft (25.5m) schooner.

Island Queen Cruises, *Bayside Marketplace* (tel: 305/379-5119). Narrated 90-minute cruises feature Millionaires' Row and cruise ships in the Port of Miami. Daily departures on the hour from 11–6, plus Friday–Sunday at 7pm and Monday–Thursday at 7.30pm. Luxury yachts for charter.

Kelley Fishing Fleet, *Haulover Resort Marina, 10800 Collins Avenue, North Miami Beach* (tel: 305/945-3801). Half- and full-day deep-sea fishing trips (9–12.30, 1.45–5.30, 8pm–midnight) for individuals and groups. Also two- to three-day fishing and dive trips to the Bahamas.

Still on the water

Jet Ski Tours of Miami (tel: 305/345-5770, www.jetskitoursofmaimi.com) offers guided tours around the Miami intercoastal waterways or jet-ski rental.
Tropical Boat Tours (tel: 786/218-3030, www.tropicalboat.com) has trips daily between 7am and 11.30pm on a range of craft from small sports or 'power' boats to 72ft (22m) luxury yachts.

Water taxis

The Miami water taxi service is no longer operating. A water taxi service links Fort Lauderdale with Miami for day trips to South Beach. This is the South Beach Water Express (tel: 954/467-6677, www.watertaxi.com). The taxi runs Tuesday and Saturday. You will set off in the evening (on the shuttle's return to Fort Lauderale) and will need to arrange accommodations and explore the town the following day.

KAYAKS AND CANOES
For a chance to paddle your own canoe up the unspoiled Oleta River or explore the islands of Biscayne Bay, contact Crandon Park Aquatic Center, Key Biscayne (tel: 305/365-3067). They also hold kayak workshops. Canoes can also be rented directly from the Blue Moon Outdoor Center at Oleta River State Recreation Area, 3400 N.E. 163 Street, North Miami (tel: 305/919-1846). The park has a sandy beach, fishing and picnicking facilities, and is often visited by Atlantic bottlenose dolphins and, in winter, manatees.

The Bayside Marketplace is excellent for boat tours and water taxis

DAY CRUISES
Take a minicruise to the Bahamas for the ultimate day out. Discovery Cruise Line (tel: 305/477-2867 or 888/213-8253) offers minicruises ranging from one-day excursions to the Bahamas to a couple of hours "to nowhere," from Miami and Fort Lauderdale.

Bus tours

Duck Tours Miami, *1661 James Avenue, South Beach (tickets from the Art Deco Welcome Center)* (tel: 786/276-8300 or 877/DUCK-TIX, www.ticketing.ducktoursmiami.com). Daily departures for the 3-hour The Great Miami tour stopping at Miami Beach and the Art Deco District, Coral Gables and Coconut Grove. Reserve in advance.

Miami Sunshine Tours, *12805 N.W. 42nd Avenue, Opa Locka* (tel: 304/681-2394, www.miamisunshinetours.com). City attractions, art deco and shopping tours, plus trips to the Everglades and Florida Keys. Reserve in advance.

Bicycling and in-line skating

Several neighborhood districts of Miami can be explored by bike. Be sure to take plenty of water.

The **Miami Beach Bike Center**, *601 5th Street, Miami Beach* (tel: 305/674-0150), offers a wide range of beach cruisers and mountain bikes for hourly, daily or weekly rental. Also guided cycle tours of the Art Deco District are available on the first and third Sundays of each month, departing at 10.30.

Another popular option is to explore the parks and paths of Key Biscayne on bikes rented from **Key Cycling**, *61 Harbor Drive, Key Biscayne* (tel: 305/361-0061), or from the concession within the **Bill Baggs Cape Florida State Recreation Area** (which also rents in-line skates).

In-line skating is the coolest (and an increasingly popular) way to travel on Ocean Drive; even the Miami Police Department do it! Rentals are available from the kiosk on Lummus Park opposite 14th Street, or from **Fritz's Skate & Bike Shop**, *730 Lincoln Road* (tel: 305/532-1954).

Another fun way of getting around

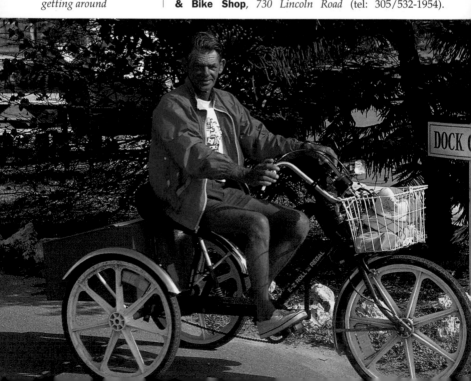

Be sure to include hand- and knee-guards for safety.

Driving tours

Miami is so spread out that visiting just a handful of sights can take a whole day. For some great scenery, take the S. Bayshore Drive–Main Highway–Old Cutler Road route around **Biscayne Bay** to the popular South Miami attractions near Homestead. **Miami Beach** is easily explored by car, from the art deco fixtures along Ocean Drive (see panel) to Bal Harbour, the pricey hotels and beaches of upper Collins Avenue. The only way to get a real feel for **Coral Gables** is by car; maps are available from the Coral Gables City Hall on Miracle Mile. Or get a feel for **Little Havana** with a drive down Calle Ocho (S.W. 8th Street).

Two superb national park sites are an easy day trip away beyond the Greater Miami city limits. **Biscayne National Park** (9 miles/14.5km east of Homestead) is a 181,550-acre (73,470ha) aquatic preserve with glass-bottom boats and diving tours. Several gateways provide access to the famous **Everglades National Park** (see pages 90–91). The eastern entrance and park headquarters are 10 miles (16km) southwest of Homestead; the northern entrance at Shark Valley lies 25 miles (40km) west of downtown Miami via the Tamiami Trail (U.S. 41).

The **Gold Coast** begins just north of Miami with Route A1A providing a slow route along the coast and the fast I–95 thundering north–south a few miles inland. The yachts and shops of **Fort Lauderdale** can be reached in under an hour, and the exclusive millionaires' enclave of **Palm Beach** is well worth a day's outing.

(For car rental information, see page 84.)

Walking tours

Art Deco Welcome Center, *Ocean Front Auditorium, 1001 Ocean Drive, Miami Beach* (tel: 305/531-3484). The Miami Design Preservation League's information center welcomes visitors to the famous Art Deco District with a tiny store full of postcards, posters and art deco memorabilia. This is the place to find a self-guided audio tour that makes a narrated round of 14 significant deco sites (allow around one hour).

For an extended version, try to catch one of the excellent 90-minute guided tours that depart at 10.30am Thursday to Sunday; or by request for groups.

Historical Museum of Southern Florida, *101 W. Flagler Street* (tel: 305/375-1492). Tours galore—from walking and bicycling excursions to moonlit gourmet canoe trips—balance fun with insight. Call ahead for prices and schedules.

Coconut Grove Ghost Tours, *departure from Tuscany Trattoria Restaurant, 3484 Main Highway, Coconut Grove* (tel: 786/236-9979, www.ghostgrove.com) Ninety-minute walking tours of Coconut Grove accompanied by ghoulishly dressed guides. Learn about the district's more colorful past.

DECO ROVERS
The latest transportation fad in terminally trendy SoBe and the Art Deco District is a cartoonish little electric buggy known as a Deco Rover. They can be rented from 215 6th Street (between Washington and Collins); tel: 305/538-0202. Scooter rentals are also available.

Snorkeling at Shark Reef, Biscayne National Park

By the mid-1970s, Miami Beach was almost beachless. Development on the island and erosion by the ocean had brought hotels and other buildings literally to the water's edge.

ENTER THE CAVALRY
The city called for the cavalry, and between 1977 and 1981, the U.S. Army Corps of Engineers mounted a vast $51 million beach reconstruction operation dumping millions of tons of sand along the ocean-shore to form a 100-yard-wide (90m) stretch of beach. From Sunny Isles in the north to South Pointe Park, the 10-mile (16km) strip is divided into a series of beaches, each with its own character. Key Biscayne and its island neighbor, Virginia Key, offer an additional 4 miles (6.4km) of beach space; there is Oleta River State Recreation Area north of the city, and the oceanfront Matheson Hammock Park in the south.

Miami Beach and North Miami

South Pointe Park Washington Avenue. Not the best beach, but there is good fishing and snorkeling from the pier (beware of currents), as well as picnic areas with barbecues, footpaths, children's playground, fitness course and a scenic view of the Port of Miami across the bay.

First Street Beach The epicenter of Miami's surfing culture. A beach bar-restaurant pumps up the volume. Volleyball.

Lummus Park Sixth to 14th streets. On the beach side of Ocean Drive, there are windsurfing and deck-chair rentals, refreshments and a playground.

21st Street Beach Start of the 2-mile (3km) **Miami Beach Boardwalk**, this is a favorite with many members of the gay community. Unofficially, topless bathing is more or less tolerated between First Street Beach and Surfside. Refreshments are available.

35th Street Beach Hemmed in by high-rise buildings, but relatively peaceful. Refreshments and good swimming.

46th Street Beach Near the Fontainebleau Hilton. A happy-go-lucky crowd of watersports fans from Miami University makes its presence felt; refreshments available plus excellent swimming.

North Shore State Recreation Area 79th to 87th streets. A 40-acre (16ha) oasis of subtropical vegetation and sandy shores. Picnic areas with barbecues, playground, bike trail, fitness course, fishing and boat rental.

Surfside Beach 93rd Street. A quieter neighbor of the Bal Harbour area beaches that fill up with wealthy northerners in the winter. Fine swimming can be had; popular with French-Canadians.

Haulover Beach 10800 Collins Avenue. Combines beach, dunes and parkland with facilities including picnic areas, playground, boat rentals, tennis and golf.

Sunny Isles 157th to 197th streets. Two miles (3km) of blustery beach, with windsurfing, jet-ski and sailboat rentals. Fishing from the pier; refreshments are available.

Oleta River State Recreation Area 3400 N.E. 163rd Street. On the mainland, with good swimming from a man-made beach. Bike trail, canoeing, boating and picnic facilities; dolphins, manatees and land mammals can also be seen.

Running for the big one: surfing is the archetypal Florida sport

Key Biscayne, Virginia Key and South Miami

Bill Baggs Cape Florida State Recreation Area Key Biscayne. On the southern tip of the island, this preserve has ocean beaches, a historic lighthouse, walking trails, windsurfing and bike rentals, fishing on the bayside, picnic areas and refreshments (see also page 63).

Crandon Park 4000 Crandon Boulevard. Parkland and beach at the northern end of Key Biscayne, which has picnicking and refreshment facilities, playground, biking trails, fitness course and boat rental.

Hobie Beach Rickenbacker Causeway. Windsurfers and surfboaters skim across the bay around the causeway, and picnic on narrow, pine-fringed strips of sand along the roadside. You will find picnic tables, refreshments and watersports equipment for rent (see also page 63).

Virginia Key Beach At the island's south end, running northeast from the causeway, this area has picnic facilities with barbecues and walking trails, plus a number of secluded coves edged by woodlands.

Matheson Hammock Park 9610 Old Cutler Road. A beautiful bayside beach in a country park south of Coral Gables. Picnic tables, refreshments, playground, walking trails, fitness course, fishing, boat rental, golf, tennis.

FLEA MARKETS AND FACTORY OUTLETS
One of the largest flea markets in South Florida, the Opa-Locka/Hialeah Flea Market, 12705 N.W. 42nd Avenue, gathers 1,200 wholesale and retail vendors on its sprawling site seven days a week. For factory outlet bargains, head 30 minutes south of Miami to Prime Outlets at Florida City, 250 E. Palm Drive (S.W. 344th Street), where you will find 60 brand-name outlets including a Nike Factory Store, Levi's Outlet by Design and OshKosh B'Gosh (*Open* Mon–Sat 10–9, Sun 11–6).

Shopping

Shopping is big news in Miami, and there are numerous huge shopping malls. Neighborhood shopping is fun, too, with a wide array of fashion boutiques, small galleries and specialty stores.

On the souvenir front, South Florida's subtropical surroundings have spawned a flourishing business in Florida kitsch, with flamingo and palm-tree motifs appearing on just about everything from T-shirts and tableware to flashing flamingo Christmas tree lights.

Downtown going north Downtown's pride and joy is **Bayside Marketplace**, *401 N. Biscayne Boulevard* (see also page 59). This 16-acre (6.5ha) waterfront site combines shopping with live entertainment and international dining opportunities. The latest fashions and sportswear rub price tags with great crafts and fun gifts. Look for brightly colored South American appliqué cotton jerseys, jewelry and leather items.

Out near the airport, Miami's largest megamall is taking shape: The 1.4 million square foot (126,000sq m) **Dolphin Mall** features more than 200 outlets, dining and entertainment venues and comes complete with theme park-style rides. You'll find discount outlets for some of the biggest designer brands.

On the bargain trail, take a detour to the **Fashion District**, *N.W. Fifth Avenue between 24th and 29th streets*, where designer clothes, accessories and locally made fashions are offered at factory outlet shops and discount stores. More department stores and boutiques are gathered in the popular **Aventura Mall**, *19501 Biscayne Boulevard* in North Miami, which is the largest regional mall in south Florida with department stores Bloomingdales, Macy's, Lord & Taylor, JC Penney and Sears, plus more than 200 specialty stores. The mall offers entertainment in the form of a 24-screen cinema complex and a children's playground.

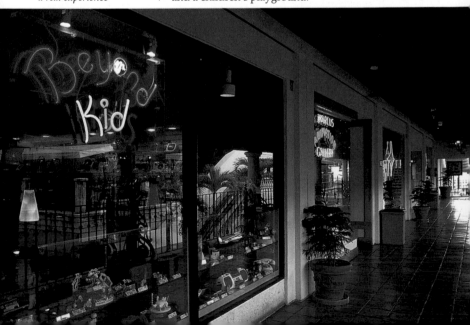

Shopping in CocoWalk is a real experience

Miami Beach On Miami Beach, the Art Deco District is a shopper's delight. A two-block strip of Collins Avenue between 6th and 8th streets has attracted fashion luminaries such as Nicole Miller and Kenneth Cole. A historic gem in its own right, **Española Way** features a clutch of alluring antiques stores and small galleries crammed with 1930s and 1940s furniture, furnishings and kitsch.

Big spenders should head straight for the shops at **Bal Harbour**, *9700 Collins Avenue* (see also page 58). A limo's length from Millionaires' Row, the darlings of European design, along with America's top stores—including Florida's largest Neiman Marcus—cater to well-heeled residents and visitors in a very upscale setting.

North Miami Beach is home to the three-level **Mall at 163rd Street**, *1421 N.E. 163rd Street*, the world's first Teflon-coated indoor mall.

Coconut Grove Coconut Grove's metamorphosis from hippie to hip has made it a front-runner for the title of sunglass capital of the world. These Florida essentials have been raised to an art form, and a whole fleet of chic optical boutiques can be found anchored amid the fun atmosphere of the Grove.

Cascades of greenery, Mexican-tile fountains, chic boutiques, restaurants and several sophisticated late-night clubs inhabit the exclusive **Streets of Mayfair**, *2911 Grand Avenue*.

A further galaxy of trendy nightspots, bars and café-restaurants is perched above two levels of boutiques at the Grove's other hotspot, **CocoWalk**, *3015 Grand Avenue*. The clothes-conscious will find everything from Western wear to lingerie on the shelves, and there is a good book and map store as well. **Main Highway** is crammed with both everyday and outlandish fashions, as well as poster and card shops, great T-shirts and amazing children's toys.

Another favorite shoppers' haunt is **Commodore Plaza**, whose tempting galleries sell colorful South American and Haitian art, Native American jewelry, furnishings and toys.

Coral Gables going south On Coral Way, between LeJeune and Douglas, the four-block **Miracle Mile** shopping district is lined with antiques stores, galleries, boutiques and interior design emporiums. For something a little more affordable, head for the modernistic **Miracle Center**, *3301 Coral Way*. To the south, you'll find **The Shops at Sunset Place**, 5701 Sunset Drive, South Miami—fun and family oriented with an FAO Schwarz toystore, Virgin Megastore, Barnes & Noble and an IMAX theater among its attractions.

West of U.S. 1, the **Dadeland Mall**, *7535 N. Kendall Drive*, is a long-favored shopping center with five department stores, 165 shops and a well-stocked food court. Also in the Kendall area, **The Falls**, *U.S. Highway 1 at S.W. 136th Street*, is home to a million-gallon (4.5 million liter) waterscape and 100 prestigious stores and restaurants set among tropical surroundings.

Miami's top shopping malls are generally open from Monday to Saturday 10–9, and from Sunday 11am or noon–5 or 6.

Mobile stalls sell cheap, fun souvenirs

LINCOLN ROAD

Once the Fifth Avenue of the South, Miami Beach's Lincoln Road shopping district fell on hard times until its stunningly successful multimillion-dollar face-lift. Along this pedestrian concourse, which runs west from Washington Avenue between 16th and 17th streets, are 12 landscaped blocks decorated with fountains, trees, sculpture and eye-catching sidewalk designs. There are dozens of boutiques and more than 20 galleries, plus restaurants and outdoor cafés that offer mile-long alfresco dining at night.

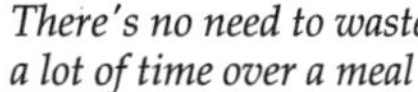

Food and drink

In recent years, Miami has emerged as one of the hottest culinary crucibles in the United States, if not the world—and this has nothing to do with chili, but everything to do with inspired cooking. Floribbean cuisine is a light and delicious marriage of fresh local ingredients, New American style and Caribbean and Asian flavors. It was perfected in the stylish restaurants and hotels of Miami Beach, but can now be found in good dining spots throughout the city, and, indeed, the state.

When eating out in Miami, keep in mind the fact that variety is the spice of life. Cuisines from Argentina, Brazil, Cuba, France, Greece, Haiti and Thailand are served in a diverse spread of eateries. Fresh fruit and vegetables are locally grown, steak is trucked in from the ranches of central Florida, fish and shellfish arrive fresh every day from the docks, and adventurous eaters can sample exotic Florida specialties such as alligator meat and Everglades frogs' legs.

Stop for a meal The food-lover's day begins with breakfast, normally served between 7 and 11am. It may consist of a sticky Danish pastry and muffins; a less sugary alternative is a bagel or buttered English muffin. Late breakfast at a café table on the sidewalk is a popular feature along Miami Beach's Ocean Drive and in Coconut Grove, where eggs Benedict and a plate of fresh fruit accompany a leisurely session with the morning paper.

Serious lunching has become a lost art in many North American cities, but Miami's Latin and European inhabitants have ensured that it remains an important feature of their day between 11.30 and 2. However, even recent arrivals have tended to gravitate towards a lighter, healthier American eating style, and there are plenty of imaginative salads and sandwiches on restaurant menus. The snacking population grabs a double-decker bus-size Cuban sandwich, piled high with ham, pork and cheese, a burger or, alternatively, a deli sandwich. Snacking is big in Miami—everywhere there are concession stands, juice bars, delis and health-food stores.

There's no need to waste a lot of time over a meal

In the evening, most Cubans eat late, but dinner is a running buffet in Miami, which starts at 5pm with cut-price "early-bird" special menus, and lasts until the Latin restaurants and late-night cafés switch off the stove at around midnight or 1am—though many dining spots do not take orders after 10pm. There are also several 24-hour chain restaurants, usually found near busy truck routes such as U.S. 1.

Choosing where to eat This is almost as confusing as choosing what to eat. Miami is well supplied with restaurants, bistros and cafés in every price range and a plethora of styles. There can be no doubt that the greatest concentration of dining options is found in the Art Deco District and SoBe on Miami Beach. You can dine at an art deco treasure on Ocean Drive, a 1950s-style deli or one of the many alfresco café-restaurants lining the Lincoln Road Mall. There is trendy Coconut Grove for cafés and reasonable prices; or Coral Gables, considered a gastronomic

Bayside bar in Miami

center with a raft of exclusive restaurants. Or you can sample traditional Cuban cuisine amid the palm fronds of a colonial Havana-style restaurant.

Dress in Miami is casual, and it is a rarity to spot a jacket and tie, but some of the more formal hotel restaurants might frown on blue jeans.

Cuban cuisine Cuban cuisine is one of the highlights of dining Miami-style. Throughout the day, Cuban sandwiches and thick, sweet thimbles of *café Cubano* keep locals on the go. In the evening, you can be sure of a lovely dining experience in one of the city's numerous Cuban restaurants.

For an early evening snack, experiment with *tapas* (a sampling of the restaurant's fare); there are several bars and restaurant lounges on Little Havana's Calle Ocho (S.W. 8th Street) that will make up a mixed platter of these savory specialties for *tapas* novices to try. There is plenty of time to taste everything in a leisurely way—dining rooms in the Cuban quarter do not fill up until around 10pm.

Cuban cuisine is generally hearty and filling. Favorite menu items include *sopa de frijoles negros*, traditional black bean soup; *arroz con pollo*, roast chicken with saffron rice; *arroz con camarones*, rice with shrimp; *piccadillo*, spicy ground meat with pimento, olives and raisins; and *palomilla*, thin Cuban steaks. *Tostones*, fried green plantains, or *platanos*, ripe plantains, are popular accompaniments.

Top of the scale Sunset in Miami is thoughtfully accompanied by Happy Hour, between 5.30 and 7.30pm, which brings some of the most expensive views in town within reach of most pockets.

No mistaking what this bar is selling

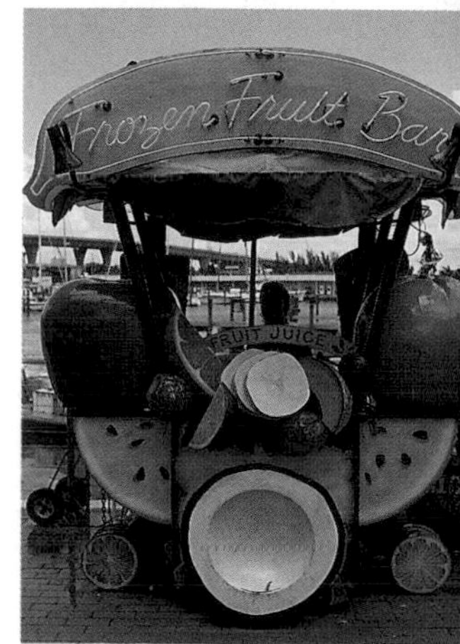

NEON NIGHTS
When it was first switched on in the 1930s, Miami Beach's art deco neon lighting knocked the socks off locals and visitors. After dark, Ocean Drive is still an electrifying sight. For real magic do not miss The Crescent, 1420 Ocean Drive; The McAlpin, 1424 Ocean Drive; and The Fairmont, 1000 Collins Avenue. The Waldorf Towers, 860 Ocean Drive, has a pseudo lighthouse, and the nearby Breakwater sports an impressive ship's prow.

It's electrifying… Ocean Drive at SoBe, the nightlife capital of the city

Nightlife and the performing arts

As evening approaches, Miami prepares for another night on the town, and cocktail shakers and conductors' batons set the pace. Miami's major performing arts venues are downtown, with outposts in Miami Beach and Coconut Grove. Miami Beach is undoubtedly the epicenter of Miami's clubland, with dozens of nightspots offering a full range of music and dance styles. The hippest clubs can come and go in the blink of an eye, so ask around if you want to find the latest 'in' scene.

Cocktails, clubs, discotheques and shows Start off in fashionable Coconut Grove, where there are Latin, reggae and hip-hop nights at **La Boheme**, *3138 Commodore Plaza* (tel: 305/448-1288). Head to **Quench**, *2801 Florida Avenue* (tel: 305/448-8150) for hot sounds or go underground to **Oxygen Lounge**, *2911 Grand Avenue* (tel: 305/476-0202) or **Streets of Mayfair** (tel: 305/476-0202, www.oxygen-lounge.biz). There's live jazz Thursday through Sunday at **Café Tu Tu Tango**, *CoCoWalk, 3015 Grand Avenue* (tel: 305/529-2222, www.cafetututango.com) or, on a more sophisticated note, **Alcazaba**, in the Hyatt Regency Coral Gables, *50 Alhambra Plaza* (tel: 305/569-4614) summons dancers to the floor with disco, salsa and merengue.

Downtown, Miami's oldest bar, **Tobacco Road**, *626 S. Miami Avenue* (tel: 305/374-1198), is famous for gritty live jazz and blues but several new clubs draw huge crowds, including **Space**, *34 N. E. 11th Street* (tel: 305/373-9378, www.clubspace.com) and **The Pawn Shop**, *1222 N.E. 2nd Street* (tel: 305/373-3511, www.thepawnshoplounge.com).

Celebrities and surfers stalk the sidewalk cafés, hole-in-the-wall clubs and power discos of Miami Beach's fashionable Art Deco District. This is a seemingly ever-changing scene but **Penrod's Beach Club**, *1 Ocean Drive* (tel: 305/538-1111) has been reeling them in with Top 40 and rock 'n' roll longer than most. Hot dance/clubbing spots include **Crobar**, *1445 Washington Avenue* (tel: 305/672-8084); **Mynt-Ultra**, *1921 Collins Avenue* (tel: 786/276-6132, www.myntlounge.com); **Amika Loft Lounge and Disco**, *1532 Washington Avenue* (tel: 305/534-1499, www.amikamiami.com); **Opium Garden**, *136 Collins Avenue* (tel: 305/531-5535, www.mansionmiami.com); gay-friendly **Score**, *727 Lincoln Road* (tel: 305/535-111) and celebrity-friendly **Bash**, *655 Washington Avenue* (tel: 305/538-2274).

For live jazz, check out **Jazid**, *1342 Washington Avenue* (tel: 305/673-9372), which attracts a stylish clientele from around 10.30pm onward; and the **Van Dyke Café**, *846 Lincoln Road* (tel: 305/534-3600), which features live music nightly from jazz to blues to Brazilian music. There are Latin sounds at **Mango's Tropical Café**, *900 Ocean Drive* (tel: 305/673-4422); and **Café Nostalgia at The Forge**, *432 41st Street* (tel: 305/695-8555), featuring Cuban musicians who splice the traditional Havana sounds of pre-revolutionary Cuba with contemporary numbers (also in Little Havana at *2212 S.W. 8th Street* (tel: 305/541-2631); check schedules for both clubs in advance.

Many Miami Beach hotels offer nightly entertainment in a number of guises, from piano bars to stage shows but for the real hot spots follow the crowds after midnight and dress for the occasion.

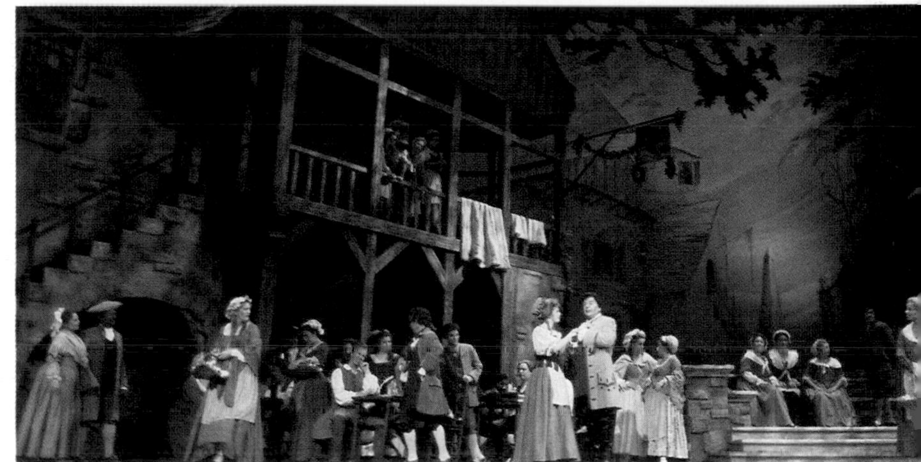

The Miami-Dade County Auditorium offers a program of opera during the winter months

Classical music The Concert Association of Florida, *1470 Biscayne Boulevard* (tel: 877/433-3100), plays host to the annual **Prestige Series of Concerts** at the **Miami-Dade County Auditorium**, *2901 W. Flagler Street* (tel: 305/547-5414). The auditorium is also home to the **Florida Grand Opera** (www.fgo.org), one of the country's oldest companies. The Grand also performs at the **Colony Theater**, *1040 Lincoln Road, Miami Beach* (tel: 305/674-1026). The Gusman Center Olympia Theater for the Performing Arts, *174 E. Flagler* (tel: 305/374-2444), hosts the **Florida Philharmonic Orchestra** for a season of music and children's programs. The young musicians of Michael Tilson Thomas's **New World Symphony** perform classical and contemporary works at the Lincoln Theatre, *541 Lincoln Road, Miami Beach* (tel: 305/673-3331, www.nws.org).

Dance Former New York City Ballet principal dancer Edward Villella directs the **Miami City Ballet**, *2200 Liberty Avenue, Miami Beach* (tel: 305/532-4880), in an acclaimed program of classical and contemporary choreography. And as evidence of Miami's multicultural society, flamenco flourishes at the **Flamenco Theatre La Rosa**, *13126 West Dixie Highway, North Miami* (tel: 305/899-7729).

Film Several of Miami's shopping malls have multiscreen theaters, including Coconut Grove's **Cocowalk 16**, *3015 Grand Avenue* (tel: 305/466-0450), **Regal Mayfair 10**, *3390 Mary Street* (tel: 305/447-9969) and **Sunset Place 24**, *5101 S.W. 72nd Street* (tel: 305/466-0450). In Miami Beach, check out the **South Beach Cinema**, *1100 Lincoln Road* (tel: 305/674-6766).

Theater Premieres, experimental productions, comedy and revues light the stage at the **Coconut Grove Playhouse**, *3500 Main Highway* (tel: 305/442-4000). The **Broadway in Miami Beach**, at the Jackie Gleason Theater, *1700 Washington Avenue, Miami Beach* (tel: 305/673-7300), puts on touring productions of hit Broadway shows. Also, the University of Miami's drama department stages four productions a year at the **Jerry Herman Ring Theater**, *1312 Miller Drive, Coral Gables* (tel: 305/284-3355).

LISTINGS AND TICKETS
The free *Miami New Times* covers everything from theater and movies to live music, clubs and restaurants. The *Miami Herald* also has daily listings. Tickets for major local sports and entertainment events are available through Ticketmaster (www.ticketmaster.com).

SoBe STYLE
A 2sq mile (5sq km) chunk at the southern tip of Miami Beach, SoBe (South Beach) is the hippest, most happening neighborhood in the city. Small boutique hotels set in art deco gems are the preferred lodgings in this neck of the woods, which is a favorite haunt of visiting movie stars, musicians and models. One of the most exclusive SoBe hotels is the gorgeous Delano, an Ian Schrager/Philippe Starck co-production and celebrity hang-out.

Miami Beach's art deco hotels are stylish places to stay

Accommodations

Beachfront luxury or beachfront budget, accommodations in Miami come in all shapes and sizes. The city currently packs in around 60,000 guest rooms in an impressive variety of hotels, motels and spas. There has been a major hotel boom in the last decade with a regiment of upscale properties from huge resorts to bijou boutique delights. Ritz-Carlton, Four Seasons, Mandarin Oriental and Conrad have made major investments here pumping billions of dollars into the local economy.

Miami's more luxurious resorts offer a full range of recreational activities, five-star dining and spectacular views, while even the humblest motel generally provides air-conditioning, TV, telephones and a pool. Most visitors are here for the sunshine, and sunshine means the beach, so it is not surprising that Miami Beach is where most of the area's smartest hotels are found. Exclusive neighborhoods such as Coral Gables, Key Biscayne and lively Coconut Grove also have their share of upscale accommodations, as does Downtown Miami, which features several spectacular modern hotel complexes aimed at the corporate sector, with prices pitched correspondingly high.

Miami's peak season lasts from December 15 to Easter, and even in summer, hotels can fill up over the 4th of July and Labor Day weekend.

A Greater Miami area resort tax of two to four percent is added to hotel bills, and there is an additional six-and-a-half percent sales tax.

Keeping down the cost Miami Beach offers the greatest choice of accommodations both in style and price range. The central, and most expensive, section of the Beach—from Lincoln Road to Surfside and Bal Harbour—is known as "Hotel Row." Farther north, the Sunny Isles beaches front "Motel Row," where prices are more reasonable and considerable discounts can usually be found during the summer season.

South of Hotel Row, the Art Deco District offers some real gems, with some rooms going at moderate prices but less chance of summer discount rates. There is also good news for real budget travelers, as the area's two youth hostels, the **Clay Hotel** and The Creek and Banana Beach Bungalows, are both on Miami Beach.

There are few bed and breakfasts in the area, but you could check into the charming and historic **Miami River Inn** downtown.

There are several money-saving tips to bear in mind when choosing your accommodations. The view, for example, can add a considerable amount to the bill. Beachfront properties and ocean views may add as much as 25 to 50 percent to the price of a room. Many hotels and motels do not charge for children under 18 sharing a room with their parents, and the excellent range of suites with separate bedroom and living areas makes this an ideal cost-cutting arrangement. Ask about **family plans**; you might find that a minimum stay may be required. A popular option on Motel Row, **efficiencies** generally sleep 4–6 people and provide kitchenettes.

When booking accommodations, always inform the

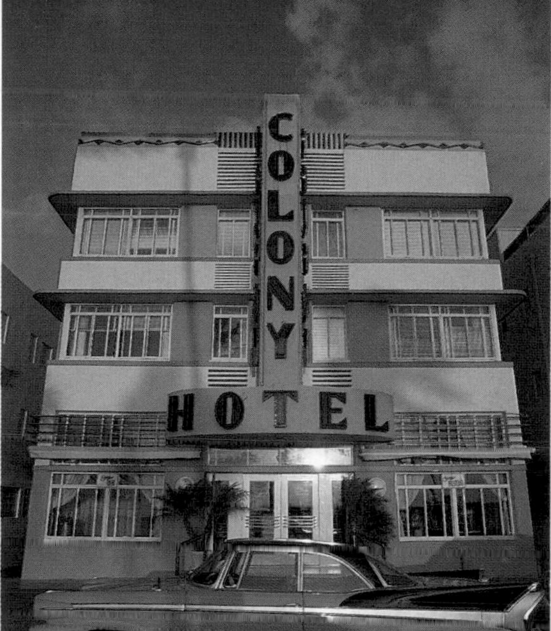

Stay at an Ocean Drive hotel for fine sea views

hotel of your estimated time of arrival. You may lose your room if the hotel has not been informed of a late arrival. Checkout is normally 11am.

Luxury and style If money is no object, several of Miami's finest hotels deserve a special mention. Downtown is dominated by the magnificent glass-and-steel tower of the **Conrad Hotel** while the **Eden Roc** is the grand dowager of Miami Beach. This area is also home to several of teh world's finest boutique hotels—chic, small properties with artsy interiors and personal service—including the Victor with its 91 luxurious rooms set next door to the old Versace mansion in the heart of the action.

Some Art Deco District favorites are **Essex House, Cardozo,** the **Delano**, and luxurious renovation **The Tides**.

More recent buildings are receiving the same treatment. The signature 1950s designed Catalina Hotel and Beach Club has recently benefited from a multi-million dollar renovation and refit, and the rooms are now filled with 21st century technological touches. However, the beach area hasn't turned its back on new builds. Two excellent examples are the beachfront **Shore Club** and **The Setai**.

In Coconut Grove, Luciano Pavarotti's split-level suite, complete with baby grand piano, is available at the **Grand Bay Hotel** when the maestro is out of town, or you can survey the bay from the rooftop pool at the all-suite **Mayfair House**.

Both the Mediterranean-style **Biltmore Hotel** and the elegant **Hotel Place St. Michel** in Coral Glades were built in the 1920s. Key Biscayne's jewel is the 300-room **Sonesta Beach Resort**; out to the west of the city, sports lovers cannot get enough of **Doral Golf Resort and Spa**; and if pampering is what you're after, head for the **Fisher Island Club**, a 220-acre (88ha) harbor island resort created as a winter retreat for William K. Vanderbilt in 1925.

BILLETED AT THE BILTMORE

Crowned by an imposing Spanish-style tower, the magnificently restored Biltmore Hotel was the showpiece of George Merrick's Coral Gables development, and remains the grand dame of Miami's luxury hotels. Opened in 1926, it played host to Roosevelt, the Vanderbilts, and royalty in its Jazz Age heyday before serving as a World War II veterans' hospital. Its marbled halls are supported by a veritable army of Corinthian columns, and the fabulous swimming pool measures almost 20,000sq ft (1,800sq m).

One of the restored Art Deco District hotels

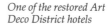

Miami is crazy about sports. From surf to stadium, the city's sporting calendar is packed with local and world-class events. There are plenty of opportunities for golfers, joggers, horseback riders, tennis players and watersports fanatics to follow their chosen hobbies every day of the year.

Fishing Deep-sea fishing is a major draw, but before you cast a line, check whether you need a license. Sail fish, kingfish, dolphin, snapper, grouper and tuna are common catches. **Bill Baggs Cape Florida State Recreation Area** on Key Biscayne and **Haulover Beach Park** on Miami Beach are two popular fishing spots.

Golf The Greater Miami Convention and Visitors Bureau (see page 85) can provide information covering the two dozen or so public courses in the area. Several 9- and 18-hole courses operate year-round; green fees vary, and advance reservations are recommended in winter. **The Crandon Golf Course**, 6700 Crandon Boulevard, Key Biscayne (tel: 305/361-9129), is one of Florida's best public courses.

Golfers can also test their skills on the famed "Blue Monster" and the new "Great White," the southeastern U.S.'s first desert-scape golf course, a 130-acre (52ha), par-72 redesigned by Greg Norman and opened in spring 2000 at the exclusive **Doral Golf Resort and Spa**, 4400 N.W. 87th Avenue (tel: 305/592-2000). The Doral hosts the Professional Golf Association's (P.G.A.) Ford Championship each spring.

Jogging Bayside parks are plentiful and popular, and many offer a fitness course, as well as scenic jogging trails. Favorites include **Haulover Beach Park**, 10800 Collins Avenue, Miami Beach (see pages 61 and 72); **Crandon Park**, 4000 Crandon Boulevard, Key Biscayne (see pages 63 and 73); **Matheson Hammock Park**, 9610 Old Cutler Road, south of Coral Gables (see page 73); and downtown's **Bayfront Park** on Biscayne Boulevard (see page 59).

Miami Jai-Alai players (or pelotaris) playing what is probably the fastest game in the world

Spectator sports The game that Miami has made its own is *jai alai* (pronounced *hi-ali*). Invented by Spanish Basques three centuries ago, the world's fastest game was introduced to Miami via Cuba. The pelota, or ball, is propelled at speeds of up to 175mph (282kph) with *cestas* (curved wicker slings) attached to players' hands. The betting is as furious as the play at **Miami Jai-Alai**, 3500 N.W. 37th Avenue (tel: 305/633-6400).

The Florida Marlins baseball team (tel: 305/623-6100) and the NFL's Miami Dolphins pack the **Pro-Player Stadium**, 2269 N.W. 199th Street (tel: 305/452-7000). Local NBA contenders Miami Heat moved into state-of-the-art quarters at the new bayfront American Airlines Arena, 601 Biscayne Boulevard (tel: 786/777-1000) in spring 2000. There is horse racing at **Calder Race**

The Orange Bowl, home to football games and the Orange Bowl Festival

Course, 21001 N.W. 27th Avenue (tel: 305/625-1311); and **Gulfstream Park**, 901 S. Federal Highway, Hallandale (tel: 954/454-7000); and greyhound racing at **Flagler Greyhound Track**, 401 N.W. 38th Court (tel: 305/649-3000). Autoracing fans should not miss the world-class **Toyota Indycar 3000**, held at the **Homestead-Miami Speedway**, 1 Speedway Boulevard, Homestead (tel: 305/230-7223), each spring.

Tennis Miami's biggest tennis event is the annual springtime NASDAQ-100 Open, at the **Tennis Center at Crandon Park**, 7300 Crandon Boulevard, Key Biscayne (tel: 305/365-3200). The tournament is televised and beamed to more than 200 countries. The City of Miami Parks and Recreation Department (tel: 305/416-1308) can provide information about its three tennis centers offering high-class instruction, and 50 free first-come-first-served courts. Or contact the City of Miami Beach Parks and Recreation Department (tel: 305/755-7800), which operates the North Shore Tennis Center, and South Beach's Flamingo Park courts among others.

The seas off Miami's coast are ideal for scuba diving

Watersports Virginia Key is the watersports center of Miami, and there are plenty of facilities available. You can waterski and rent windsurfing equipment, surfboards and jet skis. Surfing is a Miami Beach specialty, with the biggest waves around **Haulover Beach** and **South Pointe Park**.

Many resort hotels offer a range of watersports facilities to non-residents as well as guests, and there are beach-front concessions offering waterskiing, wave runners and banana boat rides. Scuba diving and snorkeling excursions are arranged by **South Beach Divers**, 850 Washington Avenue, Miami Beach (tel: 305/531-6110); and **Tarpoon Lagoon**, 300 Alton Road, Suite 110, Miami Beach (tel: 305/532-1445). For swimming, see **Beaches**, pages 72–73.

RIDING THE WAVE
In an effort to combat the appalling traffic and parking problems in the SoBe area of Miami Beach, the ELECTROWAVE Shuttle Service offers a daily two-way shuttle along Washington Avenue, between 11th and 17th streets. It operates Monday to Saturday 8am–1am, Sun and hols 10am–1am, costs 25c a ride, and includes public parking garages and park-and-ride lots on its route.

Policeman on the beat on Miami's streets

Practical points

Airport and transfer Miami International Airport is 8 miles (13km) west of downtown. Some overseas flights arrive at the International Satellite Building, linked to the main terminal by an automated shuttle. The airport's upper level has a currency exchange, 24-hour information desk, duty-free shops, luggage lockers, restaurants, and snack-bars. There are taxis and shuttle-buses on the lower-level concourse. The 15- to 20-minute taxi ride to downtown costs $19; south Miami Beach takes 25 minutes and is around $28; north Miami Beach is around $46, while 24-hour **SuperShuttle** buses provide service to all destinations within the Greater Miami area. It costs $10–12 to get downtown, and $14–16 to reach South Miami Beach and Coconut Grove (tel: 305/871-2000).

Car rental Miami's car rental agencies are based near the airport and offer free shuttle-bus transportation from the terminals to the parking lots. Rates are very reasonable but advance reservations are advisable. Be prepared to line up if several international flights have just arrived. For further details, see **Travel Facts**, page 264.

Crime As in other large cities, the best advice is to be alert. Do not walk alone along dark, unpopulated streets at night; lock car doors when traveling; ask for directions at public places, such as gas stations, rather than from passersby; keep cash in a moneybelt; and if you are asked for your wallet, don't resist; don't answer your hotel door until you are sure of the caller's identity; don't leave anything on show in rental cars; don't leave items unattended when on the beach; leave valuables in the hotel safe. Don't leave cameras and other valuables unattended on the beach when swimming or on café tables. When in your room, keep the secutiry chain on and if you get a knock at the door verify who is there by ringing the hotel/motel front desk.

Getting around Car rental is cheap, but Central Miami also has a very good public transportation system.

By car Miami's attractions are spread over a large area, so a car makes good sense. The city is laid out on a grid system with four quadrants (N.W., N.E., S.W., and S.E.) divided by Miami Avenue and Flagler Street. Numbered avenues run north to south, and streets run east to west. A network of expressways makes traveling from one side of town to the other, or even around it, fast and direct. Note that parking is in short supply downtown. In Coral Gables, all the streets have names, and it is very difficult to get around without a map (pick up one at the City Hall, on Miracle Mile). Hialeah has its own grid system. Parking is difficult and expensive in its central district, but metered parking is widely available elsewhere.

By public transportation More than 25,000 people use Miami-Dade County's public transportation system every day. The elevated **Metromover** circuit (free) serves a 26-block area of the downtown district. Fully automated cars operate daily between 6am and midnight (every 90 seconds in peak hours), and connect with the Metrorail at Government Center station. The **Metrorail** has 22 stops on its 21-mile (34km) journey between Kendall and Hialeah. Trains run every 20 minutes (5 minutes at rush hours) daily between 5am and midnight.

Metrobus operates 91 routes around the city and suburbs Monday through Friday from 4.30am to 2.13pm; Miami's commuters use the peak-hour **Tri-Rail** service (tel: 954/942-7245 or 800/TRI-RAIL). For information on all other services, tel: 305/770-3131 (6am–11pm).

By taxi Though taxis aren't cheap in Miami, they can come in handy. Miami's taxis do not cruise the streets looking for fares. Allow time to call one of the following:
Central Cab, tel: 305/532-5555
Metro Taxi, tel: 305/888-8888
Yellow Cab Company, tel: 305/444-444.

Hotel reservations Most hotels take reservations on their own websites, but if you are searching for a cut-price or last-minute hotel room, try www.expedia.com, www.ebookers.com, www.priceline.com or www.lastminute.com.

Tourist information The **Greater Miami Convention and Visitors Bureau**, *701 Brickell Avenue, Suite 2700, Miami, FL 33131* (*Open* Mon–Fri 8.30 6; tel: 305/539-3000 or 888/766-4264, www.TropicoolMiami.com) publishes a glossy annual *Vacation Planner* with up-to-date information on sights and services. The Miami Beach Tourist center is located at the Miami Beach Chamber of Commerce, *1920 Meridian Avenue, Miami Beach, FL 33139* (*Open* Mon–Fri 9–6, Sat–Sun 10–4; tel: 305/672-1270, www.miamibeachchamber.com). Other local chambers of commerce (listed in the telephone directory) can also supply maps and information for their areas.

THE DAILY NEWS
There are two daily papers printed in Greater Miami, the *Miami Herald* and its Spanish-language version *El Miami Herald*, plus another major Hispanic paper, *Diario Las Americas*. Other major papers are available at newsstands and from vending machines. The weekly free *Miami New Times* takes an uncompromising look at local issues.

Metromover, downtown's light-rail mass-transit system, is the easiest way of getting around this part of town

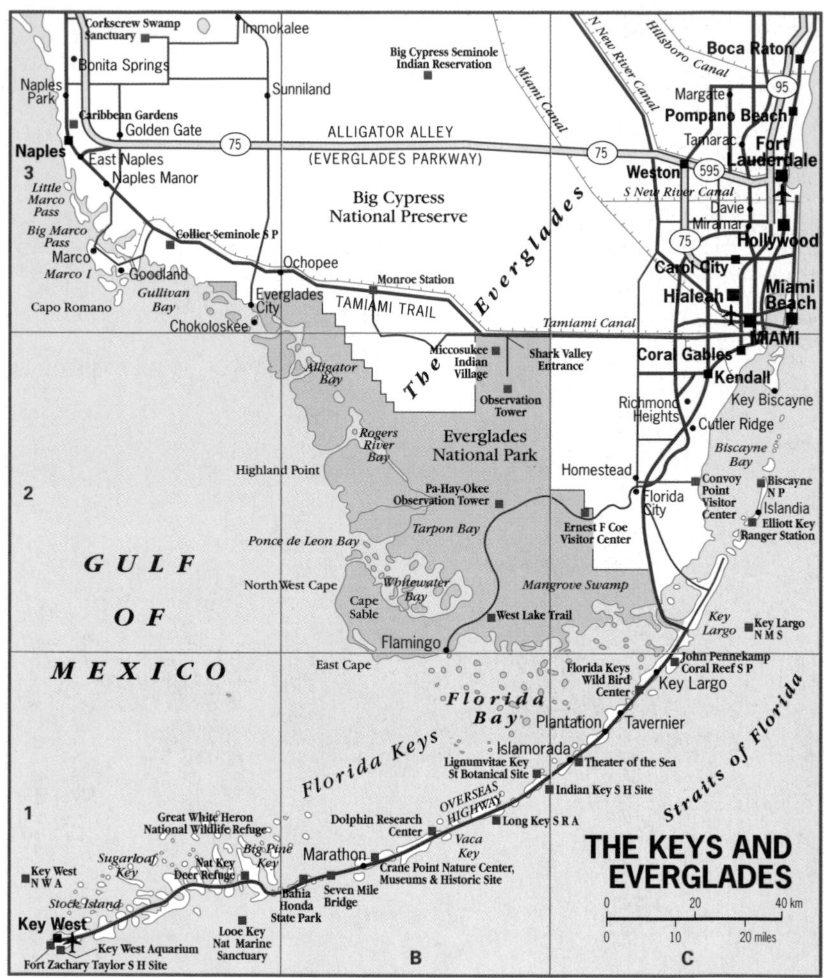

86

PRECIOUS TIME
A useful tip on driving in the Florida Keys: the Overseas Highway (U.S. 1) is the only road between Key Largo and Key West. Some sections of the drive are single lane in each direction, and speed limits (maximum 5mph/ 88kph) are quite rigorously enforced. It is best to set aside a whole day to make the trip with stops along the way (non-stop trip around 2.5 hours). Traffic on weekends and holidays can be a bumper-to-bumper nightmare.

AN HOUR'S DRIVE south of Miami, the Florida Keys angle off the peninsula in a spectacular chain of islands set in shimmering blue-green seas. This is the American Caribbean, home to tropical birds, flowers and exotic fish that dart around the only living coral reef in the Continental United States.

In the early days, pirates overran this isolated and treacherous maze of reefs and keys. Later, the sea captains and merchants of Key West profited handsomely from shipwrecks and trade on the route between the Gulf and Cuba (just 90 miles/145km to the south), and tourism arrived with Henry Flagler's "Railroad That Went To Sea" in 1912. The railroad was destroyed by a hurricane in 1935 and replaced by the Overseas Highway (U.S. 1), named for the 43 bridges that link the island chain from Key Largo to Key West.

This chapter is arranged in geographical order starting on the mainland with two exceptional national parks an easy day trip away from Miami. On the Atlantic Coast, the **Biscayne National Park** is the nation's largest aquatic

The Keys and Everglades

park and a haven for divers and snorkelers. To the west lies the **Everglades National Park**, bordering Florida Bay on the Gulf of Mexico.

Once you leave the mainland, the first stop in the Upper Keys is **Key Largo**, largest of the 42 islands and gateway to the undersea delights of the John Pennekamp Coral Reef State Park. Heading south are **Tavernier**, with a wild bird rehabilitation facility and the sportfishing center of **Islamorada**. **Marathon** is the hub of the Middle Keys, another diving and fishing center with a natural history museum and restored railroad workers' camp on Pigeon Key. The Lower Keys start at the southern end of Seven Mile Bridge where the beachfront **Bahia Honda State Park** makes an appealing break on the road south and **Big Pine Key** is home to the National Key Deer Drive refuge, before culminating at journey's end in funky and fun-loving **Key West**.

Roadside Mile Markers (MM) will help you navigate along U.S. 1 from MM 126 just south of Florida City right down to Key West at MM 0.

Above: Airboats skim the waterways of the Everglades

REGION HIGHLIGHTS

►► Big Cypress National Preserve *86 B3*

Oasis Ranger Station, Tamiami Trail (U.S. 41 east of Monroe Station); tel: 941/695-2000, www.nps.gov
Open: daily; Visitor Center daily 9–4.30

Big Cypress, northern neighbor to Everglades National Park, is a 720,567-acre (288,227ha) wedge of wet and dry prairie, marshlands, slash pine and hardwood hammocks. Nearly one-third of the preserve is covered with cypress trees, aquatic deciduous conifers that can tolerate long periods of immersion in the swamp's seasonal high-water periods (see panel opposite). Big Cypress is a favorite home of alligators, bobcats, deer, rare black bears and a few remaining Florida panthers. Spectacular bird life includes the endangered Everglades kite, which feeds exclusively off the apple snails found in the preserve.

The main drainage swamp west of Big Cypress is **Fakahatchee Strand**, which is a separate state preserve area. It contains the largest stand of native royal palms in North America and a rare concentration and variety of epiphytic orchids.

Just west of Copeland on Route 29, **Janes Memorial Scenic Drive** is a 20-mile (32km) dead-end excursion into the backwoods, where a boardwalk gives access to an impressive stand of virgin cypress. Unusual wildlife includes the mangrove fox squirrel and Everglades mink.

Road access is provided by the **Loop Road** (Route 94) from Forty Mile Bend (just west of Shark Valley) to Monroe Station, which is paved for 13 miles (21km) of its 24-mile (39km) route. There is also **Turner River Road** (Route 839), a graded dirt track running due north to Alligator Alley (note: rental-car drivers are not insured here) and hiking trails from the Oasis Ranger Station.

Big Cypress National Preserve—a contemplative view

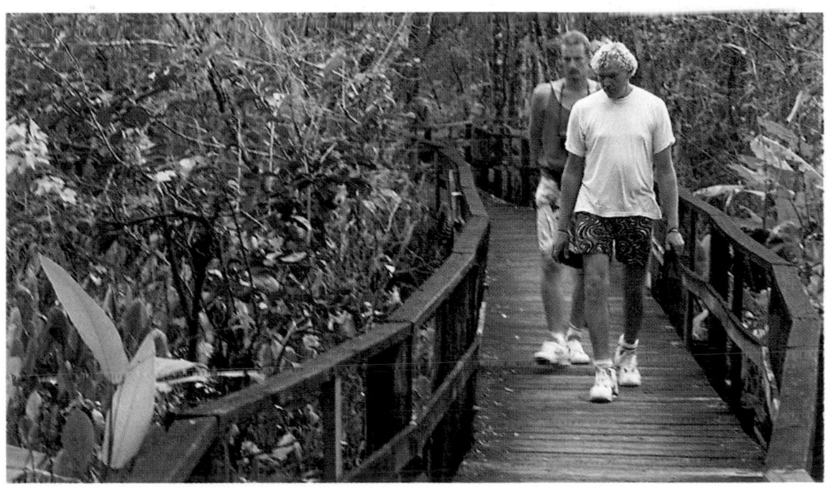

Visitors to Florida's wet wilderness areas can explore swamps and hammocks on raised boardwalk trails

►►► Biscayne National Park 86 C2

Convoy Point, S.W. 328th Street (9 miles/14.5km east of U.S. 1); tel: 305/230-1144, www.nps.gov
Open: park daily 8–5.30, Visitor Center daily 9–5. Admission free; overnight docking fees for Boca Chita and Elliott Key

Occupying 180,000 acres (72,000ha) along the southern portion of Biscayne Bay, 95 percent of Biscayne National Park is under water. The remaining 5 percent is an 18-mile (29km) chain of 44 keys, hemmed in by tangled mangroves and surrounded by the dazzling azure sea. Only a few of the Keys can be visited: Elliott, Boca Chita, Adams and Sand Keys. Boat trips, snorkeling and scuba diving are the best ways to fully explore this fascinating underwater world. Most of the park is accessible only by boat. Boat launches are found at Homestead Bayfront Marina and at Black Point Marina. Elliott Key has a 36-berth harbor, and there are anchorages off the keys. Canoe rentals are available at Convoy Point for exploring and birdwatching along the mainland mangrove shoreline.

The brackish water trapped in the mangrove nurtures an enormous variety of life. Just offshore, live coral reefs teem with an array of creatures in waters from 10 to 60ft (3–18m) deep. Hundreds of species of fish, sponges and soft corals thrive in Biscayne Bay, and manatees frequent the warm shallows. Fishing is exceptional, with snapper, snook and barracuda the most common catches.

The **Convoy Point Visitor Center** has a museum with exhibits covering the park's cultural and natural histories, and also offers ranger-led activities. There is a ranger station and two self-guided walks on Elliott Key, one along a boardwalk and the other along a short nature trail. An old road runs the length of the island (7 miles/11km), and rangers lead hiking sessions during the winter months.

Offshore, **Elkhorn Reef** is a good site for inexperienced snorkelers; other popular sites include **Schooner Wreck Reef** and **The Drop**. Daily 3-hour glass-bottom boat tours and 4-hour scuba and snorkeling trips to the reefs can be reserved through **Biscayne National Underwater Park Inc.** (tel: 305/230-1100), which can also arrange equipment rental for independent divers.

NOT SO BIG CYPRESSES

The "big" in Big Cypress refers to the size of the preserve rather than the height of the cypress trees seen here. The most common variety, found in the broad belts of trees edging the wet prairies and gathered on dome-shaped hammocks, is the dwarf pond cypress. Few mighty bald cypresses, which can grow to well over 100ft (30m) tall, survived the Everglades logging boom of the 1930s and 1940s.

►►► Everglades National Park *86 B2*

Open: daily 24 hours. Admission: moderate, tickets valid for one week, www.nps.gov

The Everglades region starts at Lake Okeechobee, where a freshwater river 6in (15cm) deep and 50 miles (80km) wide begins a slow creep seaward. However, the large national park preserve commences below the Tamiami Trail (U.S. 41), and extends south to the tip of the peninsula and west to the Gulf of Mexico. The best time to visit is the winter dry season, when low water levels make wildlife spotting easier, as animals and birds concentrate around the deeper pools and sloughs for food. In spring, temperatures rise uncomfortably, and during the summer wet season, as water levels rise, wildlife ranges farther afield and bloodthirsty clouds of mosquitoes descend.

The Visitor Center (see below), west of Homestead, is the park's most popular access point. Walking trails off the road between the center and Flamingo on Florida Bay explore the six different ecosystems that constitute the Everglades' overall habitat—the Anhinga and Gumbo Limbo Trails are favorites. Check ranger schedules, and follow the trails with an experienced guide.

Tram tours depart daily from the northern **Shark Valley** entrance on a 15-mile (24km) circuit that is also open to hikers and bikers. To the west, the **Gulf Coast Ranger Station** provides backcountry camping permits and access to the Ten Thousand Islands.

Entrances and information centers

Ernest F. Coe Visitor Center/Park Headquarters, 10 miles (16km) southwest of Florida City and Homestead via S.R. 9336 (*Open* daily 9–5; tel: 305/242-7700). The center presents a 15-minute introductory film on the ecology of the park at regular intervals and offers free information brochures and park activity schedules, including details of boat tours, guided walks and canoe rentals. Nearby, the **Royal Palm Visitor Center** (*Open* daily 8–4.15) is the starting point for

Raised hammocks provide island footholds for a variety of native trees and plants in the Everglades wetlands

several ranger-guided walks, and **Flamingo Visitor Center** (*Open* Nov–Apr 8.30–5.30) provides information on accommodations, camping, sightseeing cruises, charter fishing boats and bike rentals. **Shark Valley/Northern Entrance** (*Open* daily 8.30–6 tel: 305/221-8776), 35 miles (56km) west of downtown Miami via Tamiami Trail (U.S. 41). Year-round tram tour departures daily (schedules vary seasonally so reservations recommended, tel: 305/221-8455), nature trail and bicycle rental.

Gulf Coast Visitor Center/Western Entrance (*Open* daily in winter 8–4.30; reduced opening mid-Apr to mid-Nov; tel: 941/695-3311). Near Everglades City, 80 miles (129km) west of Miami on C.R. 29 via Tamiami Trail (U.S. 41). A Ranger Station offering marine and shore life displays, maps, information about boat tours and canoe rental.

A mangrove, the only tree that can extract fresh water from salt water

General information

Accommodations There are 103 rooms and 24 cottages at **Flamingo Lodge**, 1 Flamingo Lodge Highway, Flamingo, FL 33034-6798 (tel: 239/695-3101 or 1-800/600-3813).
Boating Excellent on Florida Bay and in the Ten Thousand Islands; canoe trails around Flamingo and Everglades City. Boat and canoe rental from **Flamingo Marina** (tel: 239/695-3101), and **Everglades National Park Boat Tours**, Gulf Coast Visitor Center (tel: 239/695-2591).
Camping Official campgrounds are available at Flamingo, and Long Pine Key. Permits must be obtained from ranger stations for overnight stays in the park.

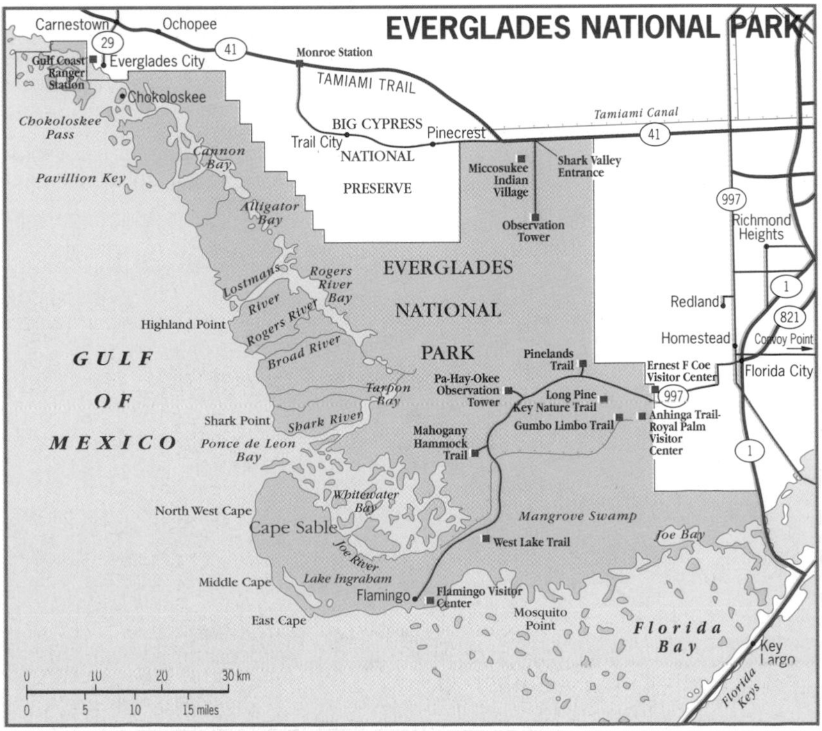

"The miracle of light pours over the green and brown expanse of sawgrass and of water, shining and slow-moving below, grass and water, that is the meaning and central feature of the Everglades ... It is a river of grass." Marjorie Stoneman Douglas, The Everglades: River of Grass *(1947).*

FRIEND OF THE EVERGLADES
A month before the Everglades National Park was dedicated by President Truman in December 1947, Marjorie Stoneman Douglas (1890–1998) published *The Everglades: River of Grass*. With a single phrase she transformed many people's perception of the Everglades from pestilential swamp to a living entity with a vital role to play in the ecology of southern Florida.
A founding member of the Friends of the Everglades campaign in 1969, she became a leading lobbyist in the conservation field during her 80s and 90s from her home of more than 70 years in Miami's Coconut Grove. Stoneman Douglas' autobiography, *Voice of the River*, with John Rothchild, is a fascinating account of an eventful life, and her collections of short stories paint a vivid portrait of Florida in the 1920s and 1930s.

Native Americans called the Everglades region *Pa-Hay Okee*, "grassy waters"; it is an apt description. Vast and mysterious, a carpet of waterlogged sawgrass punctuated by cypress swamps and hardwood hammocks, the Everglades stretches to the horizon criss-crossed by secretive waterways. Many Floridians once saw the Everglades as a challenge to be overcome, tamed, drained and reclaimed into "useful" land. But the region is a perfectly balanced ecosystem, and its unique habitat supports myriad species of native flora and fauna and aquatic creatures. The Everglades' subtropical climate is the key to its success. There are two distinct seasons—the summer rains, followed by the winter dry period. This ancient pattern of deluge and drought is essential to the well-being of the entire South Florida region.

Seasonal variations The shorter days of October and November herald the start of the dry season in southern Florida. As the waters recede in the back country, animals and birds congregate to feed around the remaining deep-water sloughs (pools). This is the mating season, but if water levels are too low and there is too little food, mating will not occur. When the rains begin in May and June, the withered brown sawgrass pushes up new shoots and algae and plankton flourish around its roots. Mosquito larvae, tadpoles and small fish start filling out the lower end of the food chain, and animals and birds disperse from dry-season refuges to rear their young. Water is the Everglades' lifeblood, and in the past, the summer downpours would overflow Lake Okeechobee, flood the prairies and gravitate towards the sea at a rate of around 0.5 miles (800m) a day. Eventually, the invisible 50-mile-wide (80.5km) river would discharge into Florida Bay.

Disappearing water Ever since Governor Napoleon Bonaparte Broward launched his campaign to drain the Everglades in 1905, the "river of grass" has been under threat. The completion of the Tamiami Trail in 1928 allowed lumber barons to log the Everglades' cypress hammocks; they were followed in the 1940s by oil explorers. By 1948, the natural flow of water from Lake Okeechobee was effectively harnessed by a 1,400-mile (2,254km) network of levees and canals. Ranchers to the north drained tracts of wet prairie for pasture, and contractors along the East Coast claimed vast acreages of land for housing and industrial development. Agriculture, in particular, posed a two-fold threat by syphoning off huge volumes of precious water and polluting run-off with high levels of phosphates and nitrates.

Boats for touring the Everglades

Wildlife in peril Another pressing reason to preserve the Everglades is its treasure of plant and animal life. Some 2,000 diverse plant species, around 45 of which are found nowhere else in the world, rely on the sunlight and rainfall of southern Florida. The dazzling flocks of snowy egrets and pink-feathered roseate spoonbills recorded by celebrated naturalist and painter John James Audubon in 1832 have dwindled to just a handful. Wood storks, herons, bald eagles, ospreys, the Everglades mink, the Florida panther, manatees, American crocodiles and green sea turtles are also threatened.

Signs of change There are signs of a positive change in attitudes toward the Everglades. Environmental pressure groups and government agencies are joining forces to tackle some of the major issues, from flood control to conservation. The 1989 Everglades National Park Protection and Expansion Law directed the Army Corps of Engineers to disassemble part of South Florida's flood-control canal system and restore areas of wetlands, and the Everglades Forever Act requires agricultural areas to dramatically reduce fertilizer run-off, among other vital measures. The year 1998 saw $26 million spent buying land to complete the East Everglases Expansion Area, increasing the viable footprint of the park. In 1999 a long-term management plan went before Congress and the Commission for the Everglades was created by Florida Governor, Jeb Bush.

There is still much to be done but there is at least a chance the Everglades will last forever.

THE WILDERNESS WATERWAY

This 99-mile (159km) inland boating trail between Flamingo and Everglades City is a real backcountry adventure. The trip can be made by canoe in 8–10 days (rentals available in Everglades City) or by small outboard craft up to 18ft (5m) in length (6–8 hours). Numbered markers indicate the route along narrow channels between mangrove forest and dozens of islands. Free backcountry camping permits are required for overnight stops.

UNDERWATER SHRINE
The 9ft-tall (3m), 4,000-pound (1,800kg) bronze *Christ of the Deep* statue at the John Pennekamp Coral Reef State Park is a copy of a famous Italian submarine sculpture, *Christ of the Abysses.* A gift to the Underwater Society of America, it has become one of the most photographed sites in the world. It is also a favorite location for underwater weddings.

The Upper Keys

▶▶▶ Key Largo *86 C1*

Across Blackwater Sound, 30-mile (48km) long Key Largo (*largo* means long in Spanish) is the largest of the Keys, and achieved widespread fame as the setting of the 1948 screen classic *Key Largo,* with Humphrey Bogart and Lauren Bacall. Film buffs on the nostalgia trail can stop by the original steel-hulled *African Queen,* moored by the Holiday Inn at MM 100, which starred alongside Bogart and Katharine Hepburn in 1951.

Key Largo's present-day claim to fame lies in the spectacular John Pennekamp Coral Reef State Park and Florida Keys National Marine Sanctuary (see below), where some of the nation's premier dive sites attract thousands of visitors every year. The island has benefited from an artificial reef site, the *Speigel Grove,* a navy transport ship that was purposely sunk just offshore in 2002. It now provides a home for a growing number of fish and coral species. More than 25 local dive outfits arrange daily excursions and rent equipment.

In November, Key Largo's **Harry Harris Park** plays host to the annual **Island Jubilee**, a nine-day festival of special events with music, food and crafts stalls, off U.S. 1 at MM 92.6.

Accommodations in Key Largo are plentiful and varied; advance reservations are advisable.

Jacobs Aquatic Center, *320 Lagauna Avenue* (*Open* daily 10–5. *Admission: moderate*; tel: 305/453-SWIM) This small three-pool water adventure park features Olympic-size racing areas and a children's play area with pirate ship. The park provides swimming and scuba-diving lessons.

John Pennekamp Coral Reef State Park, *MM 102.5* (*Open* daily 8am–dusk, Visitor Center 8–5. *Admission:*

(Continued on page 96)

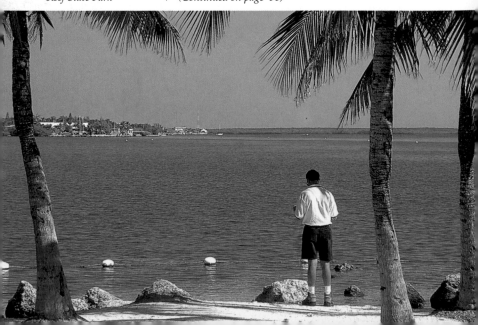

Looking out over the underwater world of the John Pennekamp Coral Reef State Park

Coral reefs are built by polyps, primitive soft-bodied relatives of the sea anemone and jellyfish, which secrete limestone to form an exterior skeleton. They cannot survive at temperatures below 68°F (20°C).

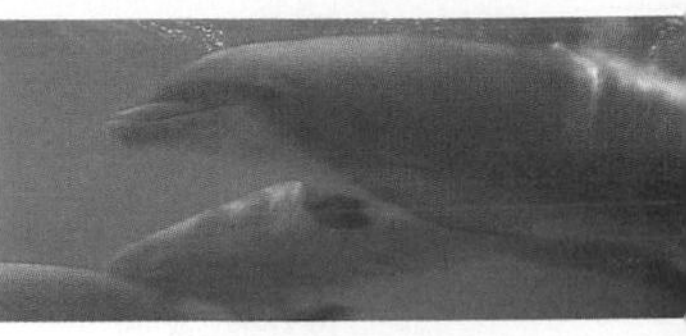

Polyps feed on tiny phytoplankton that they snare with stinging cells on their tentacles, and they receive oxygen and nutrients from algae. In return, the algae extract carbon dioxide for photosynthesis and give coral its colors. Hard coral grows slowly as each generation builds on the skeletal deposits of its ancestors. A large brain coral can take several centuries to build (branching coral advances at a rate of only 3in/7.5cm a year).

Inner reefs Known as patch reefs, inner reefs develop in calm shallow waters. Inner reefs comprise the more delicate coral formations, such as the sea fan, mountain star, and the unnervingly lifelike brain coral. Angelfish, wrasse, tang, damsels, butterfly fish and spiny lobster are some of the more colorful inshore residents; farther out, barracuda and shark cruise around massive outcrops of staghorn and elkhorn coral. Every nook and cranny of a coral reef is a potential hiding place for camouflaged moray eels, which dart out from murky crevices to snap up passing fish.

Milleflora dichotoma: *fire coral*

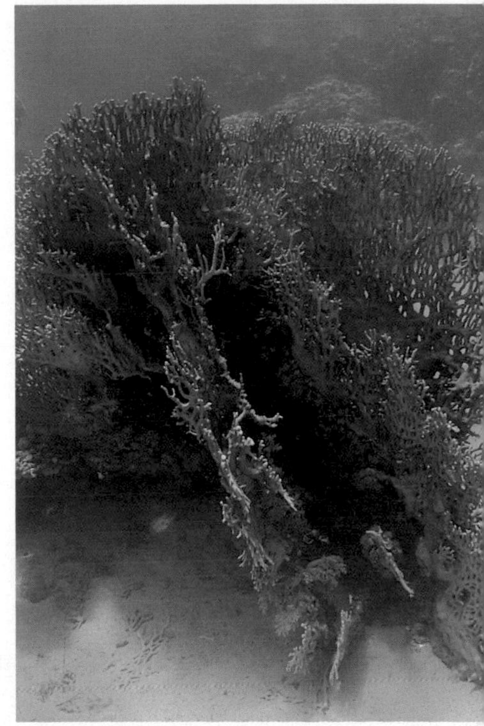

A friendly habitat Corals are functional as well as beautiful. They form a vital breakwater, diffusing the destructive force of storm-whipped seas, and provide a safe anchorage for mollusks, sea anemones, barnacles, and sponges. Colorful parrot fish graze on coral, biting off chunks with their powerful beaks and grinding it up to extract polyps and algae. Fish nibbling on corals produce more than 2.5 tons of sand per acre (0.4ha) annually. The sea grasses which grow on the sandy ocean floor are a source of food for turtles, manatees and thousands of other marine plant and animal species.

Threats to the system The delicate ecosystem of a coral reef is easily damaged. Boat anchors, propellers, and careless divers are an obvious threat. More insidious is the chemical run-off from the mainland and drifting oil from deep-sea shipping lanes. Pollution and sediment from dredging operations can smother living coral polyps, destroy the lower end of the food chain and, as a result, gradually threaten the entire population of the reef.

WHEN IS A CONCH NOT A CONCH?
Conch (pronounced "conk") is a rubbery mollusk often used by Key chefs for conch fritters, chowder, and conch seviche, which is cured with fresh Key lime juice. But a conch is also a native Keys resident. You become an honorary conch when you have lived in the Keys for seven years or more.

(Continued from page 94)

inexpensive; tel: 305/451-1202, www.floridastateparks.org). America's first underwater park and the adjoining **Florida Keys National Marine Sanctuary** total some 178 nautical square miles (611sq km) of the Atlantic Ocean. Warmed by the Gulf Stream, the coral reefs and seagrass beds support more than 500 species of fish, 55 varieties of coral and around 27 types of gorgonians, or marine life forms such as sea anemones. It is a fabulous undersea world that is a major attraction for scuba divers and snorkelers. Nonswimmers can enjoy the excellent aquariums and displays in the Visitor Center, and the glass-bottom boat trips out to the main reef areas.

The park has several popular diving sites, some with underwater wrecks. They include **Molasses Reef**, with its network of tunnels and towering coral formations; **French Reef** with its Christmas Tree Cave; the **Benwood Wreck**, a freighter torpedoed in 1942; **Grecian Rocks**; and the *Christ of the Deep* statue under 25ft (7.5m) of water at **Dry Rocks**. There are several daily dive-boat departures.

Other facilities, such as windsurfer, sailboat and canoe rentals, are available from the sandy beach area; scuba gear rentals and snorkeling trips can be arranged through the dive shop.

A campground is also available (P.O. Box 1560, Key Largo, FL 33037; tel: 800/326-3521).

Dolphins Plus, *off U.S. 1 at MM 100* (*Open* daily, call for schedules. *Admission: programs expensive, observers moderate*; tel: 305/451-1993) Divers in the Key Largo area often tell of encounters with playful bottlenose dolphins. There are also several marine research facilities in the Keys that offer a chance to swim with these friendly and intelligent creatures. One of them is low-key Dolphins Plus, which offers two dolphin encounter programs. Observers can watch the proceedings and attend the pre-swim orientation seminar exploring the marvels and myths attached to the dolphin. Participants in the encounter sessions must know how to use a mask and flippers. For information and reservations: 31 Corrine Palce, Key Largo FL 33037 (www.dolphinsplus.com; e-mail: info@dolphinsplus.com).

UNDERWATER PHOTOGRAPHY
Amateur photographers should not be afraid to try their skill under water to record the beauties of a coral reef. As well as purpose-built underwater cameras, waterproof cases are sold that will protect most types of normal cameras, and even video cameras, to depths of up to 35ft (10.5m). The best time to shoot below the surface is between 10 and 2, when the sunlight is strongest; at depths below 10–20ft (3–6m) use a flash. For the best results, get close to the subject and, if possible, use a wide-angled lens.

Florida Keys Wild Bird Center, *MM 93.6*, Tavernier (*Open* daily dawn–dusk. *Admission: donation*; tel: 305/852-4486) A rehabilitation facility and sanctuary for disabled birds unable to be returned to the wild, the center offers a great opportunity to get a really close look at native birdlife, from peregrine falcons and osprey to pelicans, cormorants and gulls. The enclosures flank boardwalk trails through forest hammock, wetlands and mangrove swamp areas to the shore, where a short nature trail leads to birdwatching hides overlooking a salt pond where roseate spoonbills, herons and stilts come to feed.

▶ Islamorada *86 C1*

Named *islas moradas* (purple isles) by the Spanish, Islamorada is a collection of pine-fringed islands, including Windley and Upper and Lower Matecumbe Keys. Rumor has it that early explorers found concentrations of *Janthina janthina*, a violet sea snail, here—hence the town's name. Others believe it was named for the orchid trees. Now Islamorada is chiefly known as a sportfishing center with a pedigree dating to the day when author and avid fisherman Zane Grey persuaded Henry Flagler to convert his Long Key railroad camp into a fishing lodge.

Indian Key State Historic Site and Lignumvitae Key State Botanical Site, *access by private boat, ferry or kayak from Robbie's Marina, MM 78.5*; tel: 305/664-2540, www.floridastateparks.org. A brace of offshore islands that make a popular day out. On the Atlantic side, Indian Key was once a county-seat town and base for 19th-century shipwreck salvagers, known as wreckers, until a Native American attack wiped out the settlement in 1840. Botanist Dr. Henry Perrine was one of the victims and his plants now grow wild among the ruins that are explored on ranger-led walks (Thu–Mon 9 and 1. *Admission: inexpensive;* tel: 305/664-4815).

Lignumvitae Key is on the bayside, and the 280-acre (112ha) key is a rare preserve of virgin tropical forest surrounding the 1919 Matheson House, built as a holiday retreat. (There are ranger-led tours Thu–Mon at 10 and 2. *Admission: inexpensive;* tel: 305/664-9814).

Theater of the Sea, *MM 84.5* (*Open* daily 9.30–4. *Admission: expensive*; tel: 305/664-2431) The world's second oldest marine park, created in pools and lagoons formed by railroad excavations, this is a popular attraction. Tours acquaint you with creatures from sea urchins to sharks. You can take a "bottomless" boat ride, swim with dolphins and watch a sea lion and dolphin show. Reserve ahead for the **Dolphin Adventure-Swim**.

FANTASTIC FOSSILS
Windley Key is one of the highest islets in the Florida Keys chain and when Henry Flagler's railroad workers began quarrying the ancient limestone reef here they discovered a fantastic treasury of fossilized corals in the rock. Visitors can now explore the quarry and take rubbings of the petrified reef creatures at the Windley Key Fossil Reef State Geological Site, MM 85.5 (*Open* Thu–Mon 8–dusk, Visitor Center 9–5. *Admission: inexpensive;* tel: 305/664-2540).

All together now…one of the popular sea lion shows at Theater of the Sea

Shrimp boats in the Middle Keys

The Middle Keys

The Middle Keys stretch southwest from the 2.5-mile (4km) Long Key Bridge, to the famous Seven Mile Bridge, beyond Marathon. Moving down the chain in north–south order, **Conch Key** has a rustic fishing dock, and its picturesque cluster of whitewashed cottages is a deservedly popular subject with photographers. Neighboring **Duck Key** once thrived as a salt producer. Though **Grassy Key** is not particularly verdant, its **Dolphin Research Center**, *MM 59* (*Open* daily 9–5; reservations, tel: 305/289-1121) offers more dolphin encounters; and **Crawl Key** was named for the turtle cages, or kraals, used to store live turtles until they were converted into soup or jewelry in the days before preservation. Capital of the Middle Keys, **Marathon** is a well-developed small town with an airport, shopping malls, a marina, golf course and public beach, plus a wide range of accommodations, campgrounds and trailer parks. An interesting stop here is the Pigeon Key National Historic District, reached via the Old Seven Mile Bridge, which also serves as a fishing pier.

►► Crane Point Nature Center, Museums and Historic Site, *MM 50.5, Marathon* (*Open* Mon–Sat 9–5, Sun noon–5. *Admission: moderate*; tel: 305/743-9100, www.cranepoint.org) This woodland museum complex presents an overview of the natural history of the Keys. User-friendly displays explain geology, geography, history and wildlife; exhibits include a Skylab photograph of the region, reef dioramas and tales of shipwrecks. A specially-designed outdoor area for children has touch tanks, iguanas and a playroom. A mile-long (1.6km) nature trail explores **Crane Point Hammock**, which covers some 63 acres (25ha) and supports a wide range of tropical vegetation and ten endangered animal and plant species. Among the mangroves, palms and hardwood trees, a 19th-century Bahamanian coach house has been restored. Evidence indicates this site has been inhabited by pre-Columbian and prehistoric Native American peoples.

PIGEON KEY CAMP

Tucked beneath the Old Seven Mile Bridge, which used to link the Middle and Lower Keys, the Pigeon Key National Historic District (*Open* daily 9–5. *Admission: moderate*; tel: 305/743-5999) was once a camp for construction workers building Henry Flagler's Overseas Railway. The 5-acre (2ha) island is accessible by tram (from 10am), or on foot across a 2.2-mile (3.5km) section of the bridge. A self-guided walking tour (call ahead for guided tour schedules) explores various 19th-century buildings, one of which houses a small museum.

The Lower Keys

The magnificent **Seven Mile Bridge** marks the transition from the Middle to the Lower Keys. Built in 1982, the present structure is actually just short of 7 miles (11km), and affords dazzling views of the bay, the ocean and the islands. Beaches are a rarity on the Keys, but just south of the bridge, Bahia Honda State Park is fringed by beautiful white-sand beaches. A large area of **Big Pine Key** has been declared a preservation area for the endangered Key deer (see page 101). Here, the speed limit on the main road drops to 45mph (72kph), 35mph (56kph) after dark, in an effort to protect any of the tiny deer that wander away from the refuge. In the middle of the refuge, Blue Hole is the largest body of fresh water in the Keys. Accessible from Big Pine, Little Torch, Ramrod and Summerland Keys, the Looe Key National Marine Sanctuary (see page 101) is another diver's delight. **Cudjoe Key** is the home of the U.S. government's zeppelin look-alike *Fat Albert*, which watches for drug traffickers.

Bahia Honda State Park, *MM 37* (*Open* daily 8–dusk. *Admission: inexpensive;* tel: 305/872-2353, www.floridastateparks.org) Bahia Honda, from the Spanish "deep bay," fronts onto the Looe Key National Marine Sanctuary. Stop off for a swim or a picnic—the sandy shore has been ranked among the top one percent of the nation's beaches. There are snorkeling tours and dive shop rentals; pelicans, egrets, herons and terns are frequently spotted, and rare plants dot the nature trail. Also fishing, bike rentals, a boat ramp and a campground.

PERKY BAT TOWER
When Righter C. Perky set up a fishing camp on Sugarloaf Key in 1929, the mosquitoes were such a menace that something had to be done. Mr Perky wracked his brains and finally hit upon a cunning plan: He imported a colony of insect-eating bats and released them into a purpose-built tower. But the ungrateful creatures ignored their new home and swiftly disappeared, leaving Perky's quirky bat tower down a dirt track just past the Sugarloaf Lodge at MM 17.

There's good swimming and good views of the Old Seven Mile Bridge to be had at Bahia Honda

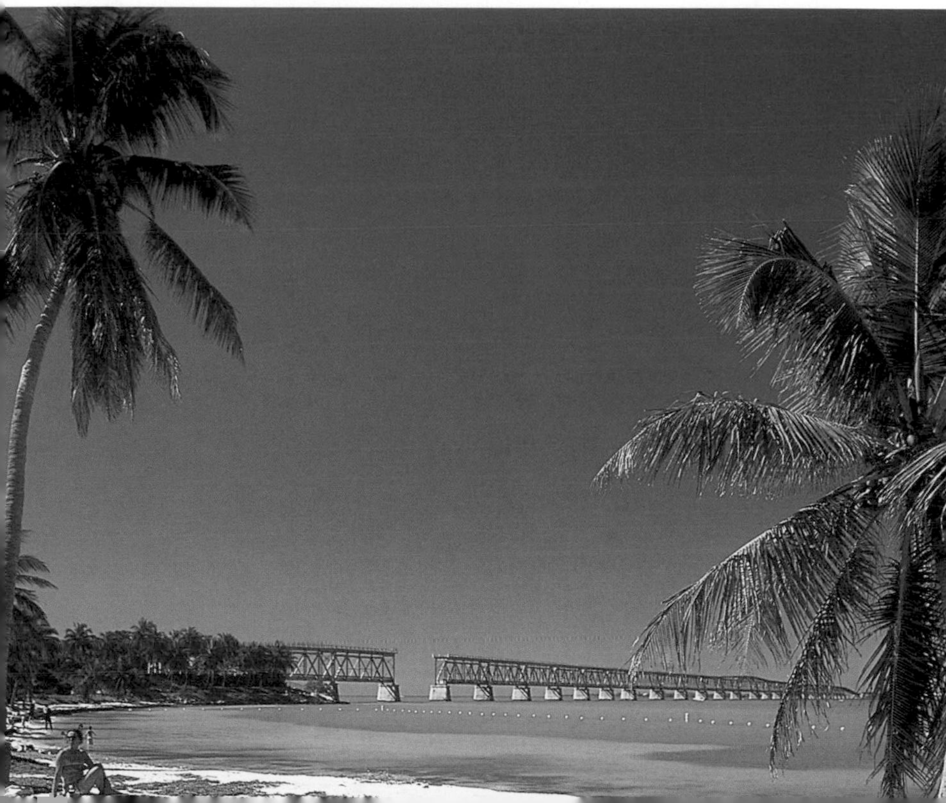

Walk

Exploring Key West

Start on Front Street, at the head of Whitehead Street, outside the imposing red-brick facade of the 1891 Old Custom House.

The former customs building has been restored to house the changing exhibitions of the **Key West Museum of Art & History**. Opposite is the **Mel Fisher Maritime Museum**, a stone's throw away from **Audubon House**.

Turn right on Front Street for the Truman Annex, entering the leafy residential quarter through a pair of gateposts.

Straight ahead is the **Harry S. Truman Little White House**, where the president once made the most of Key West's relaxing informality. Stop off for one of the regular tours.

Turn left and leave the Annex, crossing Whitehead Street onto Caroline Street. On the corner is the first office of Pan American Airways, whose Flight No. 1 from Key West to Cuba took off on October 28, 1927.

A few paces down the road, the **Heritage House Museum & Robert Frost Cottage**, 401 Caroline, is housed in a traditional Key West home dating from 1832. The interior is furnished with a marvelous array of antiques and objects gathered by seven generations of the Porter family. Poet Robert Frost used to winter in the garden cottage. Another lovely house farther down the street is the **Curry Mansion Inn**, 511 Caroline Street.

At Simonton Street, take a quick detour to the left for a visit to **The T-Shirt Factory**, 316 Simonton. Then continue on Caroline past a collection of handsome historic homes framed by mature trees, frangipani and bougainvillea.

Caroline Street continues onto the Historic Seaport district, where a boutique has become the last in a succession of businesses to occupy the 1868 **Red Doors Building**, 800 Caroline Street, which has functioned as a cigar factory, ships' chandlery, and shrimpers' bar in its colorful past. Next door, **Pepe's**, 806 Caroline Street, claims to be the oldest eating house in the Keys, and is a great place to pause for a cold drink or snack. Across the parking lot, **Flagler Station Over-Sea Railway Historeum**, 901 Caroline Street, makes an interesting stop for railroad and local history enthusiasts.

The Historic Seaport Boardwalk follows the waterfront back to Front Street.

Period furnishings in the nursery of Audubon House, a shrine to wildlife artist John James Audubon

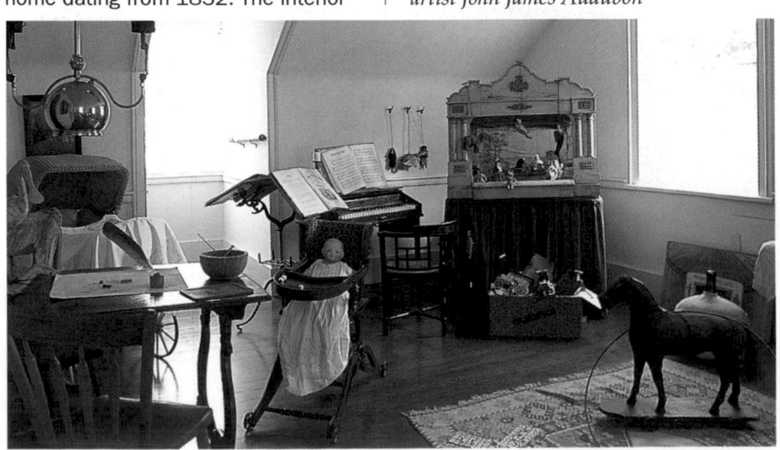

►►► **Looe Key National Marine Sanctuary** *6.5 miles (10.5km) off Big Pine Key at MM 27.5* This oceanside marine preserve is one of the most popular dive sites along the Keys. It surrounds part of a coral reef and several different undersea habitats from sea-grass beds and patch reefs to sand flats. Clear waters and moderate sea conditions make for great snorkeling on the surface, while the wide range of depths within the park makes it equally exciting for beginners and for experienced divers. In addition to the reef, there are wrecks to explore, including British frigate HMS *Looe,* which struck the reef and sank in 1744 (see panel).

► **National Key Deer Refuge and Blue Hole,** *Big Pine Key, 1.5 miles (2.5km) west at MM 33.5. Tel: 305/872-3675, www.nationalkeydeer.fws.gov* An estimated 800 Key deer remain on Big Pine Key and the 16 islands that surround it, but dozens are killed by drivers every year. At just 24 to 28in (61–71cm) high, Key deer are the smallest subspecies of the Virginia white-tailed deer. The Bambi-like creatures mate in the fall, giving birth to tiny fawns in spring. You can look for traces of antler velvet in late August and early September. The deer feed off native plants and berries, and although they can tolerate a small amount of salt water in their diet, fresh water is essential—feeding them is strictly prohibited (there is a $250 penalty for doing so).

There is a short nature trail, and the best time to spot deer is early in the morning and in the evening. The ranger knows from day to day where is the best pace to see them.

LOOE KEY ACCESS

A number of local dive and charter operators offer trips to the marine sanctuary. Among them are Looe Key Reef Resort and Dive Center, MM 27.5, Big Pine Key (tel: 305/872-2215; www.diveflakeys.com; e-mail: looekeydiv@aol.com); and Paradise Divers, MM 39, Sunshine Key Resort & Marina (tel: 305/872-1114; www.paradivers.com; e-mail: paradivers@aol.com). For snorkel and glass-bottom boat trips, contact Strike Zone Charters, MM 29.5, Big Pine Key (tel: 305/872-9863 or 1-800/654-9560, www.strikezonecharter.com).

There are only around 800 Key deer left on Big Pine Key and the surrounding islands

Blue Hole (*Open* daily 8–dusk) is an old limestone quarry at the heart of the Key Deer Refuge. Material for most of the roads on Big Pine Key was removed from here, and the quarry's freshwater supply is vital to the Key deer's survival. Although some salt water seeps into the lower levels of Blue Hole, freshwater species that thrive happily in its depths include bass, blue gills, mosquito fish and alligators. Herons, cormorants, ducks, moorhens and osprey constitute Blue Hole's varied bird life.

Unusual souvenirs for sale on Duval Street

►►► Key West 86 A1

The southernmost point in the Continental United States, Key West is an intriguing blend of laid-back locals and international sunseekers, quiet, leafy backstreets and tourist kitsch.

Pirates and wreckers laid the foundations of the town, and by the 1890s Key West had developed into the wealthiest city in Florida. Sponge-diving and cigar-making were already flourishing industries, when in 1912, tourism arrived via Henry Flagler's $50 million railroad.

After the devastating hurricane of 1935, Key West was saved by the intervention of the Florida Emergency Relief Administration, which replaced the railroad with tarmac and launched an ambitious plan to turn the city into a resort for authors and artists. Ernest Hemingway was already here, and it did not take long for a colony of artists to develop alongside the revitalized tourist industry.

To get a feel for Key West, jump aboard one of the frequent trolley or miniature train tours which circulate around town. Alternatively, you could rent a bike. Along mile-long (1.6km) **Duval Street**, the heart of downtown, visiting cruise passengers plunder the boutiques, bars and eateries, including Hemingway's favorite watering hole, **Sloppy Joe's**, 201 Duval. Take a stroll around the waterfront **Historic Seaport**, and do not miss sunset at **Mallory Square**—the ultimate Key West experience, for which half the population seems to turn up.

KEY WEST ARCHITECTURE

Local "conch" architecture was introduced to Key West by Bahamian settlers in the early 19th century. Houses were built from imported hardwoods or salvaged lumber and set on coral rock piles out of danger from flooding; roofs were designed to channel rainwater into cisterns. During the Classical Revival period, symmetrical facades adorned with columns, pediments, and gables were all the rage, and many houses still display decorative gingerbread detailing. Windows and doors were protected from sun and rain by wooden louvered blinds, which together with other local adaptations developed into a distinctive vernacular style.

Audubon House and Gardens, *205 Whitehead Street (Open daily 9.30–5. Admission: moderate*; tel: 305/294-2116 and 877/281-2473, www.audubonhouse.com) This handsome house was built by prosperous wrecker John H. Geiger in 1830. Self-guided audio tours explore the Geigers' home from top to bottom, and every room is beautifully furnished in period style with numerous examples of John James Audubon's splendid bird illustrations (see panel opposite). Upstairs a fine arts gallery sells original hand-painted Audubon lithographs for a few hundred dollars to a couple of thousand. After the tour, take time to wander around the enchanting tropical garden.

Curry Mansion Inn, *511 Caroline Street (Open tours, daily 10–5. Admission: inexpensive*; tel: 305/294-5349, www.currymansion.com) Home of an early Florida millionaire, William Curry, who made his fortune in the wrecking and lumber businesses, this is one of the loveliest buildings in town and now functions as a bed and breakfast, but opens for tours. A portion of the original homestead erected in 1855 is at the rear. Milton Curry added the gracious facade in 1899. The house has been exquisitely furnished with period antiques, with Tiffany glass, patchwork quilts on brass beds and a pool table in the attic. There are great views of the surrounding area from the roof.

East Martello Museum and Art Gallery, *3501 S. Roosevelt Boulevard* (*Open* daily 9.30–4.30. *Admission: moderate*; tel: 305/296-3913, www.kwahs.com) During the 1840s, the U.S. Army began work on a series of coastal defenses to protect Key West, including downtown Fort Zachary Taylor and two Martello towers. The East Tower, the only remaining example of its type on the eastern seaboard, houses an eclectic little local history museum which focuses on local industries, including Henry Flagler's railroad, and a welter of nautical memorabilia.

Climb to the top of the citadel for the views. The building also contains Stanley Papio's wacky scrap-iron folk art. A separate gallery displays Mario Sánchez's colorful carved and painted local street scenes.

Fort Zachary Taylor State Historic Site, *Truman Annex (entrance at the west end of Southard Street)* (*Open* daily 8–dusk. *Guided tours* at noon and 2pm. *Admission: inexpensive*; tel: 305/292-6713, www.floridastateparks.org) Founded in 1845, this fort took 21 years to complete. Although most of Florida supported the Confederacy, the fort was controlled by Union forces during the Civil War.

Today the grounds offer a sizable public beach, barbecue grills, and picnic tables. A small museum traces the fort's history, and excavations have uncovered a buried arsenal comprising the largest collection of Civil War cannons in the United States.

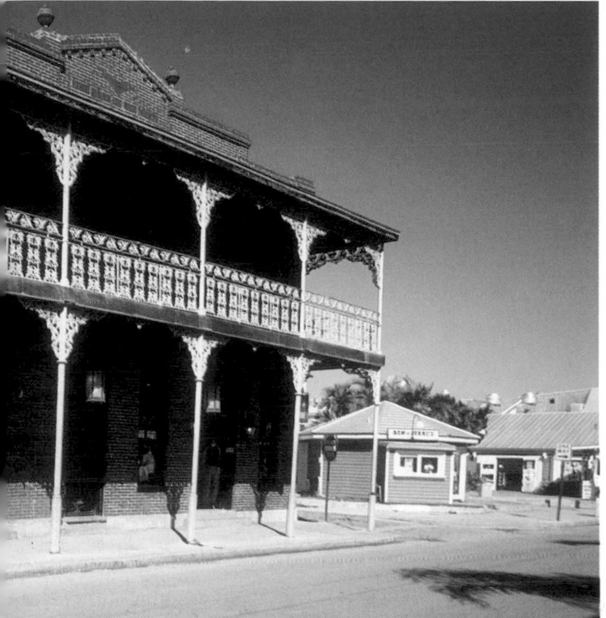

Typical southern architecture in Key West

FORT JEFFERSON
The largest coastal fortress in the United States encircles the island of Garden Key in the Dry Tortugas, 60 miles (97km) west of Key West. Fort Jefferson was founded in 1851. Its eight-foot-thick (2.5m) walls rise 50ft (15m) with three gun tiers, and its 70ft-wide (21m) moat was once patrolled by sharks and barracudas. The fort is accessible by ferry (a full-day excursion) and by boat or seaplane from Key West. The plane trip is spectacular. On arrival you can enjoy a sand beach and diving, and watch turtles and birds.
Fort Jefferson, tel: 305/242-7700. The fort also offers camping.

ARTIST AND ORNITHOLOGIST EXTRAORDINAIRE
John James Audubon was born in Haiti in 1785, the son of a French planter. To escape the Napoleonic draft, he moved into a family property in Pennsylvania and began traveling extensively to record native bird life. The result was the famous series of engravings, *Birds of America*. During a trip to Florida in 1832, Audubon recorded 18 new species of birds and worked in the gardens of John Geiger's Key West home.

When novelist John Dos Passos rode Henry Flagler's railroad into Key West in the 1920s, he later described it in glowing terms, saying it was "one of the most exhilarating experiences of my life; coming into Key West was like floating into a dream."

It was mainly Dos Passos's recommendation that lured Ernest Hemingway to Key West in 1928 and marked the beginning of a long and fruitful association between Key West and many leading 20th-century American writers.

Fishing and booze When Hemingway arrived in Key West with his second wife, Pauline, he joined the local seafaring community with enthusiasm. A turn-of-the-century boomtown, Key West was on the decline. Its population had dropped from 22,000 in the town's heyday to around 10,000, and the stream of winter tourists had dried up with the 1929 stock market crash. Fortunately for "Papa" Hemingway, Prohibition meant nothing in Key West. Cuban rum enhanced fishermen's tales of mighty marlin, tarpon and wily bonefish, and lent local bars an alluring pioneer flavor. Hemingway's fishing trips became legendary. One of his favorite fishing cronies, Joe Russell, was also the proprietor of Sloppy Joe's bar.

A place to write Pauline's uncle bought the house at 907 Whitehead Street (see page 105) for the couple in 1931. Between trips abroad, Hemingway returned here to write *For Whom the Bell Tolls*, *A Farewell to Arms*, *The Snows of Kilimanjaro* and *Death in the Afternoon*, among others. The three stories that make up *To Have and Have Not* are his only fiction with an American setting. In 1936, Hemingway met journalist Martha Gellhorn in Sloppy Joe's. She would become his third wife and influence his move to Cuba in the 1940s.

A writer's retreat: the lounge in Hemingway's house

A literary haven The Florida Emergency Relief Administration's post-hurricane scheme to attract promising writers to Key West was a wild success: 10 Pulitzer Prizes have been awarded to a succession of visiting and resident writers. In the late 1930s, poet Elizabeth Bishop spent a brief sojourn in Key West; Robert Frost, Gore Vidal and Kurt Vonnegut Jr. all enjoyed a respite from northern winters in the town; and playwright Tennessee Williams lived near Duncan and Leon streets from 1949 until his death in 1983.

Hemingway House, *907 Whitehead Street* (*Open* daily 9–5, last tour at 5. *Admission: moderate*; tel: 305/294-1136, www.hemingwayhome.com) Ernest Hemingway acquired this mid-19th-century Spanish Colonial-style house in 1931. He and his second wife, Pauline, decorated the interior with furnishings and mementos gathered on trips to Spain, Africa and Cuba, and Hemingway penned several novels and short stories in an airy study above the carriage house. Regular guided tours provide interesting detail and anecdotes about Hemingway. An extensive colony of cats, introduced to the homestead by the writer, still has the run of the house and gardens. Check out their enormous feet—some of them have as many as eight toes—a genetic hiccup that attracted Hemingway's attention when he adopted his first feline from a sea captain.

Key West Aquarium, *1 Whitehead Street* (*Open* daily 10–6. *Admission: moderate*; tel: 305/296-2051 and 800/868-7482, www.keywestaquarium.com) Hundreds of brightly colored tropical fish and other sea creatures are on display here in exhibits that will make you an expert on Florida's marine life. In addition to a 50,000-gallon (227,000-liter) coastal mangrove tank, various smaller glass-fronted aquariums line the walls. There is a touch tank, tours and shark-feeding demonstrations.

FUN

Hemingway fever hits town in July, when hundreds of Ernest Hemingway look-alikes converge on Key West for the annual Hemingway Days Festival. The week-long celebration of the writer's life includes seminars, a look-alike contest, fishing competitions, and storytelling. Later in the year, the October Fantasy Fest honors Halloween with a costume party, parade, and a town fair. Make hotel reservations well in advance.

Marine encounters in the touch tank at the Key West Aquarium

Climb the 88 steps of the Lighthouse Museum for the superb vista over historic Key West

Key West Lighthouse Museum, *938 Whitehead Street* (*Open* daily 9.30–5. *Admission: moderate*; tel: 305/294-0012, www.kwahs.org) For a bird's-eye view of Key West, look no farther than the 86ft-tall (26m), 19th-century lighthouse. It's an 88-step ascent to the viewing balcony; another 10 steps lead to the light itself. At ground level, the former Keeper's Quarters, paneled with rock-solid Dade County pine, house interesting and eclectic memorabilia from past keepers, including Barbara Mabrity who worked the lighthouse until the age of 82. She survived the 1946 hurricane that killed six of her children.

Lazy Dog Island Outfitters and Kayak Guides, *310 Duval Street* (tel: 305/294-7178, www.mosquitocoast.net) A great way to get to grips with nature, this is a must for nature-lovers and outdoorsmen; experience is not necessary as instruction and easy-to-use kayaks are provided. Kayakers and all necessary equipment are transported to Geiger Key or Sugarloaf Key, where knowledgable guides lead four- or five-hour tours into the backcountry, exploring mangrove islands and crystal-clear waters teeming with birds, marine life and other wildlife. Snorkeling gear is supplied for those who want to investigate seldom-dived coral and hard-bottom mangrove channels—be sure to bring along plenty of sun block, as well as mosquito repellent, hats, UV-protective sunglasses and waterproof camera cases.

Little White House Museum, *111 Front Street* (*Guided tours* daily 9–5. *Admission: moderate*; tel: 305/294-9911, www.trumanlittlewhitehouse.com) Tucked in the Truman Annex, part of an old naval station, this was President Harry S. Truman's alternative White House. Truman took 11 working vacations here during his 6 years of office. The house dates from 1890. Refurbished in 1940s style, living areas and bedrooms contain Truman-era relics, such as his custom-made poker table with shell cases for ashtrays, and there is an excellent film presentation before the guided tour. Dwight D. Eisenhower worked on his State of the Union address here in 1956.

Mallory Square Pier, *off Wall Street* Key West locals don't just watch the sun go down, they celebrate it. For this daily party, locals and visitors alike gather on the dockside at Mallory Square to watch the fiery sun slide into the Gulf of Mexico. Street entertainers roll up in force—washboard strummers and bongo players set feet tapping, and jugglers, mimes, and unicyclists show off their skills.

Mel Fisher Maritime Museum, *200 Greene Street* (*Open* daily 9.30–5. *Admission: moderate*; tel: 305/294-2633,

SHIPWRECK AHOY!

For an entertaining look at Key West's notorious wrecking era, check out the Key West Shipwreck Historeum on Mallory Square (*Open* daily 9.45–4.45. *Admission: moderate*; tel: 305/292-8990). There are displays of objects raised from the wreck of the *Isaac Allerton*, which sank in 1865 carrying the richest manifest of any ship of its time, as well as shows and a 65ft (20m) observation tower with fine views of Old Town Key West and out to sea.

www.melfisher.org) "Today's the day!" is Mel Fisher's motto, and it kept him going through 16 long years of determined exploration before he finally hit the jackpot with the discovery of the Spanish galleon *Atocha* in 1985. There had been several finds before, but nothing to match this $400 million in gold, silver and jewels—the cargo that sank with the ship off the Keys in 1622. Domestic objects retrieved from the *Atocha* and her sister ship the *Santa Margarita* present a microcosm of daily 17th-century life, and then there is the real treasure: Gold and silver tableware, emeralds from the Muzo mines of Colombia and fabulous jewelry such as a 12ft-long (3.5m) gold wedding chain that weighs 4.5 lbs (2kg) and is valued at a mere $500,000. Take in the video presentation, handle a gold bar and visit the shop selling objects and replicas.

Oldest House Museum, *322 Duval Street* (*Open* daily 10–4. *Admission: inexpensive;* tel: 305/294-9502) Built in the early 19th century, this building, which claims to be the oldest house in Key West, is a fine example of early Key West architecture, with its distinctive maritime flavor. The interior is lined with horizontal planks reminiscent of a ship's hull, while furnishings and objects trace the history of the one-time owner of the house, Captain Francis B. Watlington. The original outdoor kitchen is the last in the Keys.

I TOLD YOU I WAS SICK
Between Olivia and Angela streets, Key West City Cemetery is a surprising repository of local humor. As well as a litany of quirky nicknames, there are some irreverent epitaphs such as B. P. Robert's "I told you I was sick," and one honest widow's revenge: "At least I know where he's sleeping tonight." If it all looks a little disorganized, blame the local bedrock, which has left several stone caskets resting above ground. The shortage of space means that an estimated 100,000 people have been buried in the 15,000 plots.

A bird's-eye view of Key West

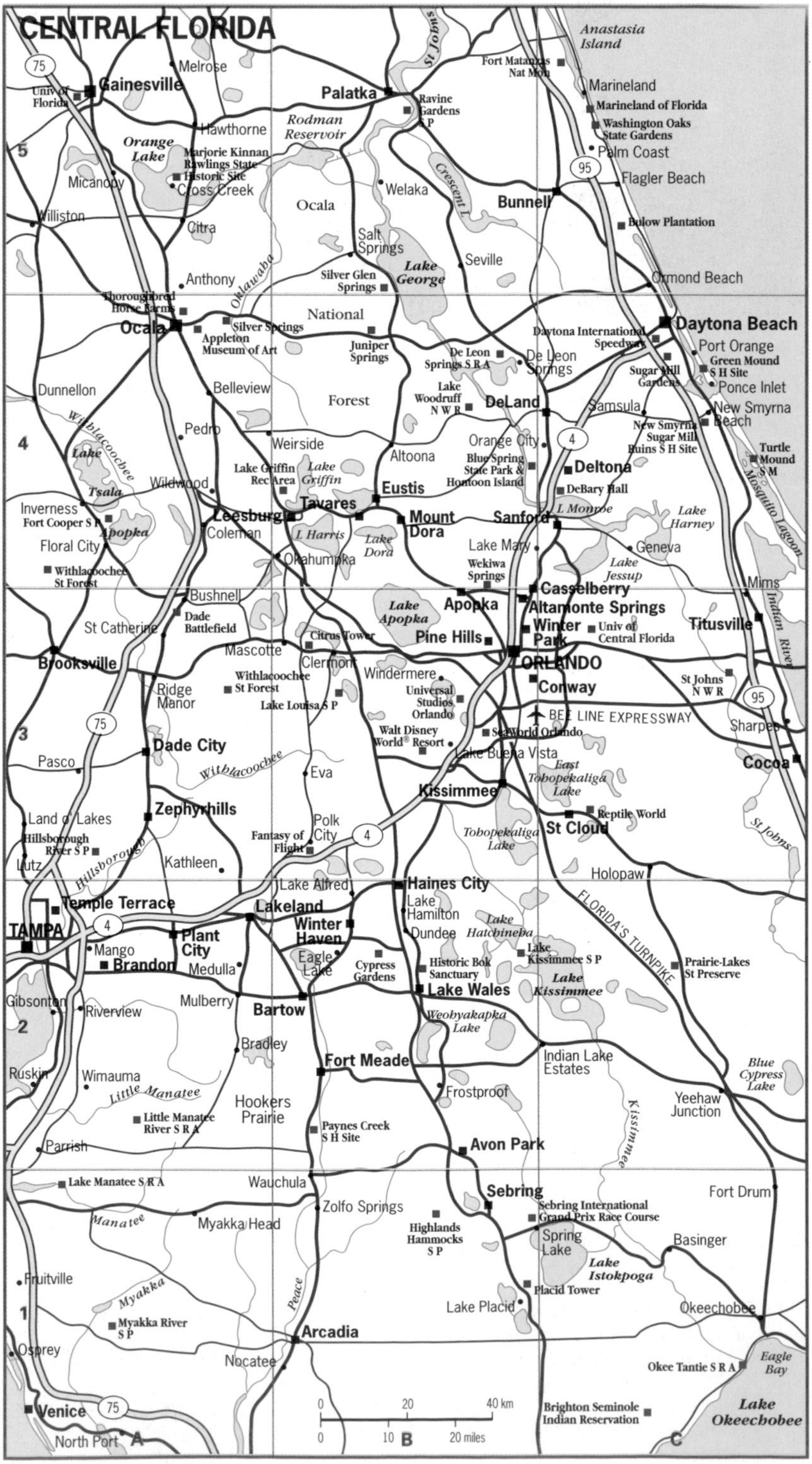

CENTRAL FLORIDA

Anastasia Island
75
Melrose
Fort Matanzas Nat Mon
Univ of Florida
Gainesville
Palatka
Ravine Gardens S P
St Johns
Marineland
Marineland of Florida
5
Hawthorne
Rodman Reservoir
Washington Oaks State Gardens
Orange Lake
Marjorie Kinnan Rawlings State Historic Site
Palm Coast
95
Micanopy
Cross Creek
Welaka
Crescent L
Flagler Beach
Ocala
Bunnell
Williston
Citra
Bulow Plantation
Salt Springs
Seville
Oklawaha
Lake George
Anthony
Silver Glen Springs
Ormond Beach
Thoroughbred Horse Farms
National
Ocala
Silver Springs
Daytona Beach
Appleton Museum of Art
Daytona International Speedway
Juniper Springs
Port Orange
De Leon Springs S R A
De Leon Springs
Green Mound S H Site
Dunnellon
Belleview
Sugar Mill Gardens
Ponce Inlet
Forest
Lake Woodruff N W R
DeLand
Samsula
New Smyrna Beach
Withlacoochee
Pedro
New Smyrna Sugar Mill Ruins S H Site
4
Weirside
Orange City
Turtle Mound S M
Lake Tsala
Altoona
Lake Griffin Rec Area
Lake Griffin
Blue Spring State Park & Hontoon Island
Deltona
Wildwood
Eustis
DeBary Hall
Mosquito Lagoon
Inverness
Tavares
L Monroe
Lake Harney
Fort Cooper S P
Leesburg
Mount Dora
Sanford
Apopka
Coleman
L Harris
Lake Dora
Floral City
Lake Mary
Geneva
Okahumpka
Withlacoochee St Forest
Wekiwa Springs
Lake Jessup
Mims
Bushnell
Casselberry
Lake Apopka
Apopka
Altamonte Springs
Dade Battlefield
Indian River
St Catherine
Citrus Tower
Winter Park
Univ of Central Florida
Titusville
Pine Hills
Mascotte
Brooksville
Clermont
ORLANDO
Windermere
St Johns N W R
Ridge Manor
Withlacoochee St Forest
Conway
Universal Studios Orlando
Lake Louisa S P
95
75
BEE LINE EXPRESSWAY
Walt Disney World® Resort
SeaWorld Orlando
Sharpes
3
Dade City
Lake Buena Vista
Cocoa
Pasco
East Tohopekaliga Lake
Withlacoochee
Eva
Kissimmee
Zephyrhills
Reptile World
Land o' Lakes
St Cloud
Polk City
Tohopekaliga Lake
Fantasy of Flight
4
St Johns
Hillsborough River S P
Hillsborough
Kathleen
Lutz
Holopaw
Lake Alfred
Haines City
Temple Terrace
FLORIDA'S TURNPIKE
Lakeland
Lake Hamilton
TAMPA
4
Winter Haven
Mango
Plant City
Dundee
Lake Hatchineha
Lake Kissimmee S P
Brandon
Eagle Lake
Medulla
Cypress Gardens
Historic Bok Sanctuary
Prairie-Lakes St Preserve
Lake Kissimmee
Gibsonton
Lake Wales
Riverview
Mulberry
Bartow
2
Weohyakapka Lake
Bradley
Indian Lake Estates
Ruskin
Fort Meade
Blue Cypress Lake
Wimauma
Frostproof
Kissimmee
Little Manatee
Hookers Prairie
Yeehaw Junction
Little Manatee River S R A
Paynes Creek S H Site
Parrish
Avon Park
Lake Manatee S R A
Wauchula
Sebring
Fort Drum
Zolfo Springs
Sebring International Grand Prix Race Course
Manatee
Myakka Head
Highlands Hammocks S P
Spring Lake
Basinger
Fruitville
Lake Istokpoga
Peace
Placid Tower
Myakka
Lake Placid
Okeechobee
1
Myakka River S P
Arcadia
Osprey
Nocatee
Okee Tantie S R A
Eagle Bay
0 20 40 km
Brighton Seminole Indian Reservation
Lake Okeechobee
Venice
75
0 10 20 miles
North Port
A
B
C

Central Florida

CANE FIELDS AND CITRUS GROVES, cartoon characters and cowmen—Central Florida has it all, yet most visitors come for one thing only. Orlando is Central Florida's first city. Settled as a fortress during the Seminole Wars, it developed into a relatively prosperous citrus and cattle town ringed with lakes, and earned its nickname, the City Beautiful. When Walt Disney selected Florida as the location for his second theme park in the 1960s, Orlando was the perfect site, with year-round good weather and good transportation and communication links close to huge tracts of undeveloped land.

Today, Walt Disney World® Resort is the world's biggest tourist destination, attracting millions of visitors every year. There has been an inevitable onslaught of tourist-related industries and tacky spin-offs, notably in **Kissimmee**, a small town-turned-sprawling-budget-dormitory at Disney's back door, a half-hour drive south of Orlando. However, it is surprisingly easy to leave the theme parks and find tranquility in a state park or sophistication in the attractive suburb of **Winter Park**. Orlando is also within easy reach of both the east and west Florida coasts: **Kennedy Space Center** (pages 192–193) is an hour's drive east; while the Gulf of Mexico, **Tampa** (pages 226–233) and **St. Petersburg** (pages 216–219) lie 90 minutes west.

Citrus country stretches west and south of Orlando. Here, **Lake Wales** is renowned among the faithful for its simple, devout annual Passion Play, and there are two marvelous gardens nearby: Bok Tower Gardens; and Cypress Gardens, which incorporates a distinctly kitsch theme park element, near Winter Haven. **Arcadia**, 65 miles (105km) west of Okeechobee City, is in the heart of cattle country. Facades straight out of a Western movie line the main drag, and it is wall-to-wall blue jeans and Stetsons during the All-Florida Championship Rodeo. A vital link in the Everglades ecosystem, expansive **Lake Okeechobee** has been dangerously tamed, but it is still a haven for bird-watchers and fishermen.

North of Orlando is **Ocala**, surrounded by lush countryside and thoroughbred farms.A fine art museum is on the edge of town, which is bordered by the vast expanses of Ocala National Forest. Rolling hills and ranches encircle historic **Gainesville**, a college town that has hardly been touched by tourism. Enthusiastic sports fans flock here to support the University of Florida football team, the mighty Gators.

Top: Neon signs at Universal Studios in Orlando

▶▶▶ REGION HIGHLIGHTS

▶ Arcadia *108 B1*

Detour off Route 70 for a look at this sleepy cattle town. Past the imposing **DeSoto County Courthouse**, downtown **Oak Street** has been restored, and there are some lovely old houses beyond the shopping district. If you want to stock up on genuine cowman outfits, such as Resistol and Stetson headgear, boots, belts and ladies' leather Annie-Get-Yer-Gun skirts, visit **Eli's Western Stores** at *1003 East Oak Street, on Highway 70 East*.

North on Route 17, **Peace River** is a shallow waterway where **Canoe Outpost** (tel: 863/494-1215) rents out water-sports equipment. On Route 72, just east of Sarasota, is **Myakka River State Park**. One of the state's largest parks, at 35,000 acres (14,000ha), it can be explored on foot, on horseback, by tram or by boat trips on the Myakka River as it flows through the park. The highlight is a canopy walkway that allows you access to tree-top level.

▶ Gainesville *108 A5*

Surrounded by cattle ranches, stud farms and Florida-style rolling hills, Gainesville is home to the University of Florida. On the attractive, tree-shaded university campus, the **Florida Museum of Natural History**, *Hull Road at S.W. 34th Street* (*Open* Mon–Sat 10–5, Sun 1–5. *Admission free;* tel: 352/846-2000) presents a 12ft (3.5m) mammoth skeleton together with bronze casts of a saber-toothed tiger and giant upright sloth, as well as a full-scale Florida limestone cave exhibit. Well-presented displays and interactive stations transport visitors to a variety of Florida ecological and cultural experiences including a Butterfly Rainforest with 60 species.

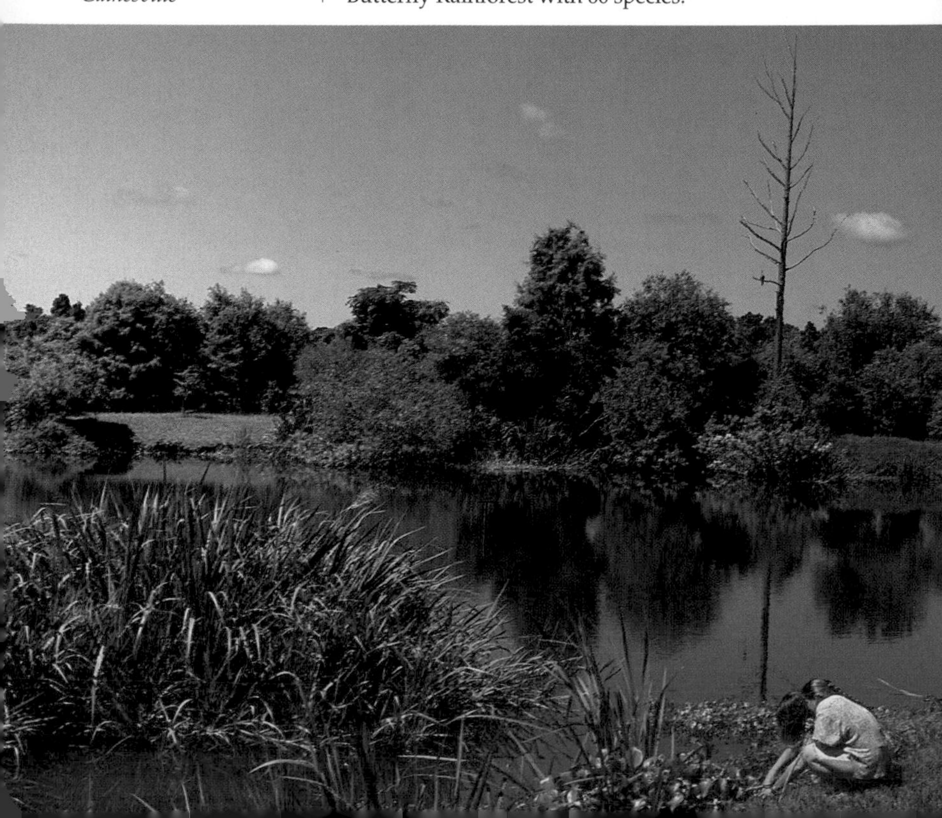

Lake Alice, near Gainesville

Neighboring **Samuel P. Harn Museum of Art** (*Open* Tue–Fri 11–5, Sat 10–5, Sun 1–5. *Admission free*; tel: 352/392-9826, www.harn.eft.edu) is a campus feature with a semipermanent collection of American, Oceanic, African and pre-Columbian art, plus contemporary works.

On the outskirts of town, the scenic and unusual **Devil's Millhopper State Geological Site**, *4732 Millhopper Road* (*Open* Wed–Sun 9–5. *Admission: inexpensive*; tel: 352/955-2008, www.floridastateparks.org), is a 500ft (150m) wide, 120ft (36m) deep sinkhole festooned with lush plants and giant ferns, cooled by a dozen little waterfalls.

The lovely **Kanapaha Botanical Gardens**, *4700 S.W. 58th Drive, off Archer Road* (*Open* Mon, Tue, Fri 9–5, Wed, Sat, Sun 9–dusk. *Admission: inexpensive*; tel: 352/372-4981, www.kanapaha.org), meander across a sloping lakeside site where a profusion of azaleas and camellias blooms each spring. There are forest and desert areas, bamboo groves and a colorful hummingbird garden.

▶▶ Lake Wales *108 B2*

North of Lake Wales, it is worth making a short detour west to **Chalet Suzanne**, *on ALT 27* (*Cannery Open* Mon–Fri 9–4; tel: 863/676-6011 and 800/433-6011, www.chaletsuzanne.com), a rambling country restaurant -hotel with craft shops and a home-made soup business. It is not just any old soup—it is so popular that it accompanied the crew of *Apollo 15* to the moon in 1973.

A few miles south, do not miss beautiful **Historic Bok Sanctuary**, *C.R. 17-A* (*Open* daily 8–6, last entry 5pm). *Admission: moderate*; tel: 863/676-1408, www.boksanctuary.org). Created by Dutch-born philanthropist Edward W. Bok in the 1920s, these peaceful woodland gardens spread over the gentle slopes of Iron Mountain, the highest point on the Florida peninsula at a modest 298ft (89m). Visitors are invited to explore the 157-acre (63ha) spread on winding footpaths with spectacular views of the massed springtime blooms of azaleas, camellias, magnolias and ferns, shaded by slender palms, pines and oaks. The centerpiece is a 205ft (61.5m) pink and gray marble and coquina tower, whose 57-bell carillon chimes every half hour from 10, with a full recital daily at 3. A program of events includes Moonlight Recitals and an International Carillon Festival (February). An additional highlight of a visit is **Pinewood Estate**, a romantic Mediterranean Revival mansion built in 1931. Named for the splendid pine trees on the Great Lawn, the house is surrounded by landscaped gardens inspired by an eclectic combination of formal Italian-style plantings and a burgeoning English walled garden of the type perfected by English country house gardener, Gertrude Jeckyll.

▶ Micanopy *108 A5*

Once named Wanton, but now as decorous as they come, this lovely little town offers a tantalizing glimpse of Old Florida. Handsome Victorian homes and giant shady live oak trees line Cholokka Boulevard as it makes its way into the town center, where the old red-brick storefronts now harbor a selection of antiques and collectibles dealers. The town was the first white settlement in Alachua County when it was founded on the site of a former Timuca Native American village in 1821, and the name Micanopy

CROSS CREEK
In 1928, New York authoress Marjorie Kinnan Rawlings moved to Cross Creek, a quiet rural community, where she bought a small homestead and settled down to learn about backwoods Cracker life. The fruits of her labors were a series of evocative novellas, including *The Yearling*, which won her a Pulitzer Prize. Her home, the Marjorie Kinnan Rawlings State Historic Site, lies 21 miles (34km) southeast of Gainesville on C.R. 325 (*Open* daily 9–5. Tours inexpensive; tel: 352/466-3672). It has been preserved just as she left it, with an ancient typewriter on the porch, rum by the fireplace and canned food on the shelves.

was adopted in honor of a Native American chief. Many of the town's early residents were buried in the quiet, moss-carpeted cemetery off Seminary Avenue.

▶ Mount Dora *108 B4*

On the shores of Lake Dora, 20 miles (32km) northeast of Orlando, this picturesque small town was founded on a low rise overlooking the waterfront by Northern settlers in the 1870s. The oldest surviving building is the **Lakeside Inn**, dating from 1883, where President Calvin Coolidge once stayed, and there are many lovely old buildings. Mount Dora is also a favorite haunt of antiques collectors. The Chamber of Commerce, 341 Alexander Street, has walking maps of the restored downtown shopping and antiques district, and neighboring Victorian mansions. One of the finest is the impressive 1893 Queen Anne-style **Donnelly House**, on Donnelly Street, a riot of fancy ironwork and gingerbread decoration, gables, balconies and steeply pitched roofs with a cupola.

Mount Dora was initially known as Royellou, a made-up name derived from the three children of the local postmaster, Roy, Ella and Louis Tremain. Just off Fifth Avenue, Mount Dora's main drag, the **Royellou Museum**, *Royellou Lane* (*Open* Fri–Sun 1–5. *Admission: inexpensive*; tel: 352/383-5228) displays local history exhibits in the old Town Fire Station.

Down on the shores of Lake Dora, there are boat and bicycle rentals available in Gilbert Park, close to Grantham Point with its red and white-painted mini lighthouse. **Palm Island Park** has a nature trail and boardwalks for a close up look at water birds and the occasional alligator or otter.

Mount Dora also prides itself on a busy calendar of events throughout the year which range from the February Art Festival through April's Sailing regatta to the charming Christmas Lighting when more than 100,000 tiny lights illuminate the downtown area.

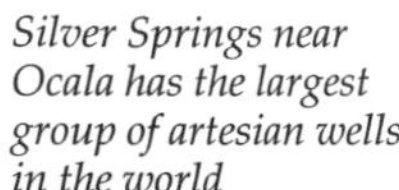

Silver Springs near Ocala has the largest group of artesian wells in the world

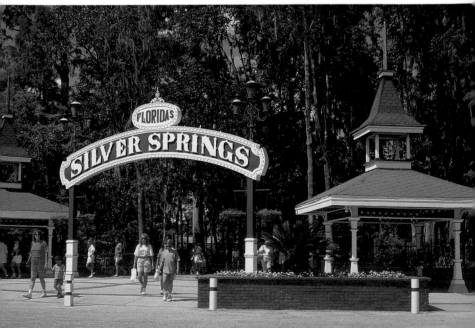

►► Ocala *108 A4*

Marion County's 600-plus thoroughbred horse farms are home to almost 58,000 horses. Every road to Ocala is lined with white-painted railings and grassy paddocks, where glossy equine fortunes graze peacefully in the shade of spreading live oaks. For information about local farm visits and the region's busy calendar of equestrian events, check with the Chamber of Commerce, *110 E. Silver Springs Boulevard* (tel: 352/629-8051).

A popular family day out just east of town, **Silver Springs**, *5656 East Silver Spring Boulevard* (*Open* daily 10–5. *Admission: expensive*; tel: 352/236-2121, www.silversprings.com) can lay claim to being "Florida's Original Attraction." In 1878, local entrepreneur Hullum Jones launched an ingenious idea when he installed a glass viewing box in the flat bottom of a dugout canoe offering tourists a fish's-eye view of the head of the world's largest artesian spring formation. Glass-bottom boat rides with sightings of freshwater fish and turtles as well as ancient fossils remain a favorite pastime, and cruises explore the peaceful, tree-shaded Silver River. Other diversions include Jeep safaris in the backwoods with animal encounter opportunities such as the Panther Prowl, home to rare Florida panthers, and an alligator swamp, plus a variety of animal shows and demonstrations, and a summer season weekend concert program. The wave pool and water flumes of the adjacent **Wild Waters** family water park are very inviting on a hot day.

On a completely different tack, **Don Garlits' Drag Racing and Museum of Classic Automobiles**, *13700 S.W. 16th Avenue* (*Open* daily 9–5. *Admission: moderate*; tel: 352/245-8661 and 877/271-3278, www.garlits.com) feature mean drag racing machines and classic vehicles.

The **Appleton Museum of Art**, *4333 E. Silver Springs Boulevard* (7 miles/11km east of I–75. *Open* Tue–Sun 10–6. *Admission: inexpensive*; tel: 352/291-4460), is an unusual regional art museum. A stunning Italian travertine marble museum houses exhibits from Ancient Greek and Etruscan pottery to African ceremonial masks, Japanese ivories, Chinese jade and Tiffany lamps.

Stretching east from Ocala to the St. Johns River, the 383,573-acre (153,429ha) **Ocala National Forest** is a woodland delight for hikers, birders, fishermen and canoeists. As well as a terrific choice of walking trails and boardwalk excursions, there is excellent bass fishing, sailing and watersports; the canoe trails are among Florida's best.

► Okeechobee *108 C1*

Down at the southern extent of the central region, **Lake Okeechobee** is the second largest expanse of fresh water in the United States, covering 730sq miles (1,883sq km). It is possible to drive around the entire lake, with stops on the eastern side at **Port Mayaca** and at **Pahokee State Recreation Area** for picnicking, camping and boat rentals. The lake is popular with birdwatchers and with fishermen on the trail of largemouth bass. The southern end of the lake is sugar country, where **Belle Glade mill** produces some 2,000 tons of raw sugar daily. **Clewiston** is a sugar town with a sideline in cabbage palms. Along the northwest lakeshore, the road traverses **Brighton Seminole Indian Reservation**.

Pre-Columbian exhibit in the Appleton Museum of Art

ORLANDO Orlando, the land of theme parks, also offers a number of other attractions, from historical and science museums to botanical gardens, water parks and themed restaurants. Take time out for a stroll by lovely downtown **Lake Eola** with its remarkable fountain, or a boat trip on Kissimmee's Lake Tohopekaliga, renowned for its birdlife (see page 116). There are accommodations to suit every pocket; look out for especially good deals in the Kissimmee/Maingate area.

Orlando's International Drive Resort Area (off I–4) is the main tourism, shopping and transportation hub. There is a helpful Visitor Information Center at the *Gala Center, 8723 International Drive at Austrian Row* (*Open* daily 8–7; tel: 407/363-5872), which sells discounted admission tickets to many local attractions and theme parks. A handy trolley service, the **I-Ride**, operates shuttles the length of International Drive (I-Drive) between Orlando Premium Outlet Mall in the south, and the Belz Factory outlet mall every 5–10 minutes, daily 7am–midnight.

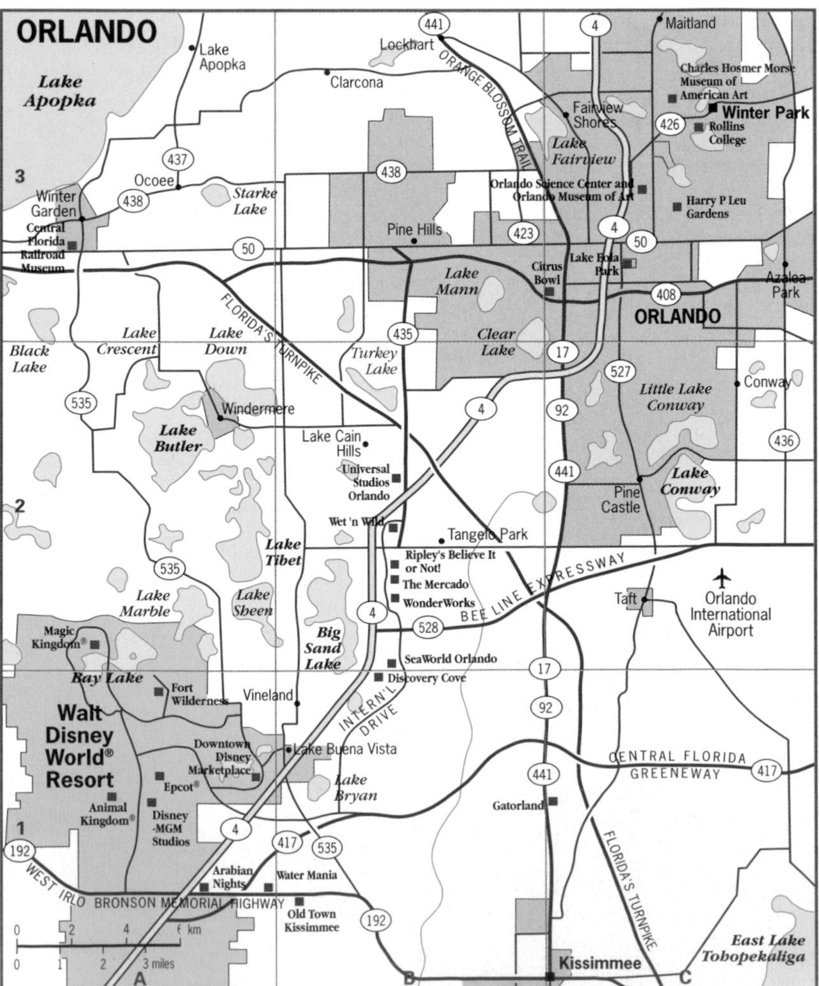

►► Discovery Cove

6000 Discovery Way; tel: 407/363-3380 or 877/4 DISCOVERY, www.discoverycove.com
Open: daily 8–5.30, twilight sessions 3–9pm.
Admission: expensive

Sibling of SeaWorld, Discovery Cove was opened in 2000. The park is designed around a tropical lagoon with white-sand beaches and swaying palms and hammocks, accessible to only 1,000 visitors each day. The Dolphin Encounter is the highlight, a personal interaction with these loveable creatures. While you wait for your encounter you can swim with shoals of tropical fish at Coral Reef or with rays at Ray Lagoon. Tropical River offers warmer waters and cascades, while the Aviary has more than 250 colorful birds, many of which will feed from your hand.

►► Gatorland 114 C1

14501 S. Orange Blossom Trail (U.S. 441); tel: 407/855-5496, www.gatorland.com
Open: daily 9–5 Admission: expensive

Just north of Kissimmee, a monster alligator jaw marks the entrance to 55 acres (22ha) of pens and pools teeming with alligators and a breeding marsh area that can be observed safely from a raised boardwalk. There are daily alligator shows in the "Wrestlin' Stadium." Other touristy attractions include Florida crocodiles and caimans, a selection of venomous snakes and native turtles.

►► Harry P. Leu Gardens 114 C3

1920 N. Forest Avenue; tel: 407/246-2620, www.leugardens .org
Open: daily 9–5. Admission: inexpensive

These lush gardens in the heart of Orlando are just the place for a quiet stroll. Explore the camellia and azalea woods, the ornamental flowering-tree garden, sweet-scented Mary Jane's Rose Garden and the native wetland garden. The floral clock is a popular attraction, as is the Orchid Conservatory, and there are tours of **Leu House**, a carefully restored turn-of-the-century farmhouse.

Lake Tohopekaliga, better known as Lake Toho, hosts water sports events

Scaly resident at Gatorland

LOCH HAVEN PARK MUSEUMS
Loch Haven Park is also home to the Orlando Museum of Art (*Open* Tue–Fri 10–4, Sat–Sun noon–4. *Admission: inexpensive*; tel: 407/896-4231, www.omart.org), containing notable collections of pre-Columbian art and works by leading 19th- and 20th-century American artists.

RIPLEY'S BELIEVE IT OR NOT! MUSEUM
From the strange to the bizzare to the barely credible, exhibits at this museum-cum-freak-show set out to lift the lid on some of life's little oddities. Among the interactive exhibits, holograms and illusion, this is the place to find authentic shrunken heads, chunks of the Berlin Wall and video nasties of truly revolting feats of human endurance. Kids love it.
8201 International Drive; tel: 407/363-4418, www.ripleysorlando,com Open: daily 9am–1am. Admission: expensive

► Kissimmee *114 C1*

Kissimmee is a popular vacation base south of Orlando and a few minutes from Walt Disney World. The center of town, **Broadway**, still has historic shopfronts and there are cattle auctions at the Livestock Market on Wednesdays. Down by Lake Tohopekaliga (better known as Lake Toho), boats and fishing tackle can be rented from **Big Toho Marina**, *101 Lakeshore Boulevard*, and **Aquatic Wonders Boat Tours** depart for 2-hour nature safaris and bass fishing trips (tel: 407/846-2814).

Between I–4 and the town center, U.S. 192 is known as Irlo Bronson Memorial Highway. To help visitors find their way around, there are numbered guide markers (#) set approximately a mile (1.6km) apart: the "Tourist Trap Trail." Heading east from I–4, the landmark waterslides of **Water Mania**, *6073 W. Irlo Bronson #8. Admission: expensive;* tel: 407/396-2626, www.watermania.com) are easy to spot. **Old Town, Kissimmee**, *5770 W. Irlo Bronson #9.* www.old-town.com) is a period-style mall with a vintage Ferris wheel. **Green Meadows Petting Farm**, *1368 S. Poinciana Boulevard* (*Open* daily 9.30–5.30. *Admission: expensive;* tel: 407/846-0770, www.greenmeadowsfarm .com), offers hayrides, 200 farm animals, pony rides and cow-milking lessons. **Boggy Creek Airboat Rides**, *3702 Big Bass Road* (*Open* daily, tours every half hour 9–5.30. Reservations required for night tours. *Admission: moderate, night expensive,* tel:407/344-550, www.bcairboats.com) takes you across the lake shallows in a US Coastguard accredited airboat to spot gators and other wildlife. Day tours last 30 minutes, night tour 1 hour.

►► Orlando Science Center *114 C3*

777 E. Princeton Street, Loch Haven Park (I–4/Exit 43); tel: 407/514-2000, www.osc.org
Open: Tue–Thu (and school holiday Mon) 9–5, Fri and Sat 9–9, Sun noon–5. Admission: moderate

This impressive complex is crowned by an observatory and anchored by the CineDome, an eight-story domed theater designed to showcase large-format films, planetarium presentations and 3-D laser light shows. The complex has plenty of hands-on exhibits, plus live science demonstrations, such as Bodyworks.

►►► SeaWorld® Orlando *114 B2*

7007 SeaWorld Drive; tel: 407/351-3600 or 800/4-ADVENTURE, www.seaworldorlando.com
Open: daily 9–7, extended in summer. Admission: expensive
This is one of the world's largest and most popular marine-life parks. It is huge—200 acres (80ha) in all, divided among a variety of different features, including marine stadiums, lagoons, aquariums, botanical gardens, restaurants and cafés—and it deserves a whole day. There are a couple of rides, but most of the attractions are walk-by viewing areas or shows, so lines are rare.

The park is laid out around a central lagoon, used for daytime waterskiing and aquabatic displays and the night-time laser and firework shows. Favorite stops include **The Shamu Adventure** killer whale show; the wacky Clyde and Seamore Take Pirate Island performance in the **Sea Lion and Otter Stadium**; and the rocky shores of **Pacific Point Preserve**, a naturalistic setting for California sea lions and seals. The **Wild Arctic** polar experience and the **Penguin Encounter** deliberately manufacture freezing conditions in order to provide a suitable habitat for their inmates, which include polar bears, beluga whales and penguins. **Manatees: The Last Generation?** investigates the plight of Florida's endangered sea cows; and **Terrors of the Deep** provides a scary cast of barracudas, sharks and razor-toothed moray eels.

SeaWorld is also home to the **Kraken**, a mega sea serpent-design roller coaster. The park's other thrill ride is **Journey to Atlantis**, which takes visitors on a trip to the lost world, combining high-speed water ride and roller coaster elements with state-of-the-art special effects.

►► Wet 'n Wild *114 B2*

6200 International Drive
Open: daily from 9 in summer (10 in winter). Call for schedules, tel: 407/351-WILD or 800/992-9453, www.wetnwild.com. Admission: expensive
One of the liveliest areas here is the **Kids' Park** water playground, which gives children their turn on scaled-down versions of adult rides like **Mach 5**: The "grown-ups" version features 2,500ft (750m) of twists and turns. Nerves of steel are required for the **Bomb Bay**, a near free-fall drop down to a 76ft (23m) slide; multi-passenger rides include the interactive **Hydra Fighter**; and check out the **Fuji Flyer** speed toboggan adventure. Or cram the family into the **Bubba Tub** for a giant inner-tube ride.

►► WonderWorks *114 B2*

*Pointe*Orlando, 9067 International Drive; tel: 407/351-8800, www.wonderworksonline.com*
Open: daily 9–midnight (extended at holidays)
Admission: expensive
It is hard to miss this eye-catching attraction, which seems to be disappearing upside down into a Florida sinkhole. Once inside, things are none too straightforward either, with dozens of interactive games, virtual reality experiences and earthquake and hurricane simulators.

SHOP TILL YOU DROP
Around South Orlando's International Drive, there are some amazing bargains to be had. An attraction in its own right, Belz Factory Outlet, 5401 W. Oakridge Road, houses 170 outlet stores selling discounted fashions, electronics, books and toiletries. This is the place to pick up Disney character T-shirts at prices around *three-quarters* less than on Disney property. The most upscale mall in the city is Mall at Millennia while you'll find bargains galore at Orlando Premium Outlet with designer names at a fraction of high street prices.

THE MARCH OF THE PEABODY DUCKS
Very few attractions in Orlando are free but people flock to the Peabody Hotel (9801 International Drive, tel: 407/352-4000) to watch the resident ducks go about their business, Playing in the lobby fountain during the day, they are ceremonially marched from their second-floor luxury accommodations at 11am, and marched home again at 5pm to the stirring music of John Philip Souza.

CITYWALK
Universal's 30-acre (12ha) shopping, dining and entertainment complex offers something for everyone. Specialty shops run the gamut from fossils, cigars, sportswear and silver jewelry to Glow!, a store selling things that, well, glow. There is a Hard Rock Café, and Hard Rock Live Orlando, a 2,200-capacity performance venue, plus jazz, reggae and Motown spots. Or you can chill out Keys-style at Jimmy Buffett's Margaritaville. Racing fans can dine out amidst auto memorabilia at the NASCAR Café; Pat O'Brien's re-creates the legendary New Orleans watering hole, complete with dueling pianos; and the Universal Cineplex has 20 screens showing the latest box-office hits.

CityJazz, Universal Studios CityWalk

▶▶▶ Universal Studios Orlando *114 B2*

1000 Universal Studios Plaza (I-4/Exit 29 or 30-B); tel: 407/363-8000 or 1-888-U-ESCAPE, www.universalorlando.com)
Open: daily, check schedules. Admission: expensive. One-day one-park ticket, or both parks with a 2- or 3-Day Escape Pass
The umbrella title for Universal's Florida theme park and resort complex, Universal Studios Escape now covers the original **Universal Studios** park (see below), the **Islands of Adventure** park (see pages 120–121) opened in 1999, **CityWalk** (see panel), and a growing portfolio of on-site hotels. Though Disney has the higher profile, Universal is a clear winner in the eyes of many visitors to Orlando. Both the Universal parks are strong on rides and ideally suited to teen and adult visitors in search of serious thrills and fun.

UNIVERSAL STUDIOS FLORIDA

A movie-oriented theme park grafted onto a working film and television production facility, Universal Studios invites guests to "ride the movies" on a 444-acre (180ha) site divided into six themed districts, covering the Deco and palm trees of Hollywood, to Fisherman's Wharf meets New England San Francisco/Amity.

Hollywood Heading up the clutch of popular diversions in the Hollywood section is the absolutely unmissable **Terminator 2:3-D Battle Across Time™**, a $24-million 3-D adventure scenario that reunites the original *Terminator 2* team in an electrifying combination of new film footage, special effects and live action. The **Universal Horror Make-Up Show** reprises revolting oozy bits from favorite movie monsters. On a brighter note, **Lucy: A Tribute℠** presents memorabilia from the life and works of that zany redhead, Lucille Ball.

New York Take the incredible effects of the Mummy series of movies, combine it with a high-speed roller coaster, and you have the sensory feast that is **Revenge of the Mummy℠–The Ride**, the star attraction in New York. Derived from a movie favorite of the 1990s, **TWISTER...Ride It Out®** re-creates the power of a five-story-high cyclone; while **The Blues Brothers** show brings back Jake and Elwood to perform a selection of their hottest hits.

Production Central® Stop off here for high jinks with the cartoon characters of **The Funtastic World of Hanna-Barbera™**. Guests touring **Nickelodeon Studios®**, production center of the popular children's T.V. network, get to test out new games, visit the Gak Kitchen to learn about slime production and may be able to attend the taping of a show, which is regularly watched by millions of children across the United States. Around production you are bound to run into one of Hanna-Barbera's host of cartoon favorites, including Scooby Doo and Dick Dastardly.

Shrek, one of the most popular characters of the last decade, stars in his own **Shrek 4-D™** (special effects include a form of "smelly-vision"), and you can usually meet the gentle guy outside the venue for photo opportunities.

San Francisco/Amity You can ride a San Francisco subway train into **Earthquake®: The Big One** and experience fire, flood and crashing masonry in an earthquake experience that rates 8.3 on the Richter Scale. A gentle sightseeing cruise with Amity Boat Tours turns into something altogether snappier with an appearance by that notorious 32ft (9.5m) mechanical white shark in the corny, but enduringly popular, **JAWS®** ride. And there is a rollicking show nearby in **Beetlejuice's Rock 'n Roll Graveyard Revue™**.

Woody Woodpecker's Kidzone A special area dedicated to scaled-down rides, shows and games for young children (see panel). Also in the area is **E.T. Adventure®**. Adventures probably don't get much tamer than this cute "flying bicycle" ride complete with an E.T. in a basket on every handlebar, but it's great entertainment.

World Expo Here you'll find two great thrill rides, one a Universal classic and the other the new kid on the block. First up is **Back To The Future The Ride®**, a four-minute, 21-jigowatt blast in Doc Brown's backup DeLorean, rescuing civilization as we know it from the awful Biff. Unveiled in 1993, this remains one of the most ambitious theme-park rides ever created. Universal's latest thriller is the interactive **MEN IN BLACK™ Alien Attack™**, where guests fight it out with alien invaders through the streets of New York in an all-out battle for the security of the planet. You can ride this again and the ending will be different—it has alternative endings

KIDS' STUFF

Families with young children may need to make several forays to Woody Woodpecker's KidZone℠. Here tots can sing along with the purple dinosaur in A Day In the Park With Barney™, follow in the footsteps of a cheeky monkey in the Curious George Goes To Town℠ water-based interactive play area (bring dry clothes), explore Fievel's Playland®, and take a ride on Woody Woodpecker's Nuthouse Coaster℠. For a well-needed time-out, take a break at the Animal Actors Stage®, where trained dogs, chimps, and birds show off their tricks in an excellent live performance.

Cyborg from Terminator 2:3-D

AMAZING ROBOTICS

Inspired by Steven Spielberg's *Jurassic Park*—to date one of the most successful motion picture of all time—the special effects wizards at Universal have employed state-of-the-art technology to create the amazing robotic creatures featured in the various Jurassic Park district attractions. As well as incredibly realistic and fluid movements, the creatures' lifelike responses include blinks, muscle flinches and, in the case of the lurking Spitters, some pretty accurate spitting at passing guests.

Face to face with a T-Rex at the Jurassic Park River Adventure[SM]

UNIVERSAL STUDIOS ISLANDS OF ADVENTURE

A larger-than-life, primary-colored cartoon world straight out of the comics (and blockbuster movie *Jurassic Park*), Islands of Adventure is hailed as the world's most technologically advanced theme park. There is an additional feather in the park's elaborate and distinctly wacky cap, too: it boasts producer/director Steven Spielberg as its creative consultant. Like its sister park, Universal Studios Florida, Islands of Adventure is arranged into themed "islands" around a central lagoon, known as the Inland Sea. Guests arrive in the souk-like Port of Entry and travel from island to island via boats or footbridges.

Jurassic Park® The **Jurassic Park River Adventure**[SM] is the big one here and one of the top rides in the park. A raft trip through lush dinosaur habitats harboring remarkably lifelike robotic creatures (see panel) goes dramatically wrong when the T-Rex gets loose, and there is an 85ft (25.5m) plunge down a long, fast, steep water descent. Back on *terra firma*, **Triceratops Encounter**[SM] allows guests to get a close look at a "live" 10ft (3m) high "animatronic" Triceratops undergoing its bi-annual check-up with a Jurassic Park vet; the interactive **Jurassic Park Discovery Center**[SM] encourages guests to scan a dinosaur egg, create their own dinosaur and watch a "real" raptor hatching in the shadow of a skeletal T-Rex. Head for the **Camp Jurassic**[SM] adventure play area for more dino encounters and the chance to ride the **Pteranodon Flyers®** aerial runway.

Lost Continent™ A fantasy lost world combining elements of medieval dungeons-and-dragons sorcery, the Holy Land crusades and Ancient Greece, the Lost Continent's entertaining offerings are equally eclectic. Roller coaster fans should join the queues for **Dueling Dragons®** (see panel opposite), while little kids can enjoy the scaled-down **Flying Unicorn**[SM] coaster as it speeds through a mystical forest scenario. The entrance to **Poseidon's Fury: Escape From the Lost City**[SM] is marked by the crumbling ruins of the sea god's statue before a chilly walk-through adventure to Atlantis. Visitors pass through a whirling 17,500-gallon (79,625-liter) water tunnel for a fiery encounter between Poseidon and Zeus. There are plenty more fire and water effects, plus great stunts in the action-packed **The Eighth Voyage of Sindbad℠** show.

Marvel Super Hero Island™ Laid out beneath the landmark green aerial spaghetti of the **Incredible Hulk Coaster℠** (see panel), join the ranks of comic strip super heroes in experiencing the three other mega rides grouped here. A tour of the *Daily Bugle* offices leads into **The Amazing Adventures of Spider-Man℠** and an epic combination of rides, 3-D film action and special effects as the goodies battle the baddies for control of the Statue of Liberty. Meanwhile, the twin towers of **Doctor Doom's Fearfall®** set the scene for rocketing 200ft (60m) trip to the top and back down at terrific speeds. In comparison, **Storm Force Acceletron℠**, an indoor attraction starring super heroine Storm in a thunderous special effects spectacular, is a walk in the park.

Dueling Dragons

Seuss Landing™ This visually appealing, whimsical 10-acre (4ha) island is where Dr. Seuss's much-loved children's book characters are brought to life. The elaborate **Caro-Seuss-el™** sports 54 colorful character mounts with state-of-the-art interactive animation features, while the gently entertaining **One Fish Two Fish Red Fish Blue Fish™** ride features Seussian-style, two-passenger fish that must be guided along to a special tune to avoid a soaking from "squirt posts" dotted about the course. Kids can let off steam in the **If I Ran The Zoo™** interactive playland, where Toe Tickle stations allow junior guests to tickle the toes of giggling Seussian creatures; and don't miss a journey on a moving couch through the classic tale of **The Cat In the Hat™** as Thing 1 and Thing 2 wreak havoc when they come to play while Mom's away.

Toon Lagoon™ First take a stroll down **Comic Strip Lane**, with its giant cartoon cut-outs, then hop aboard **Popeye & Bluto's Bilge-Rat Barges℠** for a white-water raft ride (and a guaranteed soaking) that includes a kitschy-horror encounter with an 18ft (5.5m) tall octopus brandishing 12ft-long (3.5m) tentacles. **Me Ship, The Olive℠** is a family-friendly interactive play area set on board Popeye's three-story boat. And in **Dudley Do-Right's Ripsaw Falls℠**, a rip-roaring log flume ride follows the 1960s Canadian Mountie character on a wet and wild rescue attempt to save his gal.

COASTING TO NEW HEIGHTS

At Islands of Adventure, Universal has extended the highly competitive world of roller coaster design to new heights. Dueling Dragons offers two entirely different rides (Fire and Ice) over intertwined tracks that appear to be on a collision course; riders are slammed through a camelback, double helix and compound inversion. The Incredible Hulk Coaster blasts riders from zero to 40mph (65kph) in two seconds, with the same thrust as a US Air Force F-16 fighter jet, and follows up with a weightless, zero-G heartline inversion, seven roll-overs and two plunges into subterranean enclosures.

SAVE TIME WITH A FASTPASS
Save time waiting for the most popular rides in all four Disney theme parks with a FASTPASS. Pop your regular park ticket into the FASTPASS machine at the rides offering this complimentary service and you will receive a designated ride time with no need to line up. The FASTPASS allows a one-hour window from the time printed on the ticket. At the allotted time, just present yourself at the FASTPASS entrance with your ticket and sail straight through. Each member of a party must get his or her ticket authorized by the FASTPASS machine, and you can only have one FASTPASS running at any one time, i.e. you must have used (or exceeded the time allocation for) one FASTPASS before you can collect another.

▶▶▶ Walt Disney World® Resort 114 A1

It is another world—there's no doubt about it. The Walt Disney World Resort is vast and completely self-contained: a 30,500-acre (12,200ha) site housing 4 major theme parks, 3 water parks, 27 resorts, lakeside beaches, shopping, nightlife and entertainment areas, and enough good times to last a lifetime. Mickey Mouse is out to play, and the whole world (so it seems in peak season) has followed suit. Young and old can happily exchange the everyday for the pure fantasy of **Magic Kingdom®**, the futuristic vision and international flavors of **Epcot®**, a sprinkling of stardust in the Tinseltown setting of **Disney-MGM Studios**, and the wildlife and exotic landscapes of **Disney's Animal Kingdom®**.

Admission Daily One Day/One Park admission tickets are valid for one park only on the stated day. For longer-stay guests, multiday tickets offer greater flexibility.

The **5-Day Park Hopper Plus Pass** covers a) unlimited admission to any combination of major theme parks for the duration of the ticket, b) use of the W.D.W. Resort transportation system and c) a choice of two entries to Disney's water parks, Pleasure Island, or standard admission to Disney's Wide World of Sports Complex.

The **7-Day Park Hopper Plus Pass** covers all of the above, but a choice of four entries under category c). Unused days never expire and can be used on a future visit.

W.D.W. Resort guests can purchase the **Disney Unlimited Magic Pass with Flex Feature**, which provides admission to all Disney's theme parks, water parks and entertainment zones for the duration of their stay.

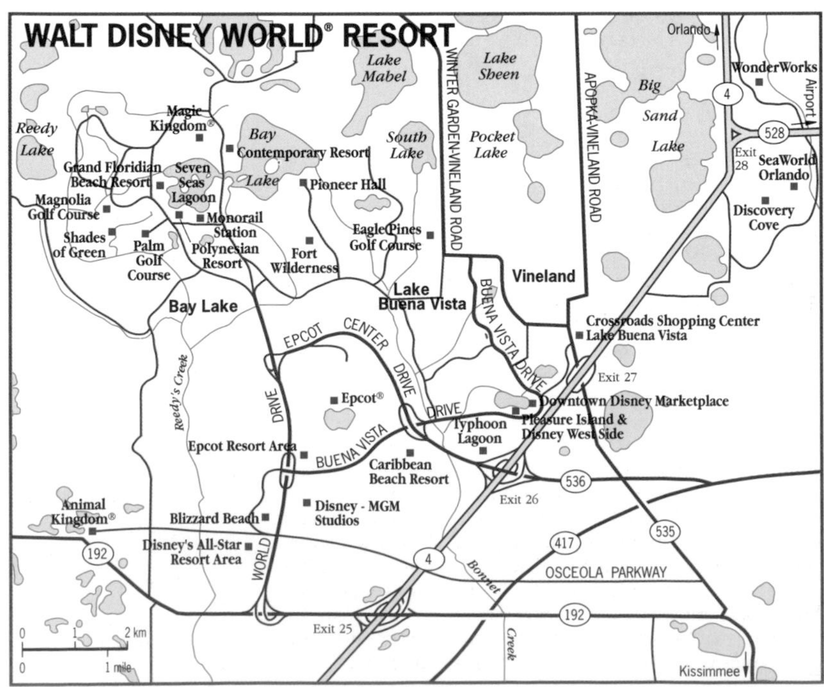

Tracking down Africa's wildlife with Kilimanjaro Safaris

Information and reservations For general information in advance, request an informative *Vacation Guide* from Walt Disney World Guest Information, *Box 1000, Lake Buena Vista, FL 32830-1000* (tel: 407/824-4321). Hotel, campground, show and ticket reservations can be made through Central Reservations (tel: 407/W-DISNEY). Dining reservations can be made up to 60 days in advance (tel: 407/939-3463).

When to go If you want to avoid W.D.W. Resort's busiest periods, the best times to visit are from September to early November, on either side of the Easter holiday peak period and from the Easter peak until early June. If you must visit during holiday periods or the summer vacation, expect big crowds and long waiting times in all the theme parks (see panel opposite).

DISNEY'S ANIMAL KINGDOM®
Disney's latest theme park showcases more than 200 animal species in magnificently re-created naturalistic habitats, and combines its zoological role with a strong eco-educational message. From **The Oasis** entry point, the park is laid out in five themed districts.

Africa In the African-inspired Harambe Village even the ice-creams come with an imprint of Simba's paw, and this is the start point for some serious wildlife spotting with **Kilimanjaro Safaris®**. This safari lorry journey through the African veldt reveals lions, giraffes, wildebeest, rhinos and more. Along the leafy **Pangani Forest Exploration Trail®**, there is a close-up look at hippos and meerkats and a wonderfully lush and misty gorilla habitat. The **Wildlife Express to Conservation Station** is a train ride around the "backlot," where the animals take a break from their public duties. At **Conservation Station®** itself, peek into the veterinary suite and hatchery and learn how the conservation battle continues on behalf of endangered creatures from Siberian tigers to bluefin tuna.

Asia An imaginatively re-created rain forest is the setting for this attractive rural village scenario, complete with rickshaws and ornately hand-painted and decorated Indian trucks. The **Maharajah Jungle Trek®** takes visitors on a stroll around "ancient" temple ruins, past a bat colony, tapirs and tigers, and through aviaries where the heliconias, hibiscus and flowering orchid trees are as gorgeous as the birds. If it is time to cool down, head for the white-water rafting thrills of **Kali River Rapids®**, and

PARK TIPS

- It really does pay to make an early start at Disney's Animal Kingdom, as the animals are more active in the cooler part of the day.
- A character breakfast buffet with Mickey Mouse, Goofy, Pluto and Donald Duck is served daily at Donald's Breakfastosaurus in DinoLand U.S.A.
- Make use of the FAST-PASS system (see panel, page 122) for Kilimanjaro Safaris, Kali River Rapids and DINOSAUR.
- Information on behind-the-scenes educational programs is available from Guest Relations in The Oasis (or tel: 407/WDW-TOUR).

STRICTLY FOR KIDS!
Disney offer a number of activities for 4–10-year-olds that give the adults some "alone time." There are several supervized child clubs with arts and crafts and Disney movies, cookery lessons at the Grand Floridian Resort and Disney's Pirate Cruise Adventure takes children out on the "high seas" of Bay Lake.

thunder down the Chakranadi River past bamboo tunnels, giant boulders and pumping water jets. Or take the weight off your feet at the **Flights of Wonder** bird show, where trained birds of prey display their incredible prowess overhead.

Camp Minnie-Mickey This Frontier-style stockade is great for little kids, with character-greeting areas inhabited by the likes of Mickey, Minnie and Goofy, and characters from *The Lion King* and *The Jungle Book*, plus a couple of shows. **Pocahontas and Her Forest Friends** is aimed firmly at junior visitors, with plenty of cute animals included in the show. There is something for everyone at **Festival of The Lion King**, a high-energy song, dance and acrobatic spectacular featuring specialist acts such as fire-jugglers and stilt-walkers.

DinoLand U.S.A. A 40ft (12m) *Brachiosaurus* skeleton, known as the Oldengate Bridge, spans the entrance to DinoLand U.S.A., where things get distinctly prehistoric. **DINOSAUR** is the big ride here, traveling back in time for a last look at the dinosaur era before the meteorites strike. The audience's mission is to bring back a live dinosaur and there are all sorts of thrills, spills and meteorite showers along the way, from "animatronic" dino thrills to the real thing, as genuine paleontologists demonstrate their work with dinosaur remains and answer questions in the **Fossil Preparation Lab**. The hangar-like exhibition space of **Dinosaur Jubilee** is used to display towering casts of dinosaur skeletons, fossilized dino eggs, claws and even coprolites (that's dung to the uninitiated). Kids can clamber, slither and crawl around the jumble of boulders and bones that make up **The Boneyard®** playground; and **Tarzan® Rocks!** unites Tarzan, Jane, Terk and a cast of jungle gymnasts in a high-energy acrobatic rock show.

The Oasis The hub of Disney's Animal Kingdom complex, Safari Oasis's centerpiece is **The Tree of Life**, a 145ft-tall (43.5m) symbol for the park, adorned with 325 animals carved into its twisting branches, roots and

Festival of The Lion King, Camp Minnie-Mickey

giant trunk. **Safari Village Trails** meander around the giant tree past enclosures housing lemurs and capybaras. Another gentle trail with close-up views of animal carvings and tropical plantings leads into the tree's root system and a theater where Pik and Hopper from the movie *A Bug's Life* return to star in **It's Tough to be a Bug!**®, an entertaining (and frequently surprising) 3-D insect's-eye view of the world. Not recommended for anybody, particularly small children, with a fear of creepy-crawlies.

DINING TIPS II
A favorite stop for a quick lunch in Future World is the Sunshine Season Food Fair, a food court in The Land pavilion.

DISNEY-MGM STUDIOS

From the tips of the Mickey Mouse ears perched on the water tower to the shops and eateries of Hollywood Boulevard, Disney-MGM Studios celebrates the movies. Guest Relations, on Hollywood Boulevard, provides a dining reservations service.

Backlot Tour This ride is a must, but try to get here first thing in the morning or later in the afternoon. Before boarding the backlot tram, there is a visit to the splash tank and an opportunity to discover how special effects are created in movies with images of the sea. Then sit back for the ride through the wardrobe, props and special effects departments, and a side trip to Catastrophe Canyon to witness special effects in action (passengers on the left may get wet).

Backstage Pass A walk-through tour that kicks off with an introduction to animatronic animals, from cutesy puppies to incredibly realistic sheep used in the movie *101 Dalmatians*. Volunteers help illustrate "bluescreen" editing techniques, which mix live action with previously filmed footage. Guests then continue past Production Sound Stages containing sets from recent and current film and T.V. productions. The tour winds up in a storeroom packed with costumes, props and detailed designers' sketches and models for *101 Dalmatians*.

The Great Movie Ride Housed in a full-scale replica of Mann's Chinese Theater in Hollywood, Audio-Animatronics figures do their best to re-create great moments from film classics, such as Gene Kelly getting drenched in *Singin' in the Rain* and Bogie and Bergman in *Casablanca*. Though there's commendable attention to detail, this is a disappointing ride.

Muppet*Vision 3D Kermit, Miss Piggy, Fozzie Bear, Gonzo and the Electric Mayhem Band strut their stuff with the help of sensational special effects and 3-D film wizardry. A huge hit with kids.

Hollywood Boulevard A pastiche of the 1930s and 1940s "Hollywood that never was and always will be." Shopping is the name of the game along the boulevard. Star-struck movie buffs can pick up authentic memorabilia from Sid Cahuenga's One-of-a-Kind—at a price.

"Honey, I Shrunk the Kids" Movie Set Adventure This imaginative adventure play area is equipped with giant apparatus that dwarfs the kids, who can also frolic in cooling water jets.

VISITORS WITH DISABILITIES
Special parking areas and 'handicap vans' with platforms for loading wheelchairs are provided on request. A WDW *Guidebook for Guests with Disabilities* details additional facilities and makes helpful suggestions.

PARK TIPS II

• Use the FASTPASS system (see panel, page 122) for the Rock 'n' Roller Coaster Starring Aerosmith, The Twilight Zone Tower of Terror, Voyage of The Little Mermaid and Indiana Jones Epic Stunt Spectacular.

• Disney-MGM Studios offers several more shows than those listed here. Check the free park guides available at the entrance for details and schedules.

• There is a daily afternoon parade on Hollywood Boulevard; and the spectacular night-time Fantasmic! firework show in the Hollywood Hills Amphitheater.

• Disney-MGM Studios' rides are not particularly suitable for young children. The shows fare rather better and the Honey, I Shrunk the Kids playground is a good place to let off steam.

GREEN THUMBS

Plant lovers who want more after the greenhouse boat tour at The Land pavilion can sign up for an hour-long Behind the Seeds guided walk, which explores the futuristic greenhouses in more depth. Make reservations for the tours (*Admission moderate*).

Indiana Jones® Epic Stunt Spectacular! Plenty of fire, brimstone and death-defying live stunt work in this intriguing look at the tricks of the trade. Volunteers from the audience take part in scenes from *Raiders of the Lost Ark;* the rest of the crowd feels the heat of the explosive finale.

Magic of Disney Animation Hugely popular, this fascinating walk through the Animation Building lays bare every stage of the animation process. From the sidesplitting introduction to animation basics, right through to the final presentation in the **Disney Classics Theater**, this is one of the best attractions in Walt Disney World Resort.

Rock 'n' Roller Coaster® Starring Aerosmith Fronted by a giant red electric guitar, this roller coaster takes the form of a motorized dash across town to catch an Aerosmith concert. Mega thrills and sound track by the old rockers themselves.

Sounds Dangerous Join funnyman Drew Carey in a pilot for a new investigative TV show and spend most of the time in the dark experiencing the action through sound alone. Take a trip to the barber, or hear a swarm of killer bees on the loose. Highly recommended.

Star Tours—the ultimate Star Wars™ thrill ride Hang on to your seats for this bone-shaking trip through space in an out-of-control Starspeeder vehicle on loan from *Star Wars* travel agent duo R2D2 and C3-PO.

Theater of the Stars Check showtimes to find out what's on (*Beauty and the Beast—Live on Stage* is a long-running favorite) in this handsome Sunset Boulevard covered theater, which stages all-singing, all-dancing Broadway-style musical productions. Naturally, Disney characters take the various roles, and it is all a lot of fun.

The Twilight Zone Tower of Terror™ A nightmarish visit to the 199ft (60m) Hollywood Tower Hotel culminates in a thrilling adventure in the elevator shaft.

Voyage of The Little Mermaid Ariel's undersea adventures brought to life in a cute combination of animation, live performances and puppetry, with lasers and other special effects for good measure.

EPCOT®

This was Walt Disney's greatest dream. Inspired by his vision of an "experimental prototype community of tomorrow," Epcot is divided into two separate "worlds". **Future World** explores the role of communications, transportation, agriculture and energy, and delves into the realms of the imagination. **World Showcase** tackles the world around us, re-creating the sights and smells of far-off places, such as Britain and Beijing, all bathed in uncharacteristic Florida sunshine. Here the culture of 11 nations has been transposed to specially designed pavilions that have themed shops and restaurants. With nearly 70 stores, World Showcase is a veritable international shopping mall.

The high-speed Rock 'n' Roller Coaster® Featuring Aerosmith

Future World

Imagination! If it is possible, the new **Journey Into Your Imagination** ride is even less engaging than its predecessor, but there is fun to be had in the interactive ImageWorks area and the 3-D film misadventure *Honey, I Shrunk the Audience*.

Innoventions A much more successful update of these twin pavilions has resulted in a colorful, fully interactive and child-friendly look at how science and technology influence and improve our lives.

The Land Food, glorious food, is under the microscope on a boat trip through experimental greenhouses (see panel opposite); upstairs the **Circle of Life Theater** presents an entertaining eco-concious film.

The Living Seas An illuminating study of man and the sea. The 5.7 million gallon (256.5 million liter) central aquarium is home to more than 2,700 tropical fish, as well as sharks, dolphins and manatees.

Spaceship Earth Housed in Epcot's trademark 180ft-tall (55m) silver geosphere, this ride spirals 18 stories through the development of earthling communications, through time and space before releasing its captive audience into the interactive computer-video wonderland of the **Global Neighborhood**.

Test Track High-speed auto action in the longest and fastest ride ever created by the Walt Disney Imagineers.

Wonders of Life Ricochet through the bloodstream on the **Body Wars** ride, or experience a day in the life of a 12-year-old boy in **Cranium Command**.

PARK TIPS III

- There are two FASTPASS (see panel, page 122) attractions at Epcot: the popular Test Track ride and Honey, I Shrunk the Audience.
- Dining out in one of the international restaurants in World Showcase is a major attraction. Reservations can be made in advance (tel: 407/939-3463), or through Guest Relations at the entrance to the park or in Spaceship Earth.
- A host of international entertainments, from music and Japanese drumming to acrobatics, take place around the World Showcase "villages" throughout the day. Check the free map guide for details.
- The World Showcase Lagoon at the center of the park is the setting for dramatic nightly firework and laser shows (check schedules).

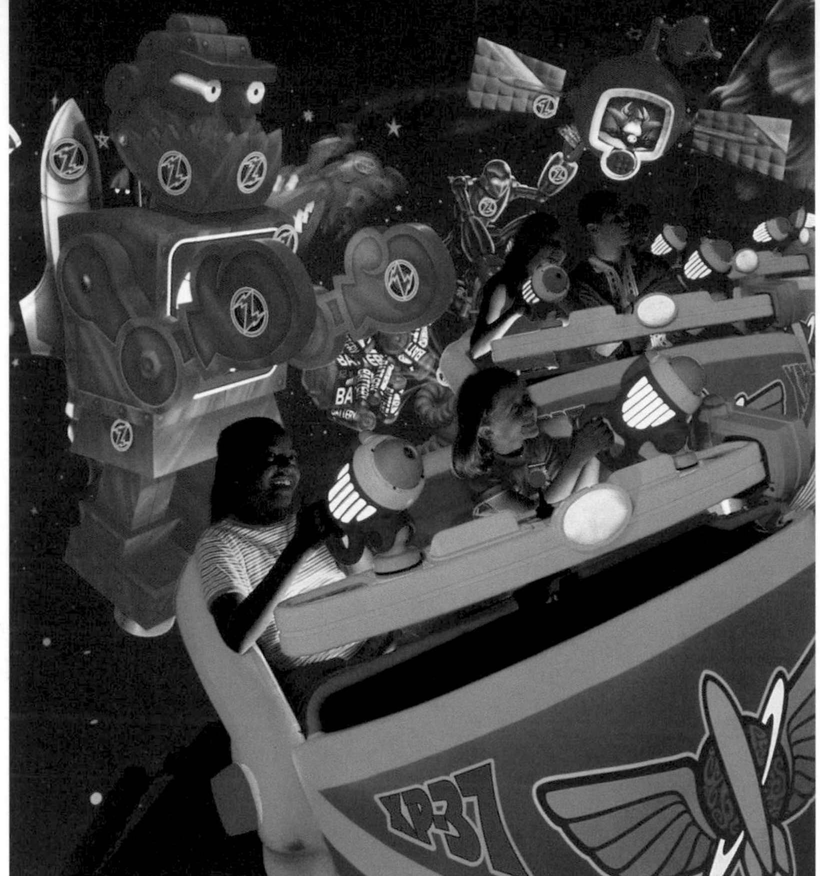

Buzz Lightyear's Space Ranger Spin transports guests to the playful world of "Toy Story"

Universe of Energy Not-to-be-missed journey back in time to the dinosaur era on the trail of fossil fuels. Ellen DeGeneres stars alongside realistic dinosaurs and terrific big-screen effects.

World Showcase

American Adventure Theater Show A generously proportioned Georgian-style building houses a 30-minute Audio-Animatronics show that celebrates the "spirit of America" from the Pilgrim Fathers to John Wayne. Attractive souvenirs from **Heritage Manor Gifts**.

Canada A Rocky Mountain, a totem pole and a flourish of native trees precede the CircleVision 360° presentation, *O Canada!* Buy lumberjack shirts and maple syrup from **Northwest Mercantile**.

China A curtain of bamboo and the colorful **Gate of the Golden Sun** front a dazzling world of ornate green and gold curved roofs, carp-filled lily ponds and one of the Showcase's top features, **Reflections of China**, a CircleVision 360° journey through China.

France Belle Époque Paris in the shadow of an Eiffel Tower (to scale): a Pont des Arts-esque bridge, a sidewalk café, a poster-plastered kiosk and a deliciously scented bakery. Very chic shopping (fragrances, cosmetics, wine) and some serious cuisine at **Les Chefs de France**.

Germany Fairy-tale facades, oompah music, red geraniums, lederhosen and a pungent and unmistakable whiff

of sauerkraut from the **Biergarten Restaurant** all add up to a very convincing scene.
Italy Venice's **St. Mark's Square** and the **Doge's Palace** re-created in extraordinary detail. Enjoy the fine piazza, then try the pasta at **L'Originale Alfredo di Roma Ristorante**.
Japan The Japanese pavilion is a vision of tiered pagoda roofs, bonsai, monkey-puzzle trees and enormously elegant music and dance demonstrations. Galleries exhibit Japanese arts, crafts and mechanical toys.
Mexico Take the **El Río Del Tiempo** (River of Time) boat trip and visit a re-created **Mayan Temple**, then enjoy the music provided by the sombrero'd mariachi bands on the lakeshore.
Morocco Wander around the bazaar and take time to admire the cool, tiled courtyards of the **Medina** (Old City). Constructed by Moroccan artisans, this is one of the most impressive buildings in the Showcase.
Norway Take ***Maelstrom***, a Viking longboat ride into Norse history and the land of the midnight sun. The Norway pavilion's craft shop is well-stocked with trolls and toys, and the bakery makes a good snack stop.
United Kingdom Half-timbered facades, old red telephone boxes and warm beer in a traditional pub are just the ticket, but Anne Hathaway's Cottage taken over by a tea shop? It's just not cricket!

MAGIC KINGDOM®
The first of the Walt Disney World Resort parks to open (in 1971), the 107-acre (43ha) Magic Kingdom site is based on the original Disneyland design. Mickey Mouse reigns over singing bears, pirates, Cinderella and a host of fun-loving characters from the magical world of Disney cartoons. Maps and information are available from **City Hall** at the start of Main Street U.S.A., near the entrance. It's easy to navigate and you'll find it much easier if you arrive early, since lines will be significantly longer by mid-morning.

Adventureland Outlandish African Colonial-Middle Eastern-Moorish architecture, exotic plants and tropical juice bars take second place to the action-packed fun offered here. Explore the roomy, vine-covered **Swiss Family Treehouse**, perched in the boughs of a gigantic concrete, steel and plastic banyan tree; then hop aboard a launch at the last outpost river landing for a steamy **Jungle Cruise** down the Nile and into the Amazon jungle. **Pirates of the Caribbean** is a favorite ride in Adventureland; it is a rollicking encounter with one-eyed buccaneers, treasure troves and a sighting of the world's first raid by pirates under the influence of Audio-Animatronics. Crooning flowers and chattering totem poles join assorted Audio-Animatronics feathered friends for a Tropical Serenade in **The Enchanted Tiki Room**. The show itself lasts about nine minutes, and is a must for small children.

Fantasyland In the style of the Brothers Grimm, Disney classics centered around **Cinderella Castle** include **Cinderella's Golden Carousel**, the **Mad Tea Party**, **Dumbo the Flying Elephant** and **Peter Pan's Flight**. **The Many Adventures of Winnie the Pooh** takes a honey-laden,

PARK TIPS IV
- Use the FASTPASS system (see panel, page 122) for Adventureland's Jungle Cruise, The Many Adventures of Winnie the Pooh, Buzz Lightyear's Space Ranger Spin, Space Mountain and Splash Mountain.
- Keys to the Kingdom is a fascinating four-hour, behind-the-scenes tour of the park which takes guests backstage and beneath the Magic Kingdom (minimum age 16; additional charge). For information and reservations (up to six weeks in advance), tel: 407/939-8687.
- The daily Disney's Share A Dream Come True Parade on Main Street U.S.A. (popular with under 8s) at 3pm is a good time to sneak onto some of the more popular rides.
- The nighttime Fantasy in the Sky fireworks displays are amazing; so is the Main Street Electrical Parade. Check with City Hall for showtimes.

cuddly trip to the Hundred Acre Wood to visit Pooh, Piglet, Owl and Eeyore. On a hot day, make tracks for **Ariel's Grotto**, where kids can cool off among the bouncing water jets and pose for photos with (and collect autographs from) the famous mermaid. Other diversions include the ride-through **Snow White's Adventure**, which stars the wicked queen and could well frighten little children; the **Legend of The Lion King** involves some highly skillful puppetry; and a totally renovated show entertains at **It's a Small World**. This is the obvious place to raid the toy shop, though never at discount prices.

Frontierland® Here you will find boardwalks and the **Frontierland Shootin' Arcade**; plenty of hootin', hollerin' and belly-laughing entertainment in the hilarious **Country Bear Jamboree**. There is also a runaway mine train charging down **Big Thunder Mountain**. **Splash Mountain** is a hair-raising experience: a log flume ride with a 47° drop and speeds of nearly 40mph (64kph) with a very wet finale. A raft-ride away, wooded **Tom Sawyer Island** offers a fort-stockade Mystery Mine Shaft to explore; or take to the water with **Mike Fink Keelboats**.

SINCE 1971 WALT DISNEY WORLD RESORT HAS ...
—welcomed more than 500 million visitors
—planted 25 million flowering annuals and 100,000 trees
—clocked up enough monorail journeys to equal the equivalent of 30 round-trips to the moon
—sold 35 million souvenir T-shirts
—found an estimated 1.5 million pairs of lost sunglasses.

Liberty Square In the 19th century, while half the U.S. was whooping it up in the local **Diamond Horseshoe Saloon Revue** in Frontierland, complete with high-stepping dance-hall belles, the other half built gracious colonial-style homes, embroidered flags and brewed great pickles. Brush up on American history with a presentation featuring Audio-Animatronics presidents in **The Hall of Presidents** (less impressive to children than their parents). There is a relaxing cruise through history on a sternwheel steamer at **Liberty Belle Riverboats**. The most popular ride in this land is **The Haunted Mansion**. After gravestone humor has provided a diversion from waiting in line, sidle past creepy greeters, take time to check out the horror wallpaper and climb aboard a doom buggy. Although the start is unimpressive, the trailing cobwebs and shrieking holograms ensure that this soon develops into a memorably kitschy ghost-train ride.

Main Street U.S.A. This is the hub of the Magic Kingdom from which the other lands radiate, and **Cinderella Castle** (see page 129) is its focus. With more than a hint of mad King Ludwig of Bavaria's turreted folly Neuschwanstein, this 180ft (54m) steel-and-fiberglass fantasy castle encapsulates the park's storybook allure.

Main Street re-creates a pristine Victorian village of "olde worlde" shopfronts and color-coordinated floral displays, barbershop quartets, ice-cream parlors and hot dog stands with striped awnings. The shops are real, and sell trifles, treasures and fancy foodstuffs. The scent of freshly baked croissants and cookies from the **Bake Shop** makes it hard to concentrate, but do not hurry away too soon.

Other diversions include barbershop quartet serenades and concerts in Town Square, and for a gentle circuit of the Magic Kingdom domain take a trip on the **Walt Disney World Railroad®**, which departs from the station near the main entrance and stops in Frontierland and Mickey's Toontown Fair.

Fireworks over Cinderella Castle

Mickey's Toontown Fair A popular photo-stop with its colorful, outsize attractions and Disney topiary, Toontown offers a rare opportunity to visit the world's most famous mouse "at home." Take a stroll around **Mickey's Country House** and **Minnie's Country House**, then catch up with favorite Disney cartoon characters at the **Toontown Hall of Fame**. There is watery fun at the **Donald's Boat** play area, where hot tots can work off some energy, while the **Barnstormer at Goofy's Wiseacres Farm** is a scaled-down roller coaster.

Tomorrowland® Fantasy-oriented Tomorrowland offers a full complement of escapist rides and antagonistic aliens. Set in a time pre-Disney's animation "Lilo & Stitch," **Stitch's Great Escape!** attraction sees Stitch causing mayhem at the Galactic Federation Prisoner Teleport Center. It's a light-hearted fun but really action-packed. For more light relief, visit **The Timekeeper**, hosted by a jocular robot and his flighty sidekicks, which whisks you back and forth through time to meet famous inventors and visionaries in Circle Vision 360°.

Buzz Lightyear's Space Ranger Spin blasts off from Star Command Headquarters on an interactive mission to defeat the evil Zurg and his minions as passengers get to test their laser shooting skills.

That old favorite, **Space Mountain**, a terrific roller coaster, rockets through the darkness past meteors and shooting stars. This is a rough ride, so batten down the hatches and take off your glasses. If there's no line when you're done, do it again.

Goodyear's **Tomorrowland® Speedway** is also popular: its mini racing cars race around four 2,260ft (678m) tracks (good for kids only). You can ride a rocket at **Astro Orbiter**; play video games galore at the **Tomorrowland Arcade**; take in variety shows at **Galaxy Palace Theater**; and sit through the shamelessly nostalgic **Disney's Carousel of Progress**, a celebration of 20th-century domestic developments.

MORE ENTERTAINMENT AT DISNEY'S BOARDWALK
A waterfront dining and entertainment district in the Epcot Resorts area, Disney's BoardWalk re-creates 1940s Atlantic City with a collection of shops, restaurants and nightspots, including a sports bar, the ESPN Club (tel: 407/939-4363). After dark, guests can sing along and admire the dueling-pianos routine at Jellyrolls (minimum age 21, tel: 407/560-8770).

CHARACTER DINING
Dining with Disney cartoon characters is a memorable treat for both the young and the young at heart. Try Donald's Breakfastosaurus in Disney's Animal Kingdom; Hollywood & Vine at Disney-MGM Studios; the Garden Grill, in The Land pavilion at Epcot; and several locations at the Magic Kingdom, including The Crystal Palace Buffet. Different characters show up in different places; pick your character and plan accordingly. Reservations are advised for these and other Disney resort character dining locations (tel: 407/939-4363).

RAVE REVUES
There is never a spare seat in the house for the rollicking Hoop-Dee-Doo Musical Revue dinner show at Fort Wilderness. This is family entertainment at its best, and reservations for the three daily shows (5, 7.15 and 9.30pm) should be made at least several months in advance. Enjoy the verve and energy of the Pioneer Hall Players along with the generous barbecue-style banquet of ribs, chicken, corn on the cob and strawberry shortcake that arrives at intervals during the two-hour show. To book seats, write to or telephone Central Reservations.

Other WDW Resort attractions include these:

Blizzard Beach

Disney's third water park takes its inspiration from Florida's first (and last) imaginary ski resort. The slopes of towering **Mount Gushmore** feature waterborne slalom courses, toboggan and watersled runs, chair lifts with skis and sun umbrellas, and **Teamboat Springs**, the world's longest family white-water ride. From the 120ft-high (36m) **Summit Plummet** "ski jump" tower, there is a 60mph (97kph) plunge down a slide; or you can take the slightly shorter and less severe **Slush Gusher**. There is also 1-acre (0.4ha) **Melt-Away Bay** pool; **Cross Country Creek**, which makes a circuit of the entire park (you float in inner tubes); and scaled-down **Tike's Peak**, for kids.

Open daily 10am–5pm, longer in summer and on holidays. For schedules, (tel: 407/824-4321). Admission is included with Park Hopper Plus passes.

Downtown Disney

WDW Resort's mega shopping, dining and entertainment district on the shores of Lake Buena Vista, Downtown Disney is divided into three parts. Moving from right to left along the waterfront, first up is **Marketplace** (a shopping area) with its landmark steaming volcano housing the Rainforest Café. Here, you can raid World of Disney, the largest Disney merchandise store on earth, sample a variety of restaurants and gawk at the feats of creativity displayed at the LEGO Imagination Center®. In Downtown Disney's mid-section, **Pleasure Island** is WDW Resort's Nightlife Central (see opposite).

At the far end of the complex, **West Side** is home to an assortment of shops, including a Virgin Megastore, the House of Blues® live music and dining operation with a concert venue next door (information, tel: 407/934-7781), plus, on the restaurant front, Planet Hollywood®, Wolfgang Puck® Café and Gloria Estefan's Bongos Cuban Café™. For sheer entertainment, there is a 24-screen movie theater, and a purpose-built theater to house the Cirque du Soleil®'s stunning high-energy acrobatic and dance productions (reservations, tel: 407/939-7600). Another key element to the West Side is DisneyQuest®, a five-story indoor interactive theme park packed with techno wizardry and virtual fun.

(*Open* daily. General stores 9.30am–11pm. Restaurants for lunch and dinner. *Admission free* if you are only dining in one of the restaurants, otherwise there's a charge.)

Fort Wilderness

The official W.D.W. Resort campground with some 784 campsites and 406 wilderness homes, Fort Wilderness is also an activities center, though use of many of the facilities is restricted to guests who are staying in WDW Resort-owned properties.

Sailboats, pedal boats and little Water Sprites can be rented from the Bay Lake marina. Daily fishing excursions are arranged on the lake, and anglers can try their luck on the canals around the camp's domain. There are bike and canoe rentals, jogging circuits, horseback trail rides, basketball, tennis and volleyball facilities.

Evening entertainments include the **Hoop-Dee-Doo**

Musical Revue (see panel opposite); a popular **Campfire Program** with a sing-along; and Disney cartoons and movies.

Pleasure Island

Connected to the rest of Downtown Disney by foot-bridges, Pleasure Island is WDW Resort's offshore home of late-night entertainment, though its stores and restaurants remain open all day. The island harbors eight clubs offering a whole range of musical styles, discos and comedy, plus the West End Stage that occasionally lures top-name talent to the Disney empire, and a New Year's Eve party every night from 11.45pm.

Pleasure Island's musical line-up kicks off with the **BET SoundStage™ Club** serving up the hottest R&B and hip hop around. For the Top 40 backed by videos thrown on a massive wall screen, head to **Motion**. Also on the dance front, for the latest sounds, **Mannequins Dance Palace**

Blizzard Beach's Summit Plummet

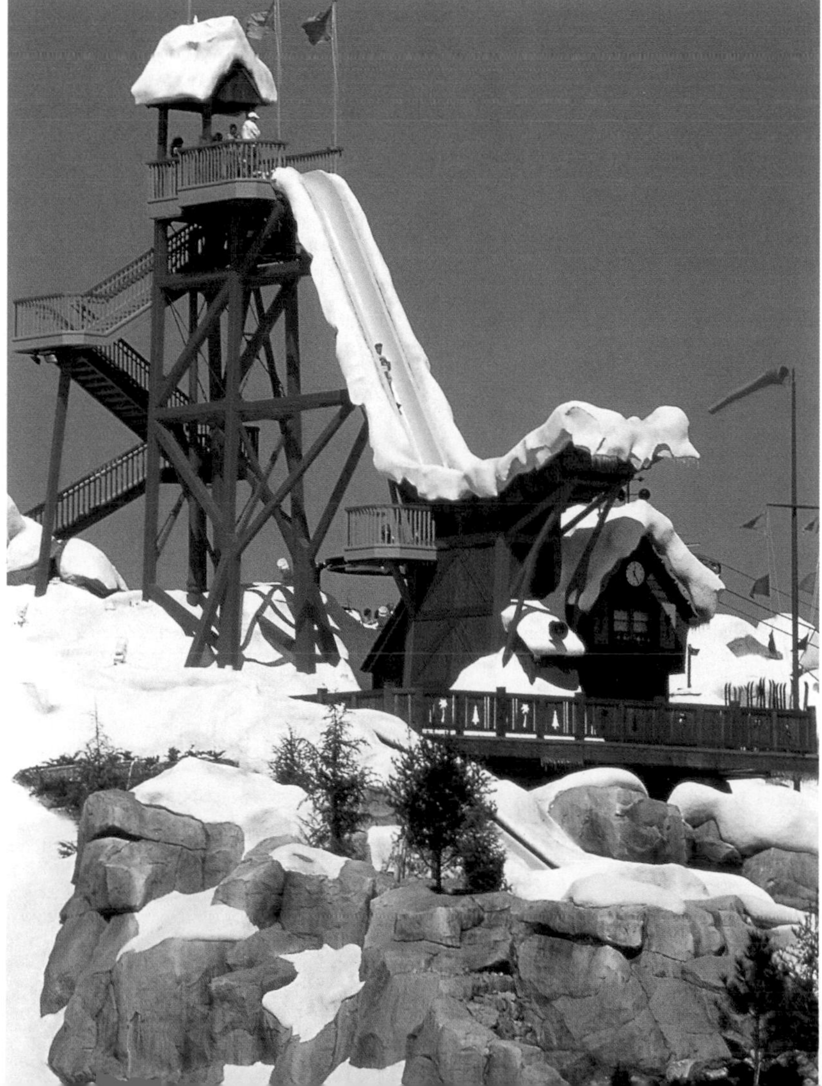

SPORTING DISNEY
It began with the Walt Disney World Marathon and Indy 200 races in January, and now Disney's Wide World of Sports Complex hosts a packed calendar of top sporting events throughout the year. The 200-acre (80ha) site features a 7,500-seat baseball and softball park (where the Atlanta Braves move right in each year for spring training), as well as tennis, and indoor and outdoor sports facilities for more than 30 sports.

SCENIC BOAT TOURS
Winter Park sits on the shores of Lake Osceola, one of a chain of six little freshwater lakes linked by narrow, leafy canals navigable by small craft. At the foot of Morse Boulevard, Scenic Boat Tours (*Open* daily 10–4) operates hour-long sightseeing trips on Lake Osceola, Lake Virginia and Lake Maitland, affording fine views of the neighborhood's most impressive waterfront homes and occasional wildlife-spotting as added extras.

does the high-tech thing with a rotating dance floor. Pack your bell-bottom trousers and enjoy 70s style dancing surrounded by lava lamps and mirror balls at **Trax 8**; while all-time rock classics get an airing at the **Rock 'N' Roll Beach Club**.

When it's time to chill out, there are zany stories at the exotic-nostalgic **Adventurer's Club**. Or let the funny men (and women) take the strain at the **Comedy Warehouse**.

(*Open* daily. Shops 10am–1am, restaurants 11.30am–midnight, clubs 7pm–2am. *Admission: expensive* (covered by Park Hopper Plus Passes), including all clubs. Under 18s must be accompanied by an adult; minimum age 21 at BET SoundStage and Mannequins Dance Palace.)

Typhoon Lagoon

This area features typhoon-ravaged tropical landscaping and a vast lagoon as a centerpiece, with 4ft (1.2m) waves that crash onto the surrounding broad beach every 90 seconds. **Castaway Creek** describes a lazy 2,100ft (630m) tube ride around the lagoon—it takes about 25 minutes. There are places to stop along the route and a dripping rain-forest section. Scale Mount Mayday for a dare on **Humunga Kowabunga**—two 214ft (64m) water slides that send willing victims rocketing down the mountainside and through a series of caves at speeds of anything up to 25mph (40kph). Three storm slides take a less hair-raising route down to pools around the lagoon. There are also three white-water raft adventures.

Rent fins and a mask to explore **Shark Reef**. This 326,000-gallon (1.5 million liters) saltwater coral-reef environment is teeming with exotic marine life, including odd-looking but harmless nurse sharks. Children (aged two to five) enjoy **Ketchakiddie Creek**'s scaled-down slides, geysers and fountains, and **SS *Squirt***, the interactive tugboat.

(*Open* daily 10–5, later in summer and on holidays. For schedules, tel: 407/824-4321. Admission is included with Park Hopper Plus passes.)

► Polk City

Head west from Orlando to this small town to visit **Fantasy of Flight**, 1400 Broadway Boulevard West (*Open* daily 9–5. *Admission: expensive*; tel: 863/984-3500), the premer private aircraft collection in Florida. The personal dream of acrobatic pilot Kermit Weeks, the collection encompasses years of aviation from the early decades of flight to the 1950s including many examples from World War II, both Allied and German. Excellent room-size dioramas immerse visitors in the dark days of war. You can also take biplane or balloon rides, weather permitting.

►► Winter Haven/Cypress Gardens *108 B4*

Near the unassuming town of Winter Haven lies Florida's oldest theme park—**Cypress Gardens**, 6000 Cypress Gardens Boulevard (*Open* daily 10–6, with extended hours in summer. *Admission: expensive*; tel: 407/863-2111, www.cypressgardens.com) was founded in the 1930s as a botanical garden with side-shows, but received a total restructure to reopen as **Cypress Gardens Adventure Park** in 2005. Today there are 39 rides to enjoy ranging from white-knuckle exhilaration to family fun. The signature ride is Triple Hurricane, the park's old-style bone-shaking wooden coaster. New designs include Inverter with its 360° twists and turns; Swamp Thing, a suspended coaster which is more than 1,250ft (380m) long; Thunderbolt where you drop like a stone from 120ft (36m) above ground. The park hosts eight shows with water and ice playing their part, although not all shows run every day. The park still has wonderful botanical gardens to enjoy, graced by the crinolined "Southern Belles" who have been part of the experience since the early days.

The adventure park's sister attraction **Splash Island Adventure Park** makes a perfect watery contrast, just the place to cool off after all the excitement.

►► Winter Park *114 C3*

Founded as a winter resort just north of Orlando at the turn of the century, Winter Park is a delightful full- or half-day excursion from the teeming theme parks. Around the compact town center, there is excellent shopping along Park Avenue.

The **Charles Hosmer Morse Museum of American Art**, *445 Park Avenue North* (*Open* Tue–Sat 9.30–4, Sun 1–4. *Admission: inexpensive*; tel: 407/645-5311, www.morsemuseum.com), has a superb collection of Tiffany glass, much of it rescued from a fire at Louis Comfort Tiffany's home on Long Island. Stained-glass windows filled with roses and fruit-and-vegetable "still lifes" are shown alongside jewelry, lampshades and "drapery" glass (which is folded when soft). Other art nouveau artists with work on display include Lalique, Emile Gallé and Maxfield Parrish.

Moravian-born sculptor Albin Polasek spent his retirement at his 3-acre (1.2ha) lakefront estate, now the Albin Polasek Museum, *633 Osceola Avenue* (*Open* Sep–Jun, Mon–Sat 10–5, Sun 1–4. *Admission: expensive*; tel 407/647-6294, www.polasek.org). The artist's work is scattered throughout the grounds and you can also tour the villa decorated with Polasek's personal art collection.

CAMPUS DELIGHT

Don't miss a stroll around the pastoral campus of Rollins College (Holt Avenue, Winter Park). By the entrance, a Walk of Fame features stones from the birthplaces and homes of famous people. There is a Spanish Mediterranean-style College Chapel and the Cornell Fine Arts Museum, which houses collections of European Old Masters, 19th-century American paintings, sculpture, modern prints and graphics and Native American objects (*Open* Tue–Fri 10–5; Sat and Sun 1–5. *Admission free*; tel: 407/646-2526).

Cypress Gardens has a number of year-round events such as this water ski show on the lake

The Gold Coast

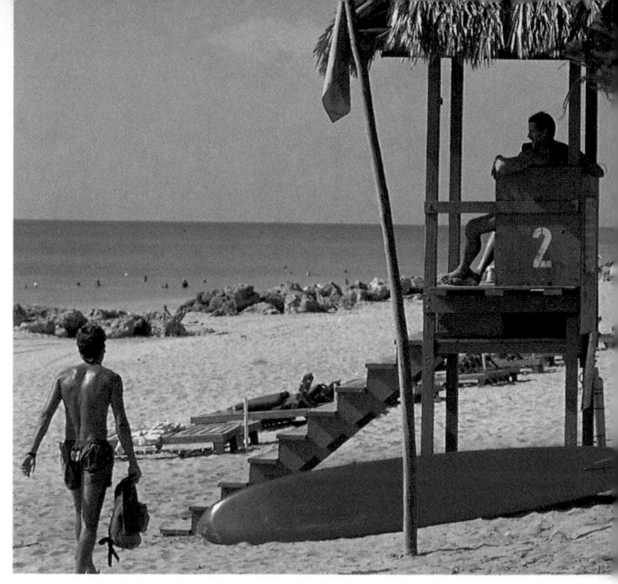

Sun, sea, sand and palm trees on the Gold Coast

GOLDEN SUN, GOLDEN SAND and golden opportunities are the stuff the Gold Coast is made of. A vacation mecca and rich man's retreat, it spreads its wares along a narrow coastal strip between two very different cities bordered by the Atlantic Ocean and the Everglades.

At the southern extreme, **Fort Lauderdale**, a high-rise success story built on a maze of inner-city canals carved from the swamps is one of the fastest-growing cities in the state. A few minutes' drive from the glittering downtown skyscrapers and arts and entertainment districts, Fort Lauderdale beach is lined with swanky resort hotels, condominiums, beachfront motels and a minor miracle—180 acres (72ha) of natural preserve fronting the shore. To the south is Port Everglades, the second largest cruise port in the world, while the city's marinas harbor 44,000 yachts and sportfishing vessels. Fort Lauderdale is expanding west and reclaiming land with a rapacious enthusiasm that is turning small country towns like horse-mad Davie into suburban satellites.

Davie is the Gold Coast's very own Wild West show. While surfers are riding the Atlantic rollers, the residents of Davie are more likely to be testing their skills at steer wrestling or bronco riding at the Thursday night rodeo.

Head north of Fort Lauderdale, and more than a dozen oceanside communities stretch out along A1A, fronted by a strip of golden sand. **Pompano Beach** is a noted sportfishing center named for the fish that frequent its shores. At **Deerfield Beach**, there is a chance to explore an unspoiled oasis of coastal hammock, where armadillos can be seen trotting across the nature trail.

Then there is **Boca Raton**, with its superb beach parks and small but excellent Museum of Art. "Pretty in pink" is the motto of this exclusive community, where elegant villas are painted to resemble strawberry ice cream; polo is the name of the game, and shopping is best left to the professionals. Palm Beach architect Addison Mizner planned to build the "Greatest Resort in the World" here, but was cheated of his dream by the collapse of the 1920s land boom. Although Mizner managed to

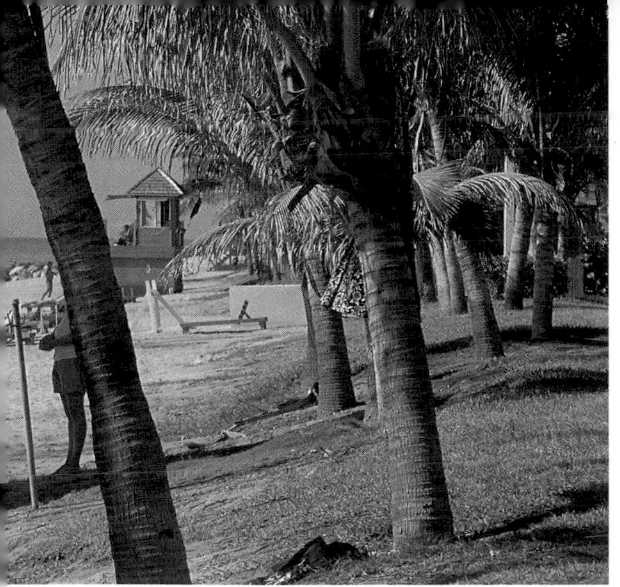

complete only one hotel, the town has honored its founder with a wealth of Mediterranean-inspired architecture in the same fashion—painted with oceans of pastel pink, naturally—and it is well worth a visit. For a change of pace, **Delray Beach** is a good place to collect shells and has a hidden treasure in its peaceful Japanese gardens and Museum of Japanese Settlement on the Gold Coast.

The Gold Coast's other main focal point, the island community of **Palm Beach**, is not expanding anywhere. This spectacularly wealthy enclave is notoriously insular. Railroad king Henry Flagler founded West Palm Beach on the mainland specifically to keep the riff-raff out of his exclusive resort, and that is the way the present-day residents intend to keep it, even though most of them only visit for three months of the year. An hour's drive north of Fort Lauderdale by car, Palm Beach is light years away in style. While the nouveaux riches of the former are charging about on their yachts, the seriously rich of the latter are planning charity croquet tournaments and packing picnic baskets for the polo game.

Palm Beach wins all the landscaping points, but **West Palm Beach** is not without its attractions, and it is the place to look for an affordable hotel. Its Norton Gallery of Art is a must for culture vultures; the Clematis Street shopping and dining district is a major attraction day and night; and polo, African safari and Everglades adventures are all to be enjoyed in the vicinity. **Juno** and **Jupiter** sound like Space Coast satellites, but turtle-watching is more common than stargazing in these relaxed beach communities at the northern end of the Gold Coast.

Sports are big on the Gold Coast. As well as spectator sports like polo, jai alai and greyhound racing, there are superb tennis and golf facilities throughout the area. If you're interested in sports, you should investigate the excellent resort packages offered, with particularly competitive rates available during the summer. Traditional off-season accommodations savings are a major attraction, and senior citizens will also find special deals.

Boardwalk in Boca Raton's oceanfront Red Reef Park

►►► REGION HIGHLIGHTS

BOCA HISTORY
The Boca Raton Historical Society is housed at the historic Boca Town Hall (71 North Federal Highway, tel: 561/395-6766) and has exhibitions about Boca's history plus a vast collection of archival material.

►►► Boca Raton *136 A2*

Boca Raton's name dates back to the Spanish explorers, who called it a "rat's mouth" for the razor-sharp rocks guarding the bay. During the 1920s land boom, Addison Mizner gathered a coterie of blue-chip backers, including the Vanderbilts and Elizabeth Arden, to launch a luxury 16,000-acre (6,400ha) project that was to be an American Venice. He built a collection of pretty Mediterranean-style homes in the exclusive Old Floresta neighborhood, off Palmetto Park Road. The superb Cloister Inn was also completed (now the swank **Boca Raton Resort and Club**), but the project collapsed along with the boom, though Boca's wealth of pink Mediterranean-inspired architecture is still very much in keeping with Mizner's plan.

Boca Raton is booming again. The "Winter Capital of Polo" is endowed with elegant shopping malls, restaurants and golf, as well as drama, musicals and revues at the **Caldwell Theatre**, tel: 561/241-7432, and 5 miles (8km) of superb ocean beaches. Special events include a springtime explosion of activity with February's **Annual Outdoor Juried Art Festival**, which attracts artists from near and far, and the jazzy **Meet Me Downtown** event in March, a large, free arts and crafts show and festival.

Boca Raton Museum of Art, *501 Plaza Real* (*Open* Tue, Thu–Fri 10–5, Wed 10–9, Sat–Sun noon–5. *Admission: inexpensive*; tel: 561/392-2500, www.bocamuseum.org) The signature space of the museum's new home is the Grand Hall, designed to accommodate constructivist painter Al Held's 58ft-wide (71.5m) abstract mural *Mantegna's Edge* (1983). The museum's second floor houses the permanent collections including The Dr and Mrs John J Mayers Collection of Modern Masters featuring some of Europe's finest artists, including works by Edgar Degas, Pablo Picasso, Paul Klee, Henri Matisse and Amedeo Modligliani.

The museum showcases a large collection of American art, with works by early 20th-century masters. The Contemporary Gallery features more than 70 prominent artists of the last 40 years including colorfield works, and post-painterly abstraction, Realist and Expressionist works and photo-realism.

The photography collection spans the history of art with earliest examples from 1850, while the ethnographic galleries are devoted to treasures from West African, Peruvian and North American cultures.

Children's Museum of Boca Raton, *498 Crawford Road (off Palmetto Park Road)* (*Open* Tue–Sat noon–4. *Admission: inexpensive*; tel: 561/368-6875) The museum occupies an octogenarian cottage, thought to be the oldest wooden structure in Boca Raton. It is a great rainy-day option or a treat for children, who will enjoy a couple of hours play-acting in the grocery store and the bank, and digging up fossils and objects in the Archeologists' Room.

Mizner Park, *Mizner Boulevard* (tel: 561/362-0606) This Mizner-inspired shopping, dining and entertainment complex is one of the largest pink extravaganzas to emerge in Boca Raton. This is where art galleries, jewelers, designer shoemakers and boutiques cater to the rich and the less rich, and it is a great free show for browsers. There are shaded benches where you can relax while surveying the scene, movie theaters and an open-air amphitheater. There is also a wide choice of restaurants.

Red Reef Park, *1111 N. Ocean Boulevard (A1A)* (*Open* park daily 8am–10pm, Gumbo Limbo Mon–Sat 9–4, Sun noon–4. *Admission free*; tel: 561/338-1473) Straddling A1A, the park offers almost a mile (1.6km) of pristine oceanfront beach bordered by a dense strip of palms, palmettos, sea grapes and Australian pines. You can snorkel around offshore reef formations, or in an artificial reef area. Picnicking facilities with barbecue grills are provided, and there is a golf course and plenty of parking (moderate). Surf fishing is a favorite pastime.

About 20 acres (8ha) of the park have been set aside for the **Gumbo Limbo Nature Center**, which encourages visitors to learn a bit more about their surroundings. Across

GRAPE HARVEST
The sea grape is a native, saltwater-tolerant shrub that grows naturally in coastal hammocks and along beaches in the southern part of the state. Early settlers used the distinctive round, leathery leaves as emergency notepaper, as plates, and even as headgear. The fruit was harvested to make wine and jelly, and the flowers rank in importance with those of black mangroves as nectar-producers for honey. The sea grape is now protected.

Pink is the theme in elegant Boca Raton

The old wooden cottage that houses the Children's Museum of Boca Raton

POLO

Played on a 10-acre (4ha) field between four-man teams, polo requires speed, stamina and considerable skill—most of which is provided by the strong, agile polo ponies. Matches are divided into six chukkers (periods) of seven minutes each, and they need a referee and two mounted umpires to keep up with the action. A team's all-important handicap is calculated on the ability ratings of its members, from a low of one to a high of ten.

A1A from the beach is a visitor center with interpretative displays, touch tanks, and saltwater aquariums for turtles. A boardwalk trail has been laid out through the tropical hardwood hammock, leading to a 40ft (12m) observation tower, and there are regular Saturday morning guided activities (call ahead for schedules and charges) that range from beachcombing with an eagle-eyed expert to exploring the many and varied examples of native flora and fauna that inhabit the preserve. From May through July, nighttime turtle walks take place on the beach (reservations).

Royal Palm Polo Sports Club, *18000 Jog Road* Every spring, polo players from all over the world converge on the Gold Coast, when Boca Raton's Royal Palm, one of the region's major clubs, plays host to the annual U.S.P.A. $50,000 International Cup Finals at the end of March (see panel). Games are also played at the club every Sunday from January to mid-April at 1 and 3.

For admission and box seats, pay at the grounds; for advance reservations for tailgate parking, tel: 561/994-1876. Free nonspectactor parking areas are provided.

South Beach Park, *400 N. Ocean Boulevard (A1A)* (*Open* daily) This is another lovely section of beach, but less developed than popular Red Reef and Spanish River. Walkways cut through the dense coastal undergrowth; lifeguards patrol 9–5; good swimming and some snorkeling.

Spanish River Park, *3001 N. Ocean Boulevard* (*Open* daily) Boca Raton's 95-acre (38ha) city park occupies both sides of A1A, with three tunnels linking the parking areas to a 1,850ft (555m) strip of sun-soaked beachfront. Nature trails explore an undeveloped natural hammock and woodland preserve, and picnickers will find plenty of tables and barbecue grills. Bicycle tracks and a boat dock are provided, and there is good fishing on the Intracoastal Waterway. A two-level observation tower gives impressive views of the park, the coast and the town.

Addison Mizner was a somewhat unlikely candidate for the title of most influential architectural stylist in south Florida. This 280-pound (128kg) ex-prizefighter and retired miner rolled into Palm Beach in 1918, and is today credited with introducing the 1920s vogue for Spanish-style architecture.

Everglades Club Addison Mizner's first venture, the Everglades Club in Palm Beach, was a collaboration with Paris Singer, scion of the sewing-machine fortune. Intended as a convalescent home for World War I veterans, it bears a strong resemblance to a Spanish monastery, with its battery of medieval turrets and wrought-iron curlicues. The end of the war saw it swiftly redesignated as a private club, which it remains. The club's eye-catching design was an instant hit, spawning a host of imitations, and its architect was signed up immediately to build winter residences for wealthy Philadelphia socialites—Stotesburys, Vanderbilts and Wanamakers.

OLD FROM NEW
The pecky cypress has a pitted, streaky appearance, and when attacked with wire brushes, blow torches and acids, then stained, it looks suitably antique.

Spain in the New World Mizner studied the Old World architecture of South America and traced it back to its roots in Spain. Conscious of the broad blue Florida sky as the only backdrop for his designs, he created bold pastel outlines and incorporated elegant courtyards surrounded by cool arcades. Red barrel roof tiles topped second-story galleries, fountains played into tiled pools, and decorative mosaic murals added a Roman-Mediterranean touch. Interiors had lofty vaulted ceilings with exposed beams hewn from mature pecky cypress. Buying trips furnished his creations with the trappings of Old Spain, and Mizner also set up local factories to reproduce ironwork, tiles and furniture—the accessories for his buildings—in the correct Mediterranean style.

End of a dream In 1925, with the land boom in full swing, Mizner embarked on a lavish scheme to transform land around Boca Raton into a dream resort.

"I am the Greatest Resort in the World," proclaimed the boastful advertisements, and they netted \$2 million worth of contracts on the first day of sales. Six months later, the boom was over, a devastating hurricane and a trail of dirty deals had caused the project to be renamed "Beaucoup Rotten," and Mizner was penniless.

One enduring memorial to Mizner's fantasy resort is his \$1.25 million Cloister Inn (now the Boca Raton Resort and Club), believed to be the most expensive 100-room hotel built in its time.

Mizner Park, a place for upscale shopping and people-watching

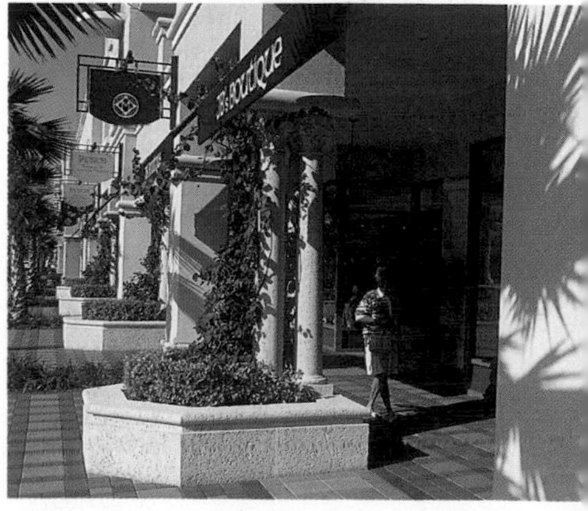

LEARNING THE ROPES
There are five standard rodeo events (see Davie), and most of them are over pretty quickly. It helps to know a couple of the finer points, such as the rule that forbids saddle bronc riders from touching the saddle, the horse or themselves with their free hand. Bull riders must stay on for a minimum of eight seconds. And just to confuse the uninitiated, steer-wrestling is also known as "bulldogging."

Cattlemen's skills and Western fashions get a regular airing at Davie's rodeos

►► Broward County

Ah-Tah-Thi-Ki Museum, *Big Cypress Reservation (I-75 west to Exit 49; 17 miles/27km north on C.R. 833 to W. Boundary Road)* (*Open* Tue–Sun 9–5. *Admission: moderate*; tel: 863/902-1113, www.seminoletribe.com) This museum offers an insight into Seminole culture through artifacts, dioramas and a film presentation. The museum's name translates to "a place to learn, a place to remember," and keeps its motto with a living village area where Seminole crafts and cooking are still practiced.

A couple of miles north, the **Billie Swamp Safari Wildlife Park** offers Everglades airboat and swamp buggy rides daily (tel: 863/983-6101, www.seminoletribe.com).

Butterfly World, *3600 W. Sample Road, Coconut Creek* (*Open* Mon–Sat 9–5, Sun 1–5. *Admission: expensive*; tel: 954/977-4400) Located southwest of Deerfield Beach and the Florida Turnpike, this attraction provides an unusual opportunity to be dazzled by the insect world. On a 3-acre (1.2ha) site, some 2,000 butterflies from more than 100 species flit around huge screened enclosures such as the dramatic 30ft-high (9m) Tropical Rain Forest Aviary equipped with observation decks, waterfalls, ponds and tunnels. Visitors can look in at the laboratory where thousands of larvae and pupae are visible at various stages of development, explore peaceful water gardens and displays of butterfly-attracting plants; a hummingbird aviary; and an **Insectarium and Museum**.

Davie A mere 10 miles (16km) from downtown Fort Lauderdale, Davie is another world. It would be unfair to call Davie a one-horse town, because it boasts enough hitching posts to secure the 7th Cavalry. This is definitely a town with horses on the brain, where even McDonald's got the idea loud and clear: The restaurant provides a "ride-through" service for locals who believe in taking their food at a gallop. To complete the picture, the local town hall boasts swinging saloon doors and a bristling display of imported cacti.

The 5,000-seat **Davie Rodeo Arena**, *6591 S.W. 45th Street* (tel: 954/680-3555, www.fivestarrodeo.com), is the scene of much of the town's horse-based activity. It provides live action in the "Jackpot Rodeo" every Thursday night at 8, and a championship rodeo event on the fourth weekend of every month. Steer-wrestling, calf-roping, bareback riding, and bronc- and bull-riding all find a place on the program, and no self-respecting cowboy should miss the **All Florida Championship Rodeo**, which takes place every fall (see box, page 23).

Everglades Holiday Park and Campground, *21940 Griffin Road* (*Open* daily 9–5; tel: 954/434-8111 and 800/226-2244, www.evergladesholidaypark.com) On the eastern edge of the vast Everglades swamplands that stretch across the state to the Gulf of Mexico, the park allows a brief Glades experience, complete with alligator shows and airboat rides. Powered by aircraft propellers, these metal-frame contraptions zip across the shallow marshes, giving ringside viewing of the weird and wonderful native flora and fauna. Boat rentals are available.

Flamingo Gardens, *3750 Flamingo Road (north off Griffin Road)* (*Open* daily 9.30–5.30, closed Mon Jun–Sep. *Admission: moderate*; tel: 954/473-2955, www.flamingogardens.org) There is a bit of everything at this popular attraction. A tram ride explores the 60-acre (24ha) site, which was one of the county's earliest citrus groves. In addition to the glossy citrus trees, there are botanical gardens where bromeliads and orchids flourish, and rare gingers and heliconias make an impressive display.

Wildlife exhibits run the gamut from alligators, crocodiles, monkeys, and otters to birds of prey and a brilliantly colored array of exotic birds including the flamingos that give the park its name. Other attractions include a pioneer homestead and a children's petting zoo.

▶ Deerfield Beach *136 A2*

Just 1 mile (1.6km) south of Boca Raton's city limits, Deerfield Beach is one of the few remaining strips of Gold Coast shoreline still of interest to shell seekers, but its best-kept secret is **Deerfield Island Park** (*Open* 8–dusk, tel: 954/360-1320). Only accessible by boat, the 56-acre (22.5ha) island sits in the middle of the Intracoastal Waterway at its junction with the Hillsboro Canal. There is a free boat service from the dock at the end of Riverview Road (off Route 810 by the Chamber of Commerce). A stone's throw from the hurly-burly of A1A and the coastal developments, this little pocket of virgin wilderness offers two beautiful nature trails with a chance to see armadillos and gray foxes in the wild. The Coquina Trail parallels the Intracoastal Waterway to a rocky bluff, while the Mangrove Trail is a raised boardwalk through areas of black, red and white mangroves and around a wooded swamp.

HOLLYWOOD NATURAL
Just south of Fort Lauderdale, the $50-million Anne Kolb Nature Center and Marina, West Lake Park, 751 Sheridan Street, Hollywood (*Open* daily 8.30–5.30. *Admission: inexpensive*; tel: 954/926-2480), offers an entertaining back-to-nature experience. There is a 1,500-acre (600ha) wetland mangrove forest habitat for ibis and herons, with an observation tower, walking, canoe and bicycle trails and narrated boat tours for the marina.

Getting away from it all by boat at Deerfield Island Park

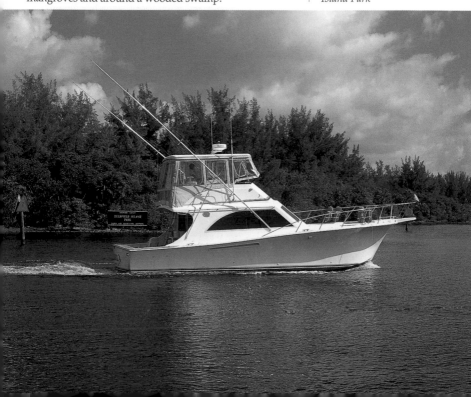

OLD SCHOOL SQUARE
Bordering Atlantic Avenue are three buildings set around this lawned complex that is now a National Historic Site. Whitewashed and smartly trimmed in aquamarine, the 1913 former Elementary School is today a showcase for the Cornell Museum of Art & History's changing exhibitions of works by national and local artists (for schedules, tel: 561/243-7922). The adjacent 1925 High School building has been transformed into the Crest Theatre (*sic*), while the former gymnasium is a community hall.

Popular and stylish cafés line the beachfront of Delray Beach

▶▶ Delray Beach *136 A2*

The earliest residents of this pleasant seaside town in the south of Palm Beach County were artists and craftsmen, and also the Yamato Colony of Japanese pineapple farmers. Flagler's railroad stopped in town, and the old Ocean City Lumber Company site is being developed into a shopping and dining district behind **Atlantic Avenue**, Delray's main thoroughfare.

A 1-mile (1.6km) section of downtown Atlantic Avenue has emerged as a popular visitor attraction. Its palm tree-lined sidewalks front an appealing collection of galleries, boutiques, specialty stores, and restaurants, and there is live music several times a week in a variety of clubs and bars. At the west end of the shops, the **Old School Square** (see panel) has been restored as a cultural arts center. There are also visits to the **Cason Cottage** (call for schedules, tel: 561/234-2577) on N.E. First Street, just across from the Crest Theatre. This typical Florida-style wooden cottage dates from 1915, and is furnished with period antiques.

Morikami Museum and Japanese Gardens, *4000 Morikami Park Road* (*Open* Tue–Sun 10–5. *Admission: moderate*; tel: 561/495-0233, www.morikami.org) These tranquil 200-acre (80ha) gardens are developing into one of the largest Japanese gardens in the US. Set amid lakes, pine forest and bonsai areas, waterfalls and lawns, the complex offers fascinating insights into Japanese art and traditions. The museum's collections include antique netsuke carvings, contemporary prints, musical instruments and folk crafts, such as origami (paper folding). You can learn about the tea ceremony and the Japanese skill of bonsai culture (growing dwarf trees).

If possible, try to time your visit so that you can attend one of the four traditional Japanese seasonal festivals celebrated here: **Hatsume Fair** (February), **Komodo No Hi** (February), **Bon Festival** (August) and **Japanese New Year** (December/ January).

Hitting the beach is an important ingredient of any Florida vacation, and although the Gold Coast was named for the Spanish treasure lost off its shores not its golden strands, visitors will still find beaches of every description, including wilderness beaches, along its coastline.

Fort Lauderdale area Even in downtown Fort Lauderdale, it's possible to relax on the beach. The **Hugh Taylor Birch State Recreation Area** is surrounded by a further 3.5 miles (5.5km) of city beach, though the backdrop is a series of high-rise hotels and condominiums. A short distance south of Fort Lauderdale, **Hollywood Beach** (on Route A1A) is a beautiful 5-mile (8km) stretch of golden sand and palm trees. It runs into leafy **North Beach Park**, which has shady picnic areas, an observation tower and sea-turtle tanks. The quietest municipal beach in the area is little **Dania Beach**, off Oak Street. **John U. Lloyd Beach State Recreation Area** has a coastal hammock nature trail (you may spot manatees in winter), and you can fish along the Intracoastal Waterway. **Pompano Beach**, with its fishing pier, is north of Fort Lauderdale, and there is **Deerfield Beach** (see page 143), which is a good spot for beachcombing.

Boca Raton area The first of the Boca Raton beaches driving north is **South Inlet Park**. It's the most secluded, good for peace and quiet during the week. Next up, **South Beach Park** (see page 140) is relatively undeveloped—in fact, it is backward compared with neighboring **Red Reef Park** (see page 139), which has a golf course and nature center across A1A. **Spanish River Park** (see page 140) is another family-oriented beach park with nature and bicycle trails. **Delray Beach** (see page 144) is good for collecting shells, and there is a great little beach at **Lantana Park** en route to Palm Beach.

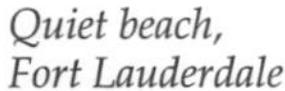
Quiet beach, Fort Lauderdale

Palm Beach area A narrow 6-mile (9.5km) strip of sand borders the ocean at Palm Beach and parking can be a nightmare. For some truly spectacular seashore head north to **John D. MacArthur Beach State Park** (see page 157), which is a favorite nesting ground for sea turtles in summer. Continue north to **Juno Beach** (see page 158) for equally stunning beaches, though parking can be tricky here. **Blowing Rocks Beach** on Jupiter Island is not a good place to swim as it is rocky and dangerous, but the scenery is marvelous; venture on to **Jupiter Beach Park** for excellent swimming and walks along the shore.

CULTURAL CENTER
The magnificent $55-million Broward Center for the Performing Arts at 201 S.W. Fifth Avenue provides world-class facilities for opera, theater, ballet, Broadway musicals, and symphony and rock concerts. Artists as diverse as Itzhak Perlman, Marvin Hamlisch, Liza Minelli and Branford Marsalis have made appearances. The Parker Playhouse, 707 N.E. Eighth Street, also stages top-of-the-line Broadway productions.

▶▶▶ Fort Lauderdale 136 A1

One of the most popular warm-weather destinations in the U.S., Fort Lauderdale also prides itself on being the "Yachting Capital of the World" and the "Venice of America" (300 miles/483km of navigable waterways). Less appealing is the nickname "Fort Liquordale," from the days when rum runners kept the town generously supplied with liquor during Prohibition. In the 1950s, droves of college students on spring break revived the Liquordale image and inspired the 1960 beach blanket movie *Where the Boys Are*, until the harrassed city fathers introduced legislation that effectively banished the student invasion in 1985. Fort Lauderdale breathed a sigh of relief as it got on with the job of promoting itself as a year-round family tourism destination.

Early days Fort Lauderdale's first known white settler was Charles Lewis, who created a plantation by the New River in 1793. Later, Major William Lauderdale came south to establish a small fort, the first of three, for the protection of local settlers during the Second Seminole War in 1838. Ohio steelworker Frank Stranahan was next on the scene. He set up an overnight camp for the Bay Biscayne Stage Line at Tarpon Bend in 1893, and founded the settlement by establishing the trading post.

For a few years, his main customers were the Seminoles, who traded pelts, alligator hides and egret plumes for provisions. The arrival of Henry Flagler's East Coast Railroad in 1896 created a mini boom. Soon there were enough children to justify having a schoolteacher, Ivy Cromartie, who later married Stranahan. Other local communities also sprang up—tomato-farming Danes congregated in **Dania**, Swedes settled in **Hallandale** and Georgians and North Carolinians migrated to **Pompano**.

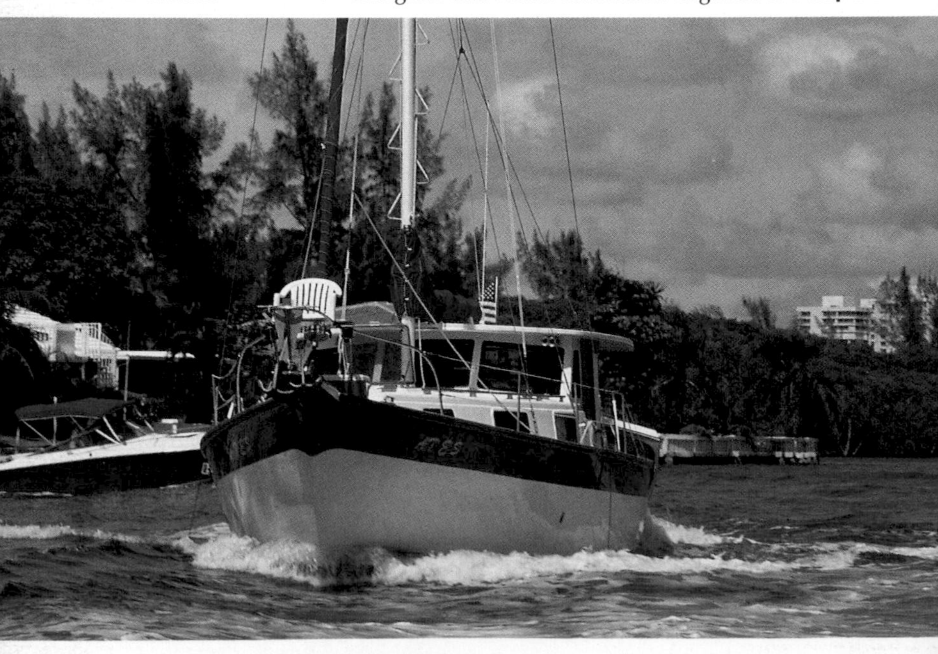

Intracoastal yacht off Fort Lauderdale

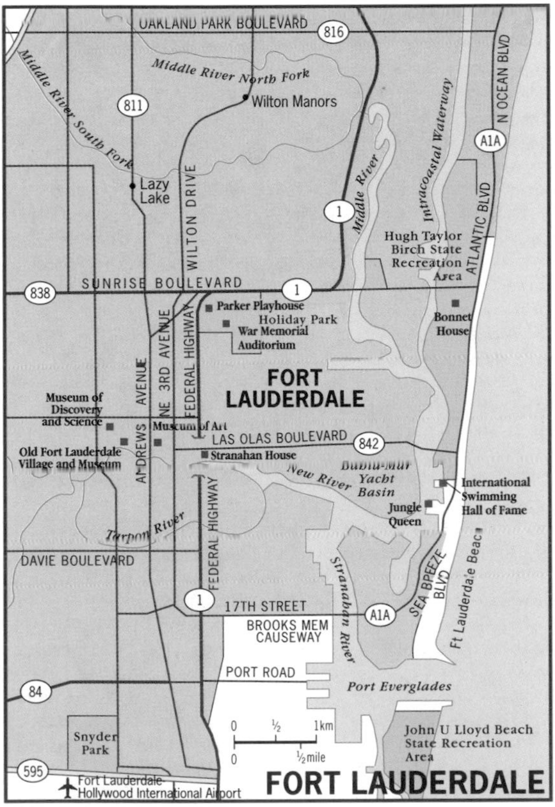

CROWD PLEASERS
In early May, Fort Lauderdale's popular Air & Sea Show, one of the largest air shows in the world, draws huge crowds with demonstrations by the U.S. Air Force, a concert on the beach, and night-time fireworks displays. In October, the Convention Center plays host to the Fort Lauderdale International Boat Show, attracting hordes of yachties.

In 1906, Florida's governor, Napoleon Bonaparte Broward, launched his much-vaunted plan to drain the Everglades, and the Roaring Twenties heralded a massive program of land reclamation. Nearby, **Hollywood-by-the-Sea** was founded by developer Joseph Young, who was also the visionary behind **Port Everglades**.

Today, Greater Fort Lauderdale is experiencing a resurgence in tourism, development, and population growth on a scale not seen since the 1920s Land Boom. Several billion dollars have been poured into an urban redesign program that extends from the renovation and expansion of the international airport to the beautification of the beachfront and the completion of the downtown **Riverwalk**, which links the city's past and future as it follows the course of the New River from historic **Stranahan House** to the state-of-the-art **Broward Center for the Performing Arts**. Fort Lauderdale is now a lively, sophisticated year-round resort.

On the accommodations front, there are around 29,000 hotel rooms; they come in all prices, ranges and styles, from deluxe resorts to great-value beachfront motels. Free Tuk Tuk Trolley services operate between the beaches and the attractive shopping and dining district on fashionable Las Olas Boulevard and do not miss the opportunity to cruise Fort Lauderdale's "Venice" and ride in a water taxi: A fun and practical form of transportation.

WHAT'S NEW
Just south of Fort Lauderdale, the I.G.F.A. Fishing Hall of Fame & Museum (*Open* daily 10–6, Wed 10–8. *Admission: inexpensive*; tel: 954/922-4212) in Dania has been drawing the crowds. Part of the state-of-the-art World Fishing Center, it provides heaps of hands-on fun and virtual sportfishing experiences, as well as objects, special exhibitions, a kids' discovery room and outdoor marina.

ACT OF GOD
Sailing off Fort Lauderdale during a storm in the 1890s, millionaire Chicago attorney Hugh Taylor Birch was blown ashore. Taking his lucky escape as a sign from God, he promptly bought up a 3-mile (5km) stretch of the oceanfront for $3,000. Today, the Hugh Taylor Birch State Recreation Area (see page 150) and the Bonnet House estate, which was a wedding gift to Birch's daughter Helen (Frederic Bartlett's second wife), are the last remnants of Old Florida on the coast between Miami and Palm Beach.

Fort Lauderdale claims to be the "Yachting Capital of the World"

Bonnet House, *900 N. Birch Road* (*Guided tours* Wed–Fri 10–1.30, Sat–Sun noon–2.30 May–Nov; Tue–Sat 10–2.30, Sun noon–2.30 Dec–Apr. *Admission: moderate*; tel: 954/563-5393) Bonnet House, named for the yellow Everglades water lilies that flourish on the 35-acre (14ha) beachfront site, is the legacy of two artists—Frederic Clay Bartlett and his third wife, Evelyn. In 1919, eschewing the Mediterranean influences of Mizner, Bartlett designed a gracious two-story plantation house around a luxurious central garden courtyard that was intended to promote an indoor-outdoor lifestyle. Broad verandas and outdoor walkways overlook the informally landscaped gardens, which can be explored with a native trail map.

The spacious, airy ground floor (tours) is decorated with the results of successful beachcombing expeditions, antiques discovered on his European travels and a menagerie of animal and bird woodcarvings and carousel beasts as well as Frederic Bartlett's artwork—murals, frescos, canvases. Evelyn's paintings hang in a small gallery, while the orchid house was her special preserve.

Old Fort Lauderdale Village & Museum, *219 S.W. 2nd Avenue* (*Open* Tue–Fri 11–5, Sat–Sun noon–2.30. *Admission: inexpensive*; tel: 954/463-4431) A collection of buildings dating from the late 18th and early 19th centuries, this collection recounts the development of the city through archives relating to the families who made the difference. Fort Lauderdale's first hotel, the New River Inn, built in 1905, forms the cornerstone of the collection. Documents include pioneer Frank Stranahan's merchant license, period photographs, landscape paintings and dozens of objects including Seminole crafts and Addison Mizner's architectural plans. The photographs are a fascinating record of changes from 1920 to 1948 as the New River marshes were transformed into today's criss-cross pattern of reclaimed land and canals.

Just down the street there is another little piece of history in the museum's **King-Cromartie House**, *229 S.W. 2nd Avenue* (*Open* for tours Tue–Sat at 2pm). This typical 1907 pioneer home is furnished as it would have been around in 1915.

Built on reclaimed Everglades marshland, Fort Lauderdale bears the proud title of "Venice of America." However, with more than 300 miles (483km) of navigable inland waterways, Fort Lauderdale and Broward County actually outrun Venice by a long shot.

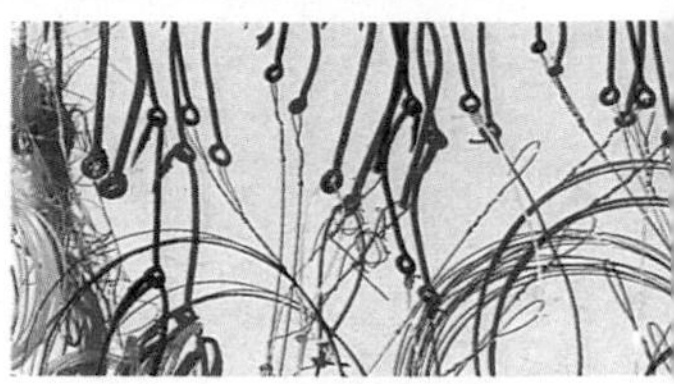

It all began with Governor Napoleon Bonaparte Broward, who won his political ticket on a promise to drain the Everglades for agricultural land. In 1906, true to his promise, he began a dredging program on the New River at Sailboat Bend, employing settlers who had worked on the Panama Canal. The veterans of Panama called the first settlement on reclaimed land Zona, later to be renamed **Davie** after a local cattle baron.

In 1912, the North New River Canal reached Lake Okeechobee, creating a brief fad for cross-state steam boat cruises to Fort Myers, but heavy silt closed the canal in 1921. In the same year, Messrs. M. A. Hortt, R. E. Dye, and Thomas N. Stilwell, inspired by Carl Fisher's Miami Beach land reclamation project, dreamed up a landfill operation for a stretch of mangrove swampland between the New River and the Intracoastal Waterway. They christened it Idlewyld, and it now forms part of downtown Fort Lauderdale.

Building an American Venice Idlewyld's success was the cue for seed-store merchant and real-estate investor Charlie Rodes to enter the arena. Using a Venetian land-building technique known as "finger-islanding," he dredged a series of parallel canals from central Las Olas Boulevard toward the river, and created narrow peninsulas with landfill from the channels. Each peninsula had a central dead-end road with waterfront plots on either side, and this grid of exclusive little fingers of land was called the Venetian Isles. It remains the most sought-after real estate in the city.

Sightseeing Forget the car—the best way to explore Fort Lauderdale's prime waterfrontage is by boat. Take a 90-minute Riverfront Cruise from Las Olas Riverfront (daily every two hours 10.30–8.30; tel: 954/463-3400) for a view of stately mansions, mega yachts, and Port Everglades, or take to the canals with the city's water taxi service. Taxis provide pick-up services for several hotels, restaurants, and sights, including Stranahan House, the Museum of Discovery and Science, and the Galleria Mall (allow 10 minutes). One-way fares are expensive, all-day passes are better value. Multijourney passes are valid for 20 trips. For information and bookings, tel: 954/467-6677.

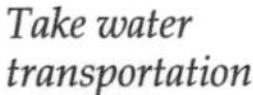

Take water transportation

Get away from the city bustle in Hugh Taylor Birch State Recreation Area

THE INTRACOASTAL WATERWAY
Florida's Intracoastal Waterway is part of a coastal boating route which runs parallel to the Atlantic Ocean and north to Chesapeake Bay in Maryland. The first section of the Intracoastal Waterway was dredged in the 1880s from preexisting natural waterways. It ran from St. Augustine to Daytona. By 1935, the channel ran the length of the state. A minimum 100ft (30m) wide and 8ft (2.5m) deep, it is maintained by the US Army Corps of Engineers.

Hugh Taylor Birch State Recreation Area, *3109 E. Sunrise Boulevard* (*Open* daily 8am–dusk. *Admission: inexpensive*; tel: 954/564-4521, www.floridastateparks.org) Fort Lauderdale residents and visitors have reason to be grateful to Hugh Taylor Birch, who provided them with 180 acres (72ha) of city-center parkland. A green oasis sandwiched between the seafront hotels of Atlantic Boulevard and the Intracoastal Waterway, the park is the ideal antidote to life in the city, with walking trails, picnic areas, canoe rentals, boating, a fitness course and an underpass to a section of ocean beach. A 1.75-mile (2.8km) circuit around the park can be walked, jogged, or driven. The 0.25 mile (400m) **Beach Hammock Trail** leads off into the natural hammock and mangrove areas.

The area provides a haven for wildlife, as well as for humans. There are around 524 species of plants and trees in the park, such as gumbo limbo, mangroves and strangler figs. Butterflies, raccoons, squirrels, marsh rabbits and owls can be spotted by eagle-eyed explorers, and wading birds frequent the lagoon and shores of the Intracoastal Waterway. This is also a good fishing spot.

Near the entrance, a visitor center housed in Birch's final residence provides a brief introduction to the park's history and flora and fauna, along with a short film and exhibits.

International Swimming Hall of Fame, *501 Seabreeze Boulevard* (*Open* Mon–Fri 9–7, Sat–Sun 9–5. *Admission: expensive*, under-12s free; tel: 954/462-6536, www.ishof.org) Do you remember Mark Spitz and his Olympic gold medals? Did you know that the legendary Johnny Weissmuller was an Olympic champion swimmer before he became the star of the *Tarzan* films? In addition to celebrating the feats of Olympic heroes, the Hall of Fame exhibits technical equipment used in professional racing, historical data and records and even swimwear—from old woolen bathing suits to modern racing apparel.

The state-of-the-art neighboring **Aquatic Complex** has two Olympic pools and diving facilities, for those who want to create records of their own.

Jungle Queen, *Bahia Mar Yachting Center, 801 Seabreeze Boulevard (A1A)* (*Open* daily. *Admission: expensive;* tel: 954/462-5596, www.junglequeen.com) The Jungle Queen riverboats provide an unusual form of transport and are a great way to explore the city and its environs. Three-hour narrated sightseeing cruises depart twice a day (at 10 and 2), and travel up the New River through downtown and into the edge of the Everglades. En route, the boats pass Fort Lauderdale's most exclusive neighborhoods, and stop at a re-created Native American village to watch alligator-wrestling bouts.

You can also take a day trip to Miami (call for schedules), or sail up the New River on the four-hour **Barbecue Ribs and Shrimp Dinner Cruise** (daily at 7pm), which docks at an island for an all-you-can-eat spread and a vaudeville revue.

Museum of Art, *1 E. Las Olas Boulevard* (*Open* Fri–Wed 11–7, Thu 11–9. *Admission: inexpensive;* tel: 954/525-5500, www.moafl.org) Designed by Edward Larabee Barnes and opened in 1986, this modern museum showcases its extensive collections of 19th- and 20th-century American and European art. Of particular note are works by the post-war CoBrA group, a collection of artists from Denmark, Belgium and Holland, whose title derives from the initial letters of their respective capitals, Copenhagen, Brussels, and Amsterdam.

There are also collections of African and pre-Columbian objects, and changing exhibitions that focus on specific periods and art forms including, for example the recent Saint Peter and the Vatican: The Legacy of the Popes display.

Souvenir hunters can enjoy browsing through the museum store for great cards, posters, art books and handcrafted jewelry.

A SHINING LIGHT ON THE ARTS
The Lighthouse Center for the Arts at tiny Tesquita (tel: 561/746-3101, www.lighthousearts.com) is Palm Beach County's oldest arts museum and offers exhibitions and hands-on experiences plus courses and guest lectures. During your visit you can dip into whatever is going on.

An easy way of seeing the sights

TEQUESTA TRACES
When Major Lauderdale founded the fort that bears his name, he chose a piece of high ground that was actually five Tequesta Native American mounds on the banks of the New River. There is evidence that the Tequestas inhabited the region between Miami and Pompano Beach some 3,000 years ago. They moved between permanent settlements on the coast and Everglades encampments, and lived off a diet of seafood, palm nuts, palmetto berries, venison, and turtle and manatee meat.

Museum of Discovery and Science, *401 S.W. Second Street* (*Open* Mon–Sat 10–5, Sun noon–6. *Admission: moderate*; tel: 954/467-6637, www.mods.org) Located in downtown's arts and sciences district, this museum is a favorite with kids. It is packed with more than 200 hands-on exhibits: On the ground floor, the walk-through Florida EcoScapes area contains one of the largest Atlantic Coast aquariums in the U.S., baby gators, turtles and a bat cave among a series of cleverly simulated natural habitats (such as a see-through beehive that you can also walk inside). The innovative and colorful games area in the Discovery Center provides entertainment for little kids.

On the upper level, dozens of interactive displays cast an educational but fun look at health, sound and myriad gizmos, from a game of virtual volleyball to computer programing. Runways to Rockets is a particular favorite where space freaks can jump on the **Manned Maneuvering Unit** space ride—but be warned that this is not recommended for the weak of stomach. There's also a 3-D IMAX theater with a five-story-high screen; a museum café; and the inevitable store.

Riverwalk, *one block west of Andrews Avenue and one block south of Broward Boulevard* (tel: 954/522-6556; www.riverfront.fl.com) River frontage is prime real estate in Fort Lauderdale, but general access was limited in the past. The Riverwalk development has changed all this by providing a delightful stretch of downtown pedestrian footpath along the New River, which extends from Stranahan House to the historic Old Fort Lauderdale district and on to the Broward Center for the Performing Arts. Landscaped with lush tropical trees, native plants, and winding walkways, Riverwalk provides a welcome interlude, with its outdoor cafés, picnic tables in gazebos, and park benches for relaxing. There are free brunch jazz sessions on the first Sunday of each month.

The latest addition to Riverwalk's attractions is **Las Olas Riverfront**, a major shopping, dining and entertainment complex with water's edge views and filled with specialty stores, sidewalk cafés, bookstores and restaurants. New River cruises depart from the wharf.

Dolphins can be seen in the waters around Florida

Drive

Fort Lauderdale to the Palm Beaches

See map on page 136.

Two main routes run the length of Florida's east coast: the fast I–95 and the seaside route A1A. Palm Beach makes an excellent day trip from Fort Lauderdale, and a good way to see more of the area is to take a gentle drive up A1A. The trip back via I–95 can be undertaken in less than an hour later in the day.

From the intersection with Sunrise Boulevard, drive north on Atlantic Boulevard (A1A) for 7 miles (11km) to Pompano Beach.

Pompano Beach is acclaimed as the "Swordfish Capital of the World," with a list of record catches just as long as one of those fishermen's tales. Its 1,080ft (324m) **Municipal Pier** is a popular spot with anglers, and during winter there is a well-supplied Farmers' Market.

The Intracoastal Waterway appears to the left at Hillsboro (2 miles/3km); to the right, luxuriant greenery conceals wealthy beachfront villas.

If it is Wednesday or Saturday and there is time to spare, the intersection with **Route 810** at **Deerfield Beach** is the cue to turn left for the boat service to **Deerfield Island Park**, a 56-acre (22.5ha) natural preserve on the Intracoastal Waterway (see page 143).

Continue on A1A for a short distance to the intersection with Camino Real at Boca Raton.

Founded by 1920s architect and developer Addison Mizner, **Boca Raton** is well worth a detour off A1A for a taste of its palm-fringed elegance (see pages 138–140).

Turn left onto Camino Real and follow the old canal route past the deluxe Boca Raton Resort and Club to the intersection with Federal Highway; turn right. At Palmetto Park Road is Mizner Park, a Mediterranean-style shopping, dining and entertainment complex, and one of Boca's top attractions. Turn right here and rejoin A1A opposite South Beach Park (see page 140), along a stretch of tree-lined roadside that continues most of the way to Highland Beach and Delray Beach (8 miles/13km).

An unusual detour at **Delray Beach** is the **Morikami Museum and Japanese Gardens** (see page 144). To get the best out of the gardens, follow the nature trails, but take it slowly. Take time to appreciate the subtle harmony of the Japanese style.

A1A continues up the coast to Palm Beach. After 16 miles (26km) the road divides: Both A1A and the right-hand fork, South Ocean Boulevard, intersect Royal Palm Way, which crosses the Intracoastal Waterway to West Palm Beach and I–95.

(See **Palm Beaches**, pages 161–169.)

You can get away from it all

The Gold Coast does not earn the name from its miles of sandy beaches, its millionaire residents or its year-round sunshine. The gold in question comes from the sea.

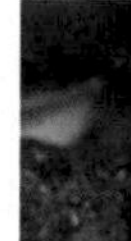

AIR MYSTERY
The likelihood of discovering a new wreck is pretty remote, but that is not to say it is impossible. One unexpected find by treasure hunters was a clutch of five World War II Avenger aircraft in some 700ft (210m) of water 10 miles (16km) from Fort Lauderdale's beach. The discovery prompted speculation that the "Lost Squadron" of Bermuda Triangle fame had been located finally, but the Avengers were from a different flight group, so the mystery continues.

Spanish treasure During the 17th and 18th centuries, Spanish treasure fleets laden with bounty from the New World started the journey homeward hugging the south Florida coastline. Their efforts to avoid offshore storms were often to no avail, and many vessels were tossed onto the reefs or sunk with their priceless cargoes of gold, silver and precious stones and a corresponding loss of life.

One of the most notable losses was the sinking of 11 vessels off the aptly named Treasure Coast between Vero Beach and Fort Pierce, north of Palm Beach, on the night of July 30, 1715. The Spanish began their own salvage operation immediately, and it continued for some years; more recently the renowned Florida marine-treasure specialists Real Eight and Treasure Salvors, Inc. have made a more comprehensive sweep.

Natural reefs The needle-sharp underwater rock formations that plagued the Spanish off the Gold Coast are the upper reaches of south Florida's three-tiered network of natural reefs, which extend 220 miles (354km) northward from the Florida Keys. This is the largest natural reef area in North America, and it is home to a magnificent variety of marine life: fish, lobsters, snails, sponges, jellyfish and sea anemones. Viewed through goggles, the reef can look like a fantasy landscape. Depths range from 12ft (3.5m)

Coral-reef scuba diving

Fish abound in Florida's coral reefs

to around 120ft (36m) within 0.5 miles (800m) of the shore. The water's low temperature is around 72°F (22°C) in winter, and visibility averages 70–100ft (21–30m) year round. Pollution and careless divers have taken a toll on the living reef in the Fort Lauderdale area, but strict controls are enforced to prevent more damage.

A sea change One of the most interesting developments aimed at preserving this natural habitat has been the growing trend for creating artificial reefs: Shipwrecks are back in fashion. These modern-day shipwrecks are intentional, and more than two dozen derelict freighters and other vessels have been sunk off the Gold Coast in recent years. Virtually any solid object, from a concrete piling to a buoy, will serve as a focal point for fish. Something as substantial as a ship can harbor an entire aquatic community, and as the soft and hard corals adhere to its steel plates, the hull is soon transformed into a veritable pillar of this community.

This "ocean reafforestation" program began in the mid-1980s with a couple of deep diving sites, including a 435ft (130.5m) freighter, the *Lowrance* (at 200ft/60m), and two Tenneco oil platforms (at 60–150ft/18–45m). Since then, artifical reefs have been interspersed with live reef areas at depths of between 15ft (4.5m) and 400ft (120m), with the purpose of providing entertainment for divers and snorkelers of all abilities and attracting deep-sea game fish, such as tuna and sailfish, from the nearby Gulf Stream.

One of the most notorious wrecks is the 200ft (60m) German freighter *Mercedes I*, which beached itself on the pool terrace of a Palm Beach socialite during a Thanksgiving Day storm in 1984. After a thorough cleanup, it was sunk in 100ft (30m) of water 1 mile (1.6km) off Fort Lauderdale beach, where its coral growths are flourishing, and a resident barracuda welcomes scuba divers. In shallower waters, snorkelers will find angelfish, sergeant majors, butterflyfish, sea turtles and octopus, all common around the rejuvenated reef.

DIVE PACKAGES

One great plus for divers visiting Fort Lauderdale is that the Broward County reefs are a lot less crowded than the Keys. Another is a range of excellent value hotel/diving packages offered by local operators. Find out more detailed information from: Parrot Island Scuba Adventures, 2705 North Riverside Drive, Pompano beach (tel: 954/942-7333 or 800/851-9106, www.parrotislandscuba.com; and Pro Dive, 429 Seabreeze Boulevard (A1A), Fort Lauderdale, FL 33316 (tel: 954/761-3413 or 800/PRO-DIVE; www.prodiveusa.com). Both companies operate fully equipped dive boats (additional charge for scuba equipment renting). Reef trips are also open to divers and snorkelers not taking part in hotel packages.

HOLLYWOOD HAPPENINGS
Every fall, jazz lovers and musicians from across the country converge on Fort Lauderdale's satellite town, Hollywood, to celebrate the Hollywood Jazz Festival (Oct/Nov). The three-day event takes place in Young Circle Park. Also in the fall, the East Coast's biggest film festival and market, the month-long Fort Lauderdale International Film Festival, is held in Hollywood and features major motion picture premieres, free film seminars, galas, and the Alamo Film Competition.

Sawgrass Recreation Park, *U.S. 27 (2 miles/3km north of I–75)* (*Open* daily 9–5. *Admission: expensive;* tel: 954/389-0202, www.sawgrassrecreationpark.com) For an excellent view of the Everglades, take an airboat tour led by knowledgable guides. You'll likely spot all sorts of wildlife, such as birds, alligators and turtles. Along with the airboat ride the entrancy fee includes admission to the Everglades nature exhibit, a Seminole village, and exhibits on alligators, and fishing equipment. You can also rent boats and fishing equipment. Bring mosquito repellent.

SeaEscape and Discovery Cruises, *Port Everglades* For a brief experience of life on the ocean wave, two local cruise ships berthed in the sprawling Port Everglades cruise complex offer day trips to the Bahamas, and daytime and dinner cruises with casino games and live entertainment. For schedules and reservations, contact **SeaEscape**, tel: 954/453-333 or 877/732-3722; or **Discovery Cruise Line**, tel: 305/477-2867 or 800/937-4477.

Stranahan House, *335 S.E. 6th Avenue (at Las Olas Boulevard)* (*Open* Wed–Sat 10–3, Sun 1–3. *Admission: inexpensive;* tel: 954/524-4736, www.stranahanhouse.com) Following his marriage in 1900, Fort Lauderdale pioneer Frank Stranahan (he set up a trading post in the 1890s for local Native Americans) built this pretty waterfront home on the banks of the New River for his bride, Ivy Cromartie, the local schoolmistress. It is the oldest surviving residence in the city, beautifully restored and furnished to re-create the period around 1913–1915. The Stranahans entertained railway baron Henry Flagler in their tiny heartpine paneled parlor, and there are numerous mementos and photographs of the early days among the Victorian and Edwardian furnishings. Frequent guided tours (full of detail and observations that really bring the period to life) give a fascinating account of the Stranahans' life in early 20th-century Fort Lauderdale.

Stranahan House, Fort Lauderdale

Walk

John D. MacArthur Beach State Park

At 10900 Route 703 (A1A), North Palm Beach, this barrier island park (*Open* daily 8am–dusk, nature center Wed–Mon 9–5. *Admission: inexpensive*; tel: 561/624-6952) was donated to the state in 1991, and has great walks along the undeveloped seashore.

Start at the visitor center on the western side of the peninsula.

There are displays and a video presentation illustrating the park's plant and animal communities.

Take the 1,600ft (480m) boardwalk across Lake Worth Cove to the coastal hammock on the Atlantic shore. A trail winds through the gumbo limbos, strangler figs and cabbage palms to MacArthur Beach.

This is a prime nesting ground for loggerhead, green and leatherback turtles from May through August (call for turtle walk schedules).

Swimming, snorkeling and shell-collecting are permitted along the 2-mile (3km) beach, and walkers may see pelicans, sandpipers, terns and other wading birds that inhabit the coastline. Serious birdwatchers should spend time scanning the mangrove-edged cove for rare roseate spoonbills, osprey, heron and ibis.

Back on the western side of the cove, there is another nature trail through a tropical hammock.

Walk

Jonathan Dickinson State Park

Situated at 16450 S.E. Federal Highway (U.S. 1), Hobe Sound (5 miles/8km north of Jupiter), this is one of southern Florida's larger parks at 11,300 acres/4,520ha (*Open* daily 8–dusk. *Admission: inexpensive*; tel: 772/546-2771). The site is named after an English Quaker who survived a shipwreck in 1696, and made it back to St. Augustine. The park's main attraction is the Loxahatchee River, an undeveloped natural waterway, which winds through the swamps and mangroves, providing refuge for manatees and a breeding ground for rare Southern bald eagles. There are areas of sand pine scrub, pine flatwoods, and Hobe Mountain (all 86ft/26m of it). Deer, marsh rabbits, otters and snakes can be spotted and alligators bask on the riverbank.

A 9-mile (14.5km) hiking trail and choice of several shorter trails explore the preserve, and rangers lead walking tours from the Trapper Nelson pioneer home site all year round.

The 30-seat *Loxahatchee Queen* riverboat makes two-hour cruises up the river; there are canoe and rowboat rentals, a campground and cabins. For information, tel: 561/746-1466.

Osprey (Pandion haliaetus)

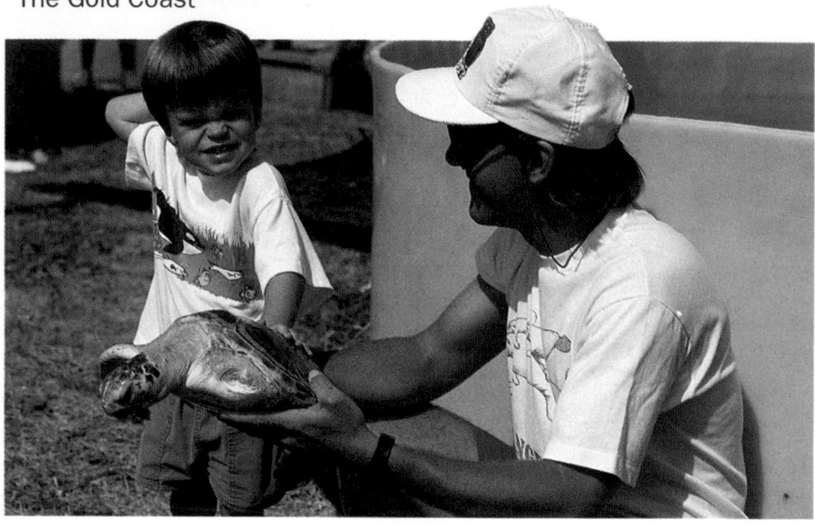

Turtle talk at Juno Beach

► Juno Beach *136 A4*

Off A1A

Once the administrative seat of Dade County, which stretched all the way down to Miami in 1889, Juno is a sleepy little town with about 2,000 inhabitants. Its main claim to fame is **Loggerhead Park**, named after the sea turtles that come ashore to lay their eggs here each summer. The **Marinelife Center of Juno Beach**, *14200 U.S. 1* (*Open* Tue–Sat 10–4, Sun noon–3; tel: 561/627-8280) is the park's focus; it has natural history and marinelife displays with a special emphasis on the sea turtles. There is a turtle nursery, where baby turtles are raised in saltwater tanks and then released into the surf, and museum staff conduct turtle walks along the beach during the nesting season (call for schedules).

►► Jupiter *136 A4*

The oldest settlement in Palm Beach County, Jupiter was founded in 1838 during the Second Seminole War. The name originated with the Jobe Native Americans, who populated the region before the Spanish and English speakers, whose tongues transformed it into Jupiter. The settlement became the northern terminal of the Lake Worth Railroad in 1888, other stops along the line including Mars, Venus and Juno. The little terminal was bypassed by Flagler's East Coast Railroad, but a small settlement remained around the **Jupiter Lighthouse** (completed in 1860). It passed almost unnoticed until the 1950s, when popular singer Perry Como began to sign off his radio and television shows with: "I'm going home to a little bit of heaven called Jupiter, Florida." The town's big draw today is the Roger Dean Stadium, out by I-95, which hosts the St. Louis Cardinals and Montreal Expos for spring training (for schedules, tel: 561/775-1818). It forms part of the ambitious Abacoa development which has plans for a major entertainment center and upscale shopping district in the near future.

Loxahatchee River Historical Society, *805 N. U.S. 1* (*Open* Tue–Fri 10–5, Sat and Sun noon–5; tel: 561/747-6639)

A collection of buildings makes up this fascinating center. Pride of place goes to the red-brick **Jupiter Lighthouse** (*Open* Sun–Wed 10–4, sunset tours last Wednesday of the month) erected in 1860 to a design by General Mead, who later went on to lead Union forces in the Battle of Gettysburg. **Little Dubois House** (*Open* guided tours Tue & Wed) offers a architectural contrast, being a pioneer home built in the late 1890s, which was found to have been built upon a Native American shell mound.

Following damage during the storms of 2004, the museum's archive of utensils, period photographs and exhibition materials on native Seminole life, Flagler Railways and other themes of local history are being renovated to be displayed in a new museum building by the lighthouse.

▶ Jupiter Island *136 A4*

Turn off A1A onto Route 707 for Jupiter Inlet Colony at the southern tip of the island and the town of Jupiter Island to the north.

These two elite residential communities have attracted the likes of Jacqueline Kennedy (who came here after President John F. Kennedy's assassination in 1963), George Bush's mother, and singer Perry Como—who forgot to mention that his "little bit of heaven" was rather richer and more secluded than ordinary old downtown Jupiter on the mainland. The real estate here is some of the most expensive along the coast, but riches lie just offshore too. The Spanish fleet was wrecked directly off Jupiter Island in 1715. The galleons were filled with gold and silver being transported to Europe. Today, pieces still wash up with the tide.

Blowing Rocks Preserve, *Route 707* (*Open* daily 9–4.30 *Admission: donation*; tel: 561/744-6668) Get here early to find a parking space and explore the preserve before the crowds arrive. Your visit should be timed to coincide with high tide, when the preserve really lives up to its name as fountains of spray are punched up through blowholes in limestone outcrops along the rocky shoreline.

A hardwood hammock borders the sand dunes, where sea grapes, palmetto and cabbage palms combine with colorful, hardy wildflowers and saltwater-resistant sea oats to anchor the sand. Woodpeckers and warblers, pelicans and osprey can all be seen. No swimming.

TURTLE TIMES

Between May and August, hundreds of female sea turtles make an annual pilgrimage to Florida's southeast coast, where they come ashore to lay their eggs in the sand. It is thought the females return to nest on the same beach on which they hatched. Loggerhead, green, and leatherback turtles all frequent the Florida shores. The leatherback is the most distinctive—capable of growing up to 6.5ft (2m) in length and weighing 1,300 lbs (585kg). It does not have a hard shell.

Royal tern, seen around the coast

Henry Morrison Flagler was born in Hopewell, New York, on January 2, 1830. The son of a struggling Presbyterian minister, he left home at the age of 14 and sought work with relatives in Ohio; by 1852, he was a partner in their grain and distillery business.

When a venture into the profitable Michigan salt industry was wiped out by the Civil War, Flagler moved to Cleveland, where he recouped his fortunes and made the acquaintance of John D. Rockefeller, owner of a small oil company. In 1867, Flagler and an Englishman, Samuel Andrews, became Rockefeller's partners. Together they launched an American legend, the Standard Oil Company, in 1870.

The East Coast Railroad Flagler originally visited Florida in the early 1880s with his first wife. After her death, he married again (there would be three wives in all) and honeymooned with his new bride in St. Augustine. The old-world charm of the city (founded by the Spanish in the 1560s), the winter sunshine and the enormous development potential captured Flagler's imagination. He chose young architects John M. Carrère and Thomas Hastings to design a fabulous Spanish/Moorish-style hotel, the Ponce de León, which opened in St. Augustine in 1888. To save his customers the indignity of abandoning their comfortable Pullman cars at Jacksonville, taking a ferry across the St. Johns River and roughing it on the rickety local railroad, Flagler bought up the existing railroad, converted it to standard gauge and built a rail bridge over the river.

Now committed to his vision of creating an American Riviera along Florida's east coast, Flagler began building hotels and buying out local railroads, extending his line down to Titusville and Cocoa in 1893 and Palm Beach in 1894. Then in 1896 Miami pioneer Julia Tuttle convinced him that he should continue the line to Miami.

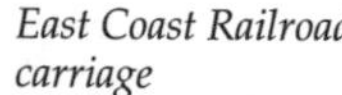

East Coast Railroad carriage

A dream fulfilled The greatest challenge was still to come—the 156-mile (251km) engineering feat that took Flagler's railroad down the Florida Keys. Three thousand workmen toiled more than seven years to carve a path through marsh and jungle, built bridges and viaducts and connected islands and hundreds of coral reefs until the first official train made the journey into Key West on January 22, 1912. Flagler was on board and announced: "Now I can die happy; my dream is fulfilled." He died on May 20, 1913.

▶▶▶ Palm Beach *136 A3*

Palm Beach has been cited as "an example of what God would do if He had money." And this magnificently manicured, palm-fringed and exclusive enclave is all about serious money. It owes its fortunes to a typical Gold Coast occurrence—a shipwreck. In 1878, a Spanish brigantine, the aptly named *Providencia*, foundered off the coast with a cargo of 20,000 coconuts. A handful of settlers planted the coconuts, named the settlement after them, and the resulting swathe of tropical palms inspired Henry Flagler to create an elite winter resort here, marked by the opening of the Royal Poinciana Hotel in 1894, since demolished (see panel).

The Mizner vision In 1918, Addison Mizner arrived in town with a vision of his own. The former miner launched his career with the Spanish Revival-style **Everglades Club** on Worth Avenue. Prone to omitting such tiresome necessities as kitchens from his house plans, Mizner was in his element when designing public spaces. The 300 block of **Worth Avenue**, one of the world's most exclusive shopping streets, is a typical Mizner creation of elegant boutiques, decorated with a sprinkling of outdoor staircases, decorative wrought ironwork, tropical shrubs and vines. This is where the rich and famous gather for lunch during the winter season in between cruising the famous name stores (see page 171).

Palm Beach practicalities Anyone can visit Palm Beach, but to feel at home on Worth Avenue or to slip into The Breakers for a cocktail, it helps to dress up. Car parking is hard to come by, and the Palm Beach traffic cops are tireless. Meters are limited to one or two hours, but Whitehall has its own parking lot.

A GRAND RESORT

Henry Flagler drew the cream of American society to Palm Beach. Princelings and presidents were entertained at Whitehall, Flagler's magnificent "seaside cottage." Others flocked to his Royal Poinciana Hotel, once the largest resort hotel in the world, and possibly the biggest wooden structure ever built. Today, the grandest hotel in town is The Breakers, 1 S. County Road, a fabulously ornate 1926 Italianate marvel and not to be missed. For a glimpse of Palm Beach's most impressive private residences, head for South Ocean Boulevard, nicknamed "Mansion Row." The biggest property of all is Mar-a-Lago (No. 1000), now an exclusive private club.

The suitably palm-shaded entrance road to Palm Beach

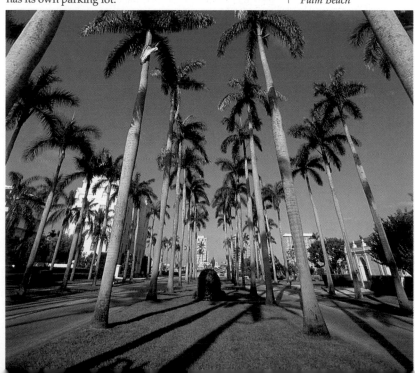

MAINTAINING STANDARDS
The battle to keep Palm Beach exclusive and genteel, started by its founder Henry Flagler, continues unabated. A series of municipal bylaws ban washing a car in public, hanging out a washing line and—horror of horrors—jogging barechested.

Bethesda-by-the-Sea Church, *141 S. County Road* (*Open daily 8–5. Admission free*; tel: 561/655-4554, www.bbts.org) Built in 1927, southeast Florida's first Protestant church is a little gem of Spanish-Gothic restraint amid the opulence. It has some lovely stained-glass windows. Behind the church, take a stroll around the formal plantings of the quiet **Cluett Memorial Gardens**.

Henry Morrison Flagler Museum, *Cocoanut Row* (*Open Tue–Sat 10–5, Sun noon–5. Admission: moderate*; tel: 561/655-2833, www.flagler.org) The Whitehall mansion, Henry Flagler's wedding present to his third wife, Mary Lily Kenan, was designed by John M. Carrère and Thomas Hastings, architects of Flagler's grandiose Ponce de León Hotel in St. Augustine. The classic two-story villa near Lake Worth took just 18 months to build and cost around $2.5 million. It is now a museum. The interior is a monument to historic European styles, some 55 lavishly decorated rooms crammed with paintings, porcelain and antiques, most of which are originals from Flagler's time.

Portraits of Flagler and his granddaughter, Jean Flagler Matthews, who rescued the building from demolition in 1959, hang in the impressive Marble Hall where the guided tours begin, passing from the Italian Renaissance Library to Mary Flagler's opulent Music Room, with its acreage of highly polished parquet and French windows to the South Porch, a favorite setting for her musical tea parties. The magnificent Louis XV-style ballroom was also designed to spill out into the courtyard. Renaissance France was the inspiration for the superb dining room. Take time to admire the extraordinary detail of the coffered ceiling created with gilded woodcarvings inset with dainty papier-mâché. Of the bedrooms, the English Arts and Crafts Movement chamber was a novel addition, and the combination of matching wallpaper and fabric in the Yellow Roses Room was also an innovation.

WALK SMALL
Flagler had the builders construct the frescoed ceiling of the Marble Hall in the Whitehall mansion 8ft (2.5m) lower than the original designs, so he would "feel at home."

Henry Morrison Flagler's magnificent Whitehall mansion

Beachside houses in the wealthy town of Palm Beach

As befitted a champion of train travel, Henry Flagler had his own railroad car, *The Rambler*, which has come to rest in the garden. It has been immaculately restored with the help of photographs from the Flagler era. Oak-paneled, plumply upholstered and fitted with carpets and chandeliers, it even boasts a copper-lined shower and a tiny private kitchen with a wood-burning stove, a sink and an icebox for preparing refreshments en route.

Palm Beach Bicycle Trail Biking is a great way to explore Palm Beach, and take a leisurely look at some of the more imposing mansions. Most of the streets are shaded by outsized palms, and, of course, the terrain is flat as a pancake—this is Florida, after all. The official breezy bike trail parallels Lake Worth, opposite the mainland.

You can venture to South Ocean Boulevard and along the ocean side of the island. Many local hotels loan bicycles to their guests, and bikes can also be rented from the **Palm Beach Bicycle Trail Shop**, *223 Sunrise Avenue* (*Open* Mon–Sat 9–5, Sun 10–5; tel: 561/659-4583). The shop also supplies a bicycle trail map, showing a route that runs parallel to the Intracoastal Waterway and loops round to the beachfront and Worth Avenue.

Society of Four Arts Gardens, *Four Arts Plaza off Royal Palm Way* (*Open* May–Oct, Mon–Fri 10–5; Nov–Apr, Mon–Sat 10–5. *Admission free*; tel: 561/655-7226) This venerable cultural institution has a beautiful series of enclosed gardens, which are filled with plants, trees and the odd carp pond. The standout is the **Philip Hulitar Sculpture Garden**, with contemporary exhibits. The center itself has an art gallery (Mon–Sat 10–5, Sun 2–5 Dec to mid-Apr) that plays host to changing exhibitions, a library, plus a theater with a music and dance program.

BEACH BREAKS

There are a couple of access points to the shore in Palm Beach. The diminutive Mid-Town Beach, 400 S. Ocean Boulevard, is found opposite the eastern end of Worth Avenue. For a more expansive stretch of sand, head south to Phipps Ocean Park, 2145 S. Ocean Boulevard, which has a handful of picnic tables and barbecue grills as well as the historic 1886 Little Red Schoolhouse.

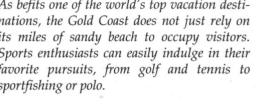

As befits one of the world's top vacation destinations, the Gold Coast does not just rely on its miles of sandy beach to occupy visitors. Sports enthusiasts can easily indulge in their favorite pursuits, from golf and tennis to sportfishing or polo.

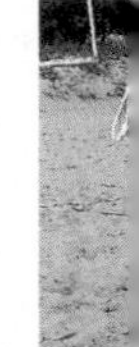

JAI ALAI
Introduced to Miami by Cuban immigrants, this fast and furious spectator sport (see page 82) is featured at one Gold Coast site: Dania Jai-Alai, 301 E. Dania Beach Boulevard/A1A (Games daily Tue–Sat at 7, Sun at noon. *Admission: inexpensive*; tel: 954/920-1511). Games last 15 minutes with a 10-minute break in between—used by spectators to place complicated bets—and there are a dozen or so games each evening.

Jai alai, Cuban-style pelota

Armchair sports fans will have a field day too, with the frenetic excitement of jai alai (see panel), excellent polo, baseball courtesy of the Florida Marlins, plus hockey action from the N.H.L.'s Florida Panthers at the National Car Rental Center, 1 Panther Parkway, Sunrise (tel: 954/835-8326). Spring training sees the St. Louis Cardinals and the Montreal Expos at the Roger Dean Stadium, 4751 Main Street, Jupiter (tel: 561/775-1818) in north Palm Beach County.

Golf Palm Beach County boasts more than 145 public and private golf courses, while Greater Fort Lauderdale can offer more than 50.

In the Fort Lauderdale area several top resorts offer all-inclusive golfing packages, including **Bonaventure Country Club**, tel: 954/389-2100; and **Palm Aire Country Club and Golf Academy** in Pompano Beach, tel: 954/975-6244. For notable nonresidential courses, try **Deer Creek**, Deerfield Beach, tel: 954/421-5550; **Inverrary Country Club**, Lauderhill, tel: 954/733-7550; and the public **Pompano Beach Municipal Golf Course**, tel: 954/786-4141. Around Boca Raton, there is the **Boca Raton Municipal Golf Course**, tel: 561/483-6100, and oceanfront **Red Reef Executive Golf Course**, tel: 561/391-5014. West Palm Beach has Fazio-designed **Emerald Dunes**, tel: 561/687-1700, and 45 championship holes at the **Palm Beach Polo, Golf and Country Club**, tel: 561/798-7000. For both golf and tennis, try the excellent **P.G.A. National Resort and Spa**, tel: 561/627-2000 or 800/633-9150.

Polo It should be no surprise that the Gold Coast is the winter home of this princely pastime; the good news is that it does not cost a fortune to watch. The season runs from December/January into April and attracts a host of celebrity fans, which makes star-spotting almost as riveting as the polo action itself. For a look at both, check out the weekend action at **Royal Palm Polo Sports Club**, 18000 Jog Road, Boca Raton, tel: 561/994-1876, and **Palm Beach Polo, Golf and Country Club**, 11199 Polo Club Road, Wellington, tel: 561/798-7000. Teams of four horses and riders compete during six 7-minute

Sportfishing off the Florida coast

chukkas (periods). If the teams are tied at 3.30, the game continues until one side wins.

Sportfishing Fort Lauderdale's **Hall of Fame Marina**, 435 Seabreeze Boulevard, tel: 954/764-3975; and **Pier 66 Marina**, 2301 S.E. 17th Street, tel: 954/525-6666, are packed with charter fishing boats. But the top fishing spot is probably Pompano Beach, where the **Hillsboro Inlet Charter Fleet**, 2629 N. Riverside Drive, tel: 954/943-8222, operates about a dozen charter vessels on the trail of marlin, pompano, shark and sailfish.

Tennis With inspiration in the form of local legend Chrissie Evert, tennis freaks will find facilities galore, with 550 local courts in the Fort Lauderdale area. Try the **Jimmy Evert Tennis Center at Holiday Park**, tel: 954/828-5378; or contact the **City of Fort Lauderdale Parks and Recreation Department**, tel: 954/828-7275. Boca Raton has some distinctly stylish courts. Try the **Boca Del Mar Country Club**, tel: 561/392-7991; **Boca Sailing and Racquet Club**, tel: 561/338-7655; or **Memorial Park**, tel: 561/393-7978. In West Palm Beach, there is **Gaines Park Tennis Center**, tel: 561/659-0735, or ask advice from the **Palm Beach Recreation Department**, tel: 561/966-6625.

You're never far from a good golf course in Florida

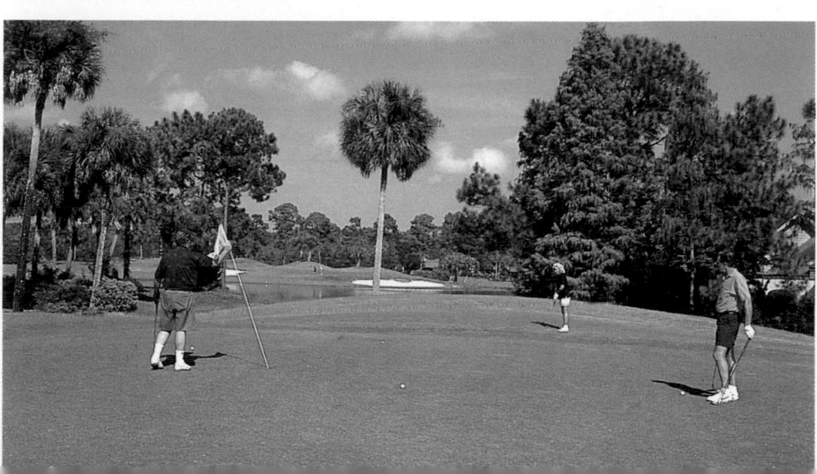

West Palm Beach, once Palm Beach's poor relation, is now an important business center

▶▶▶ West Palm Beach 136 A3

If Palm Beach was born with the proverbial silver spoon in its mouth, West Palm Beach was the poor relation. The workers and the commercial and industrial services required to keep Henry Flagler's elite resort running smoothly were conveniently housed out of sight across the Intracoastal Waterway. However, it was West Palm Beach that became the administrative seat of Palm Beach County when it was created in 1909, and West Palm has developed as a business center for law, accounting and brokerage firms, while building a new reputation for computer and electronics manufacturing.

Downtown West Palm Beach has undergone a massive redevelopment program, begun with the stunning Raymond F. Kravis Center for the Performing Arts (tel: 561/832-7469) carried through the revitalization of the Clematis Street shopping, dining, arts and entertainment district, and culminating in the $350 million Mediterranean style CityPlace (tel: 561/366-1001), a shopping and entertainment complex which anchors the western downtown. Plans in the pipeline include an $80 million opera house. The result is that West Palm Beach is now on the list of places to be in South Florida.

Beyond downtown, West Palm Beach's attractions are spread widely, particularly to the west of the city. To the north, Riviera Beach is the departure point for water taxi trips out to Peanut Island, and the water taxis also offer scenic cruises with additional departures from the busy **Sailfish Marina** complex (tel: 561/844-1724) on Palm Beach Shores, across the Intracoastal Waterway.

Sailfish Marina has one of the largest charter fishing fleets in the area and anglers will find plenty of action around the Palm Beaches. Sportfishing charters are available from Boynton Beach, Lantana, and Riviera Beach, as well as from Palm Beach Shores.

Avid fishermen can try their luck from the fish camps out at Lake Okeechobee, the headwater of the Everglades which is teeming with largemouth bass, or closer to home, Lake Worth, which is renowned for its fishing, particularly bass.

ALL THE FUN OF THE FAIR

West Palm Beach has the lion's share of festivals. January sees the South Florida Fair, a two-week-long event combining agricultural exhibits, live entertainment, and rides and games out at the Fairground. Meanwhile, February brings the Palm Beach International Film Festival, culminating in an awards gala at the Raymond F. Kravis Center. The four-day Sunfest in April–May is one of the region's biggest events, with nonstop jazz, arts and crafts, food stands, puppet shows, dance demonstrations and more.

Arthur R. Marshall Loxahatchee National Wildlife Refuge, *off U.S. 441/S.R. 7 (west of Boynton Beach)* (*Open* daily 6am–dusk, visitor center 9–4. *Admission: inexpensive*; tel: 561/735-6030, www.loxahatchee.fws.org) The closest entrance to the Everglades from the Palm Beaches, this sawgrass and hammock preserve (220sq miles/570sq km) is a haven for an impressive variety of native wildlife, and has a wilderness canoe trail on the Loxahatchee River, a federally designated Wild and Scenic River. From the visitor center, a boardwalk trail extends above cypress swamp, where you might spot alligators; the marshland trail leads to a lookout tower above a pond that is frequented by herons and other waterfowl.

Lion Country Safari, *2003 Lion Country Safari Road (S.R. 80 at U.S. 441/98 West)* (*Open* daily 9.30–5.30, last admission 4.30. *Admission: expensive*; tel: 561/793-1084, www.lioncountrysafari.com) For a fun family day out, visit this 500-acre (200ha) African wildlife park, complete with elephants, rhinos, bison, wildebeest, giraffes and chimps, as well as lions. The park opened in 1967 as the nation's first drive-through "cageless" zoo, and the 1,000-plus animals are now well established. Though it is not the Serengeti, the brilliant Florida sunshine is a good substitute for the real thing.

After the drive, the **Safari World Amusement Park** offers a further chance for animal encounters and fairground rides. Enjoy a cruise on the *Safari Queen* or navigate a pedalboat around the lagoon, with its monkey islands and flamingo colony. You can meet a llama in the petting zoo; see alligators and snakes in the reptile park; walk the nature trail; and see new arrivals in the nursery.

Mounts Botanical Gardens, *531 N. Military Trail* (*Open* Mon–Sat 8.30–4.30, Sun 1–5. *Admission: donation*; tel: 561/233-1757, www.mounts.org) These pretty gardens are a hidden treat. The 14-acre (5.5ha) plot features fruit groves, rare and flowering trees, butterfly, herb and rose gardens, as well as colorful herbaceous plantings and a central lily pond with a tiny rain forest section. There are guided tours on Saturday at 11am and Sunday at 2.30pm.

Norton Museum of Art, *1451 S. Olive Avenue* (*Open* Tue–Sat 10–5, Sun 1–5. *Admission: moderate*; tel: 561/832-5196, www.norton.org) An outstanding gallery founded by Chicago industrialist Ralph H. Norton in 1941, the Norton's extensive collections are divided into four main areas. The most important of these is the **French Collection**, broadly representative of the late 19th- to early 20th-century Impressionist and Post-Impressionist era, with works by Monet, Matisse, Pissarro and Renoir, as well as Chagall, Dufy, and Picasso.

Echoing its European counterpart, the **American Collection** includes works by Ernest Lawson, John Sloan, and Winslow Homer, Edward Hopper, Georgia O'Keefe, and Jackson Pollock. Bronzes, jade carvings, Buddhist sculpture and peerless ceramics occupy a gallery devoted to the **Chinese Collection**, and the fine **Sculpture Collection** embellishes an attractively landscaped patio garden with works by Degas, Henry Moore, Maillol and Duane Hanson.

NIGHTLIFE FOR NOTHING
Palm Beach County is streets ahead on the free outdoor entertainment front. On Thursday evenings year-round Clematis by Night brings live music and food stalls to the Clematis Street district in downtown West Palm Beach. Boca Raton's Mizner Park complex features the occasional Music in the Park series; while Art & Jazz on the Avenue livens up Delray Beach's Atlantic Avenue every Thursday evening during the winter season, switching to Summer Nights on Fridays in summer.

SCULPTURE SPECIAL
A few blocks south of the Norton Gallery are the Ann Norton Sculpture Gardens at 253 Barcelona Road (*Open* Tue–Sat 10–4. *Admission: inexpensive*; tel: 561/832-5328). The 3-acre (1.2ha) gardens are devoted to the work of Ralph H. Norton's wife, Ann Weaver. Her sculptures have been beautifully arranged against a luxuriant backdrop of native plants (many specifically chosen for their popularity with wild birds), and 300 varieties of palm trees. You can see small sculpture pieces in wood and marble in Norton's former studio.

The museum's reputation enables it to obtain some of the best traveling art shows circulating the United States, and there is a varied exhibition program that highlights established artists and new discoveries.

Palm Beach Polo, Golf and Country Club, *11199 Polo Club Road, Wellington* (tel: 561/798-7000 and 800/257-1058, www.palmbeachpolo.com) On a winter Sunday afternoon everybody who is anybody in Palm Beach County packs a picnic basket and heads for the polo ground. The Palm Beach Polo, Golf and Country Club is one of the world's classiest polo venues, where international teams compete in front of crowds that have included Dustin Hoffman, Calvin Klein and Sylvester Stallone.

Polo is not the only spectator sport offered at the club. A 125-acre (50ha) landscaped equestrian complex hosts the annual **Winter Equestrian Festival** and a wide range of other events that traditionally includes a World Cup qualifying competition. Meanwhile, golfers can take up the challenge of 45 championship holes devised by some of the top names in the golfing world.

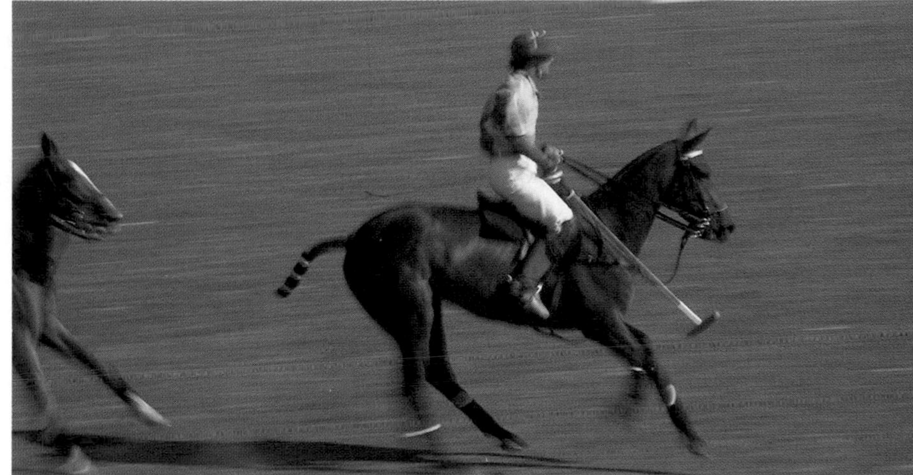

Above: Polo, a Palm Beach specialty
Left: Striking sculpture in the Norton Museum of Art

Palm Beach Zoo at Dreher Park, *1301 Summit Boulevard* (*Open* daily 9–5. *Admission: moderate*; tel: 561/574-9453, www.palmbeachzoo.org) This modest parkland setting is home to some 500 animals and birds from 100 different native and exotic species. Among the miscellaneous reptiles, a petting zoo and a small collection of butterflies, a sinuous Florida panther (on the endangered list) steals the show. A state-of-the-art tiger exhibit complete with jungle-style special effects in the Florida Pioneer area and animal encounter programs are scheduled throughout the day.

Peanut Island, *water taxi access from Riviera Beach* (*Admission free*; tel: 561/966-6600) This 79-acre (31.5ha) sand island was man-made in 1918 and was chosen by John F. Kennedy as the site for the family bomb shelter during the 1961 Cuban missile crisis, due to its proximity to Kennedy estates. In 2005 a massive redevelopment and landscaling of the island was unveiled with a mangrove swamp walk, new floating docks and tropical foliage.

South Florida Science Museum, *4801 Dreher Trail North* (*Open* Mon–Fri 10–5, Sat 10–6, Sun noon–6. *Admission: moderate*; tel: 561/832-1988) Together with the zoo (above), this provides a terrific children's day out, with lots of hands-on exhibits, flashes, crackles and surprises. Adults who never grasped the basics, let alone the principles of physics, can learn more in an hour of chasing a seven year old around here than they did in their entire school careers. All the usual skeletons and dioramas are on display, but take a break to wander through the tropical Native Plant Center. The Light and Sight Hall unleashes the true spirit of investigation, with numerous hands-on exhibits.

The **Aldrin Planetarium**, at the heart of the museum complex, takes spectators on a fascinating journey through the universe. Weekend laser concerts are another popular feature, and the 16in (41cm) Newtonian Reflector telescope in the Gibson Observatory is one of the largest in the state.

MORE ATTRACTIONS FOR KIDS

Boomers Family Recreation Center, 3100 Airport Road, Boca Raton (tel: 561/347-1888), has go-karts, bumper boats, and miniature golf. Rapids Water Park, 6566 N. Military Trail, West Palm Beach (tel: 561/842-8756), is a good place to cool off. The Children's Science Explorium, 300 S. Military Trail, Boca Raton (tel: 561/347-3913), offers plenty of hands-on fun; and the Sports Immortals Museum, 6830 N. Federal Highway, Boca Raton (tel: 561/997-2575), is a fascinating rainy-day option for sports fans.

Some years ago, when a worldwide survey discovered that the single most popular vacation pursuit is shopping, the Gold Coast took note. Department stores, discount malls, designer boutiques and flea markets abound—shopaholics should be issued a health warning and several pairs of walking shoes.

Fort Lauderdale Downtown Fort Lauderdale's finest shopping street is chic **Las Olas Boulevard**, a delightfully landscaped district of pretty designer boutiques, art and antique galleries, and a choice of elegant little café-restaurants that are just the ticket for recuperating after a tough morning scrutinizing price tags.

The **Las Olas Riverfront** shopping and entertainment complex with its selection of individual stores and boutiques and its weekend concerts and fiestas is also worth investigating, as is **The Galleria**, on E. Sunrise Boulevard near the beach, which features 150 stores and restaurants, including Nieman Marcus, Jordan Marsh, and Saks Fifth Avenue, Brooks Brothers, Polo/Ralph Lauren and the Disney Store.

Head west of downtown to the Plantation district, where the cool marble and granite precincts of **Broward Mall**, 8000 Broward Boulevard, with department stores Macy's, JC Penney and Dillards anchoring more than 100 specialty stores, icnluding Ann Taylor, Gap, Nine West, Victoria's Secrets and even a Disney Store.

A delightful shopping haven in Palm Beach

Dedicated bargain hunters should make the trek out to **Sawgrass Mills**, 12801 W. Sunrise Boulevard (9 miles/14.5km west of town), the world's largest designer outlet mall, with more than 270 manufacturers and retail outlets, plus brand-name discounters that slash prices on designer brands by up to 70 percent. Levi's, Kenneth Cole, Brooks Brothers, Off 5th Saks Fifth Avenue, and Ann Taylor all have discount stores, and there are electrical goods, toiletries, books, toys and fashions at amazing prices. But the fun does not stop there. In The Oasis area, shoppers can take a break at a Hard Rock Café, a movie or GameWorks.

Another bargain-basement shopping opportunity is the 80-acre (32ha) **Fort Lauderdale $wap Shop**, 3291 W. Sunrise Boulevard, which also has a farmers' market with local produce, fairground rides and daily circus performances.

For specialist shopping, Dania's **Antiques Row**, on U.S. 1, is a great place to browse for china, glass, furniture, silverware and jewelry. Over 100 shops occupy this atmospheric downtown district.

Shopping along Worth Avenue, Palm Beach

Boca Raton Shopping is a way of life in Boca Raton, as is the color pink. **Royal Palm Plaza**, N. Federal Highway at Palmetto Park Road, has been nicknamed "Pink Plaza" for the strawberry-ice-cream hue of its Spanish-style stucco buildings. Eighty boutiques, gift shops and specialty stores range around elegantly landscaped courtyards and ornate fountains.

A stone's throw away, a delicate shade of salmon-pink distinguishes **Mizner Park** (see page 139), with its fine array of shops and restaurants. On the women's fashion front there is a Banana Republic, and Nicole Miller has her own boutique. Reluctant shoppers can take refuge in Liberties Fine Books & Music, which provides easy chairs for book browsers. Fashionable **Town Center Mall**, 6000 W. Glades Road, has lured the likes of Louis Vuitton and Laura Ashley to join Bloomingdale's and Saks Fifth Avenue in its Mediterranean-inspired complex, which numbers 180-plus stores and an array of fine dining options. Heading north, Delray Beach's **Atlantic Avenue** is an attractive downtown shopping district with a range of specialty stores, boutiques, antiques and cafés; and art lovers may like to check out **Lake Worth**, which is rapidly building a reputation as an artists' enclave served by several interesting galleries.

Palm Beaches One of the world's most exclusive shopping streets, **Worth Avenue**, is in Palm Beach. Glittering with style, sophistication, and a richly appointed branch of the fabulous New York jeweler Tiffany's, it derives much of its charm from the landscaped sidewalks and Mediterranean-style architecture designed by Addison Mizner more than 70 years ago. Along the street, around the courtyards, and down narrow pedestrian passageways, some 200 specialty shops, a new Neiman Marcus department store, art galleries and gourmet restaurants cater to a rarified clientele (for West Palm Beach, see panel).

AND THERE'S MORE ...
Moving from the historic to the relatively recent, West Palm Beach's most impressive shopping extravaganza is the **Gardens Mall**, P.G.A. Boulevard. Beneath a glass atrium, 180 stores and restaurants fill the complex, including big department stores such as Bloomingdale's and Saks Fifth Avenue. **Palm Beach Mall**, Palm Beach Lakes Boulevard, is another tasteful collection of skylights, shrubs, department stores and boutiques. Downtown, **Clematis Street** is awash with fashion and specialty stores, and the **CityPlace** development has added even more choice.

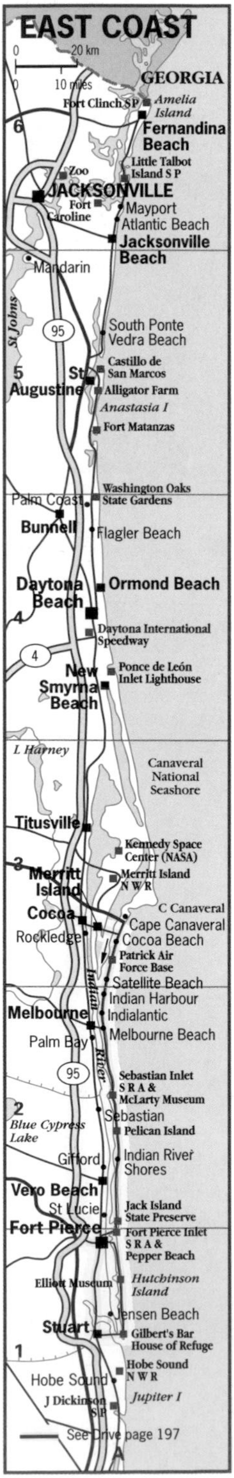

THE EAST COAST covers an area north from the top of the Gold Coast to the border with Georgia. It is a 300-mile (483km) stretch of the mainland, largely protected by a string of lush barrier islands. Here, the Floridas of past and present are juxtaposed in a series of historic old towns and modern summer season beach resorts, ancient Native American shell mounds and 21st-century space wizardry.

The East Coast is where it all began, when Spanish explorer Juan Ponce de León stepped ashore near present-day St. Augustine in 1513. This area now calls itself the "First Coast," and includes Jacksonville, on the St. Johns River, where French Huguenots established a settlement in 1564. Upon learning of the French settlers, Philip II of Spain dispatched his lieutenant Pedro Menéndez de Avilés to teach the French a lesson, and a brutal massacre of the shipwrecked French at Matanzas Bay ("Bay of Slaughter") left the Spanish to claim the territory by the founding of St. Augustine in 1565. Though at the time the mosquito-infested swamps of the East Coast were of little value, St. Augustine was a strategic link in the maritime defense of Spanish treasure fleets and a prime target of English attacks. The town was razed by Sir Francis Drake in 1586, was attacked again in 1702, and the English actually moved in for 20 years in 1763.

WAR AND TOURISTS By the early 19th century, sugar, citrus, and indigo plantations were starting to appear around Indian River and the Halifax River (as the Intracoastal Waterway is known near Fort Pierce and Daytona Beach, respectively), but the outbreak of the Seminole Wars, followed by the Civil War, led many settlers to abandon their plantations. Business picked up again in the 1870s, when the first trickle of tourists drifted down to the railhead at Jacksonville and continued south by boat down the St. Johns River or along the coast to St. Augustine, Ormond Beach and Rockledge.

When Standard Oil millionaire Henry Flagler determined to develop Florida's East Coast as a "Southern Newport" winter resort for wealthy Philadelphia socialites, the trickle became a torrent, and Flagler ferried them south on his railroad and put them up in his own luxurious hotels.

JACKSONVILLE is the original gateway to Florida. A Flagler hotel (long since gone) at Atlantic Beach was the start of today's Jacksonville Beaches resort area, and the city recovered from a devastating fire in 1901 to emerge as an industrial and trading port, the insurance capital of the South, and a vibrant cultural center. The St. Johns River meanders through the city, past Jacksonville University, where composer Frederick Delius once lived on a citrus plantation, and squeezes around a narrow bend to divide the downtown district in half. Once much maligned for the stench of its wood-pulp mills near I–95, Jacksonville's attractive center, with its Riverwalk, water taxis and neighboring beaches now justifies a detour.

A short distance north, facing Georgia across the St. Mary's River, **Amelia Island** is a charming getaway with a couple of luxury resorts and wildlife preserves as well as the historic small port of **Fernandina Beach**. Fernandina has seen eight national flags struck over its

Left: Motor racing fans pack the Daytona International Speedway, home to the famous Daytona 500

picturesque old town center. Today it is a haven for antiques browsers and for beach lovers; it also has a busy shrimping fleet.

South of Jacksonville, **St. Augustine** is the longest continually inhabited settlement in the United States. Pensacola was colonized earlier, but the settlers abandoned their encampment, and St. Augustine can claim the "Oldest House," a historic fort and a tourist park on the spot where Ponce de León is believed to have made his first footfall. The town's old Spanish Quarter is beautifully preserved, and there are beaches nearby, all of which combine to make the town a pleasant stopover.

Farther south, **Daytona Beach** is the "Birthplace of Speed," where Malcolm Campbell piloted his *Bluebird* into the record books (see page 174). Driving on the beach is no longer permitted for safety reasons, and Daytona Beach is now a popular, spring break resort.

The **John F. Kennedy Space Center** is not called Cape Canaveral. As the third biggest attraction in Florida, and home of America's Space Shuttle program, it is very particular about its title, pointing out that Cape Canaveral is a lump of sand. The Kennedy Space Center is the highlight of the **Space Coast**, which also offers a choice of good-value, family-oriented resorts and amazing wildlife flourishing in the shadow of the launch pad.

The sinking of the treasure-laden Spanish Plate Fleet off Vero Beach in 1715 caused this next section of Atlantic oceanfront to be nicknamed the **Treasure Coast**. **Fort Pierce** is the largest town on the **Indian River** mainland, but the real attractions here are the relaxed resorts, golden beaches, watersports and diving opportunities.

At the close of the 19th century, Henry Flagler bought and enlarged a grand hotel (the Ormond) on a 23-mile (37km) stretch of beach north of Daytona. He could not have envisaged that the golden sands would become one of the world's most famous racetracks or that his hotel would be a pit stop for early automobile enthusiasts.

The region's early claim to fame is the theme of a new recreation area, Birthplace of Speed Park (SR A1A and Granada Boulevard), which commemorates the first race held on the beach here in 1903, when the record was set at 68mph (110kph). Plaques offer information and there are full-scale replicas of the early racing machines.

Henry Ford, Louis Chevrolet, and Harvey Firestone were all lured south by the winter sunshine, but it was R. E. Olds, of Oldsmobile fame, who staged the first oceanside race across the hard-packed sands of Ormond Beach in 1902. Olds and Alexander Winton clocked a mind-boggling 57mph (92kph) as they tore down the beach; a year later it was more than 65mph (105kph); and by 1905 speeds had passed the 100mph (161kph) mark. In 1907, Fred Marriott recorded 197mph (317kph) in a Stanley Steamer, before crashing into the surf.

Faster and faster The original "track" began on Ormond Beach, at Granada Avenue, and ran south for 12 miles (19km) to Daytona Beach proper. Its finest hour was in 1935, when Englishman Sir Malcolm Campbell set the last land-speed record on the beach when he raced his Rolls-Royce-powered *Bluebird* to 276mph (444kph). By this time, motorcycles had also joined the fray.

After a quiet few years, beach racing was back on track in the southern beach area in the 1950s, but its popularity became a problem: Large crowds and construction along the seafront made it too dangerous, and the action was moved to **Daytona International Speedway**, International Speedway Boulevard, in 1959, the year of the first Daytona 500 Endurance Race. Today, the Daytona 500 is a world-class event and the most famous of eight-plus major car and motorcycle events staged annually at the high-banked, tri-oval racetrack; it's the high point of February's 16-day **Speed Weeks** extravaganza, which draws thousands of fans to America's Birthplace of Speed. A couple of weeks later, March's **Bike Week** brings the motorcycling fraternity rumbling into town.

Action at Daytona

▶▶ Daytona Beach 172 A4

The "World's Most Famous Beach" is 23 miles (37km) long and up to 500ft (150m) wide. The Daytona Beach resort area, which stretches down the peninsula from Ormond Beach to Ponce Inlet, is the largest resort area on the East Coast, welcoming eight million visitors annually.

Daytona's love affair with the automobile is a historic tradition. The season starts in February, with the famous formula and stock car **Speed Weeks** at the Daytona International Speedway. Several thousand leather-clad bikers transform Main Street into a week-long chrome carnival in March's **Bike Week**, followed in April by hordes of Northern students celebrating spring break. With over 16,000 hotel rooms and rental apartments, Daytona Beach is well prepared for these annual gatherings.

There is no shortage of other diversions—the beach itself is a giant amusement park, and concessions cater to every type of watersport (jet skis, windsurfers, surf boards and sailboats are all widely available), while **The Boardwalk** offers amusement arcades and go-karting, and there are aerial gondola rides on **Main Street Pier**. Nearby is the Daytona Lagoon (see panel).

For some culture, check out the impressive **Ocean Center**; the London Symphony Orchestra appears every other year at the **Peabody Auditorium**, and free beachside concerts take place at the **Bandshell** in Oceanfront Park. Natural delights include trails, boating, and fishing at **Tomoka State Park**, N. Beach Street; **Sugar Mill Botanical Gardens** in Port Orange; and excursions on the Halifax River Intracoastal Waterway with **A Tiny Cruise Line** (for schedules, tel: 386/226-2343).

The Casements, *25 Riverside Drive (at Granada)* (*Open* tours Mon–Fri at 10 and 2.30, Sat 10 and 11.30. *Admission: donation*; tel: 386/676-3716) Named for its casement windows, this modest clapboard house—the present-day Ormond Beach Cultural & Civic Center—was built in the early 1900s, and subsequently purchased by oil magnate John D. Rockefeller in 1918. The millionaire returned here every winter until his death in 1937.

Various Rockefeller-related objects have been gathered here, including his wicker beach chair with its glazed portholes. There is an exhibition gallery on the ground floor, and an extraordinary collection of scouting memorabilia is crammed into the attic.

▶▶▶ REGION HIGHLIGHTS

SPLASHTACULAR!
Daytona Beach's new Daytona Lagoon, 601 Earl Street (*Admission: expensive;* tel: 386/254-5020) is a splashtacular affair, with its high-energy tube rides, waterslides and a 17,000sq ft (1,530sq m) wave pool. The Entertainment Center has a go-kart track, mini-golf and games arcade, Laser Tag and rock climbing walls (*Open* daily 10–7 late May–early Sep, Sat–Sun Apr–early May).

The popular Daytona Beach resort

HISTORY IN THE BANK
Amateur historians will find plenty to enjoy at the Halifax Historical Museum, 252 S. Beach Street, Daytona (*Open* Tue–Sat 10–4. *Admission: inexpensive*; tel: 386/255-6976), housed in a former bank. Native American objects here include a 600-year-old Timucuan dugout canoe. There are also Spanish relics found in local plantation ruins, a 1909 time capsule, and automobile memorabilia. One of the best displays is the enchanting, marvelously detailed wooden model of the Boardwalk area as it looked in 1938.

Museum of Arts and Sciences, *1040 Museum Boulevard* (*Open* Tue–Fri 9–4, Sat and Sun noon–5. *Admission: inexpensive;* tel: 386/255-0285, www.moas.org) This classy modern museum really does have something for everyone—exhibits range from a giant ground sloth skeleton to a collection of Cuban art! The 13ft (4m) high sloth is mounted in the prehistory section where hands-on specimen drawers offer fossils, puzzles, and even a mammoth tooth and a giant ostrich egg for inspection. Elsewhere, the **Cuban Museum** records two centuries (1759–1959) of Latin American culture in vivid style, while the excellent **Dow Gallery** showcases American arts and crafts from 1640 to 1920, and there are fine collections of African and pre-Columbian objects. The museum is in the 60-acre (24ha) Tuscawilla Preserve, focus of the Window on the Wood Interpretive Center.

DAYTONA USA, *1801 W. International Speedway Boulevard* (*Open* daily 9–7. *Admission: expensive*; tel: 386/947-6800, www.daytonausa.com) Entered by replicas of Daytona International Speedway's famous under-track twin tunnels, this interactive motorsports attraction is a racing fan's heaven. Packed with hands-on activities and state-of-the-art exhibits, it is by turns a museum and a monument to the World Center of Racing. Among the highlights are NASCAR 3D, Heroes of the Track gallery and 30-minute speedway tours; an interactive pit-stop challenge; and *The Daytona 500*, a spectacular film featuring in-car camera footage and behind-the-scenes action.

Ponce de León Inlet Lighthouse, *S. Peninsula Drive, Ponce Inlet* (*Open* daily 10–4. *Admission: inexpensive;*

A giant sloth, from around 130,000 years ago, in the Daytona Museum of Arts and Sciences

Nostalgic corner in the Daytona Museum of Arts and Sciences

tel: 904/761-1821, www.ponceinlet.org) Set at the southern end of the Daytona peninsula, this 1887 red-brick lighthouse is now working again and affords great views up and down the coast from the top of its 203-step spiral staircase. Below is a keeper's cottage, furnished 1890s-style, a splendid 17ft-tall (5m) Fresnel lens in a special exhibit building, and a small museum of nautical memorabilia. The fishing village of Ponce Inlet is renowned for its seafood restaurants, and there are picnic areas, a marina and a beach in Lighthouse Point Park, at the end of Peninsula Drive.

▶▶▶ **Fernandina Beach** see page 183. *172 A6*

▶ Indian River and the Treasure Coast *172 A2*

One of Florida's quieter and more relaxed corners, the Indian River region is more famous for its citrus than its beaches. Indian River is the local name for the Intracoastal Waterway, which divides the mainland from the barrier island beaches of the Treasure Coast. South of Sebastian Inlet, the main business districts of chic Vero Beach and Fort Pierce, and laid-back Stuart are all centered on the west (mainland) bank of the Indian River, but vacationers head for the modest barrier island resort annexes strung along the A1A highway.

A pioneer military outpost founded in 1838, Fort Pierce lies across from an inlet which divides the barrier islands of North and South Hutchinson, both featuring fine sandy beaches.

North of the inlet are surfing favorites **Fort Pierce Inlet State Recreation Area** and **Pepper Beach**; nature lovers should seek out well-concealed **Jack Island State Preserve** (off A1A; see page 191), a 630-acre (252ha) mangrove island with nature trails and superb birdwatching. To the south, try **Stuart Beach**; snorkelers can explore the glassy-smooth waters around **Bathtub Reef**.

THE GAMBLE PLACE

In 1907, James Gamble built himself a modest hunting lodge on Spruce Creek, just south of downtown Daytona. The comfortable Cracker-style retreat lies hidden in a 150-acre (60ha) woodland preserve maintained by the Museum of Arts and Science. Guided tours (by arrangement; tel: 904/255-0285) visit the lodge, an old citrus-packing barn and a replica of Snow White's House from the 1938 Disney movie. There is also a nature trail and pontoon boat rides on the creek.

MARINE ENCOUNTER
Touch tanks, aquariums, and interactive computer puzzles are all part of the Florida Oceanographic Society's Coastal Science Center, 890 N.E. Ocean Boulevard (A1A) Stuart (*Open* Mon–Sat 10–5, Sun noon–4. *Admission: inexpensive*; tel: 772/225-0505, www.floridaoceanographic.org). There are also trails in the adjacent hammock and mangrove areas and plans for a turtle rescue facility.

Elliott Museum, *825 N.E. Ocean Boulevard, Stuart* (*Open* daily 10–4. *Admission: moderate*; tel: 772/225-1961, www.elliottmuseum@goodnature.org) An interesting stop on A1A, the museum is named for American inventor Sterling Elliott, the man who, for example, put four wheels on a bicycle and came up with a quadricycle. Alongside some of Elliott's inventions, you will find early 20th-century domestic dioramas, a row of old-fashioned stores imported from Massachusetts and a terrific collection of rare vintage bicycles, motorcycles and cars, including a Stanley Steamer.

Gilbert's Bar House of Refuge, *301 S.E. MacArthur Boulevard, Stuart* (*Open* daily 10–4. *Admission: inexpensive*; tel: 561/225-1875) A mile (1.6km) south of the Elliott Museum, this 1875 sailors' refuge was provided by the US Life Saving Service, forerunner of the Coast Guard. The white clapboard building is the oldest house in Martin County, and the simple living quarters have been carefully restored with Victorian furnishings. There are plans for nautical museum displays.

St. Lucie County Historical Museum, *414 Seaway Drive, Fort Pierce* (*Open* Tue–Sat 10–4, Sun noon–4. *Admission: inexpensive*; tel: 772/462-1795, www.st.lucie.lib.fl.us) In a park at the eastern end of South Bridge, this museum provides a pleasant introduction to local history. Among the nostalgic items on display, there is the restored 1907 Gardner House, a 1919 fire engine, 19th-century stores and a reconstructed Seminole tribe encampment. You can also see military hardware from Old Fort Pierce and objects from Spanish shipwrecks.

VERO BEACH
A gem of a seaside community 20 miles (32km) north of Fort Pierce, Vero Beach is home to Disney's Vero Beach Resort and Dodgertown, winter home of the LA Dodgers. However, the town's real charm lies in its luxurious real estate, tree-shaded streets, sports facilities, and upscale shopping in the boutiques and galleries lining stylish Ocean Drive. A cultural high spot is the Center for the Arts in Riverside Park, which plays host to excellent visiting exhibits.

Savannas Recreation Area, *1400 E. Midway Road* (*Open* daily 8–dusk. *Admission: inexpensive*; tel: 772/464-7855 and 800/789-5776, www.floridastateparks.org) Close by Indian River, Florida's last intact freshwater lagoon system is preserved within the Fort Pierce city limits. The 550-acre (22ha) park consists of a fragile marsh and uplands ecosystem with a diverse range of both plant and animal life. The Environmental Education Center at Walton Road, Port St. Lucie has a lot of information about the ecosystem and how it has evolved. In the park you can kayak or canoe along the freshwater channels, take to the trails to enjoy walking, cycling or horseback riding, or you can take it easy with some fishing or birdwatching. Bring a picnic and make a day of it; tables are provided.

UDT-SEAL Museum, *3300 N. A1A Fort Pierce* (*Open* Tue–Sat 10–4, Sun noon–4 year-round, Mon 10–4 Jan–Apr. *Admission: inexpensive*; tel: 561/595-5845, www.navysealmuseum.com) This is a real-life adventure story featuring the U.S. Navy's World War II Underwater Demolition Teams (UDT), and its modern-day successors, the Sea, Air, and Land Teams (SEAL). In 1943, this beach area was chosen as the training site for the Navy's elite wartime frogmen, and the museum pays tribute to this usually secretive branch of the armed forces. An impressive array of military exhibits, diving equipment, demolition apparatus, weapons, and photographs tells the story of the teams in graphic detail.

▶▶▶ Jacksonville *172 A6*

Capital of the "First Coast" (see page 172), Jacksonville is flourishing—the 16th largest city in the United States has plenty to offer family vacationers, historians and visiting culture vultures.

The city's roots run deep. A party of French Huguenot soldiers and settlers, led by René de Goulaine de Laudonnière, founded **Fort Caroline**, one of the earliest European colonies in North America, on the banks of the St. Johns River in 1564. The native Timucua people helped them construct a rough fort, but the Spanish did not take kindly to "foreign" occupation of their New World territories, and ousted the French before establishing their own settlement at St. Augustine, 60 miles (96.5km) farther south.

Jacksonville was named for General Andrew Jackson and was laid out on the site of Fort Caroline around 1822. Extending to both sides of the St. Johns River, it prospered as a river port and then as one of the earliest Florida tourist destinations with the arrival of the railroad. At the end of the 19th century, Henry Flagler built a hotel (which has now gone) at **Atlantic Beach**, part of Jacksonville's 15-mile (24km) stretch of sandy beachfront.

The downtown district is compact, divided by the river. To the north, the business district empties into **Jacksonville Landing** for shopping, dining and entertainment. Ferry services run shuttles from here to the south bank, where a **Riverwalk** meanders past several small museums of local and maritime history, and the fountains of **Friendship Park**. As the river curves south, it flows past the leafy residential enclave of San Marco, with its fine old homes and small specialty shopping district.

On the opposite bank, around St. Johns Avenue, the attractive **Riverside/Avondale** neighborhood is home to another pocket of upscale interior decorators, boutiques, antiques shops and restaurants. The lovely **Cummer**

FIT FOR THE KING

For 21 years, a suite in what is now Jacksonville's Hilton Jacksonville Riverfront and Towers was set aside for the sole use of the legendary King of Rock and Roll, Elvis Presley. The snake-hipped one slept in it six times between 1955 and 1976. The room, named the San Marco Suite, is now available (tel: 904/398-8800).

Jacksonville: modern skyline of a historic city

RIVER JAUNTS
The St. Johns River is the focal point of the city and a great sightseeing opportunity. For views of the downtown skyline, hop aboard one of the frequent water-taxi services between Jacksonville Landing and the Riverwalk. More leisurely sightseeing cruises with commentaries and musical entertainment are offered by River Cruises Inc. (tel: 904/396-2333) aboard their 1890s-style sternwheelers *Annabelle Lee* and *Lady St. Johns.*

Museum of Art and Gardens on Riverside Avenue is a must-see. Cultural events in Jacksonville include programs at the gloriously kitschy **Florida Theatre** (tel: 904/355-2787). Painstakingly restored to its 1920s grandeur, it has earned a spot on the National Register of Historic Places, probably despite rather than because of the fact that it is where Elvis Presley made his first stage appearance.

Downtown the **Times-Union Center for the Performing Arts** is one of the state's finest cultural showcases and frequent host to the highly regarded **Jacksonville Symphony Orchestra** (tel: 904/354-5547). In October, jazz lovers are treated to one of the world's largest free jazz events during the annual three-day **Jacksonville Jazz Festival**, in Metropolitan Park.

Cummer Museum of Art and Gardens, *829 Riverside Avenue* (*Open* Tue and Thu 10–9, Wed, Fri and Sat 10–5, Sun noon–5. *Admission: inexpensive, free Tue 4–9;* tel: 904/356-6857, www.cummer.org) This is your excuse to visit the attractive Riverside district. One of the greatest attractions is its lovely gardens, a mixture of formal Italian and English landscaping, wisteria arbors, a superb old live oak with a canopy spreading over 175ft (52.5m), and brick paths leading to the water's edge.

The 10 galleries display fine arts and antiquities from the Cummer's permanent collection of over 5,000 pieces, making it the largest museum in northeast Florida. Exhibits span ancient, medieval, Renaissance, baroque, rococo, Impressionist and contemporary art from Europe and America, and pre-Columbian ceramics, while there are also notable Asian collections. The Cummer also boasts the Wark Collection of 18th-century Meissen tableware, one of the largest publicly displayed collections of its kind in the world. The hands-on education program allows kids to have a lot of fun in the interactive Art Connections area.

Bicyclists on the sand at the edge of the Kathryn A. Hanna Park, a beachfront park

Fort Caroline National Memorial, *12713 Fort Caroline Road (off S.R. 10)* (*Open* daily 9–4.45. *Admission free*; tel: 904/641-7155, www.nps.gov) Historic site of de Laudonnière's French Huguenot colony, this park has a scale model of the original Fort Caroline, as well as three walking trails, and pleasant picnic spots. A granite marker commemorates French explorer Jean Ribaut. This is a good place to look for bottlenose dolphins in the river.

One mile (1.6km) southeast of Fort Caroline, the Theodore Roosevelt Area has been designated a **Timucuan Ecological and Historic Preserve**, encompassing wetlands, river systems, historic sites and several hiking trails through maritime forest and salt marsh.

Jacksonville Museum of Modern Art, *333 North Laura Street* (*Open* Tue and Fri 11–5, Wed–Thu 11–9, Sat 11–4, Sun noon–4. *Admission: inexpensive*; tel: 904/366-6911, www.jmoma.org) This museum took possession of its renovated six-story building in 2003 and showcases the latest artistic trends alongside its growing permanent collection. The changing arts program includes avant-garde English- and foreign-language films, artists in residence, guest speakers at lunchtime lectures, a theater and a café. The ArtsExplorium Loft offers hands-on learning with 16 areas that aim to increase the understanding and enjoyment of art, and explore its influence within society.

Jacksonville beaches *(12 miles/19km east via U.S. 90/S.R. 10)* Jacksonville's Atlantic beaches were established as a resort area with the arrival of the railroad in the 1880s. Fifteen miles (24km) of dazzling sand, sun and fun link the three distinct beachfront districts of **Atlantic Beach**, **Neptune Beach**, and **Jacksonville Beach** (together with its southern annex, **Ponte Vedra Beach**). The first two are bordered by residential communities and are quieter than the more commercial Jacksonville Beach section, which offers a full range of shopping, sports facilities and family entertainment (see panel).

The official beach season opens in April with a round of festivals and entertainment. Watersports enthusiasts will find a host of beachfront surf shops renting surfboards and sailboards; boat rentals for water-skiing and diving are also available at the beach. **Jacksonville Beach Pier**, at *6th Avenue South* (*Open* daily 6am–10pm. *Admission: expensive*), is a great spot for fishing, and is well supplied with tackle rental and bait shops.

Jacksonville Landing, *Independent Drive* (*Shops open* Mon–Thu 10–8, Fri and Sat 10–9, Sun noon–5.30; tel: 904/353-1188, www.jacksonvillelanding.com) Downtown's shopping, dining and entertainment complex, the horseshoe-shaped festival marketplace sits on the northern bank of the St. Johns River, below Main Street Bridge. By day, the mall is packed shoppers visiting the more than 40 retail stores, which include many well-known names. The Food Hall's wide range of restaurants and take-out joints caters to all tastes, including Japanese, Mexican and Italian, and offer generous deli sandwiches. At sunset, the Landing is transformed from a shopping mall into a live entertainment venue, with a variety of events staged in the central courtyard.

FAMILY ADVENTURES

Rain or shine, Adventure Landing, 1944 Beach Boulevard, Jacksonville Beach (*Open* Sun–Thu 10am–11pm, Fri–Sat 10am–midnight. *Admission: expensive*; tel: 904/246-4386), offers family entertainment from outdoor adventure golf, batting cagers and go-karting to an indoor video arcade and laser tag. In hot weather, the shipwreck-themed waterpark is a good place to cool off—arranged around a 65ft (19.5m) tall Caribbean play village with a dozen waterslides, wave pool, and 200 water-squirting nozzles for added drenching power.

Shells are a popular souvenir. You can also pick up your own from the beach, but be aware of the restrictions

On the African veldt at Jacksonville Zoo

NAUTICAL MAYPORT
On the south bank of the St. Johns River where it flows into the Atlantic is Mayport, one of the nation's oldest fishing communities. Famous for its seafood restaurants, the shrimp dock is dwarfed by neighboring Mayport Naval Station (tel: 904/270-5226), the fourth largest naval base in the United States. A popular outing with children, the base offers free tours of navy vessels, which can include home-based aircraft carrier U.S.S. *John F. Kennedy* (call for weekend schedules).

Children enjoy Jacksonville Zoo's miniature train

Jacksonville Zoo and Gardens, *370 Zoo Parkway* (*Open* Mon–Fri 9–5, Sat–Sun 9–6 Mar 6–Sep 6; daily 9–5 rest of the year. *Admission: moderate*; tel: 904/757-4463, www.jaxzoo.org) A short drive north of the city on the interstate, Jacksonville Zoo has worked hard to replace old-style animal cages with natural open "environments" where non-predatorial species interact as they would in the wild. You can find more than 2,000 animals in total, with over 1,000 plant species in the verdant landscape.

The Birds of the Rift Valley Aviary is an example of the care the zoo has taken, with 20 species enjoying a large enclosure where the landscape mimics that of East Africa. The Range of the Jaguar opened in 2004 and in addition to this elusive wild cat, you'll find other animals, insects and amphibians of the Central American jungles. The latest attraction is the Giraffe Overlook, where you can climb to a walkway above these majestic creatures in their 2-acre (0.8ha) compound as if you were flying over the plains.

Kathryn A. Hanna Park, *500 Wonderwood Drive* (*Open* daily 8–8 Apr–Oct; 8–6 Nov–Mar. *Admission: inexpensive*; tel: 904/249-4700, www.coj.net) A 450-acre (180ha) beach-front park south of Mayport Naval Station, this is a highly recommended alternative to the main public beaches. Dunes crested with sea oats stretch for over 1 mile (1.6km) along the shore, while behind the beach woodland hiking and bicycle trails extend throughout the nature preserve, which also encompasses more than 60 acres (24ha) of freshwater lakes. As well as good fishing spots, there are lakeside picnic tables and barbecue grills (picnic supplies are available from the park campers store), summer concessions and no fewer than 300 campgrounds.

Museum of Science and History, *1025 Museum Circle, Southbank (Riverwalk)* (*Open* Mon–Fri 10–5, Sat 10–6, Sun 1–6. *Admission: moderate*; tel: 904/396-6674) This interest-packed museum complex offers a broad range of displays and hands-on exhibits illustrating local and natural history and the physical sciences. The Florida Naturalists Center is inhabitaed by more than 60 native species from snakes to skinks to birds, and there may be snapping turtles and tarantulas, as well. The **Atlantic Tails: Whales, Dolphins, and Manatees of Northeast Florida** is an informative section, relating the story of five endangered marine animals native to the region. Local NFL heroes the Jacksonville Jaguars also warrant a shrine packed with memorabilia and interactive playstations.

Moving up a floor, there are hands-on science pods and a motion simulator that provides virtual explorations of the dinosaur era and the moon. On the historical front, **The Current of Time** delves into Jacksonville's history through objects and dioramas. There are daily displays in the **Alexander Brest Planetarium** (seating passes from the front desk) and 3-D musical laser shows.

Follow this coastal route for exciting glimpses into history, views of beautiful architecture, excellent food, and stunning scenery. Northeast from Jacksonville, Route A1A takes a scenic trail up the coast to historic Fernandina Beach. This makes a great day trip, starting with a short ferry ride from Mayport as far as Fort George Island. Ferries operate daily every 30 minutes, from 6.20am (6am Mon–Fri) to 10.15pm.

The first stop is **Kingsley Plantation**, 11676 Palmetto Avenue (*Open* daily 9–4.45), the oldest plantation house in the state, owned by slave trader Zephaniah Kingsley from 1813 to 1839. He grew cotton, sugar cane, sweet potatoes and citrus fruits; his 200 slaves lived in tabby cabins, made from a mixture of shells and lime, 23 of which still exist, in a neat row in a clearing in the woods.

Follow A1A north, along the **Buccaneer Trail**, by Little Talbot Island State Park, where 5 miles (8km) of wide sand beach, salt marshes and coastal hammock harbor bobcats, otters, marsh rabbits, water fowl and superb fishing opportunities. A causeway crosses the Nassau Sound to **Amelia Island** (www.ameliaisland.com), named by the British in 1735 after George II's daughter. Host to legions of Spanish, French, British and Mexican invaders, the island is now a quiet resort offering bed-and-breakfast accommodations, small hotels and deluxe resorts.

The historic town center of **Fernandina Beach** lies on the west side of the island, with a wealth of fine Queen Anne stick-style and Victorian buildings, antiques and crafts shops, boutiques, galleries, restaurants and purportedly the state's oldest continuously operated hostelry, **The Palace Saloon**, 117 Center Street. This is a good place to sample local shrimp delivered to the docks daily. The best way to explore the 50-block historic district is on foot. The **Amelia Island Museum of History**, 233 S. Third Street, offers walking tours and strolls; for information, tel: 904/261-7378, or pick up a map from the Chamber of Commerce, 102 Center Street.

East of the center, **Fort Clinch State Park** (*Open* daily 8–dusk) lies on the south bank of Cumberland Sound, the border with Georgia. Dating from 1847, the brick fortress has worn well, and park rangers, dressed in Civil War uniforms, cook, clean and take turns standing guard. There are picnic grounds, a nature trail, a beach area, a fishing pier and a campground. (For camping information, tel: 904/277-7274.)

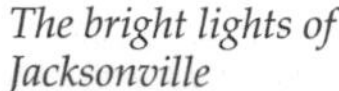

The bright lights of Jacksonville

To find Florida as it used to be, you need to take a step back from the popular coastal strip and explore an area of the state that flourished in the pre-railroad era, but has been largely overlooked for almost a century.

RIVER OF LIFE
The St. Johns River has been an important landmark and highway for a very long time—there is evidence of a human presence along its banks as early as 5000BC. Archeological research has pieced together a picture of these early Floridians. They were tall, dark-skinned people who ate a lot of clams and oysters (mounds of shells bear vivid testimony to that). The shells themselves were used to make tools and to hollow out wooden canoes.

There are various ways of enjoying the river

Florida's largest and most important natural watercourse, the St. Johns is also one of the few rivers in the United States to flow north. It rises in St. Johns Marsh, 8 miles (13km) north of Fort Pierce, and flows parallel to the Atlantic coast for 250 miles (402km) or so before curving east through Jacksonville to reach the ocean.

By the time the first Europeans tried to settle Florida's east coast in the mid-16th century, Timucua Native Americans occupied the northeast corner of Florida. They helped French settlers to build a fort near the mouth of the St. Johns River (which the French called the River of May), and provided them with native corn. The original site of the fort was destroyed during dredging operations in the 1880s, but a reconstruction of the rough wooden stockade based on contemporary drawings is the centerpiece of the **Fort Caroline National Memorial** on the outskirts of Jacksonville (see page 181).

A strategic gateway To control the lower St. Johns River was to control the interior of Florida (and the backdoor to St. Augustine), but until the 19th century, pioneer settlers generally restricted their incursions to the immediate coast. During the 1820s, however, Jacksonville was founded, and trading posts were established upriver. Lumber, sugar cane and citrus, which flourished along the fertile river banks, were shipped north, and the steamboat era brought luxurious passenger steamers south. A popular stop was the fashionable spa at **Green Cove Springs** (www.greencovesprings.com). Its natural spring attracted the patronage of President Grover Cleveland and of chain-store magnate J. C. Penney.

The river is more than 1 mile (1.6km) wide as it rounds an S-bend about **Palatka**. The town was named for the

Steamboat on the St. Johns River

Native American word *pilaklikaha*, meaning "crossing over." Confederate troops trounced a Unionist outpost here in 1864, but this old lumber town is better known as a top bass fishing spot.

South of Palatka, the river runs through Lake George, with the vast 383,573-acre (153,429ha) wilderness of **Ocala National Forest** spreading off to the west. Then it squeezes past the citrus center of **De Land** (see panel).

CITRUS POWER
De Land was founded by a baking powder manufacturer, but is more notable as the scene of Chinese citrus culturist Lue Gim Gong's experiments with cold-weather grapefruit and cherry-sized currants in the 1880s and 1890s. He succeeded in both cases.

Manatees and shell mounds French marine biologist Jacques Cousteau was lured to the St. Johns River to film its endangered manatee population. One of the best places to watch these hefty sea cows is Blue Spring.

Blue Spring State Park (www.floridastateparks.org) at 2100 W. French Avenue, 2 miles (3km) west of Orange City, is a popular winter resort with manatees, which escape the cooler main river to bask in the 72°F (22°C) spring from November to March. For human visitors, there are swimming, fishing and canoeing opportunities here, as well as picnic areas, boat tours, and trips to **Hontoon Island State Park** (www.floridastateparks.org). This 1,650-acre (660ha) island has been a boatyard, cattle ranch and settlement. The Timucua Native Americans built shell mounds, visible from the trail.

Sanford, 200 miles (322km) south of the St. Johns River mouth at Mayport, is the last navigable stretch of the river. When steamboats ceased to ply the river, Sanford settled for raising celery and quiet obscurity. However, things are changing today, with a revival of interest in St. Johns River cruises. This is the place to hop aboard a riverboat for a short narrated sightseeing trip, and keep an eye out for bald eagles, alligators, manatees and deer. For details, contact **Rivership Romance**, 433 N. Palmetto Avenue, Sanford (tel: 407/321-5091 or 800/423-7401).

The St. Johns continues upstream from Sanford, through Lake Harney, to its headwaters in **St. Johns Marsh.** West of Cocoa and Melbourne, there are river camps and recreation areas, such as **Lone Cabbage Fish Camp** (Route 520) and **Camp Holly** (Route 192), which provide fishing and boating facilities, airboat rides and campgrounds.

LITERARY LANDMARK
As early tourists made their way upriver on steamboats, they passed Harriet Beecher Stowe's house on the bank at Mandarin. A famous author since the publication of *Uncle Tom's Cabin* In 1852, she was paid by the riverboat companies to sit out on the lawn and wave to their passengers.

►►► St. Augustine 172 A5

The oldest continuously occupied European settlement in the Continental United States, St. Augustine is definitely "Historyville, USA." It was named in 1565, after the feast day of St. Augustine (August 28), by Pedro Menéndez de Avilés, the Spanish governor of Florida. The settlement predates the British colony at Jamestown by 42 years and the Pilgrims by 55 years. None of the earliest buildings remain, but the 17th-century **Castillo de San Marcos** and a few early 18th-century dwellings have survived in the old Spanish Quarter. These dwellings housed Spanish soldiers garrisoned at the fort, and then British soldiers during their brief occupation of Florida from 1763 to 1783.

When the Spanish returned, they planted citrus trees, built courtyards off the narrow streets, and added balconies to the simple whitewashed houses. The **Cathedral of St. Augustine**, in the town center, contains the oldest written records in the United States, dating from 1594.

St. Augustine was a scruffy little garrison town when the Americans finally acquired Florida in 1821. Yellow fever epidemics and the outbreak of the Seminole Wars discouraged early speculators. After the Civil War, tourists began to venture farther south. A significant visitor in the early 1880s was Standard Oil millionaire Henry Flagler, who later launched his Florida resort hotel chain here with the luxurious **Ponce de León Hotel** in 1888.

Although the grand resorts have had their day—the famous hotel is now a college—tourism is still the city's prime industry. The best way to explore the old town center is on foot, but sightseeing trams and horse-drawn carriages offer an alternative method of getting round the main sights. Across the **Bridge of Lions**, on A1A, St. Augustine's beach annex provides an additional choice of restaurants and accommodations near the landmark black-and-white striped 1874 **lighthouse**.

The Old World arts and crafts area of St. Augustine

GLORIOUS GOLF

Golf is a major visitor attraction in the St. Augustine area, and a handful of top professional golfers make their home here. The first golf course in St. John's County was built in St. Augustine in 1916, and now the centerpiece of World Golf Village, just outside town, is the World Golf Hall of Fame (*Open* Mon–Sat 10–6, Sun noon–6. *Admission: moderate*; tel: 904/940-4000), which celebrates the history of the game and great players through antiques, objects and interactive displays. The Village boasts designer courses, a golf academy, a spa, accommodations and dining.

Castillo de San Marcos, *1 Castillo Drive East* (*Open* daily 8.45–4.45. *Admission: inexpensive;* tel: 904/829-6506, www.nps.gov) St. Augustine's most significant historic site, this star-shaped fortress stands on the foundations of nine previous wooden structures, the earliest dating back to 1565. The foundation stone of the present fort was laid in 1672, and it was constructed of coquina, a soft seashell "rock," which proved a remarkably efficient defensive building material. Assailants' cannon balls simply buried themselves in the walls, so they could be dug out and re-used by the defenders. Linked by curtain walls, diamond-shaped bastions allowed cannons to set up a deadly crossfire. The fortress is surrounded by a moat with a single point of entry (the sallyport), backed up by a portcullis. Around the gun decks, long-barreled cannons and short-nosed mortars were supported by musket fire, and the central courtyard, where soldiers drilled, is enclosed by guardrooms, stores and the powder magazine. A program of costumed events take place throughout the year, bringing the castle's history to life.

Flagler College, *74 King Street* (*Open* foyer daily 8–5, guided tours in summer at 10 and 2. *Admission: inexpensive;* tel: 904/823-3378, www.flagler.edu) Henry M.

Flagler visited St. Augustine during the winter of 1883–1884, and liked what he saw. He returned a year later to build the Ponce de León Hotel, a monumental Spanish/Moorish Revival affair that now houses Flagler College. It was the first major U.S. building to be constructed using poured concrete. The interior was decorated with imported marble, carved oak and Tiffany stained glass. An elegant courtyard leads to the foyer where an elaborately gilded and pointed cupola displays symbolic motifs representing Spain and Florida. Beyond this, the Rotunda has been transformed into a grand college dining hall.

Fountain of Youth, *11 Magnolia Avenue* (*Open* daily 9–5. *Admission: moderate*; tel: 904/829-3168) It is a matter of record that Ponce de León discovered neither legendary Bimini (see page 36) nor the source of eternal youthfulness. But he did discover a spring: There is one in this touristy park. Archeological digs have revealed the existence of early Timucua tribes here and evidence of Christian Native American burial grounds, but guided tours merely scratch the surface of local history. They also include a film show, a planetarium visit which reconstructs the position of the heavens as seen by Ponce de León and an opportunity to sample the famous spring water.

DRESSING UP

St. Augustine residents find any excuse to dress up in period costume. In Spanish Night Watch (third Saturday in June), there is a torchlit procession through the old Spanish Quarter, with "troops" dressed in 18th-century costume, reenacting colonial customs. September's Menendez Landing marks the 1565 Spanish landing on the grounds of the Mission of Nombre de Dios, and the British Night Watch (first weekend in December) marks the British occupation of St. Augustine with a three-day living history reenactment.

Reconstruction of the arrival of explorer Ponce de León at the Fountain of Youth

DOMESTIC ARRANGEMENTS
In 1821, Dr. Seth Peck moved his family to St. Augustine, where they took lodgings in a boarding house at 20 Aviles Street, now known as the Ximenez-Fatio House. Later, the family moved to Pena-Peck House, 143 St. George Street, built for the Spanish Royal Treasurer in 1740. Both houses have been imaginatively restored and provide an intriguing insight into 19th-century domestic life.

Lightner Museum, *75 King Street* (*Open* daily 9–5, last ticket 4pm). *Admission: moderate;* tel: 904/824-2874. www.lightnermuseum.org) Opposite Flagler College, the Lightner displays the decorative arts collections of Chicago newspaper baron Otto C. Lightner in the third of Henry Flagler's former grand hotels. (The second was the restored Casa Monica Hotel across Cordova Street.)

This is a real treasure trove, best visited from top to bottom. The highlight of the collection is the glass on the second floor, featuring the largest gathering of American cut glass: On display are superb Tiffany lamps and other decorative pieces; delicate Venetian glass; and scalloped, frilled, satin-finish, colored and copperized glass. In the basement, the Lightner Antiques Mall occupies the impressive former swimming pool.

Oldest House, *14 St. Francis Street* (*Open* daily 9–5. *Admission: moderate;* tel: 904/824-2872) Also known as the Gonzalez-Alvarez house, after former occupants—Tomas Gonzalez, an early 18th-century artilleryman, and Geronimo Alvarez, who bought the house in 1790—this is one of the best documented houses in the United States. It has a fascinating story, told with great gusto and plenty of incidental detail on the frequent guided tours.

There are traces of a crude palm-thatched wooden habitation here dating from the early 1600s. Some time after the great fire of 1702, this was overlaid with a single-story coquina structure, constructed of blocks made of compacted shell material quarried on Anastasia Island, shipped to the mainland and then cemented into place with "tabby," a mixture of lime, shells and sand.

A wooden second story was added in the mid-18th century by Maria Peavett, the wife of an English soldier. Maria operated a successful tavern and boarding house, and her extraordinary life was the basis for the novel *Maria* by Eugenia Price (on sale in the gift shop). Each room in the house has been furnished in a period relevant to the building's long and colorful history. The gardens are beautiful, with deliciously cool arcades and a picnic area. There is also a **Museum of Florida's Army**, which displays uniforms and weaponry.

Once a luxury Flagler hotel—the Lightner Museum

Some of the curiosities in Ripley's "Believe it or Not!" Museum in St. Augustine

Old Florida Museum, *254 D San Marco Avenue* (*Open* daily 10–5. *Admission: moderate*; tel: 904/824-8874 or 800/813-3208, www.staugustinehistoricalmuseum.org) The most recent museum of history in the city is perhaps one of the most enjoyable. It's an exploration of Native and early Spanish life, where you can try your hand at carving a dugout canoe, grinding corn, making candles or pulverizing shells to make "tabby" used on the floors of Spanish homes. St Augustine's oldest general store has been renovated and also forms part of the complex.

Old St. Augustine Village, *246 St. George Street* (*Open* daily 9–5. *Admission: moderate*; tel: 904/823-9722, www.old-staug-village.com) A preserved block of the city, this open-air museum takes you through 400 years of history. The nine extant buildings date from between 1790 and 1910 and five have period furnishings. At ground level we move to an earlier era, with archeological sites of a 16th-century hospital and early cemetery. The grounds also protect the site where the Emancipation Proclamation, which freed Florida's slaves, was read in 1863. You can explore the objects displayed inside the buildings or wander the shady avenues admiring the architecture.

Ripley's Believe it or Not! Museum, *19 San Marco Avenue* (*Open* end May–Sep 6 daily 9–8 : Sep 7–Memorial Day Sun–Thu 9–7, Fri–Sat 8–9. *Admission: moderate*; tel: 904/824-1606, www.staugustine-ripleys.com) Robert L. Ripley was born in California in 1893, and his story is no less peculiar than most of the strange-but-true exhibits in his museums. He graduated from a career as a cartoonist to become America's master of trivia, collecting weird and wonderful tales and objects from some 198 countries. Opened in 1950, this museum was the first permanent display of his finds and includes such oddities as a shrunken head, grotesque film footage of freaky circus acts and Van Gogh masterpieces re-created in jelly-beans—get the idea?

SMALLER ATTRACTIONS
St. Augustine's trade in things historical extends to a host of smaller attractions, such as the creaky Oldest Wooden Schoolhouse, 14 St. George Street, dating from 1763. The Old Jail, 167 San Marco Avenue, retains its 19th-century cage-like cell block.

FOOD, GLORIOUS FOOD
In 18th-century colonial St. Augustine, food cooked on outdoor fires was provided by hunting, fishing, and kitchen gardens, such as those in the Colonial Spanish Quarter. They are planted with chilis, beans, eggplants, onions and pumpkins, and even the odd citrus tree that the Spanish originally imported to counter the risk of scurvy.

St. Augustine Alligator Farm, *A1A (1 mile/1.6km east of Bridge of Lions)* (*Open* daily 9–5. *Admission: expensive*; tel: 904/824-3337, www.alligatorfarm.com) The alligator farm is the only place where all the planet's 23 species can be viewed. Founded in 1893, the "World's Original Alligator Farm" has added a few interesting extras to its menagerie. There are still plenty of crowd-pulling crocodilians of all shapes and sizes, but visitors will also have the opportunity to see monkeys and tropical birds from South America, giant Galapagos tortoises and snakes from all around the world. There is a boardwalk nature trail leading through the swamps, alligator and reptile shows throughout the day and a petting zoo.

Colonial Spanish Quarter, *Triay House, 33 St. George Street* (*Open* daily 9–5.30. *Admission: moderate*; tel: 904/825-6830, www.historicaugustine.com) Tucked away toward the City Gate end of St. George Street, this is a great living history complex. Plan to spend extra time in this museum, in whose buildings and gardens costumed interpreters explain how life was lived in old St. Augustine.

A group of seven historic buildings dating from the 18th century has been restored and sparsely furnished to recreate colonial life in St. Augustine around the 1740s. Visitors are free to explore the grassy plot and nose around the old houses, and staff in period costumes are on hand to answer any questions and to perform demonstrations. There is a blacksmith in the smithy, sweating over ancient bellows as he fashions cooking utensils and tools. The spinning demonstration includes an explanation of wool dyeing from locally available materials, such as onion skin and bark. Tours are frequent and are worth waiting for.

A five-minute walk away, the **Spanish Military Hospital**, 3 Aviles Street (off the Plaza), depicts the fate of a soldier-patient in the 18th century

Costumed bandsmen lead visitors back to St. Augustine's colorful past in the restored historic Spanish Quarter

Jack Island State Preserve

Slow down and keep a sharp look out for the concealed entrance to this wilderness refuge on A1A, north of Fort Pierce Inlet. It is on the Indian River side of A1A. The 630-acre (252ha) island (*Open* daily 8–dusk. *Admission: inexpensive*; tel: 561/468-3985) is accessible by footbridge from the parking lot and offers a network of trails. The mile-long (1.6km) **Marsh Rabbit Run** is named for a local resident. Marsh rabbits are smaller than their cottontail cousins, with shorter ears and hind legs and darker fur, and can be spotted in the river and the coastal hammock area.

A boardwalk crosses patches of black, red and white mangroves to an observation tower overlooking Indian River, which is an excellent vantage point for birdwatching.

Osprey, brown pelicans, great blue herons and ibis are among the many water birds to feed here.

Walk

Washington Oaks State Gardens

Sandwiched between the Matanzas River and the Atlantic, on both sides of A1A 20 miles (32km) south of St. Augustine, these fine gardens (*Open* daily 8–dusk. *Admission: inexpensive*; tel: 386/446-6780) are a hidden treasure with three distinctly individual walking habitats; it is easy to take in all three within a couple of hours.

Starting in the west, the nature trail makes a loop along the river through lush coastal hammock woods and tidal marshes inhabited by a host of water birds.

Woodpeckers and red cardinals flit among the trees, and there is a good chance that you will spot raccoons and opossums. (A word of warning, however: This is prime mosquito territory.) To the north, part of the hammock has been transformed into a marvelous formal garden round a faintly smelly spring.

Shaded by towering mature live oaks and palms, soft sawdust paths and luxuriant ferns encircle beds of azaleas, camellias, hydrangeas and a headily scented rose garden. On the beach side, a boardwalk traverses a swathe of coastal scrub alive with butterflies and the flash of brilliantly colored scrub jays. At low tide, its yellow-orange sand is coarse with crushed seashells and strewn with seams of coquina that form well-stocked rock pools. Look for starfish, tiny crabs and sea anenomes. Beware of hidden rocks when swimming.

Marshlands at dusk

192 *Kennedy Space Center: getting together with an astronaut...*

...and close encounters with the Space Shuttle

▶▶▶ Space Coast *172 A3*

Sandwiched between the "First Coast" to the north and the "Treasure Coast" in the south is the "Space Coast," home of the **Kennedy Space Center**. In addition to the high-tech marvels of the National Aeronautics and Space Administration (NASA), the area has rapidly developed into a family-oriented vacation center, offering every possible Florida tourist attraction with Walt Disney World just an hour's drive away.

The four principal communities, **Cocoa**, **Melbourne**, **Rockledge** and **Titusville**, all lie on the west bank of the Indian River, linked to the coastal peninsula by bridges. To the south, Melbourne is home to the **Brevard Zoo**, *8225 N. Wickham Road* (*Open* daily 9.30–5. *Admission: moderate*; tel: 321/254-9453, www.brevardzoo.org), which features shaded boardwalks through a Latin American jungle area, and Expedition Africa, a kayak ride through wetlands and plains. To the north, **Cocoa Beach** is "Surf City" (don't miss the **Ron Jon Surf Shop**, 4151 N. Atlantic Avenue); and **Port Canaveral** is a cruise-line terminal.

Nature lovers will be amazed by the beauty of **Merritt Island National Wildlife Refuge**, which shares a boundary with the Kennedy Space Center, as does undeveloped **Playalinda Beach** on the Canaveral National Seashore. The best dive spots are in the south of the region, around **Sebastian Inlet**. Things cultural have not been overlooked either, with Melbourne's fine modern **Maxwell C. King Center for the Performing Arts**, *3865 N. Wickham Road* (tel: 321/242-2219) playing host to concerts, dance and theater productions.

Cocoa Village On the west bank of the Indian River, just south of S.R. 520, the historic Cocoa Village district has been attractively restored, with cobblestone streets, brick sidewalks and Victorian shopfronts. There is plenty of browsing to do among the 50 art and antiques galleries, crafts stores, and boutiques. Elegant **Porcher House**, built in 1916 by citrus-grove owner Edward Postell Porcher, is on the National Register of Historic Places and is open to visitors, as is the 1924 **Cocoa Village Playhouse**.

Guided tours of the area are offered by the **Brevard Museum of History and Natural Science**, *2201 Michigan Avenue* (*Open* Tue–Sat 10–4, Sun noon–4; tour information, tel: 321/632-1830, www.brevardmuseum.com). Here exhibitions trace local history from the original Native American inhabitants through 16th-century Spanish incursions to the pioneers. There is also a hands-on Discovery Room for children, and 22 acres (9ha) with nature trails laid out around the museum grounds.

Kennedy Space Center Visitor Complex, *NASA Parkway (S.R. 405)* (*Open* daily 9–dusk. *Admission: expensive*; tel: 321/449-444, www.ksc.nasa.gov) An armchair astronaut's dream and launchpad for bus tours of the third most popular visitor destination in the state, the Kennedy Space Center's visitor facility offers a fascinating journey through the history of America's space program from the 1950s up until the present, with a hint of what is to come. Arrive early to beat the crowds and book tickets for the bus tours and IMAX films before the lines start to stretch around the block.

Rocketry on display

LIFT OFF
Cruised Miami Beach? Dived the Keys? Eaten alligator and done Disney? Here is a chance to sample one more Florida specialty, a Space Shuttle launch from the Kennedy Space Center. Advance information about schedules can be obtained from Florida Launch Information, Kennedy Space Center, FL 32899 (tel: 321/449-4400, www.kennedyspacecenter.com; www.pafb.af.mil or www.floridatoday.com/space). The limited number of launch passes allowing viewing from inside the security gates is usually booked well in advance, but there are excellent vantage points along U.S. 1 at Titusville and from Cape Canaveral City (Route A1A). Titusville permits roadside parking from 24 hours before launch time.

Once you've bought your tickets, the first stop is the Visitor Complex, which offers a range of exhibits and shows as well as ticketing, and shopping and dining opportunities. Take time to stroll around the **Rocket Garden**, with its towering bunch of original manned and unmanned craft. Exhibits include Mission to Mars, where NASA has made great strides since the year 2000, and Exploration in the New Millennium, where the cooperative venture, the International Space Station, is among the topics explored.

Do not miss a chance to see the stunning 35-minute **The Dream Is Alive** IMAX presentation, with seat-shuddering footage of a shuttle launch, astronauts working in space, and shots of the Earth translated onto a screen five-and-a-half stories high and 70ft (21m) across. Astronaut Encounter is your change to meet a real off-world explorer, and have your photograph taken with a suited astronaut.

Tours Two bus tours depart from the Visitor Complex. The must-do **Kennedy Space Center Tour** runs throughout the day and ventures to the heart of NASA's Florida facility to **Launch Complex 39**. Along the way, the tour passes the vast **V.A.B. (Vehicle Assembly Building)**, one of the largest-volume structures in the world (129.5 million cubic feet/3.7million cubic meters), where Space Shuttles are assembled before being rolled by monster Crawler

(Continued on page 196)

STAR SPOTTING
For a view of the heavens right up close, take a trip to the Astronaut Memorial Planetarium and Observatory, 1519 Clearlake Road, Cocoa (*Open* evenings, call for schedules. *Admission: inexpensive*; tel: 321/433-3732). Observe the rings of Saturn and study the surface of Mars 450 million light years away. Then catch an Iwerks movie presentation or a rock laser show.

A distinctive peninsula that juts out from the Florida coastline into the Atlantic, Cape Canaveral was named by Spanish sailors for the hollow reeds that grow abundantly in the area. Contrary to the widespread misconception, this region is by no means all given over to the space business; in fact, most of it is devoted to wilderness and wildlife.

BEYOND CANAVERAL
Away from Cape Canaveral, downtown Melbourne seems an odd place to go manatee watching, but the Crane Creek Promenade boardwalk along Melbourne Avenue (west of Front Street Park) is a prime site to spot these gentle vegetarian giants. At the Audubon Society's Turkey Creek Sanctuary in Palm Bay, a 4,000ft (1,200m) boardwalk traverses three distinct Florida plant communities that attract a wealth of native wildlife. There is another chance to go turtle-watching with the Sea Turtle Preservation Society (tel: 321/676-1701), which organizes nesting-season walks along the coast between Satellite Beach and Spessard Holland Park.

Merritt Island is located between the cape and the mainland, marooned to east and west by the Banana and Indian rivers, and bordered to the north by Mosquito Lagoon and the **Canaveral National Seashore**. The southern portion of this island houses the **Kennedy Space Center**. An area of 220sq miles (570sq km) in the north is given over to the **Merritt Island National Wildlife Refuge** (*Open* daily dawn–dusk). For an introduction to the wildlife and native flora found in the reserve, stop in at the Visitor Center, off S.R. 402 (*Open* Mon–Fri 8–4.30, Sat–Sun 9–5. *Closed* Sun in May–Oct. *Admission free*; tel: 321/861-0667, www.merrittisland.fw.org).

Since it emerged from the ocean around 1 million years ago, this 25-mile-long (40km) barrier island has been battered and sculpted by the elements. It has protected the coastline and has developed a wide variety of habitats that harbor around 330 species of birds, 31 kinds of mammals, 117 types of fish and 65 kinds of amphibians and reptiles. A sad statistic is that 21 of these species are endangered, more than in any other single wildlife refuge in the whole United States.

Merritt Island's diverse habitats range from pocket-size freshwater lagoons to vast saltwater estuaries; brackish marshes give way to hardwood hammocks and to areas of pine flatwoods. Flourishing within the shallow marshlands, a nutritious smorgasbord of worms, snails, crabs, clams and fish attracts crocodiles and shore and wading water birds. During winter, a further 23 species of migratory waterfowl take advantage of these open-water feeding grounds, while pelicans, cormorants, great blue herons, egrets and wood storks live here year-round. The well-watered hardwood hammocks provide an ideal environment for a lush backdrop of exotic bromeliads (air plants) and tropical and subtropical plants. Pileated woodpeckers, squirrels and armadillos are also common.

Walks and trails For a closer look at hammock environments, there are two walking trails off S.R. 402, east of the visitor center. **Oak Hammock Trail** is a 0.5 mile (800m) stroll through a subtropical forest, with interpretative signboards along the route. The **Palm Hammock Trail** is a more interesting 2-mile (3km) hike that includes hardwood forest, cabbage palm hammocks and boardwalk sections over open marshland. Early morning and late

Watching whales is a fascinating spectacle

afternoon are the best times to undertake the **Black Point Wildlife Drive**, a 7-mile (11km) one-way circuit off S.R. 406. There are parking areas for observing the mud flats and lagoon areas, which bustle with bird activity during the height of the winter migration (January/February). A 5-mile (8km) marsh hike, the **Cruickshank Trail**, begins at Stop 8; there is an observation tower a 5-minute walk from the parking lot. The optimum time to visit the park is October to April; bring mosquito repellent year-round.

Canaveral National Seashore Extending north for 24 miles (38.5km) from Merritt Island toward Daytona, this is one of Florida's few remaining areas of undeveloped coastal dunes. The 57,000-acre (22,800ha) preserve also contains **Mosquito Lagoon**, a shallow saltmarsh estuary with particularly interesting wildlife, reflecting its location at the point where temperate and tropical climates meet. Animals and birds typical to both habitats coexist around the marsh and areas of coastal forest, which are thick with oaks, cedars and wild orange trees. White-tailed deer, bobcats, raccoons and rattlesnakes hide out in the woodlands, while dolphins, manatees, osprey and roseate spoonbills enjoy the rich lagoon feeding grounds.

From May through August, the warm sandy beaches are an ideal nesting ground for green and leatherback sea turtles. Starting in September, the original "snowbirds" —bald eagles, warblers, even Arctic peregrine falcons— journey up to 6,000 miles (9,660km) to winter here. In early spring, migratory right whales calve offshore. There is parking and access to the seashore from **Playalinda Beach** (S.R. 402). Visitors should keep to official beach access points and not climb the dunes, or pick seagrasses which anchor the fragile environment. During summer, guided **turtle walks** are led by Merritt Island rangers.

CRUISE FROM CANAVERAL
The closest port to the Orlando area, Port Canaveral is booming. The growing popularity of two-destination vacations has not escaped Disney, whose two fun-packed cruise ships offer seven-day land-and-sea packages, combining a stay at Walt Disney World with a cruise to the Bahamas. Other major cruise operators serving Port Canaveral include Cape Canaveral Cruise Line, Carnival Cruise Lines, Premier Cruise Lines, Royal Caribbean International and Sterling Casino Lines.

(Continued from page 193)

Transporters to the launchpad. The highlight of the tour is a visit to the spectacular $37-million **Apollo/Saturn V Center**, which you can explore for as long as you wish. In addition to the 363ft (584m) Saturn V rocket in the main hall, there are interactive exhibits, the dramatic Firing Room Theater presentation, and a re-created moon walk. On the return trip to the Visitor Complex, there is a stop at **International Space Station Center** where components for the 21st-century space facility are made and tested. Aboard the tour bus, the recorded commentary is by James Lovell, Commander of Apollo 11.

The **Cape Canaveral Then & Now Tour** (several departures daily; check schedules) visits Cape Canaveral Air Force Station, where NASA launched its operations in 1958. The tour explores the site of the early Mercury and Gemini space projects.

U.S. Astronaut Hall of Fame, *NASA Parkway (S.R. 405)* (*Open* daily 10–7, last admission 5. *Admission: expensive;* tel: 321/269-6100) A short drive from the Kennedy Space Center, the Hall of Fame, a showcase for the country's astronauts and their historic missions, is particularly user-friendly for children. Objects and rare video footage turn the spotlight on the men of the Mercury space program, and there is plenty of stomach-churning fun to be had in a variety of simulators, including a full-scale replica orbiter. The complex is also home to **Camp KSC** (information, tel: 321/449-4400), which offers live-in five-day camp programs for children in grades 4–7.

Valiant Air Command Warbird Museum, *6600 Tico Road (at Space Coast Regional Airport, S.R. 405), Titusville* (*Open* daily 10–6. *Admission: moderate*; tel: 321/268-1941, www.vacwarbirds.org) More than 350 vintage World War II and postwar military planes are housed here. Each March the collection comes alive for the **Valiant Air Command Warbird Airshow**, when fans can see the planes put through their paces.

A shuttle replica at the Astronaut Hall of Fame

Drive

Along the East Coast

An easy day's excursion from the Space Coast, this drive follows A1A from Cocoa Beach down to the Treasure Coast around Fort Pierce.

Cocoa Beach is a bastion of surfie culture and fluorescent beachwear—both in and out of the water. Just south of Cocoa Beach, the huge **Patrick Air Force Base** borders A1A to the west for the next 5 miles (8km). A display of military rocketry is set up outside the Technical Headquarters.

A seamless run of beach communities continues to spill down the coast: Satellite Beach, Indian Harbor, Indialantic and Melbourne Beach, where A1A does a little signposted jig slightly inland before the road narrows. It is 14 miles (22.5km) from the southern city limits of Melbourne Beach to the entrance to Sebastian Inlet State Recreation Area.

This is a great place to stop off. The premier saltwater fishing location on the East Coast boasts two Atlantic jetties and a catwalk, giving access to waters teeming with bluefish, redfish, snook and Spanish mackerel. Surfers flock to a reserved beach area, and there are plenty of opportunities for snorkeling and excellent swimming off sparkling white beaches.

To visit the McLarty Museum, continue on A1A, then follow the signs.

On the site of an old Spanish salvage camp, the **McLarty Treasure Museum** (*Open* daily 10–4.30. *Admission: inexpensive*; tel: 772/589-2147) is the place to check out the history of Spanish shipwrecks off this part of the coast. There are several more beach-access points carved through the thick coastal barrier of palms, oaks, sea grapes and pines.

Rejoin A1A and continue for 14 miles (22.5km) to Vero Beach.

Vero Beach (see panel, page 178) is a wealthy resort town off A1A. The main street is **Ocean Drive**, with its exclusive shopping district and the eccentric **Driftwood Inn**.

Drive 20 miles (32km) to Fort Pierce.

There is more fishing, snorkeling, and swimming at **Fort Pierce Inlet State Recreation Area**. The Treasure Coast itself has several attractions such as the **Elliott Museum**, right on A1A before Stuart, and **Gilbert's Bar House of Refuge**, at the southern tip of Hutchinson Island.

A1A rejoins U.S. 1 at Stuart.

F4-4 Fighter Race Corsair on show at Valiant Air Command Museum

REGION HIGHLIGHTS

SKILLED MARINERS
Southwest Florida was once Calusa territory. Skilled mariners and fishermen, these Native Americans ranged far and wide, sometimes venturing as far south as Cuba. Archeologists have discovered Calusa objects from around 5000BC in some of the many ancient ceremonial, burial, and refuse shell mounds dotted about the barrier islands and mainland back bays of the region.

LAPPED BY THE warm, translucent waters of the Gulf of Mexico, Florida's West Coast is an alluring mix of white-sand beaches, water sports, world-class museums and wildlife. Once the butt of retirement jokes, it has developed into a cosmopolitan vacation destination offering a broad range of accommodations and diversions, including areas of exceptional natural beauty.

The early Spanish explorers—Juan Ponce de León, Pánfilo de Narváez and Hernando de Soto—all stopped by, but were discouraged by warring Native Americans and steaming, insect-infested mangrove belts. Coastal navigation was perilous because of reefs and shoals. This was to the advantage of legendary 18th-century pirate Gasparilla, who was able to operate unhindered.

The US Army arrived in the 1820s, and a handful of fishing settlements began to grow along the coast. **Tampa**, the Gulf Coast's largest city, was put on the map by Henry Plant's railroad in the 1880s. Vincente Martinez Ybor and his cigar industry added the city's Cuban connection, which remains strong even today. Across the bay, **Pinellas County**, with its 28 miles (45km) of barrier-island beaches, St. Petersburg, Clearwater and Largo, is Tampa's Gulf shore playground. To the north, Dunedin and **Tarpon Springs** provide a further touch of cultural diversity—Scottish and Greek, respectively—and the Manatee Coast continues up to Crystal River.

South of Tampa, **Sarasota** is a cultural capital, and is where circus king John Ringling built a fabulous estate and an Italian Renaissance-style museum to house his art collection. Sarasota's two performing arts centers feature nationally acclaimed programs. The "City of Palms," **Fort Myers** is renowned for being the winter home of inventor Thomas Alva Edison and for its offshore islands. The South Seas paradise of the Lee Island Coast is shelling heaven for seashell seakers, and Edison earned the city its nickname by planting the first royal palms along McGregor Boulevard. At the southern end of the coastal strip, elegantly manicured **Naples** luxuriates in social circles and shopping malls worthy of Palm Beach. There are excellent golfing opportunities, too, and it is also an ideal base for excursions into the Everglades.

Fun and games on the coast: Naples Beach

West Coast

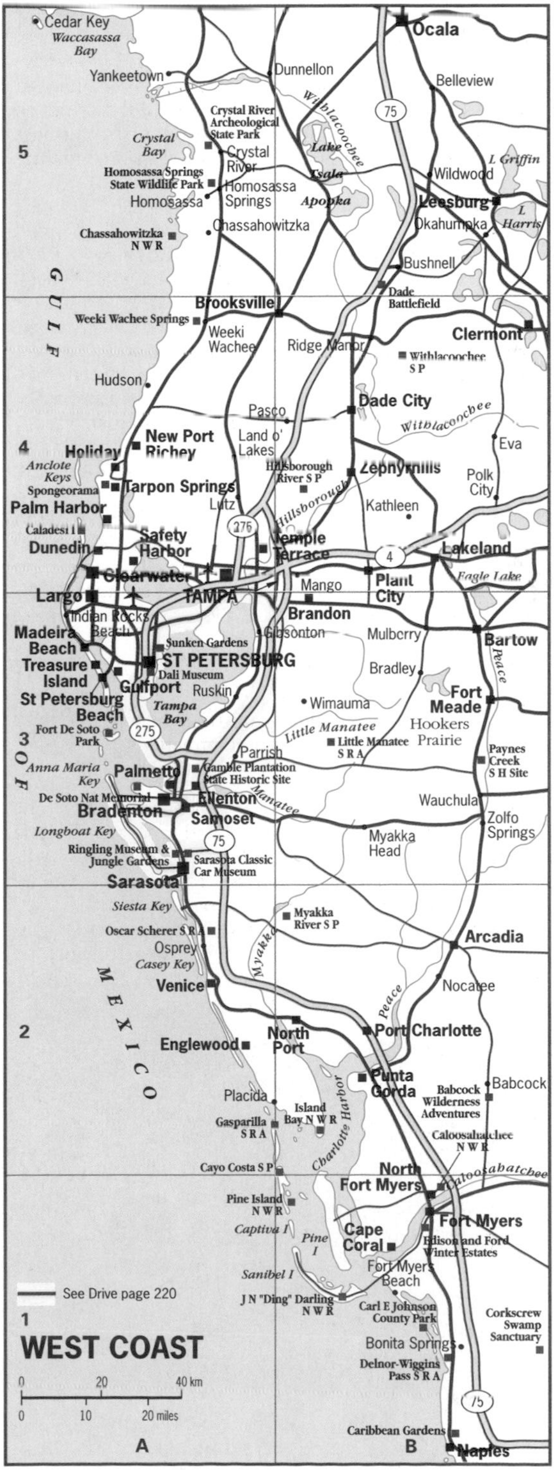

Cedar Key
Waccasassa Bay
Yankeetown
Dunnellon
Ocala
Belleview
75
Withlacoochee
Crystal River Archeological State Park
Crystal River
Lake Tsala Apopka
Crystal Bay
Homosassa Springs State Wildlife Park
Homosassa
Homosassa Springs
Wildwood
L Griffin
Leesburg
Okahumpka
L Harris
Chassahowitzka NWR
Chassahowitzka
Bushnell
Dade Battlefield
GULF OF MEXICO
Brooksville
Weeki Wachee Springs
Weeki Wachee
Ridge Manor
Clermont
Withlacoochee SP
Hudson
Pasco
Dade City
Withlacoochee
Eva
New Port Richey
Land o' Lakes
Holiday
Anclote Keys
Spongeorama
Tarpon Springs
Hillsborough River SP
Zephyrhills
Polk City
Hillsborough
Kathleen
Palm Harbor
Lutz
275
Caladesi I
Dunedin
Safety Harbor
Temple Terrace
4
Lakeland
Clearwater
TAMPA
Mango
Plant City
Eagle Lake
Largo
Indian Rocks Beach
Brandon
Madeira Beach
Gibsonton
Mulberry
Bartow
Sunken Gardens
Treasure Island
ST PETERSBURG
Dali Museum
Bradley
Peace
Gulfport
Ruskin
Fort Meade
St Petersburg Beach
Tampa Bay
Wimauma
Hookers Prairie
Fort De Soto Park
275
Little Manatee
Little Manatee SRA
Paynes Creek S H Site
Parrish
Anna Maria Key
Palmetto
Gamble Plantation State Historic Site
De Soto Nat Memorial
Ellenton
Manatee
Wauchula
Bradenton
Samoset
Zolfo Springs
Longboat Key
Myakka Head
75
Ringling Museum & Jungle Gardens
Sarasota Classic Car Museum
Sarasota
Siesta Key
Myakka River SP
Oscar Scherer SRA
Arcadia
Osprey
Myakka
Casey Key
Venice
Nocatee
Peace
North Port
Port Charlotte
Englewood
Punta Gorda
Babcock
Babcock Wilderness Adventures
Placida
Island Bay NWR
Charlotte Harbor
Gasparilla SRA
Caloosahatchee NWR
Cayo Costa SP
North Fort Myers
Caloosahatchee
Pine Island NWR
Fort Myers
Captiva I
Pine I
Cape Coral
Edison and Ford Winter Estates
Fort Myers Beach
Sanibel I
See Drive page 220
J N "Ding" Darling NWR
Carl E Johnson County Park
Corkscrew Swamp Sanctuary
WEST COAST
Bonita Springs
Delnor-Wiggins Pass SRA
0 20 40 km
0 10 20 miles
75
Caribbean Gardens
Naples
1
2
3
4
5
A
B

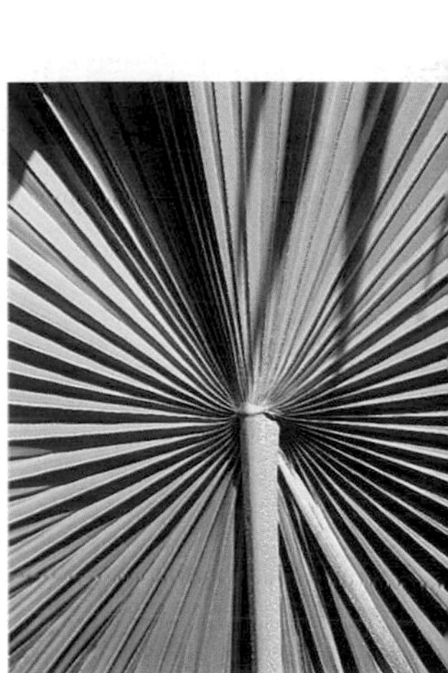

ESTERO BAY BOAT TOURS
A fascinating introduction to local natural history, Charlie Weeks runs a one-man boat tour that combines knowledgable commentaries with a spot of showmanship. There is not a nesting spot, manatee playground or fishing hole on the back bay that he doesn't know about, and you'll learn about Calusa Indians, too. Daily tours morning, afternoon and dusk; call for information and schedules, tel: 941/922-2200. The Weeks' Fish Camp is 4.7 miles (7.5km) north of Bonita Springs, off U.S. 41 at the end of Coconut Road.

Bonita Beach

► Bonita Springs *199 B1*

Sandwiched between the ever-encroaching cities of Naples and Fort Myers, Bonita occupies a rare pocket of the southwest Gulf shore, where large-scale development has been kept to a minimum. The virgin coastline of the **Carl E. Johnson Country Park**, off Hickory Boulevard, is one of the few remaining stretches of natural shell beach, or take a hike around **Lovers' Key State Recreation Area**. Bonita's back-bay estuary area is teeming with bird life; there are also manatees here, and the fishing is great. For after-dark entertainment the **Naples/Fort Myers Greyhound Track**, *1601 Bonita Beach Road (at Old U.S. 41;* tel: 239/992-2411) lures in the spectators and speculators for its races.

Corkscrew Swamp Sanctuary, *Route 846 (20 miles/32km east of U.S. 41)* (*Open* daily 7–7.30 Apr 12–Sep; 7–5.30 Oct–Apr 11. *Admission: moderate*; tel: 239/348-9151, www.audubon.org) Corkscrew was once the northern tip of southwest Florida's immense Big Cypress Swamp. The 11,000-acre (4,400ha) sanctuary preserves America's largest remaining unspoiled stand of bald cypress trees and is a unique natural wildlife habitat. The National Audubon Society recognized the area's importance in 1912, when poachers roamed the swamp slaughtering wood storks and egrets for their feathers—much in demand as fashion accessories. Today, the swamp is one of the Society's greatest treasures and home to large populations of rare woodstorks as well as several species of wild orchid that can be seen during the winter months. The best time to visit is early morning before the heat of the day drives the wildlife into the protective shade. (See Walk on page 215.)

Lovers' Key State Recreation Area, *8700 Estero*

Boulevard/C.R. 865 (*Open* daily 8–dusk. *Admission: expensive*; tel: 239/463-4588, www.floridastateparks.org) Encompassing two islands and a couple of uninhabited islets, this Gulf-side preserve combines recreational activities such as canoeing, biking and hiking trails, shell-collecting and fishing with birdwatching and wildlife-spotting ranging from manatees and dolphins to turtles. There are snack-bar and picnicking facilities, too.

▶ Bradenton *199 A3*

Bradenton lies on the southern bank of the Manatee River and makes a good starting point for a trip to west Florida's only true antebellum building, the **Gamble Mansion** at Ellenton (see page 204). Bradenton's beach lies out to the west, on **Anna Maria Key**, a real old-fashioned narrow beachfront lined with clapboard houses, fast-food and ice-cream stands, plus a few surfies who do their best to ride the relatively tame Gulf waves. A detour via the beach makes a change from the highway if traveling to or from Sarasota.

De Soto National Memorial, *75th Street* (*Open* daily 9–5. *Admission free*; tel: 941/792-0458, www.nps.gov) This memorial park commemorates Spanish explorer Hernando de Soto, who is said to have landed at this very spot in May 1539. His 600-man expedition also included 350 horses, bloodhounds and greyhounds for hunting, pigs, weapons and tons of supplies. Park rangers dress up in period costumes (December to April) and reenact life in an early settlement. There is also a good nature trail (see Walk on page 215).

South Florida Museum and Bishop Planetarium, *201 W. 10th Street* (*Open* Tue–Sat 10–5, Sun noon–5. *Admission: moderate*; tel: 941/746-4131, www.southfloridamuseum.org) The museum's main attraction is Snooty, an 8ft-long (2.5m), 700 lb (315kg) male manatee, who has lived here since 1949. Born in captivity at the Miami Seaquarium in 1948, Snooty is fed four times a day—some 24 heads of lettuce, 16 apples, two vitamin pills and a pineapple—and after years as a solitary bachelor has recently acquired a series of poolmates who are raised and released into the wild. The museum itself provides good dioramas of Native American life displayed together with archeological finds—a reconstruction of a midden (shell mound) and a burial mound and the Tallant Collection of 15,000 Native objects collected from more than 130 sites around the state in the 1930s and 40s.. The **Bishop Planetarium** presents daily astronomy shows and weekend laser light shows (Fri–Sat).

▶▶ Clearwater and the Pinellas County Beaches *199 A4*

Twin pole of the Pinellas County beaches with St. Petersburg to the south, Clearwater proper is on the mainland, but all the action is along Clearwater Beach on the barrier islands lining the Gulf of Mexico.

Beaches Pinellas County boasts 35 miles (56km) of coastline, most of it maintained under the public parks system. In fact, it is so well cared for that beach scientists regularly

GREAT EXPECTATIONS

In 1894, Dr. Cyrus Teed and followers of his eccentric religious sect, the Koreshan Unity, moved to a site near Bonita Springs, where they planned to build a city for 10 million people. At the height of its popularity, the settlement attracted around 250 inhabitants. Tours of the Koreshan State Historic Site, U.S. 41 at Corkscrew Road, include descriptions of Teed's bizarre belief that mankind lives on the inner surface of a hollow globe containing the galaxy at its heart. The sect's commendable belief in equal rights for women was considered just as outlandish in 19th-century Florida.

HIGHLAND GAMES
Not much more than a caber's throw from Greek Tarpon Springs is a corner of Florida with strong Scottish roots. Dunedin's Hibernian links were forged in the 1860s, when Scottish merchants founded the first settlement here and gave it the Gaelic name meaning "peaceful rest." Each spring, the town pulls in the crowds for Highland Games, complete with bagpipes, a military tattoo and much swaggering around in kilts.

rank Clearwater Beach, Caladesi Island State Park and St. Petersburg's Fort De Soto Park among the Top Ten beaches in the U.S.

North of Clearwater, **Honeymoon Island** and **Caladesi Island** (see below) are two of the last natural barrier islands on the coast with beautiful white-sand beaches. **Clearwater Beach** is reached from the mainland via the Memorial Causeway; then head south for **Sand Key**'s fabulous Gulf-shore beach; fashionably sedate **Belleair Beach**, and **Belleair Shores**; **Indian Rocks Beach**, with its 41ft (12m) fishing pier, the longest in the state; **Redington Shores Beach**, where the famed Suncoast Seabird Sanctuary houses around 500 rescued birds; and **Madeira Beach**, which fronts funky John's Pass Village, a shopping and dining enclave with a scenic waterfront stroll along the boardwalk. Treasure hunters be warned: **Treasure Island**, a section of beach and hotels, was just a name dreamed up as a promotional gimmick in the land-boom era, and hopes should not be raised too high.

Next stop along the shores is **St. Petersburg Beach**, the busiest of all, dominated by the vast pink outline of the 1928 Don Cesar Hotel. This land-boom folly of staggering proportions was a playground for the rich and famous, from F. Scott Fitzgerald to Babe Ruth. Finally, top-rated **Fort De Soto Park** encompasses the tip of the peninsula.

Caladesi Island State Park (*Open* daily 8am–dusk. *Admission: inexpensive*; tel: 727/469-5918, www.floridastateparks.org. Information from Honeymoon Island S.R.A.) It is a short ferry hop to this natural barrier island, where the only inhabitants are birds, armadillos and the occasional alligator. Caladesi was once a part of a larger barrier island linked to Honeymoon Island, its neighbor to the north, but it was annexed by hurricanes in 1848 and 1921, and has remained undisturbed, save for a

The West Coast: sun, sea and palms

Sunset over Clearwater

small development near the dock and a ranger station. Visitors will find sandy swimming beaches linked by boardwalks to picnic and changing facilities, as well as diving and shell-collecting opportunities and a 3-mile (5km) nature trail. There is boat access to the island from Clearwater, and from Honeymoon Island State Recreation Area, reached by Causeway Boulevard from Dunedin.

Clearwater Marine Aquarium, *249 Windward Passage* (*Open* Mon–Fri 9–5, Sat 9–4, Sun 11–4. *Admission: moderate;* tel: 727/441-1790, www.cmaquarium.org) Not far from Clearwater Beach, this aquarium has a dual function—as a tourist attraction, showing sea creatures in huge tanks, and as a rehabilitation unit for injured sea turtles and marine mammals such as otters. Displays focus on local marine life. Among the best are the Mangrove/Seagrass Marsh Tank, with a "Window to the Sea" tank (they usually have over 30 patients). There are also aquariums of loggerhead turtles, rays and other exotic species. The aquarium also offers two-hour Sea Life Safari Cruises with a marine biologist and guided Kayak Adventures in Clearwater Harbor and St. Joseph's Sound, as well as one- to four-day Marine Life Adventures to study endangered animal and plant species.

▶ Crystal River

199 A5

North of Tampa on U.S. 19

Crystal River is best known for its warm springs. More than 100 of them rise around Kings Bay and attract manatees, especially during the winter months (Dec–Mar). These vegetarian mammals can weigh up to 3,000 lbs (1,350kg), and are quite safe to swim with. For information about diving with the manatees, boat trips and canoe

CRUISING FROM CLEARWATER

Starlite Cruises offer several options from the Clearwater Beach Marina or from St. Pete Beach. The *Starlite Princess Riverboat* makes daytime sightseeing cruises and jazz cruises (Tue, Wed, Fri, Sat), while the modern *Starlite Majesty* sets sail on dinner cruises with live entertainment (Tue–Sun). For more information and reservations, tel: 727/462-2628.

GENTLE GIANTS
The aquatic West Indian (Florida) manatee evolved from a four-footed terrestrial mammal thousands of years ago. Shaped like an Idaho potato with the face of a gentle boxer dog, and a spatulate tail like a beaver's, you can still see the outline of three or four toe nails on their fore limbs. These gentle giants can grow up to 14ft (4m) long and weigh in at over one ton, but their vegetarian diet consists of little more than aquatic grasses found in rivers and estuarine areas. When calves are born they have a pinky hue to their gray-brown skin. A healthy manatee (that avoids the propellors of power boats!) can expect to live for 50–60 years.

Storm clouds over the Crystal River

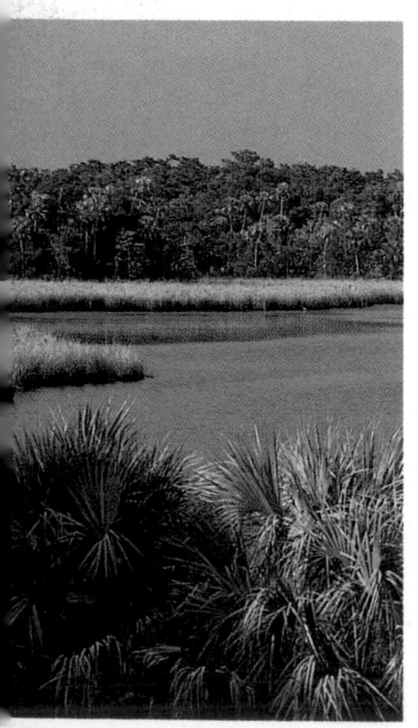

rentals in the **Crystal River National Wildlife Refuge**, contact the Citrus County Chamber of Commerce, at Crystal River, *28 N.W. U.S. 19*, tel: 352/795-3149, www.fws.gov.

Just north of the town, the **Crystal River Archeological State Park**, *3400 Museum Point North* (*Open* daily 8am–dusk; visitor center 9–5. *Admission: inexpensive*; tel: 352/795-3817, www.floridastateparks.org) is one of the oldest and longest continuously inhabited Native American sites in Florida. The six-mound complex was an important ceremonial center from around 200BC to AD1400; archeologists have uncovered more than 400 graves filled with prehistoric objects ranging from everyday tools and weapons to a sophisticated astronomical calendar.

►► Ellenton's Gamble Plantation (State Historic Site) *199 A3*

3708 Patten Avenue (U.S. 301 E.), Ellenton, tel: 941/723-4536, www.floridastateparks.org
Open: daily 8–dusk, visitor center 8–4.30; tours of house Thu–Mon. Admission: house: inexpensive ; park: free
One of southwest Florida's first settlers, Major Robert Gamble was granted the original 160-acre (65ha) plot of land here in 1844. The estate grew to 3,500 acres (1,416ha) along the Manatee River. Sugar cane was refined in the plantation's mill; citrus, wild grapes and olives were shipped to New Orleans. Gamble built himself a classic two-story antebellum mansion from tabby (limestone and shell blocks cemented with molasses, lime, sand and water) and brick, its broad verandas supported by 18 columns. To keep the house cool, he made it only one room wide, and the 2ft(60cm) whitewashed walls are lined with loose-shuttered windows aligned to catch the breeze. Great care has been taken to maintain the authentic period interior, and the house is also a memorial to Confederate secretary of state Judah P. Benjamin, who took refuge here in 1865 before he escaped to England.

►►► Fort Myers and the Lee Island Coast *199 B1*

Thomas Alva Edison, the town's most famous winter resident, had it about right when he predicted, back in 1914, that "there is only one Fort Myers, and 90 million people are going to find it out." Airport gateway to the southwest coast, Fort Myers covers a lot of ground. The historic and commercial downtown district lies on the south bank of the Caloosahatchee River, with North Fort Myers and Cape Coral across the water. Hotel-lined Fort Myers Beach is 20 miled (32km) south on Estero Island. Meanwhile, life on the offshore islands and keys is still largely a *mañana* affair of palm-fringed sands, fabulous seashells, scenic boat trips and deep-sea fishing. Sports fishermen from across the world travel to Boca Grande for a chance to lure a mighty tarpon, while the "Sanibel stoop" is an affliction of shell gatherers harvesting the treasures washed up on that island's white-sand beaches.

Babcock Wilderness Adventures, *8000 S.R. 31, Punta Gorda (9.5miles/15km north of S.R. 78)* (*Open* Nov–May, 9–3; Jun–Oct, mornings only. *Admission: expensive*; tel: 941/489-3911 or 1-800/500-5583; reservations only, www.babcockwilderness.com) An exciting swamp-buggy ride allows a unique look around the vast 90,000-acre (36,000ha) Babcock Crescent B Ranch. Logging baron E V Babcock bought the property in 1914, and logged the cypress swamp during the 1930s. However, he recognized the importance of the trees in the swamp-filtration process, and at the heart of the property, the clear, brown, tannin-rich waters of 10,000-acre (4,000ha) Telegraph Cypress Swamp—so named because the telegraph wires had to be routed around it—reflect an amazing display of curious "cypress knees," protrusions around the base of the cypress tree trunk, uncluttered by weed or grass. Here, birds and alligators thrive, and a boardwalk leads to the cougar enclosure, where native American panthers live in a natural habitat. The 32-seat swamp buggies, carved from old trucks, make a 90-minute circuit (there is also a 10-mile/16km Off-Road Eco-Bike Tour). There are normally sightings of the ranch's bison herd, unusual crossbreed Senepol cattle and quarter horses, plus unscheduled appearances by wild hogs, turkey, deer and snakes.

Calusa Nature Center and Planetarium, *3450 Ortiz Avenue (north of Colonial)* (*Open* Mon–Sat 9–5, Sun 11–5. *Admission: inexpensive;* tel: 239/275-3435, www.calusanature.com) Founded in 1970, on a 105-acre (42ha) plot, the Nature Center was specifically designed with children in mind. In the reception area, there is a collection of snakes, tree frogs, terrapins, baby alligators and American crocodiles, as well as a selection of touch

MORE FLORIDA HISTORY
The Williams Academy Black History Museum, 1936 Henderson Avenye, Fort Myers (*Open* Mon–Fri 10–4. *Admission: inexpensive*; tel 239/332-8778) puts a personal perspective on African American history with a collection of archival material and donated artifacts from local families. There is an interesting exhibit about the Union soldiers who manned Fort Myers during the Civil War.

Fort Myers beach and pier

exhibits, including shells, rudimentary musical instruments and Native American objects augmented by traditional Seminole chickee huts outside. Stop off in the shade below the main building for a look at the turtle ponds with native Florida species such as snapping and mud turtles and musk turtles, which use pungent scent as a defense.

Next, head for the bobcat enclosure and the aviary, where the Audubon Society houses a number of its injured birds. Starting from here, there are two boardwalk trails in the swamp, cypress and pine woods and a more taxing 2.5-mile (4km) Wildlands Trail without the benefit of a boardwalk.

The 90-seat planetarium (*Admission: inexpensive*) operates a busy program of astronomy and laser shows.

Examining the wares in Fort Myers' Shell Factory

ECHO, *17391 Durrance Road (off S.R. 78, east of I-75)* (*Open* tours only Tue–Sat at 10 Jan–Mar; Tue, Fri, Sat at 10 Apr–Dec. *Admission free*; tel: 239/543-3246, www.echonet.com) Under its full title, Educational Concerns for Hunger Organization, ECHO does not sound like much of a tourist attraction, but gardeners will find it fascinating. ECHO is a Christian ministry with a mission to fight world hunger by developing a seed bank of unusual food plants for use in the Third World, and promoting efficient recycling methods. An example of an ECHO success story is the moringa tree: Its leaves make highly nutritional baby food, the pods are used as a vegetable, the root makes a horseradish substitute and the seeds can purify water overnight. Ideas developed here include space-saving gardens using plastic gutters and lightweight rooftop gardens made of soft drink cans and grass clippings that can grow ginger and chilis or (without cans) radishes, lettuces and much more. Flourishing in the gardens are edible landscape plants, such as coffee, citrus, carambola (starfruit), pepper and cashew trees; and you can meet another of ECHO's special projects—the wool-free sheep.

Edison and Ford Winter Estates, *2350 McGregor Boulevard* (*Open* Mon–Sat 9–5.30, Sun noon–5.30; last tour begins at 4. *Joint admission: expensive*, river cruises additional, *inexpensive*; tel: 239/334-7419, www.edison-ford-estate.com) Inventor of the automatic telegraph, phonograph and incandescent lamp, Thomas Alva Edison can be credited

THE SHELL FACTORY

A southwest Florida institution for more than half a century, The Shell Factory, N. Tamiami Trail (U.S. 41) North Fort Myers, claims to offer the world's largest collection of rare shells, corals, sponges and fossils from the world's oceans. Some five million shells and shell-related souvenirs are on sale, from sand dollars costing a couple of cents to pricey exotica; plus beachwear, T-shirts and manatee fridge magnets. Outdoor entertainment includes miniature golf and bumper boat rides.

with "discovering" Fort Myers. Vacationing in Florida in 1884–85, he ventured down to this small, semitropical fishing village on the Caloosahatchee River. He loved the area so much that he bought a 14 acres (5.5ha) of land there. The **Edison Winter Home** was an innovation, too: Its prefabricated sections were constructed in Fairfield, Maine, transported on schooners, and erected in 1886. Edison and his second wife, Mina Miller Edison, their children and friends wintered here until he died in 1931.

The modest house retains its original furnishings, and the surrounding gardens reveal that the wizard inventor was also an expert horticulturist. Friends and colleagues were constantly producing gifts of exotic plants to add to his collection (such as Henry Firestone's monstrous banyan tree), and several varieties of rubber plant and goldenrod stand as a testament to Edison's search for a domestic source of natural rubber.

Across McGregor Boulevard is his fully equipped laboratory, still lit by the original carbon-filament light bulbs that have shone for 12 hours a day ever since they were installed. In the museum, hundreds of Edison inventions, which range from talking dolls to miners' lamps, illustrate just a handful of the 1,097 patent designs he achieved.

The Henry Fords visited the Edisons in 1915, and a year later bought the adjacent property, which they named Mangoes. The **Ford Winter Home**'s garage is used to display the cornerstone of the Ford fortunes: a 1914 Model-T, plus a 1917 Ford truck and 1929 Model A.

Southwest Florida Museum of History, *2300 Peck Street* (*Open* Tue–Sat 10–5. *Admission: moderate*; tel: 239/332-5955) The museum's collections present the history of

FUN FOR THE YOUNG
There's plenty of fun in store at the Sunsplash Family Waterpark, 400 Santa Barbara Boulevard (tel: 239/574-0557) a good summer season cooler with water slides, inner-tube rides and games. The Children's Science Center, 2915 Pine Island Road (*Open* Mon–Sat 10–4, tel 239/997-0012) is nearby, with exhibits ranging from holograms to hermit crabs.

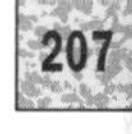

Thomas Edison's laboratory, a fitting memorial to a great scientist

ALL ABOARD
The old Fort Myers–Naples railroad has been restored betwen Fort Myers and Bayshore, allowing the old-fashioned Seminole Gulf Railway to ply the route with sightseeing excursions, lunch and dinner tours and mystery dinner theater outings. Trains depart from Colonial Station at the Amtel Mall, Metro Parkway and Colonial Drive (for schedules and reservations, tel: 941/275-8487 or 800/SEM GULF).

southwest Florida in a nutshell. The story begins with Calusa Native American objects and continues through the founding of the fort, the Seminole Wars and events of the 20th century. The museum also displays a refurbished 1930s railroad car, *The Esperanza*, and a recently excavated World War II P-39 bomber found in Estero Bay, as well as the Cooper collection of Depression and Carnival glassware, plus excellent scale models of trains and a gift shop.

Imaginarium Hands-On Museum, *200 Cranford Avenue* (*Open* Mon–Sat 11–5, Sun noon–5. *Admission: inexpensive* tel: 239/337-3332, www.cityftmyers.com) Opened in 1995 but redesigned and upgraded, the Imaginarium sits at the heart of downtown. There are more than 60 interactive exhibts, plus a range of animals to enjoy. The W-IMG TV Weather Station allows you to present forecasts and watch them on TV; feel the force of a hurricane at The Hurricane Experience; or dig for bones at Dino Dig. There are live shows and 3D movies and "Tiny Town" for the youngest visitors. Outdoors is Fish Eye Lagoon with birds and water creatures, plus a Florida citrus grove.

Island hopping Many of the highlights of the Lee Island Coast are accessible only by boat. Island hoppers can explore more than 100 offshore retreats, and are given plenty of opportunities for shell-collecting, fishing or just simply lazing.

Across Pine Island Sound, home to an abundant population of playful bottlenose dolphins, **Cayo Costa State Park** is the largest barrier island in the region and one of the largest uninhabited islands in Florida, undisturbed for the past 500 years. Acres of pine forest, oak palm hammocks and gumbo limbo are fringed with deserted sand beaches that offer excellent shell-collecting. There is spectacular bird life, and sea turtles lay their eggs here.

The Ford Winter Home at Fort Myers now forms part of a museum dedicated to Henry Ford

Cruise under sail on the tall ship Eagle

Calusa Native Americans left their mark on **Cabbage Key** with a huge shell mound. Today's visitors are more likely to leave an autographed dollar bill pinned to the walls of the island's historic inn—built on top of the mound in 1938 by mystery writer Mary Roberts Rinehart.

North of Cabbage Key, **Gasparilla Island** lies on the Boca Grande Pass, a top tarpon-fishing spot . In the Gasparilla Island State Recreation Area, the **Boca Grande Lighthouse Museum and Visitor Center** (*Open* daily 10–4 Nov–Apr; Mon–Fri 10–4 May–Oct. *Admission: inexpensive;* tel: 941/964-0375) traces the island's Native American heritage, its development as a pioneer south Florida resort and natural history.

Nature lovers should find time for a sea kayak tour with **Gaea Guides**. Guide-led trips (tel: 239/694-5513, www.gaeaguides.com) take a detailed look at aquatic bird life, dolphins, stingrays and manatees.

To get around the islands, experienced sailors will find plenty of boat-rental outfits offering everything from dinghies to motorboats. Shelling charters are available from the 'Tween Waters Inn Marina, Captiva (tel: 941/472-1051); shelling and out-island cruises are offered by **Captiva Cruises**, *McCarthy's Marina, Captiva* (tel: 239/472-5300). To explore the Estero Bay Aquatic Preserve, contact **Calusa Coast Outfitters**, *7225 Estero Boulevard, Fort Myers* (tel: 239/418-5941), who lead historical, archeological and dolphin encounter tours around the marine/island reserve. Meanwhile **J. C. Cruises**, *Fort Myers Yacht Basin* (tel: 941/334-7474), ply the Gulf and take tours up the Caloosahatchee River.

Manatee Park, *10901 S.R. 80* (1.5 miles/2.5km east of I-75/Exit 25) (*Open* Apr–Sep, 8–8; Oct–Mar, 8–5. *Admission: inexpensive*, parking fee; tel: 239/694-3537, www.leeparks.org) East of downtown Fort Myers, this winter season (Nov–Mar) manatee haven lies on the Orange River. During the cooler months, manatees are drawn here by the warm waters issuing from the Florida Power & Light plant downstream. View them from riverside observation decks (enjoy an "All About Manatees" program November–March daily 11, 2); or take a kayak tour.

SHELLING POINTERS

Here are some tips for shell seekers: Bowman's Beach on Sanibel Island is the acknowledged top spot, and Captiva Beach has piles of easily accessible washed-up shells. But both of these beaches are very popular, so why not try secluded beaches, such as Upper Captiva, Cayo Costa and neighboring Johnson Shoals? Only accessible by boat, they are great for shell-collecting. *Remember, the law limits the collection of live shells to two per species per person per day along Lee Island Coast, except Sanibel Island where collecting live shells is completely banned.*

STATE SYMBOL
The horse conch (*Pleuroploca gigantea*), also known as the giant band shell, is Florida's official state shell symbol. The conch can grow to a size of around 24in (61cm) and feeds off clams in waters from a depth of 1ft to 80ft (30cm–24m). Though the conch is protected in Florida, the locals have no qualms about eating their state symbol. Imported conch is the staple filler in local chowders and appears in various guises on menus from the Panhandle to Key West.

Sanibel and Captiva Islands Linked to the mainland by a mile-long (1.6km) scenic causeway, picturesque Sanibel and Captiva could be hundreds of miles from the busy coastal highways and condominiums. In fact, this is Florida's Tahiti, a lush island paradise where, in the 18th century, pirate José Gaspar held his female captives among the purple trumpets of morning glory and brilliant hibiscus. Life is easy on the sandy beaches and in the funky cafés, friendly restaurants and artsy-craftsy boutiques. Bicycle rentals are the most popular way to get around here, and there are a number of low-key attractions, from the 1884 lighthouse and 19th-century stilt houses on the eastern tip of Sanibel to the C.R.O.W. wildlife rehabilitation facility on Sanibel–Captiva road.

The islands' top sight is the **J. N. "Ding" Darling National Wildlife Refuge**, a 6,354-acre (2,542ha) preserve with a 5-mile (8km) scenic drive (not Fridays; good bird life in the mornings), and nature trails. Open-air narrated tram tours, kayak excursions with a naturalist guide and canoe, kayak and bicycle rentals are available from **Tarpon Bay Recreation Area**, *900 Tarpon Bay Road, Sanibel* (*Open* daily. Tram tours *moderate*, call for schedules, tel: 239/472-8900).

Near the Refuge, conchologists, or shell enthusiasts, will want to stop off at the informative and well-presented **Bailey–Matthews Shell Museum**, *3075 Sanibel Road* (*Open* daily 10–4. *Admission: inexpensive*; tel: 239/395-2233, www.shellmuseum.org).

When it comes to beaches, **Bowman's Beach** is one of the best, and there is another popular sand strip at **Blind Pass** where the islands meet. **Turner Beach** is considered a prime spot for shells, and an excellent vantage point for the spectacular Gulf sunsets.

The beaches of Captiva Island attract both amateur and professional shell collectors

It starts off with one little whelk, and before you know it you have collected a small mountain of striped, speckled, spotted and striated seashells—all begging to be taken home. Shell-collecting is not a hobby in Florida, it is a fixation. Confirmed conchologists are known to hit the beach before dawn, shuffling along with the distinctive "Sanibel stoop," armed with flashlights and bags full of treasures.

Several species of cockles, cones, moons and glossy olives are common and easy to collect. Cleaned up, the Atlantic moon bears an eerie resemblance to its nickname, shark's eye. Whelks, with their rounded living quarters and elegant tapered tails, are also a familiar sight on Florida beaches. Mature whelks can range from 3–4in (7.5–10cm) to 16in (40cm) long, depending on the variety; look for females, which lay leathery chains of eggs or shell-bearing capsules.

Conchs Conchs come in all shapes and sizes, from the delicate hues of the pink conch to the mottled hawkwing and the strangely named 3in (7.5cm) Florida fighting conch. Sheltered bays and saltwater mangrove areas harbor the crown conch, easily identified by its single or several spiky "crowns."

Sand dollars Shuffle along a sand bar, and there will be a fortune in sand dollars. To get that shop-clean look, soak the coarse green discs in a weak bleach solution and dry them in the sun.

La crème de la crème After storms, conchologists come out in force, and a prize find is the junonia, a long whitish shell decorated with evenly spaced dark brown spots. The lion's-paw scallop is another beauty—an exotic cousin of the common scallop with raised "knuckles" that give it the appearance of a paw. Keep an eye out also for delicate janthina shells, home of the violet sea snail.

Only collect dead, empty shells; it's illegal to collect live shells as the species may be threatened. Only buy shells from reputable sources.

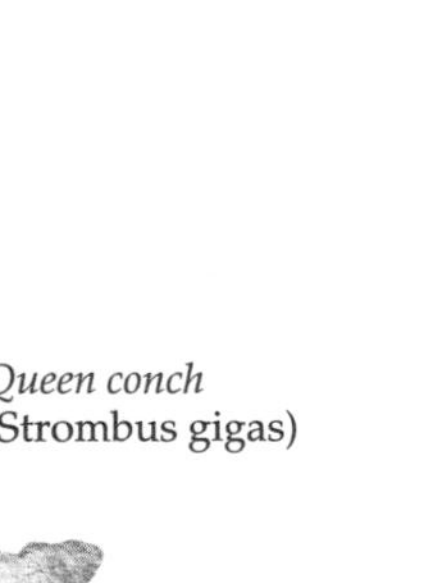

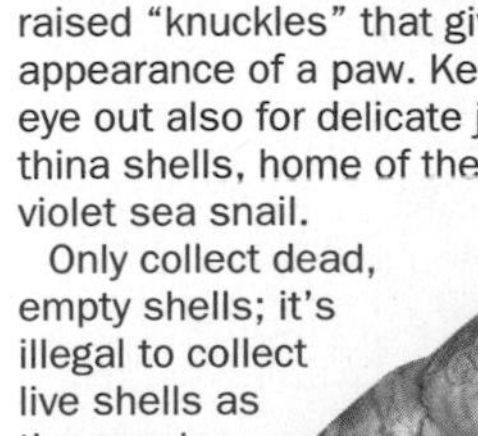

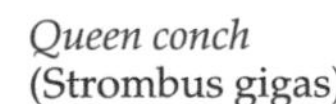

Queen conch
(Strombus gigas)

Feeding the manatees in Homosassa Springs State Wildlife Park

HISTORIC NAPLES
For a well-rounded history of the southwest region, stop off at the Collier County Museum, 3301 E. Tamiami Trail (*Open* Mon–Fri 9–5. *Admission free*; tel: 239/774-8476, www.colliermuseum.com), for displays of prehistoric fossils, Native American, Spanish, and pioneer objects. In the downtown historic district, the 1895 Palm Cottage, 137 12th Street South (*Open* Nov–Apr, Tue–Fri, Sun 1–4; May–Oct, Fri and Sun only. *Admission: moderate*; tel: 941/261-8164), has been restored and furnished in Victorian style.

►► Homosassa Springs State Wildlife Park

199 A5

9225 4150 Suncoast Boulevard , Homosassa Springs (off U.S. 19); tel: 904/352-2311, www.floridastateparks.org
Open: daily 9–5.30; last ticket 4. Admission: moderate

Homosassa Springs has been a tourist attraction since the early 1900s, when stopped by the spring so that passengers could stretch their legs.

Within the 166-acre (66.5ha) wildlife park an underwater observatory provides an unrivaled view of the 45ft-deep (13.5m) **Spring of 10,000 Fish**. The natural spring pumps million gallons of water to the surface every hour at a constant 72°F (22°C), and attracts as many as 34 different species of fish, both freshwater and saltwater varieties, and, of course, manatees.

Explore the rest of the park on pontoon boat trips and self-guided nature trails. Look for river otters, turtles and marvelous bird life; native wildlife kept in enclosures includes black bears, bobcats and deer. A Wildlife Care Center for sick and injured animals opens in 2006.

► Largo: Pinewood Cultural Park

199 A3

11909 N. 125th Street (between Walsingham and Ulmerton); tel: 727/582-2123
Open: Tue–Sat 10–4, Sun 1–4. Admission free

Three attractions have been brought together in this hidden away location, which is worth seeking out. The original attraction is the **Pinellas County Heritage Village**. Here, some 24 historic homes, barns, a schoolhouse, railroad station and store have been rescued from around the county and re-erected, restored and in many cases furnished in period style on a 21-acre (8.5ha) plot surrounded by pine woodlands and palmettos.

On a neighboring site, the **Gulf Coast Museum of Art**, *12211 Walsingham Road* (*Open* Tue–Sat 10–4, Sun noon–4. *Admission: inexpensive;* tel: 727/518-6833) hosts regular exhibitions, and takes a particular interest in Florida artists. There are plans to link the two sites with the new **Florida Botanical Gardens** (www.flbg.org), an ambitious 200-acre (80ha) scheme, still underway, which combines 18 individually landscaped areas—from rose gardens to hammock trails.

►►► Naples

199 B1

A tony and fast-developing resort city built on an appealingly small scale, Naples is rapidly earning a reputation as the Palm Beach of the Gulf. Just take a stroll down chic Fifth Avenue South or the attractively developed Third Street South shopping and historic district and you will see why. Famous for its photogenic pier, Naples also has lovely, sandy beaches—its sweeping Gulf beaches are near the Everglades—and some 50 golf courses, upscale accommodations and fine restaurants.

For getting around, **Naples Trolley Tours** provides narrated information about more than 100 points of interest, with convenient stops along the way. On the cultural front, drop in on the **Philharmonic Center for the Arts** at *5833 Pelican Bay Boulevard* (for information, tel: 239/597-1900, www.thephil.org), for a look round the sculpture gardens and galleries; and check out the varied music, theater and dance programs.

Caribbean Gardens, *1590 Goodlette-Frank Road (Open* daily 9.30–5.30, last tickets 4.30. *Admission: expensive*; tel: 239/262-5409) Straight As go to this zoo garden in a state that is well supplied with the genre. It is relatively small, so not too taxing for little kids, but the inhabitants range from antelopes to spider monkeys via rarities such as the Southeast Asian binturong, a little bear-cat related to the mongoose. Thoughtfully designed habitats have contributed to the animals' longevity and successful captive breeding programs. The stars are the big cats—cougars, lions, leopards and tigers—some of which take part in the amazing twice-daily showtimes with their trusted trainer. There are "meet the keeper" encounters, where visitors can learn more about individual animals from their carers; inexpensive zoo keys that activate audio information stations outside various exhibits; and Primate Expedition Cruises that set out (every 30 minutes) across the alligator lagoon to visit monkey colonies on wooded islets.

Naples Nature Center, *1450 Merrihue Drive (Open* Mon–Sat 9–4.30; Sun 1–5 Nov–Apr. *Admission: moderate*; tel: 239/262-0304, www.conservancy.org) Headquarters of the Conservancy of Southwest Florida, the Center doubles as a natural science museum and a wildlife rescue and rehabilitation facility. Investigate the aviaries, aquarium and boardwalk nature trail, then hire a kayak or take one of the regular mini-boat tours.

Teddy Bear Museum Of Naples, *2511 Pine Ridge Road (east off Airport-Pulling) (Open Mon, Wed*–Sat 10–5. *Admission: moderate*; tel: 239/598-2711, www.teddymuseum.com) Naples philanthropist Frances Pew Hayes opened this $2 million teddy bear preserve with her own collection in 1990, and the 5,000-teddy roll call is growing all the time. Antique and brand new bears, bear dioramas and sculpted marble bears are kept in a house in the woods.

SANCTUARY ON MARCO ISLAND

Six miles (9.5km) long and four miles (6.5km) wide, Marco Island (14 miles/22.5km south of Naples) hangs off the tip of the Florida peninsula surrounded by the scattered islets of the Ten Thousand Islands. Rampant resort development has not quite ousted nature or obliterated the memory of the island's early inhabitants, the Calusa people. Ancient shell mounds can still be seen, and bald eagles are encouraged to breed in artificial nests among the hotels and apartments. The island is a sequestered sanctuary to more than 200 species of birds, a natural haven for manatees and hatching ground for loggerhead sea turtles.

Boating is the key to exploring Florida's unspoiled coastline and island wildlife sanctuaries

Walk

Trails in Cayo Costa State Park

Access is by boat or ferry from Sanibel, Captiva and Pine islands.

Directly south of Boca Grande, this park (*Open* daily 8am–dusk. *Admission: inexpensive*; tel: 941/964-0375) occupies 2,132 acres (853ha) on the tip of Cayo Costa Island. A barrier island, Cayo Costa shelters Charlotte Harbor and Pine Island Sound from the worst ravages of the Gulf storms; it's also a major shell-collecting destination. Between the beaches and dunes of the island's Gulf shore and the bayside mangrove belt, there is a network of attractive short trails that explore the interior, comprising a mixture of pine flatwoods, oak palm hammocks and grassy regions dotted with palms.

The Quarantine Trail leaves from the Bayside Dock and works its way north to a picnic area on Pelican Bay. A tram from the dockside crosses the island to the Gulf Coast and a Gulf Trail. Cemetery Trail runs north–south, passing the site of an old pioneer graveyard. The Pinewoods Trail and Scrub Trail run east–west, and the latter links with the Quarantine Trail on the way to the picnic site.

Walk

Collier-Seminole State Park

Tamiami Trail (U.S. 41), 17 miles (27km) southeast of Naples.

On the northwestern edge of the Everglades, this superb 6,423-acre (2,569ha) park (*Open* daily 8am–dusk. *Admission: inexpensive*; tel: 239/394-3397) is frequently overlooked. Named after 1940s entrepreneur and developer Barron Collier, who first envisaged the park, and after the Seminole Native Americans who made the area their home, the park offers an introduction to the Everglades, plus fishing, canoeing and boating access to the Ten Thousand Islands in the Gulf of Mexico.

The 6.5-mile (10.5km) hiking trail leaves from the boat basin and winds its way through pine flatwoods and cypress swamp.

A special feature of the park is an unusual tropical hammock (an area slightly raised above the surrounding swamp) that flourishes with trees more commonly found in West Indian coastal forests and in Yucatan. In the woodlands, native Florida black bears and panthers keep to themselves, but wood storks, cockaded woodpeckers and mangrove fox squirrels are frequently spotted. A separate boardwalk system and observation platform overlook the salt marsh region, where bald eagles circle overhead. A word of warning: Biting insects can be a problem.

Louisiana heron

Walk

Trail in Corkscrew Swamp

Route 846, Bonita Springs (20 miles/32km east off Route 41).

This 2.25-mile (3.5km) boardwalk trail, starting at the Visitor Center, covers a minute section of the sanctuary, but offers an unbeatable opportunity to explore three contrasting native habitats. Just beyond the park headquarters, a woodland area of slash pines, palmetto and occasional wax myrtle is a great place to spot woodpeckers and tiny gray flycatchers. Then a broad swathe of wet prairie reveals alligator trails and a mass of brilliant wildflowers flourishing among a sea of grasses. In the shade of the thin, silver-gray pond cypresses, look for masses of little white apple-snail eggs, the only food of the rare Everglades kite. Corkscrew's bald cypress stand is the largest in America. These impressive trees, draped in Spanish moss, are hundreds of years old. At their feet, ferns grow in abundance, and bromeliads (air plants) nestle against the trunks, gathering nutrition from rainwater. Visit the central marsh in July, and it is aflame with red hibiscus; in the fall it is a sea of primrose willow (see page 200).

Walk

Trail in De Soto National Memorial

75th Street, Bradenton.

A short 0.5-mile trail (800m), the great charm of this walk is its breezy waterside location.

Take in the Visitor Center first (9–5).

There is a 20-minute video and display of Spanish explorers' objects, including armor, weaponry and a model shallow-draft caravel.

Set out along the beach.

You can imagine how it must have seemed to the early pioneers, attacking the mangrove thickets. Along the beach, the leaves of the sea grape trees were used by the explorers as stationery. In the undergrowth, broken blocks of tabby (the settlers' version of concrete—made from sand, limestone and shells) mark William Shaw's 1840s pioneer cottage. This area was known as Shaw Point for many years. The bayside cove is a good place to see pelicans, gulls, terns, ospreys and cormorants (see page 201).

Sentinel heron

GATEWAY TO THE SUN
For the most impressive entry to St. Pete and Pinellas County, visitors arriving from the south should take the spectacular Sunshine Skyway (I–275), north of Bradenton. The nominal toll is a small price to pay for the 4-mile (6.5km) suspension bridge, which was modeled after the Brotonne Bridge over the River Seine in France.

▶▶▶ St. Petersburg *199 A3*

On the western shores of Tampa Bay, St. Pete (as it is generally known) is the cultural center of Pinellas County, and like neighboring Clearwater is divided into two parts, with the downtown heart on the mainland linked by causeways to a barrier island beach. Downtown St. Pete looks out over Tampa Bay behind its landmark pier and new BayWalk shopping, dining and entertainment complex, which opened in fall 2000. Nearby is the world-class Salvador Dalí Museum and several more notable cultural attractions, but for most visitors the chief draw remains the beach and the county's much-vaunted average of 361 sunny days per year; the *Guinness Book of World Records* credits St. Pete with the most consecutive days of sunshine on record—some 768 during 1967–1969.

Salvador Dalí Museum, *1000 S. Third Street* (*Open* Mon–Sat 9.30–5.30, Sun noon–5.30. Friday open till 8. *Admission: moderate*; tel: 727/823-3767, www.salvadordalimuseum.org) This museum is the permanent home of the world's largest and most comprehensive collection of Spanish surrealist Salvador Dalí's art. The collection was amassed by Cleveland industrialist A. Reynolds Morse and his wife, Eleanor Reese, who first encountered Dalí's work in 1942. A year later they purchased their first canvas, *Daddy Longlegs of the Evening…Hope!*, the foundation stone of a collection that now numbers some 95 oil paintings, more than 100 watercolors and drawings, 1,300 graphics, plus posters, sculpture and decorative pieces. A 2,500-volume library is devoted to Dalí and surrealism.

The exhibits are displayed chronologically, starting in 1914, and chart the eccentrically mustachioed artist's

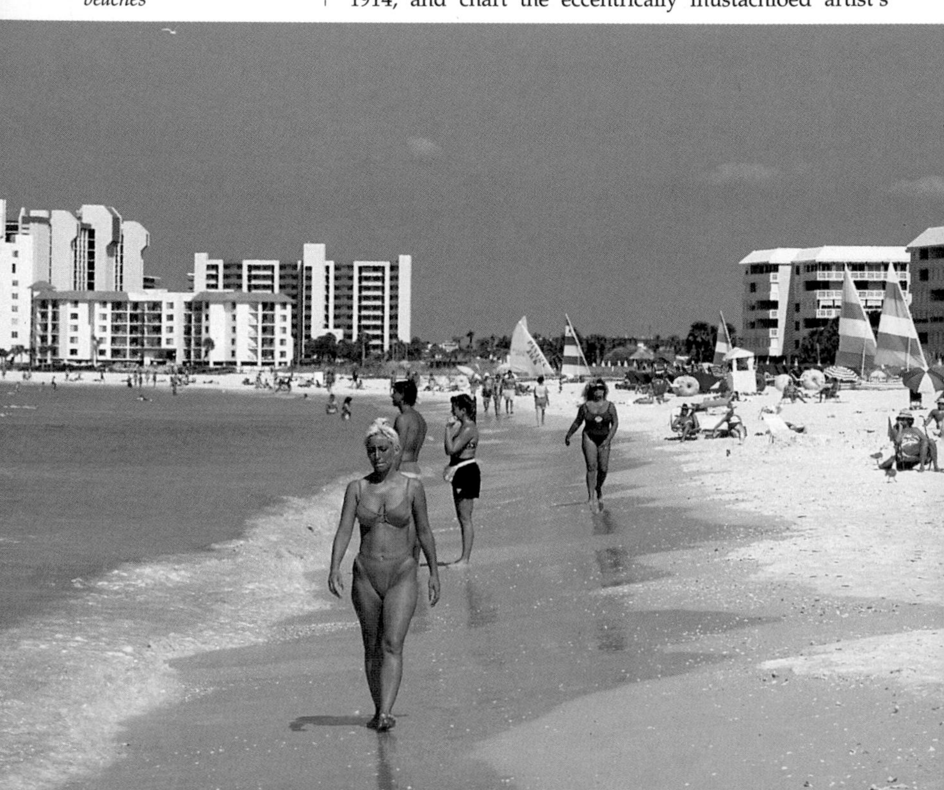

Sunshine is almost guaranteed on St. Pete's beaches

development from early dabblings with Impressionism through the theatrical 1921 *Self-Portrait*, which shows a hint of things to come, to the full-blown classical period. Here Dalí's twin obsessions—religion and science—are consummately illustrated in the *Discovery of America by Christopher Columbus* (1958) and *Nature Morte Vivante* (1956), respectively. Dalí's ability to utilize a variety of media is amply proved by the diversity of sculpture and glassware on display. There is even a hologram.

Excellent guided tours of the museum are offered throughout the day, and the gift shop provides an exhaustive range of Dalí-phernalia, from books, posters and cards to jewelry.

Florida Holocaust Museum, *55 S. 5th Street* (*Open* Mon–Sat 10–5, Sun noon–4. *Admission: moderate*; tel: 727/820-0100, www.flholocaustmuseum.org) The third largest museum of its kind in the U.S., the Florida Holocaust Museum illustrates a moving account of the period through photographs, memorabilia, film and art exhibits. The centerpiece is a boxcar used to transport people to the concentration camps.

Florida International Museum, *261 N. Second Avenue* (call for schedules and ticket reservations, tel: 727/822-3693, www.floridamuseum.org) An admirably ambitious arts project, the museum has swallowed up a whole city block of downtown St. Pete to house major artistic and historical exhibitions from round the world. Shows have included "Riches of the State Russian Museum" from Russia and "Splendors of Ancient Egypt" from the National Museum in Cairo. There is also the permanent "The Cuban Missile Crisis"exhibition. The intention is to host a major international exhibit every year, coupled with a traveling domestic show.

Fort De Soto Park, *via Pinellas Bayway (toll)* (*Open* daily dawn–dusk. *Admission free*; tel: 727/582-2267, www.fortdesoto.com) A welcome respite from the high-rise hotels lining the Gulf shore, this park is made up of five islands off the southern tip of Tampa Bay. Its strategic importance led to the construction of a fort on Mullet Key, in 1898, but the hefty 12in (30.5cm) mortars have never fired a shot in anger. The Quartermaster Storehouse Museum (*Open* 9–4), a reconstructed fort building reveals more about the fort's history. The park boasts three excellent beaches, a couple of popular fishing piers, boat ramps and picnic and camping facilities.

Great Explorations, *1925 Fourth Street North* (*Open* Mon–Sat 10–4.30, Sun noon–4.30. *Admission: inexpensive*; tel: 727/821-8992, www.greatexplorations.org) There is pure fun to be had at this splendid museum. Start your visit by creating instant images in the Phenomenal Arts section using kinetic touch or audio-activated image makers. The Touch Tunnel, approached on hands and knees in the dark, is not for the claustrophobic, but provides a satisfyingly peculiar experience as you feel your way out. In the Body Shop, testing stations check reactions and muscle tone. The latest diversion is the Mission Control: from the Moon to Mars launch experience.

RECREATIONAL TRAILS

For sporting types, how about a 47-mile (75.5km) walking, running, biking and in-line skating route? The Pinellas Trail follows an abandoned railroad track from Gulfport in the south of the county all the way north to Tarpon Springs, linking a variety of neighborhoods and green spaces off the main roads. Another option is the Friendship TrailBridge, a 2.6-mile (4km) route across the Old Gandy Bridge between Tampa and St. Pete.

The Salvador Dalí Museum is one of St. Pete's main attractions

HISTORY IN ST. PETE
During the 1920s, archeologists from the Smithsonian Institution excavated an important Native American site at Weedon Island, north of St. Pete. Objects from Weedon and from another Native American site at Safety Harbor are on display at the St. Petersburg Museum of History, 335 N.E. Second Avenue (*Open* Mon–Sat 10–5, Sun 1–5. *Admission: inexpensive*; tel: 727/894-1052), together with pioneer exhibits and a replica of the *Benoist*, the world's first commercial airliner, which flew from Tampa to St. Pete on January 1, 1914.

Museum of Fine Arts, *255 N.E. Beach Drive* (*Open* Tue–Sat 10–5, Sun 1–5. *Admission: moderate*; tel: 727/896-2667) Housed in a very attractive Mediterranean-style villa near The Pier, the museum has several notable collections, so allow enough time to do them justice. The Impressionists are well represented, as are sculptures and paintings from the 17th- and 18th-century European schools. American art from the 19th and 20th centuries includes some gorgeous Gorgia O'Keefe flower studies. Decorative arts and crafts gathered from around the world run the gauntlet from pre-Columbian objects, and Greek and oriental treasures, to Steuben crystal.

As well as the galleries, there are charming set-piece rooms, each of which has been carefully furnished in period style. Another treat is the photography collection. Guided tours are available, and the museum frequently plays host to special exhibitions from other collections.

The Pier, *800 N.E. Second Avenue* (*Open* daily, most stores open from 10–9; tel: 727/821-6443) Projecting into the bay like the superstructure of a vast turquoise-and-cream aircraft carrier, The Pier (a St. Petersburg landmark) combines shopping, dining and sightseeing opportunities all in one. Its lower-deck mall houses a variety of boutiques, toy and gift stores, a tourist information point and snack stops. Moving on up, Ybor City's famous **Columbia Restaurant** has an outpost here, serving fine Spanish-Cuban cuisine (lunch and dinner). The top-deck observation platform offers a cocktail lounge and panoramic view of downtown St. Pete and the bay. There is plenty of parking, linked by a free tram service (or valet for a fee); sightseeing boat trips; fishing along the causeway; trike, roller blade, aquacycle, windsurfer, kayak and catamaran rentals; plus a sunny afterdeck with bench seating that provides an excellent spot for outdoor snacking.

The upside-down pyramid of St. Petersburg's Pier

Suncoast Seabird Sanctuary, *18328 Gulf Boulevard, Indian Shores* (*Open* daily 9am–dusk. *Admission: donation*; tel: 727/391-6211, www.seabirdsanctuary.org) A fascinating excursion across the peninsula from downtown St. Pete, the sanctuary started with a chance encounter between Ralph Heath and an injured cormorant in 1971. Heath had the bird's wing set and nursed it back to health, though Maynard, as the bird was named, would never fly again. Soon word of the "bird doctor" spread, and injured birds were brought in from far and wide.

The aim is to release birds back into the wild unless their injuries are permanent and would affect their ability to survive. Each year the sanctuary cares for around 8,500 injured birds, of which more than 80 percent survive. Among those figures are some 500 pelicans, most of them injured by fish hooks and nylon line. Over 180 chicks have been hatched from breeding couples, and the offspring then rejoin their fellows in the wild. Other success stories have involved great blue herons and great egrets, owls, gannets, petrels, an Arctic loon and peregrine falcons.

Feeding time at Suncoast Seabird Sanctuary

Sunken Gardens, *1825 N. Fourth Street* (*Open* Mon–Sat 10–4.30, Sun noon–4.30. *Admission: inexpensive*; tel: 727/551-3100) Laid out in a former natural sinkhole, which was drained in the 1930s, this colorful profusion of exotic plant life flourishes in the rich layer of fertile soil residue. There are lush tropical corners, brilliant curtains of bougainvillea, along with carefully landscaped contours of formal gardens, replenished with around 50,000 plants each year. The hundreds of rare and exotic blooms in the Orchid Arbor are sure to be appreciated by gardeners, and there are hour-long garden tours offered daily at 10.30 and 1.30. Additional features include a flock of flamingos, turtle ponds and parrot show presentations, and there is also a walk-through aviary containing a butterfly garden.

Luxuriant growth in the exotic Sunken Gardens

Drive

Around Tampa Bay

See map on page 199.

This full-day drive around Tampa Bay starts in downtown Tampa at the **Florida Aquarium** (see page 228). This terrific state-of-the-art facility deserves a really thorough visit, so an early start is recommended.

From the Aquarium, take the Downtown Crossway east to Exit 15-A and join I–75 south (direction Naples) for 30 miles (48km). At Exit 43, follow signs for U.S. 301 south for 1 mile (1.6km) to Ellenton.

On the right-hand side of the road, you will see the **Gamble Plantation State Historic Site** (see page 204). This elegant restored plantation home is one of the few remaining antebellum houses in Florida. Tours provide an insight into plantation life and vernacular architecture especially tailored to local Florida conditions.

Rejoin I–75 south for 12 miles (19km) to Exit 40 for Sarasota. University Parkway leads directly to the gates of the Ringling Museum (7 miles/11km) across U.S. 41/Tamiami Trail.

The Venetian-inspired winter residence of a circus king is part of the **John and Mable Ringling Museum of Art** complex (see page 221) that occupies a fabulous site on Sarasota Bay. There is also a museum café-restaurant here, which makes a good lunch stop. Sarasota offers several other sightseeing opportunities (see pages 221–225), plus sweeping barrier island beaches across the bay.

From the Ringling Museum, U.S. 41/Tamiami Trail heads north to connect with U.S. 19, the direct route to the Sunshine Skyway bridge and St. Petersburg for downtown Tampa.

If you are heading for the barrier islands around Sarasota, take U.S. 41/Tamiami Trail south for 3 miles (5km) and turn right for St. Armands Key (S.R. 789 N.) across the John Ringling Causeway. Follow S.R. 789 N. up the barrier island chain.

Bradenton Beach is a good place to stop off for a swim, with its busy strip of cafés, shops and watersports concessions overlooking the Gulf.

To return to the mainland, take S.R. 64 to Bradenton; then rejoin U.S. 41 N./U.S. 19.

Spanning the entrance to Tampa Bay, the **Sunshine Skyway** is something of an attraction in its own right. The central span is a record 1,200ft (360m) and rises 183ft (55m) above the water below.

From the Skyway, I–275 cuts across downtown St. Petersburg for downtown Tampa.

A taste of Italy in Sarasota: the John and Mable Ringling Museum of Art

The skyline of culture city, Sarasota

▶▶▶ Sarasota 199 A3

Once known as "The Town the Circus Built," Sarasota is a sophisticated, cultured resort founded by early Florida pioneers in the 1840s. When a "fine hotel" was built here in the 1880s the town prospered, attracting socialites from the North, among them John Ringling, the circus king and art lover, who installed himself in predictably flamboyant style at Ca'd'Zan, a grand waterfront mansion.

One of the great joys of Sarasota for the visitor is the compact nature of the city. From a beach hotel on Longboat or Lido Key, it is only a five-minute drive to downtown and the attractive antiques district on **Palm Avenue**. Restored storefronts lure the collector to browse in more than 30 stores, and the **Marie Selby Gardens** are at the end of the street. There is waterfront dining and more shopping at downtown **Sarasota Quay**, and shoppers should not miss Lido Key's **St. Armand's Circle**. Performing arts are big news in Sarasota, with the **Asolo State Theater** blazing a trail as one of the nation's leading regional theaters; the Florida West Coast Symphony performs in the **Van Wezel Performing Arts Hall** on Sarasota Bay; and the city has its own ballet and opera companies.

John and Mable Ringling Museum of Art, *5401 Bay Shore Road* (*Open* daily 10–5.30. *Admission: moderate*; tel: 941/359-5700, www.ringling.org) Sarasota's cultural epicenter, the Ringling bayfront estate, should not be missed. On trips to Europe between 1924 and 1931, the Ringlings amassed an extraordinary collection of artwork—more than 600 paintings, plus tapestries, objets d'art and several tons of statuary—and Ringling constructed a magnificent Italian-style palazzo to house what remains of one of the largest and finest collections of European paintings in the United States. Ringling's particular passion was the Italian baroque period, but he also bought several notable examples of medieval and Renaissance art. He owned the largest collection of Rubens in the world, and commissioned a special gallery to show off his beloved Rubens cartoons. Surrounded by three wings of the museum, 20th-century copies of classical statuary adorn formal gardens.

SHARK TOOTH CITY

Once the winter home of the Ringling Brothers and Barnum and Bailey Circus, the quiet seaside town of Venice (20 miles/32km south of Sarasota) now rejoices in the unlikely sobriquet of "Shark Tooth Capital of the World." Casperson Beach, south of the airport, makes a great beachcombing spot, with rewarding shell-collecting as well as a chance to gather a haul of the distinctive fossilized shark's teeth that have washed up on the shore. They range in size from one-eighth of an inch (0.3cm)up to 3in (7.5cm)or more. There are also nature trails and scuba diving and other watersports opportunities.

Part of the Ringling art collection

ANIMAL MAGIC

For more than 60 years, the Sarasota Jungle Gardens, 3701 Bay Shore Road (*Open* daily 9–5. *Admission: moderate*; tel: 941/355-5305), have attracted visitors to their 10-acre (4ha) tropically landscaped site for bird shows, reptile displays and assorted animal encounters. Meet alligators and flamingoes, talented cockatoos and leopards. The Kiddie Jungle has an animal farm, tree house and jungle-themed playground. There is a regular schedule of shows and a shell museum.

Down on the water's edge is **Ca'd'Zan** (Venetian dialect for "House of John"), the Ringlings' winter residence. It was inspired by Mable's two favorite buildings, the Doge's Palace in Venice and the tower of P. T. Barnum's Old Madison Square Garden in New York. Around the main hall, 32 luxurious rooms and 15 bathrooms edge the 2½-story atrium. Life-size portraits of the couple hang in the court. The former garages have been transformed into a **Circus Museum**, where posters and memorablilia rub shoulders with sequined finery, calliopes, rare carved and painted circus wagons, and cannons for launching human projectiles.

Marie Selby Botanical Gardens, *811 S. Palm Avenue* (*Open* daily 10–5. *Admission: moderate*; tel: 941/366-5731, www.selby.org) These glorious gardens, overlooking Sarasota Bay, were the idea of Marie Selby, who wintered in Sarasota with her Ohio oil baron husband, William. The modest house in the middle of the property was built in 1921 as a temporary residence for the Selbys until a more substantial home could be constructed. They never bothered, and the bayfront estate was donated to the county in 1971 with a bequest and proviso that it should be laid out as a garden. Some 20,000 plants have now been introduced, and 20 distinct garden areas created. Most famous is the orchid collection, but bromeliads, hibiscus and cacti grow in profusion. There is a colorful Butterfly Garden, the waterfront Baywalk, and a tropical display house overflowing with exotic plants from around the world. A small Museum of Botany and Arts (same ticket) exhibiting botanical illustrations is housed in the neighboring **Payne House**, a gracious 1935 mansion that combines all the best features of southern architecture.

Mote Marine Laboratory, *1600 Ken Thompson Parkway* (*Open* daily 10–5. *Admission: moderate*; tel: 941/388-2451, www.mote.org) A terrific family outing, this excellent aquarium complex offers a fascinating window on the marine world. Tanks full of gruesome puffer fish and electricity-producing stargazers grab kids' attention from the start. There are outdoor touch tanks and a shark tank that houses a floating—or rather circling—population that may include lemon and nurse sharks, the hefty mottled jewfish, shoals of sardines and the occasional tarpon. The plate-glass windows make for interesting viewing, but there is nothing quite like watching one of those predatory dorsal fins slicing through the water up on the surface. Other smaller aquaria are inhabited by seahorses, clearnose skates, octopuses and more.

Take a walk through the lab area before crossing the street to the waterfront turtle hospital, aquaculture tanks and manatee facility. Additional attractions are the Shark Attack Theater, which puts the audience into the shark's "shoes" as it hunts for food. And call in advance for information about **Sarasota Bay Explorers** (tel: 941/388-4200), nature cruises with a naturalist on Sarasota and Roberts bays, where mangrove islands are home to pelicans, egrets and herons, and dolphins and manatees can be seen.

Sarasota Classic Car Museum, *5500 N. Tamiami Trail (U.S. 41)* (*Open* daily 9–6. *Admission: moderate*; tel: 941/355-6228) On show are more than 100 antique and classic automobiles, from the Model-T Ford to the Volkswagen Beetle via handsome Rolls-Royces, racy Corvettes and John Ringling's 1932 Pierce Arrow. The museum also displays old coin-operated arcade games and a collection of nickleodeons, pianolas, music boxes and an Edison's Home Phonograph.

ZOO ENCOUNTERS
There are around 200 permanent inhabitants at the Pelican Man's Bird Sanctuary, 1708 Ken Thompson Parkway, next to the Mote Marine Aquarium (*Open* daily 10–5. *Admission: inexpensive, tel: 941/388-444*). These birds can no longer survive in the wild, but the sanctuary has successfully rehabilitated thousands of injured pelicans and other birds such as herons, hawks and owls. Birders flock to Oscar Scherer State Park, U.S. 41 at Osprey, to look for endangered Florida scrub jays and bald eagles.

Elegant shopping at Sarasota Quay

John Nicholas Ringling was born on May 30, 1866, in MacGregor, Iowa, the sixth of seven sons raised by immigrant parents. His father, a German-born leather craftsman, and his mother, the daughter of a prosperous French weaver and vineyard owner, moved frequently around the Midwest until they finally settled in Baraboo, Wisconsin, in 1875. Though fortunes fluctuated, the boys were given a strict Lutheran upbringing in which the qualities of honesty, dignity and pride in a job were rigorously emphasized, beliefs which would characterize the Ringling brothers' business deals.

The traveling circus During the 1870s, the newly built railroads opened up the whole country, enabling traveling entertainment acts to reach a vast new audience. Circuses were among the first to take advantage of this new way to reach the people. In 1872, entrepreneur Phineas T. Barnum recognized the potential of railroads and purchased a fleet of railroad cars, turning his successful freak show into the "Great Traveling Museum, Menagerie, Caravan and Hippodrome." Albert, Otto, Alfred and Charles Ringling launched a variety act inspired by Dan Rice's Circus in the same year. It was called the Classic and Comic Concert Company. Their brother John joined them in 1882, and two years later the Ringling Brothers Circus was formed in Baraboo.

The Ringling mansion Ca'd'Zan has more than a touch of the Doge's Palace in Venice

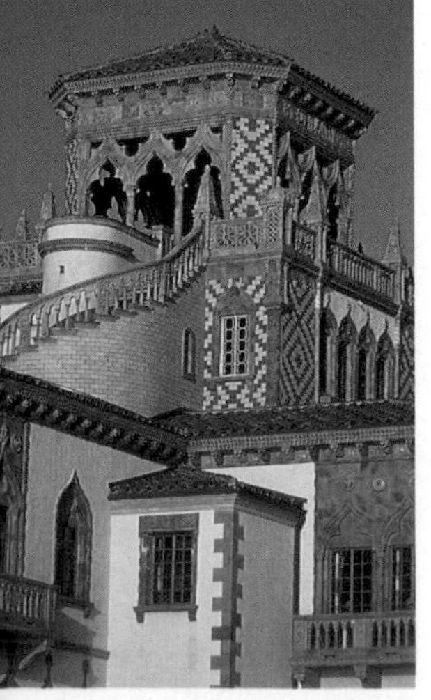

On the up Two more brothers, August and Henry, were soon added to the payroll, and responsibilities were divided. John's brains and extraordinary memory earned him the position of transportation manager. In his spare time, he invested in oil, real estate, railroads and a variety of smaller concerns. On business trips to Europe, sightseeing visits to the great European museums and palaces fueled his interest in art. While his brothers wintered in Baraboo, John busied himself in New York and Chicago among cultivated friends drawn from the ranks of artists, celebrities and politicians. By the time he first visited Sarasota in 1911, John Ringling was already a celebrity in his own right, a wealthy businessman and an imposing figure, described by a contemporary as "tall, with the chest of a sea elephant, the chin of a prize fighter and sensitive, artistic hands."

The move to Sarasota John married Mable Burton, a noted Ohio beauty, in 1905. After he bought a winter property on the Sarasota bayfront in 1912, he and Mable made annual visits, often entertaining the family. Brother Charles built a marble mansion on an adjacent lot, now the University of South Florida's College Hall. In 1917, John began to invest in Sarasota real estate. Circus elephants occasionally helped out with the heavy work as causeways were built to link his barrier-island properties to the mainland, and New York landscape architect John Watson was chosen to design the elegant St. Armands Circle shopping district: "Now Mable won't have to go to Palm Beach to shop," Ringling explained. However, other projects did not fare so well, and work on a luxurious Ritz Carlton hotel on Longboat Key was halted by the collapse of the 1920s land boom.

Mable's "House of John" Meanwhile, Mable had been fully occupied supervising the construction of Ca'd'Zan, a Venetian Gothic-style residence of grandiose proportions, truly fit for a circus king. She personally visited the kilns where the terracotta decorations for the interior and exterior of the house were glazed, accommodated shiploads of columns, doorways, balustrades and Venetian glass windows, and approved the exuberant designs by Ziegfield Follies set artist Will Pogany for the ballroom and playroom ceilings. An 8,000sq ft (720sq m) marble terrace extended west from the house, and an elegant dock was constructed for Mable's Venetian gondola. Christmas 1926 was celebrated in the newly completed house, and in the New Year work began on a museum to house additional treasures.

End of an era After the death of his brothers, John managed the circus alone, and in 1927 moved its winter quarters to Sarasota in an effort to boost the flagging local economy. The Ringlings had purchased Barnum & Bailey's Circus in 1906, and their last major rival, the five circuses of the American Circus Corp., were brought under Ringling's control in 1929. It was also the year that Mable died, after just three winters in her dream home. John Ringling opened his museum in 1930, but the last few years of his life were plagued by unhappiness and business disappointments. He had just $350 in his bank account when he died in 1936, but bequeathed his entire estate to the state of Florida, which finally accepted the $14 million legacy in 1946.

A LITTLE GEM
John Ringling would have been delighted with the Asolo Theater, a dazzling little rococo gem added to his estate in the 1950s. Originally built for the Palazzo Asolo in Italy, it seats 300 in a horseshoe arrangement of rising tiers of boxes, ornately decorated in pastels and gilt friezes and lit by small lamps. It is used for concerts, lectures and art-film screenings.

A copy of Michelangelo's David surveys the Ringling Museum of Art

Not a mosque, but the Henry B. Plant Museum in Tampa

►► Tampa

199 A4

The safe anchorage of Tampa Bay made it one of the first spots marked on early explorers' maps. In 1824, Fort Brooke was established here as a pioneer military outpost for monitoring the Seminole people, and during the Civil War a steamship service was opened between Tampa and Cuba. Henry Plant's railroad line rolled into the port in 1884. Two years later, Vincente Martinez Ybor moved his cigar industry from Key West to the growing megalopolis of late 19th-century Tampa. In just six years, the bayside fishing village was transformed into a boom town with more than 5,000 inhabitants. Plant lured wealthy Northerners south to winter in his fabulous **Tampa Bay Hotel**, and used his considerable connections in Washington to turn Tampa into a troop embarkation point during the 1898 Spanish-American War.

Today, downtown Tampa is the West Coast's commercial powerhouse, a glistening array of towering skyscrapers, modern shopping malls and the brilliant Florida Aquarium. But its history is never far away. Plant's dream hotel has survived and is now used as a university building, and 1 mile (1.6km) down the Crosstown Expressway, the Victorian facades and red-brick cigar factories of **Ybor City** have developed into a popular tourist attraction.

Adventure Island, *10001 McKinley Drive* (*Open* daily late Mar–early Sep; mid-Feb to mid-Oct, weekends. *Admission: expensive*; tel: 813/987-5600, www.4adventure.com) A one-day pass entitles visitors to try out all the facilities at this 30-acre (12ha) water park. The Rambling Bayou offers a leisurely passage through a man-made rain forest, complete with weather effects from mist to a monsoon. For more exciting watersports, check out the Tampa Typhoon, a 76ft (23m) free-fall body slide, or the Gulfstream—all 210ft (63m) of it—where sliders reach speeds of up to 25mph (40kph). Other hot favorites are Splash Attack and the Spike Zone volleyball courts. Small children are catered to in the Fabian's Funport area; there are also beaches, picnic areas and cafés.

There's fun for water babies of all ages at Tampa's Adventure Island

A Bengal tiger cools off in the water at Busch Gardens

Busch Gardens, *3000 E. Busch Boulevard (at 40th Street)* (*Open* daily from 9.30 (call for schedules). *Admission: expensive*; tel: 813/987-5082, www.buschgardens.com) Originally designed by the Anheuser-Busch Tampa Brewery for its workers, this 300-acre (120ha) African-themed family attraction now combines more than 2,700 animals from 320 species with theme park rides, creatively landscaped grounds and live entertainment. It is one of the most popular days out in the Bay area.

At the entrance to the park, there are shows and shopping in **Morocco**, then it's off to **Crown Colony** for the cable car or Nairobi Train Station, where guests can depart for tours of the **Serengeti Plain**. This is the park's focal point, home to hippos and lions, herds of graceful gazelles, zebras and giraffes, as well as the **Edge of Africa** self-guided safari. Explore a replica of King Tut's tomb in **Egypt**, take a spin aboard the hair-raising Montu roller coaster (see panel), or hop aboard a Serengeti-bound miniature train. **Nairobi** is home to the Myombe Reserve gorilla and chimpanzee habitat, and a popular Animal Nursery. To the north, there are thrill rides and shows in **Timbuktu**; bumper cars, rafting adventures and tigers in the **Congo**; flume rides aboard the Tanganyika Tidal Wave and the Stanley Falls Log Flume (this is definitely the place to cool off), and orangutans in **Stanleyville**; and a koala habitat in the **Bird Gardens**. Children have the run of **Land of the Dragons**, a colorful collection of storybook tree houses, splash zones, play areas and scaled-down rides. The latest addition to the park is **Gwazi** and you can hear the rumble of this spectacular double wooden roller coaster before you see it (see panel).

THRILLS AND SPILLS
After the Serengeti comes the really wild stuff: Busch Gardens' thrill rides are some of the mightiest movers in the business beginning with Sheikra, North America's "dice coaster," with a full Immelmann loop in the design. Then there's Gwazi with its dueling coasters careening over 15 hills, generating 3.5G and speeds of over 50mph (80kph). Kumba reaches speeds of over 60mph (95kph), while Python offers a 70ft (21m) plunge.

FESTIVALS IN TAMPA
The annual Gasparilla Festival, in early February, is Tampa's big day out. The timetable begins mid-morning when the world's only fully rigged pirate ship sets sail from Ballast Point Pier and docks downtown with a full crew of colorful "pirates" all armed to the teeth. A victory parade sets off down Bayshore Boulevard, culminating in a vast street party. There is only about a week's breathing space before festival fever breaks out again. Fiesta Day in Ybor City sees sideshows and art, craft and food stalls line Seventh Avenue, and in the evening the streets are ablaze with dozens of illuminated floats.

Downtown Tampa You will not find any priceless architectural gems or quaint backstreets in downtown Tampa, but you will find a busy, well-maintained district that has invested in quantities of public sculpture assisted by the City of Tampa Art in Public Places program.

If you are interested in local history, start your explorations at the **Tampa Bay History Center** in the *Convention Center Annex, 225 S. Franklin Street* (*Open* Tue–Sat 10–5. *Admission free*; tel: 813/228-0097, www.tampahistorycenter.org) for a 500-year overview of the Bay Area. On Tampa, at the corner of Kennedy, is Charles Perry's stainless-steel sculpture *Solstice* (1985). Beyond it is George Sugerman's *Untitled* of 1988. If you are feeling in the mood for more artistic inspiration, then head for the Tampa Museum of Art (see page 231). Two of Tampa's best buildings are the art deco Woolworth's building and the ornate Tampa Theatre (see page 231), both on Franklin. You will find more art on Franklin in the shape of the *Franklin Street 1925* mural and Geoffrey Naylor's 1973 aluminum sculpture *The Family of Man*.

Florida Aquarium *701 Channelside Drive* (*Open* daily 9:30–5. *Admission: expensive*; tel: 813/273-4000, www.flaquarium.net) Opened in 1995, this impressive downtown aquarium traces the journey of a drop of water from its underground source to the sea through a series of Florida habitats. Self-guided tours begin in the Florida Wetlands section, a steamy recreation of springs and streams, sawgrass marshes, swamps, hammocks and mangrove forests enclosed in a giant glass seashell. Turtles and bass, native birds and alligator hatchlings inhabit the living complement of wetland plants and trees. In the Bays and Beaches exhibit there are seabed close-ups providing glimpses of crabs, conch, shrimp and sand dollars, among others. The highlight of the Coral Reefs Gallery is the massive 500,000-gallon (2,275,000 liters) aquarium tank with its colorful corals and darting tropical fish. Interactive dive shows are held here several times a day, and the audience can listen to the diver explaining what's what from inside the tank.

Other denizens of the deep—sharks, rays, drifting jellyfish—occupy the Offshore Gallery, while there is a family-friendly outdoor area, Explore A Shore, which has a sandy beach for digging and giant water-squirting scallops. If you want to get into the action, the aquarium offers "Swim with the Fishes" and "Dive with the Sharks" programs.

Piratical goings-on in Tampa's Gasparilla Festival

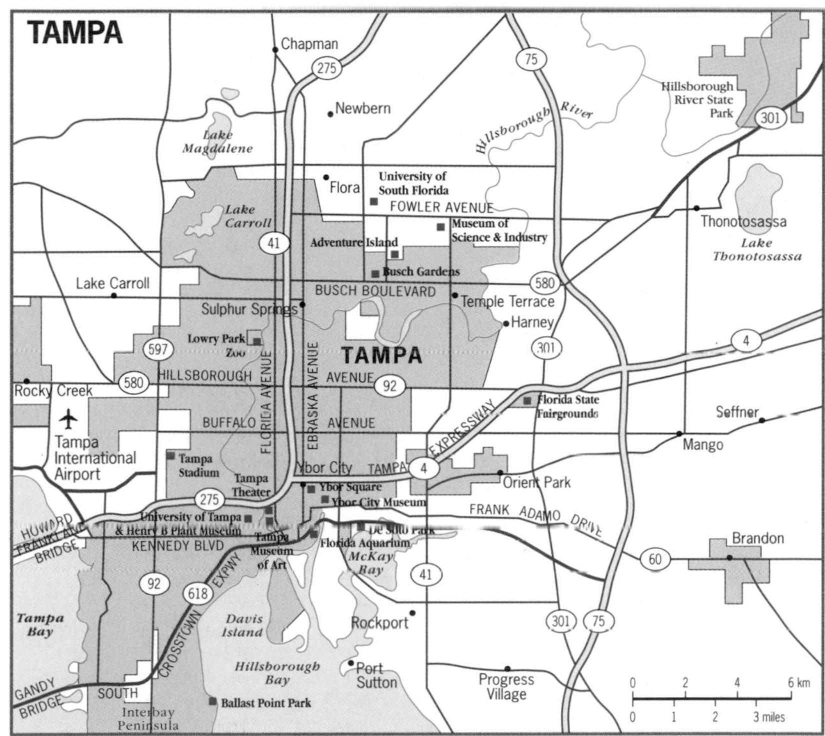

Henry B. Plant Museum, *University of Tampa, 401 W. Kennedy Boulevard* (*Open* Tue–Sat 10–4, Sun noon–4. *Admission: donation*; tel: 813/254-1891, www.plantmuseum.com) There is no difficulty locating Henry B. Plant's palatial Tampa Bay Hotel building, now part of the city's university campus. Visitors to the downtown district will have caught glimpses of its silver onion-domed minarets. Built in 1891, the 500-room hotel was a triumph of Moorish Revival architecture, from its crescent-tipped spires to its acres of red-brick and ornamental fretwork. It is surrounded by verandas, wide enough to accommodate rickshaws for the guests' convenience, and was furnished with enormous quantities of antiques and art treasures collected from Europe and the Orient.

The museum occupies only a corner of one wing, but its suite of rooms, with original furnishings, re-creates some of the splendor of this extraordinary building. (You can walk through the college sections to see the former lobby and other public areas.)

Hillsborough River State Park, *15402 U.S. 301 N. at Thonotasassa (6 miles/9.5km southwest of Zephyr Hills)* (*Open* daily 8–dusk. *Admission: inexpensive*; tel: 813/987-6771, www.floridastateparks.org) One of Florida's earliest state parks, opened in 1938, Hillsborough lies 12 miles (19km) north of Tampa. The preserve, bordering the scenic Hillsborough River, contains **Fort Foster State Historic Site**, a carefully reconstructed 1837 frontier post built during the Second Seminole War. There are weekend tours of the fort, nature trails, swimming, fishing and picnic areas.

BUY THE BUY

Shoppers will have a great time in Tampa's malls. Two of the largest are the International Plaza at West Shore Boulevard and Boy Scout Boulevard and University Mall, 2200 E. Fowler Avenue, while WestShore Plaza at Westshore and Kennedy boulevards is Tampa Bay's premier fashion mall with more than 100 shops and department stores. In the historic district, Old Hyde Park Village, just south of downtown at Swann and Dakota Avenues, offers upscale stores in an attractively restored setting. For antiques, collectibles, cigars and craft shops, check out Ybor Square, 8th and 13th streets, in a former Ybor City cigar factory.

MOSIMAX: THE BIG ONE
A giant 10,500sq ft (945sq m) gleaming blue bubble parked up against the Museum of Science and Industry (MOSI), the IMAX® *Dome* Theatre houses an 82ft (24.5m) hemispherical movie screen specially designed to maximize the IMAX film format. This is the place to get immersed in a tropical rain forest, dive deep into the ocean on the trail of a whale, or savor a moon shot from the comfort of an armchair. There are regular showings throughout the day (reservations, tel: 813/987-6000).

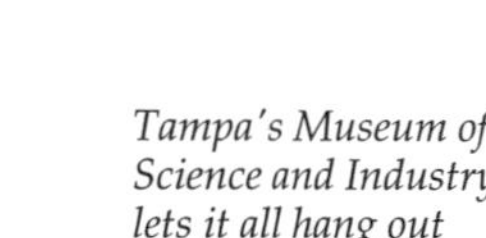

Lowry Park Zoo Gardens, *1101 West Sligh Avenue* (*Open* daily 9.30–5. *Admission: moderate*; tel: 813/932-0245) A multimillion-dollar rejuvenation project launched here in the 1980s revolutionized the old city zoo, transforming it into one of the top-ranked, mid-sized zoos in the country. Pride of place goes to the **Manatee and Aquatic Center**, with its three 25,000-gallon (113,500 liter) manatee treatment tanks and emergency rescue clinic. Natural habitats have been provided for other aquatic and wetland creatures native to Florida, including alligators, snapping turtles and river otters, while the **Florida Wildlife Center** showcases Florida panthers, black bears and fox squirrels. An 18,000sq ft (1,620sq m) **Free-Flight Aviary** houses exotic birds; orangutans, chimpanzees and lemurs hang out in **Primate World**; tigers, camels, tapirs and rhinos reside in the **Asian Domain**. Children will be enchanted by the small-scale inhabitants of **Children's Village**, such as pygmy goats and Vietnamese pot-bellied piglets; and the **Harrell Discovery Center** provides interactive exhibits and a creepy-crawly insect zoo.

Museum of Science and Industry, *4801 E. Fowler Avenue* (*Open* daily from 9am. *Admission: expensive*; tel: 813/987-6100, www.mosi.org) The southeast's largest science center is a monster, with a Grand Lobby that manages to dwarf not one but two three-story-high sauropod dinosaur skeletons. The museum is a sprawling scientific playground boasting some 450 hands-on exhibits and the largest children's science center in the country, **Kids in Charge**. Experience a hair-raising encounter with a van de Graaff generator or pedal power into a light bulb, then try the **Weather Station's** hurricane chamber, simulating winds up to 74mph (119kph). The human body comes under the microscope in **The Amazing You**; there is a trip to space at the **G.T.E. Challenger Learning Center**; and "backwoods trails" are laid out in the grounds. Last, but by no means least, check out the daily movie program in the IMAX® *Dome* Theatre (see panel).

Tampa's Museum of Science and Industry lets it all hang out with its multicolored exposed pipes

Sacred Heart Catholic Church, *509 Florida Avenue* (*Open* daily, tel: 813/229-1595) For a taste of old Tampa buried among the downtown high-rises, step off the beaten track for just a moment to this quiet oasis. Completed in 1905, the Romanesque-style edifice has fine stained glass, including scenes from the life of Christ.

Tampa Museum of Art, *600 North Ashley Drive (at Twiggs)* (*Open* Tue–Sat 10–5, Thu 10–8, Sun 11–5. *Admission: inexpensive*; tel: 813/274-8130) There are two main, and totally diverse, strands to this museum's collections: one is the display of 19th- to 20th-century American art; and the other is a significant holding of Greek, Roman and Etruscan antiquities. The latter collection of sculpture and elegantly decorated pottery is on permanent display, and ranges from two grotesque and remarkably contemporary-looking heads from the 2nd or 3rd century BC, to exquisite statuettes and gracefully fashioned urns and vases. The Florida Gallery showcases works by local artists, while other galleries house selected exhibits from the museum's collections of paintings, sculture, photography and works on paper. The museum also plays host to a wide-ranging program of traveling and special exhibitions. Don't miss the waterfront terrace, which has a terrific view across the Hillsborough River to the University of Tampa's Plant Building.

Tampa Theatre, *711 Franklin Street* (Occasional tours, call for schedules. *Admission: inexpensive;* tel: 813/274-8268, www.tampatheatre.org) Modestly hailed as "The Pride of the South," this 1926 rococo-style movie theater is a weird and wonderful addition to the downtown district. Its facade is decorated with elegant classical reliefs, while the interior is a grotto-style, low-lit Aladdin's cave, with rough walls, ornate painted ceilings and colored floor tiles. Pillars and arches are topped with gargoyles and statuary, and there is a grand old theater organ. In addition to all that, the old movie theater still operates.

ON THE WATER

Take a dinner cruise aboard the modern *Starlite Majesty*. Cruises depart from St. Pete Beach or Clearwater Beach Marina (call for schedules; tel: 727/462-2628 or 800/444-4814, www.starlitecruises.com). If you prefer to paddle your own canoe in a stunning wilderness setting, contact Canoe Escape, 9335 E. Fowler Avenue (tel: 813/986-2067, www.canoeescape.com), who can organize guided canoe trips and rentals on the Hillsborough River.

Tampa Museum of Art has displays of both ancient and modern art

UP IN SMOKE
The 110-block Ybor City historic district contains more than 1,300 significant buildings, of which more than 150 are old cigar factories that once employed nearly 13,000 people. Some 500 million cigars are still produced in Tampa annually by just 15 manufacturers with a work force of around 3,000. Annual sales are in the region of $150 million.

If it's souvenirs you're after, cigars are the obvious buy in Ybor City, and there are dozens of cigar stores to choose from. One of the most impressive is Metropolitan Cigars, 2014 E. 7th Avenue (tel: 813/248-3304), which sells local and foreign-made cigars and features one of the world's largest walk-in humidors.

Ybor City (www.ybor.org) The name Tampa means "sticks of fire," and the city's old cigar-factory neighborhood, Ybor (pronounced E-bor) City, is undergoing a renaissance. One of Florida's prized National Historic Landmark Districts (along with the likes of St. Augustine and Pensacola), this century-old Cuban district has been polished up with replica 19th-century street lamps, restored wrought-iron balconies, cobblestone streets, and an influx of artisans, boutiques and entertainment venues, all of which are designed to recapture the gaiety of its heyday.

Don Vincente Martinez Ybor moved his cigar-making operation from Key West to Tampa in 1886. Cuban workers were joined by a mixture of Italian, Spanish and German immigrants, who brought their own customs and traditions to the area, creating a vibrant, bustling community that entertained Cuban freedom fighter José Marti, Teddy Roosevelt's Rough Riders and every goodtime gal in town.

The heart of the district is La Setima (Seventh Avenue), the main shopping district, well-supplied with restaurants and cafés. This is also the nightlife strip, which comes alive after sundown, particularly on Friday and Saturday nights when the clubs are open until early morning. The Centro Ybor anchors the district. Opened in 2000 on 1600 Block, its a great dining and entertainment complex. On 13th Street, Ybor's original red-brick cigar factory, with its three-story oak and heart pine interior, has been restored and converted into another shopping and restaurant complex, **Ybor Square**. When the factory was operational, hundreds of workers (mostly men) spent long hours at the serried ranks of benches, rolling cigars by hand while a lector (reader) read novels and daily newspapers aloud to relieve the tedium.

For a look at life as it used to be lived here, visit the former bakery that houses the compact **Ybor City State Museum**, *1818 E. Ninth Avenue* (*Open* daily 9–5. *Admission: inexpensive*; tel: 813/247-6323. www.ybormuseum.org).

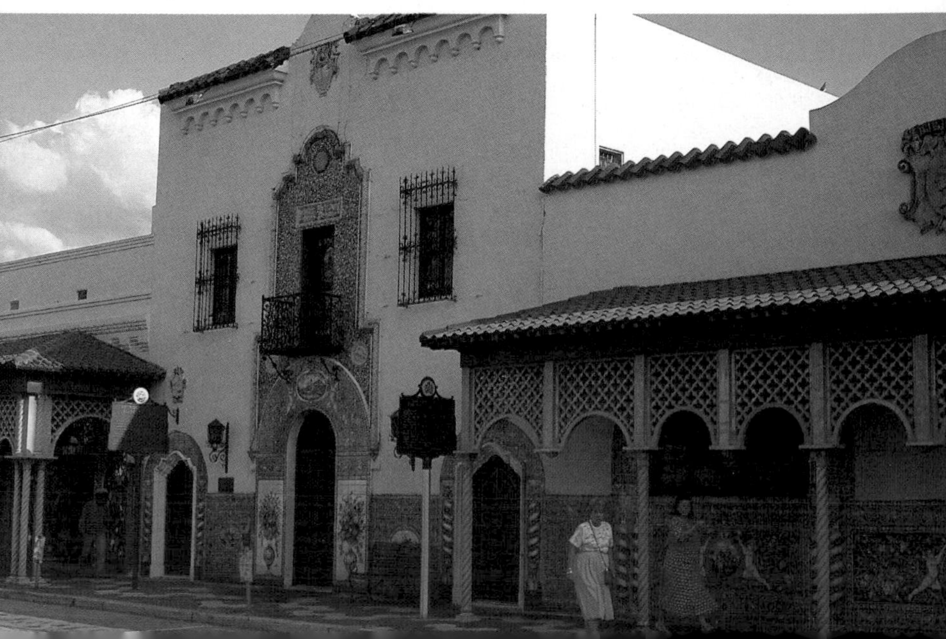

Cuban is the style in Ybor City

Do not miss the furnished worker's "shotgun" cottage a few doors down. Though the bakery no longer bakes bread, there are plenty of opportunities to sample Cuban cuisine on Seventh Avenue. Feast on a Cuban sandwich or sample traditional fare in one of the family restaurants—a historical favorite is the 1905 **Columbia Restaurant**, on 21st Street, which is decorated with wonderfully photogenic hand-painted tiles.

There are 90-minute guided walking tours from the museum on Saturdays at 10.30am (*Admission: inexpensive*; tel: 813/241-8838). Major events at Ybor include the costumed parade of Guavaween on October 29 and Thanksgiving weekend festival with trolleybus tours, street entertainment and a tree-lighting ceremony.

The Old Bakery in Ybor City, Tampa

►► Tarpon Springs *199 A4*

And now for something completely different: a Greek sponge-fishing town on the shores of the Gulf of Mexico. A stroll down Dodecanese Boulevard to the sponge docks here is like taking a Mediterranean vacation. The aroma of freshly baked Greek pastries scents the air (there is a more pungent whiff of drying sponges when the fleet is in) and *bouzouki* music accompanies coffee and ouzo in small cafés off the main street. You should certainly sample traditional Greek delicacies, such as nut and honey *baklava*, *spanakopita* (spinach) or *tiropita* (cheese) triangles wrapped in flaky phyllo pastry.

The Greek community arrived in the early 1900s to harvest the Gulf sponge beds. They imported their customs and culture, too; one example is **St. Nicholas' Greek Orthodox Cathedral**, *N. Pinellas Avenue (U.S. 19)* (*Open* daily 9–5). The present neo-Byzantine building, dating from 1943, contains marble from the Greek pavilion's display at the 1939 New York World's Fair. Its broad nave is lined with striking stained glass, and there is a miraculous weeping statue of St. Nicholas.

On Dodecanese Boulevard, take a 30-minute boat trip around the docks with the **St. Nicholas Boat Line** (*Admission: inexpensive*; tel: 727/942-6425). Frequent daily sailings include a narrated history and demonstration of diving techniques. Marine life from the Gulf and Caribbean are at the **Tarpon Springs Aquarium** (*Open* Mon–Sat 10–5, Sun noon–5. *Admission: inexpensive*; tel: 727/938-5378, www.tarponspringsaquarium.com); while **Spongeorama** (*Open* daily 10–5. *Admission free*; tel: 727/942-3771) comprises a dusty museum and movie about the sponge industry in a former wharfside factory.

The old cigar factory, the heart of Ybor City, is now a shopping and restaurant complex

► Weeki Wachee Springs *199 A4*

6131 Commercial Way, U.S. 19 (at S.R. 50); tel: 1-877-GO-WEEKI or 352/596-2062

Open: daily from 10am. Admission: expensive

While the rest of the state is getting back to nature, this is one of the original Florida fantasies, a watery wonderland of make-believe, where human "mermaids" perform Hans Christian Andersen water ballets 16ft (5m) under water, and the rain forest is nurtured by a sprinkler system. Created in 1947, the mermaid shows are now part of an entertainment package that includes exotic and birds of prey shows; a petting zoo; river cruises; and a pirate-themed water park.

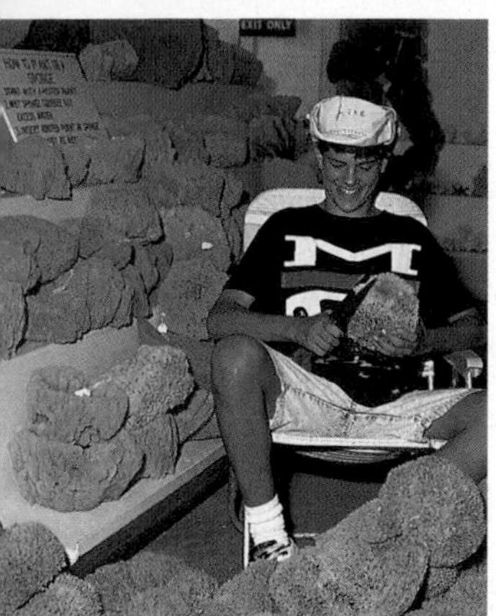

The first Florida sponges were discovered off the shores of Key West in the mid-19th century. In 1890, real-estate developer John K. Cheyney, looking for ways to promote Tarpon Springs, discovered a wealth of sponges growing off the central Gulf Coast and began his own small-scale "hooking" operation. These "hookers," or early spongers, set off in small rowboats from a mother ship, armed with a glass-bottom bucket to survey the seabed and long poles with hooks on the end that they used for gathering the sponges. Hooking required considerable dexterity, and the spongers were limited to shallow waters no more than 15–20ft (4.5–6m) deep.

Arrival of the Greeks During the Spanish-American War, spongers from Key West joined the Gulf fleet, and their haul was sold at the Tarpon Springs Sponge Exchange. John Cocoris, a Greek sponge buyer from New York, traveled south to deal with Cheyney in 1905. He stayed on and soon sent for his brothers from Greece. Together they worked for Cheyney, while surreptitiously surveying the extent of the sponge beds until they were confident enough to send back to Greece for a diving team. The Greeks had already pioneered the use of diving suits and air pipes in the Mediterranean, and Cocoris's divers revolutionized the Gulf sponge industry.

By 1936, Tarpon Springs was recognized as the sponge capital of the world, and its 200-vessel fleet set sail in the traditional Phoenician-style boats built by local Greek craftsmen. They would stay out for six months at a time, curing and cleaning their catch on board as they plied the Gulf from the Keys to the Panhandle.

The sponge-boat quay at Tarpon Springs

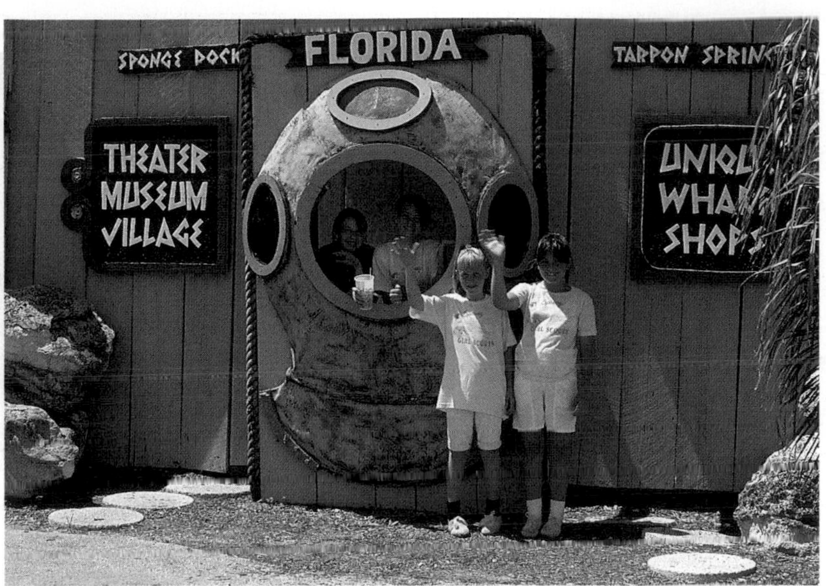

Spongeorama in Tarpon Springs

Disaster and recovery In the 1940s, a bacterial blight ripped through the Gulf sponge beds. Nothing grew for almost 20 years, until most divers had moved away, grown too old, or turned to shrimping and fishing. The recovery rate was slow, and only four or five sponge boats operated during the 1970s; they had to work up to 100 miles (160km) offshore, collecting just 200 to 300 pieces per day. In 1985, Hurricane Elena swept up the Gulf Coast and spent a couple of days churning up the seabed in the crook of the Panhandle. A year later, a boat belonging to one George Billiris was hove to in the face of a storm, about 5 miles (8km) offshore. One of the divers went down to look at the old sponge beds and discovered wall-to-wall sponges. The hurricane had redistributed the larvae, and they were flourishing. In four or five days, Billiris collected 4,000 pieces of sponge, and the Gulf sponge industry was back on its feet.

What happens to the sponges? Each sponge is protected by a membrane that solidifies if it dries out. To prevent this, when the sponges are harvested, they are graded into types, piled on deck, and covered with canvas. The membrane dies and decomposes over two to three days (a very smelly process), leaving the sponge skeleton, which is then cleaned with high-pressure hoses. Beaten, washed and turned constantly to remove all the dead matter, the sponges are then placed in big string bags and hung on the rigging until they are prepared for market. At auction, the sponger displays his catch in strings of 50 sponges, varying in size, but all of the same type. Wool sponges are the highest grade, followed by yellow, grass and wire varieties. A successful bid sees the sponges removed to a wholesaler's packing house, where they are bleached from grubby brown to a soft yellow color, cut, clipped into shape with shears and then sold for one of their 1,400 commercial uses.

MARINE HARVEST
Sponge is a living multi-celled organism, one step up the evolutionary ladder from an amoeba. Sponges are hermaphrodites: They produce both male and female cells and reproduce themselves. The main requirement is firm anchorage for the larvae—rocks are ideal, but not sand. The sponge grows at a rate of about half an inch (1.25cm) in diameter each month for four to five years, then the growth rate slows, but does not stop. It can grow up to 10ft (3m) across. Fragments left behind when a sponge is picked will grow again, and state law prohibits the harvesting of any sponge less than 5in (12.5cm) in diameter.

THE PANHANDLE

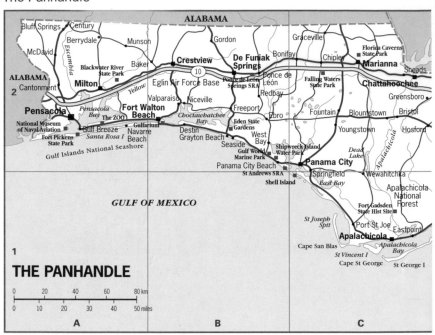

ALABAMA
Bluff Springs
Century
Berrydale
Munson
Gordon
Graceville
McDavid
Escambia
Crestview
De Funiak Springs
Bonifay
Chipley
Florida Caverns State Park
Marianna
Sneads
Baker
Blackwater River State Park
10
ALABAMA
Milton
Cantonment
Yellow
Eglin Air Force Base
Ponce de León Springs SRA
Ponce de León
Falling Waters State Park
Chattahoochee
Redbay
Greensboro
Valparaiso
Niceville
Pensacola
Pensacola Bay
Fort Walton Beach
Choctawhatchee Bay
Freeport
Ebro
Fountain
Blountstown
Bristol
The ZOO
National Museum of Naval Aviation
Gulf Breeze
Gulfarium
Navarre Beach
Destin
Grayton Beach
Eden State Gardens
Youngstown
Hosford
Fort Pickens State Park
Santa Rosa I
Seaside
West Bay
Gulf Islands National Seashore
Gulf World Marine Park
Shipwreck Island Water Park
Dead Lake
Apalachicola
Panama City
Panama City Beach
St Andrews SRA
Shell Island
Springfield
East Bay
Wewahitchka
Apalachicola National Forest
GULF OF MEXICO
Fort Gadsden State Hist Site
St Joseph Spit
Port St Joe
Eastpoint
Apalachicola
Cape San Blas
Apalachicola Bay
St Vincent I
Cape St George
St George I
1
2
0 20 40 60 80 km
0 10 20 30 40 50 miles
A
B
C

A SOUTHERN SONGBIRD
A year-round Florida resident, the common mockingbird was chosen as the state bird in 1927. About 10in (25.5cm) in length, with a 15in (38cm) wingspan, grayish upper body, white underside and patches on the wings and tail, they are great songsters, singing well into the night on balmy spring evenings.

SANDWICHED BETWEEN the Gulf of Mexico, Georgia and Alabama, Florida's Panhandle extends west from the peninsula in a dark-green ribbon of pine forest edged by pristine white quartz-sand beaches. This is "Florida with a Southern accent," where *Gone with the Wind* antebellum mansions grace historical plantations, oak-canopied roads draped with Spanish moss tunnel into the countryside and Deep South hospitality serves up grits and throws "all comers welcome" mullet fries.

In its early days, the region was bandied between foreign invaders like a shuttlecock. French, British and two terms of Spanish rule left a handful of fortresses,

Oyster boats off Apalachicola

The Panhandle

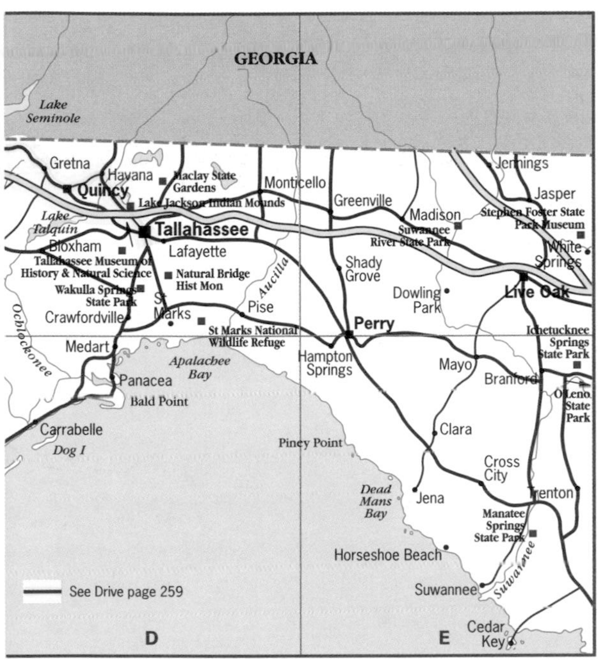

foreign place names and a clutch of shipwrecks. Historic **Pensacola** was the main settlement until the 1820s, when, midpoint between Pensacola and St. Augustine, **Tallahassee** was chosen as the site of the new state capital, and here it remains, an attractive small city, a stone's throw from the Georgia border.

Largely bypassed by Northern tourists fleeing south and by international visitors pouring into Orlando and Miami, the Panhandle is Florida's well-kept secret. Its fabulous beaches rank among the finest in the state (and, indeed, the nation), and now attract a far wider audience than the vacationers from Alabama, Georgia and Mississippi who earned the Panhandle Coast its nickname: the "Redneck Riviera." The Panhandle's main season is summer (May–Sep). When things become a little too hot and sticky down in the south, the northern reaches of the state welcome vacationers to the well-developed mainland beaches, and to the barrier islands of the **Gulf Islands National Seashore**, which preserves tracts of spectacular undeveloped shoreline in the west. The central **Emerald Coast**, named for its glassy green waters, and **Panama City Beach**, offer excellent deep-sea fishing and diving opportunities, family oriented entertainments, sports and accommodations with the emphasis on value.

In the backcountry pine forests, freshwater springs feed narrow creeks and the pristine, dark, tannin-stained rivers so favored by canoeists. The rich coastal estuaries these rivers create are a haven for fish and birdlife, and the little town of **Apalachicola** is famous for its oyster beds. The subterranean beauty of the **Florida Caverns**, near Marianna, makes them a popular outing.

(Note: West of the Apalachicola River, the Panhandle operates on Central Standard Time, one hour behind Eastern Standard Time in the rest of Florida.)

▶▶▶ REGION HIGHLIGHTS

Apalachicola and the barrier islands *pages 238–240*

Canoeing *page 244*

Cedar Key *page 240*

Eden State Gardens and Mansion *pages 241*

Grayton Beach *page 242*

Marianna/Florida Caverns State Park *page 243–242*

Pensacola *pages 249–251*

Tallahassee *pages 254–258*

OYSTER STEW

1 pint shucked oysters
quarter cup butter
1 quart milk
salt, pepper, paprika

Drain oysters; reserve juice. Remove any shell particles. Add oysters and juice to butter; cook for three minutes, or until edges of oysters start to curl. Add milk, salt and pepper. Heat thoroughly, but do not boil. Sprinkle with paprika and serve at once.

▶▶▶ Apalachicola *236 C1*

If miles of fine, sandy beach, superb fishing and wildlife, historic houses and buckets of fresh oysters daily sounds like heaven, it could be named Apalachicola. This small fishing port, 60 miles (96.5km) southwest of Tallahassee, is a real find for a quiet break. Founded as a rivermouth customs post back in 1823, the town and its history and prosperity have long been tied to the Apalachicola River, one of Florida's largest natural waterways. As settlers farther north developed plantations, so river transportation increased, and thanks to "King Cotton," Apalachicola's customs post grew to be the third largest port on the Gulf of Mexico. When the cotton bubble burst, Apalachicola turned to logging until the cypress forests were exhausted; it then hit on fishing and oystering. Mullet, pompano, mackerel, bluefish and trout were the fishermen's staples. The oystermen still harvest their catch by hand, prying oysters from the beds with long-handled tongs worked like scissors from their small boats.

Apalachicola's boom periods in the mid-19th and early 20th centuries were translated into some wonderful buildings. The crumbling cotton warehouses on the downtown docks are being restored, and the many gracious houses lining **Chestnut Avenue** (Avenue E.) and the surrounding streets evoke the prosperous Victorian lifestyle once enjoyed by the town's successful merchants. The best way to see Apalachicola is on foot. There are around 200 houses dating from 1840 to 1880, and the Chamber of Commerce, 99 Market Street (tel: 850/653-9419), provides a map of an exhaustive walking tour of the town that covers all sorts of interesting spots, from the pre-1830s **Chestnut Street Cemetery**, with its memorials to the town's early settlers, yellow-fever victims and Confederate soldiers, to the **John Gorrie State Museum** (*Open Thu–Mon 9–5. Admission: inexpensive*; tel: 850/653-9347;

(Continued on page 240)

Apalachicola, source of the Florida oyster

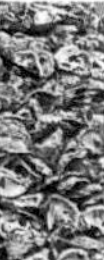

The barrier islands off the Franklin County coast protect St. George Sound, one of the most productive fishing regions on the Gulf of Mexico. Largely undeveloped—two of them are uninhabited—they are superb natural preserves.

Dog Island Set 5 miles (8km) across the sound from Carrabelle, Dog Island has the highest sand dunes in the state. Its tiny population is linked to the mainland by a daily ferry service. Most of the island is a wildlife preserve of coastal dunes, with marsh and mangrove enclaves on the protected bayside.

St. George Island The biggest of the islands (25 miles/40km long) and the most developed, St. George is reached by a 4-mile (6.5km) causeway from the east bank of the Apalachicola River. The central and western parts of the island have a clutch of shops and restaurants and a forest of weatherboard vacation homes on stilts, many of them available for rent.

Nine miles (14.5km) of undeveloped Gulf and bay beaches on the eastern end are protected by a state park. Here, the wind has sculpted the fine sand into miniature mountains, their ridges and hummocks crested with sea oats and scrub grasses. Waves and currents move 180,000 cubic yards (234,000cu m) of sand west along the island coast annually. Pine trees have been buried up to their crowns by these drifts, and the boardwalk trail completely disappears in places. On the Gulf shore, ghost crabs and the little wading birds called sanderlings scuttle around the seashells in the surf; the back bay woodlands are full of birds, and ospreys and bald eagles ride the thermals above the fishing grounds.

St. Vincent Island Nine miles (14.5km) offshore and part of the National Wildlife Refuge System, 2,358-acre (943ha) St. Vincent is the least accessible of the barrier islands and therefore the most enticing for nature lovers. Its remarkably diverse habitats, including dunes, tidal marshes, freshwater lakes, oak ridges, pine flatwoods, magnolia and cabbage palm hammocks, attract an equally diverse cross section of wildlife. Captive-breeding programs for endangered native species, such as the red wolf, exist alongside such exotic surprises as sambar deer (originally from India), introduced by hunters in the 1920s. (There is a visitor center in Apalachicola, tel: 850/653-8808.)

LITTLE ST. GEORGE ISLAND
Once part of the main island, uninhabited Little St. George Island is now separated by a channel, and can only be reached by boat.

Fishing off the islands

Busy Destin marina is a top sportfishing center

(Continued from page 238)

see panel). A reproduction of Gorrie's original ice-making machine is the centerpiece of the interesting one-room museum. Gorrie's tomb is found across the street at the **Trinity Episcopal Church**.

Finding a quiet spot away from town is easy. **St. George Island** is a short drive from downtown Apalachicola, across a 4-mile (6.5km) causeway from the fishing community of Eastpoint. Drastically developed with old Florida-style beach vacation homes in recent years, it still has several miles of magnificent white beach in the state park (see page 239). The half-million-acre (200,000ha) **Apalachicola National Forest** contains **Fort Gadsden State Historic Site** (28 miles/45km northeast of Apalachicola, off S.R. 65), whose exhibits highlight the role of Native and African Americans in armed forces in the early 19th century. Farther east, the extensive **St. Marks National Wildlife Refuge** (www.fws.gov) is a winter destination for thousands of migratory birds and has some great hiking trails (see page 253).

▶▶ Cedar Key *237 E1*

Anchored to the mainland by a 3-mile (4.8km) run of island-hopping bridges, Cedar Key looks out over the Gulf of Mexico from the southern edge of Florida's Big Bend. Where the panhandle meets the pan, this former cross-state railroad terminal and logging town is one of only a handful of small settlements and fish camps that survive along the Bend's 150-mile (241km) stretch of undeveloped coastal wetlands and forest.

Cedar Key's fortunes pretty much ran out when its cedar stands were logged to extinction in the 1870s. Fishing and low-key tourism have kept the town afloat, and it is a great place to relax, go fishing or birdwatching, or take a boat trip out to island beaches in the **Cedar Keys Wildlife Refuge** (www.fws.gov). There are some fine old Victorian homes, small hotels, shopping and dining on the dock and the landmark Island Hotel.

The little **Cedar Key Museum State Park**, at Second and D streets (*Open* Thu–Mon 9–5. *Admission: inexpensive*; tel: 352/543-5549) was the home of local historian St. Clair Whitman. It now houses his eclectic collection, including numerous Native American objects. The house is furnished in 1920s–30s style. Thirty miles (48km) north of town is **Manatee Springs State Park** (*Open* daily 8am–dusk. *Admission: inexpensive*; tel: 352/493-6072, www.floridastateparks.org) on the banks of the Suwannee River. It's a good place to spot manatees in winter, rent a canoe or follow a nature trail.

▶ Emerald Coast: Destin and Fort Walton Beach *236 B2*

The Emerald Coast unfurls in a ribbon of white-sand beaches from Fort Walton Beach in the west to the fishing village of Destin. The emphasis here is on laid-back, family fun and outdoor activities. There's shell collecting, watersports, sailing on Choctawhatchee Bay and golf. Affordable accommodations, shopping malls, dive shops and touristy attractions are strung out along the main drag, U.S. 98, which parallels the shore.

ICE MAKER

A young physician from Charleston, South Carolina, John Gorrie moved to the mosquito-infested estuary port of Apalachicola in 1833. During the next 22 years, until his death in 1855, he served as the town's mayor, postmaster, treasurer, council member, bank director and church founder and still found time to practice medicine. Ignorant of the mosquito's role in spreading yellow fever, Gorrie and others believed that humid marsh air was to blame, and he set about devising a method of cooling and purifying the air in the sickroom. En route he invented an ice-making machine, and the concept of refrigeration and air-conditioning was born.

Destin regularly plays host to fishing tournaments and an annual Seafood Festival in October. For the largest and most elaborately equipped sportfishing charter fleet in the state, look no further than Destin's East Pass marina.

Air Force Armament Museum and Eglin Air Force Base, *14 Eglin Parkway (north of Fort Walton Beach)* The largest U.S. Air Force base in the world, Eglin covers some 720sq miles (1,858sq km) of the mainland and rules the skies over a further 86,500sq miles (224,035sq km) of test area in the Gulf of Mexico. The base's Armaments Museum (*Open* daily 9.30–4.30. *Admission free;* tel: 850/882-4062, www.eglin.af.mil) displays an array of weaponry, from a 1903 Springfield rifle to the 6,000-rounds-per-minute GAU8, plus the 180-piece Sikes Antique Pistol Collection. The latter includes flintlock dueling pistols, six-shooters and firearms dating back to the Civil War. A comprehensive aircraft collection is arranged inside and around the building.

Eden State Gardens and Mansion *Port Washington, 4 miles (6.5km) northeast of Grayton Beach on S.R. 395* (*Open* gardens daily 8–dusk; house guided tours Thu–Mon 9–4, on the hour. *Admission: inexpensive*; tel: 850/231-4214, www.dep.state.fl.us) Tucked away off a back road, this lovely two-story southern mansion was built by mill-owner William H. Wesley in 1897. Timber logged in the nearby woods was floated down the Choctawhatchee River to this site until the mill was burned down and the family sold out. The antebellum house was restored in the 1960s, filled with antiques and the gardens created. Moss-draped live oaks dot the lawns and shade picnic tables by the Chocawhatchee where timber logged in the woods was sawn up in the mill and transported by barge to Pensacola. Camellias and azaleas are in bloom from late October to May; the peak flowering time is mid-March.

FISHING SEASON

When to go for "the big one":

Amberjack (1–65 lbs/0.4–29kg.): all year.

Barracuda (3–60 lbs/1.3–27kg): April–November.

Black/Red Grouper (1–60 lbs/0.4–27kg): all year.

Blue Marlin (45–700 lbs/20–315kg): May–November.

Jack Crevalle (2–40 lbs/1–18kg): May–October.

Red Snapper (1–40 lbs/0.4–18kg): all year.

Sailfish (5–100 lbs/2.2–45kg): April–November.

Tarpon (3–90 lbs/1.3–40kg): April–November.

Wahoo (8–100 lbs/3.5–445kg): April–October.

White Marlin (20–150 lbs/9–67.5kg): May–December.

But note: you need a license for sportfishing off Florida.

Fascinating hardware at the Air Force Armament Museum

The little resort of Seaside is developing a name for itself

WEDDING CAVERN
Several of the caves in Florida Caverns State Park have special names suggested by the rock formations, such as the Wedding Cavern, with its glittering white "wedding cake." Several weddings have actually taken place here in the constantly cool temperature of 61–66°F (16–19°C).

Emerald Coast Science Center, *139 Brooks Street, Fort Walton Beach* (*Open* Mon–Fri 9–4, Sat–Sun 11–4. *Admission: inexpensive*; tel: 850/664-1261, www.ecscience.org) A hands-on museum with particular appeal to children. The seven galleries are each devoted to a different branch, inlcuding 18 exhibits relating to color and light. You can fly a modern plane in a wind tunnel in the Fly and Land area; Explore Energy looks at the power of electricity; while at the Hall of Life you'll learn more about the human body and how our senses work.

Gulfarium, *1010 Miracle Strip Parkway (east U.S. 98)* (*Open* Tue– Sun 9–6, last ticket sold at 4. *Admission: expensive*; tel: 850/243-9046, www.gulfarium.com) A short distance east of Fort Walton Beach, Gulfarium was one of the area's pioneering seaside attractions, founded in 1955 but almost totally rebuilt after the hurricanes of 2004. Shows include aquabatic entertainment from performing porpoises and sea lions. The Living Sea exhibit tank has a varied collection of sharks, stingrays, sea turtles, sinuous eels and performing scuba divers, or try the Dolphin Encounter for a close up meeting with this loveable mammal. The tropical penguin colony is a must; so are the otters. Other bird colonies include the Duck and Pelican Roost and the Geese and Swan Sanctuary.

Indian Temple Mound Museum, *139 Miracle Strip Parkway* (*Open* Mon–Sat 9–4.30, Sun 12.30–4.30 Jun–Aug; Mon–Fri 10–4, Sat 9–4 Sep–May. *Admission: inexpensive*; tel: 850/833-9595) This small museum, which traces 10,000 years of Native American life, sits right next to a Native American ceremonial and burial mound dating from around 1400BC. Artifacts and displays include arrowheads, fish-hooks and pottery. A recreated thatched temple has been built atop the burial mound.

►► Grayton Beach *236 B2*

Grayton is the oldest community on the coast between Apalachicola and Pensacola. Its quiet, sandy and tree-shaded streets have been tastefully preserved. There are a couple of fine old homes, smart little boutiques, galleries and antiques shops, but Grayton's real pride and joy is **Grayton Beach State Recreation Area** (*Open* daily 8–dusk. *Admission: inexpensive*; tel: 850/231-4210, www.floridastateparks.org). The spectacular Gulf beach fronts a 365-acre (146ha) park, which offers great swimming, boating, nature trails and surf-fishing. There are also campfire interpretative programs in summer.

A mile (1.6km) up Scenic Country Road 30A, **Seaside** (www.seasidefl.com) boosted its profile when it was chosen as the set for the 1998 Jim Carrey movie, *The Truman Show*. A fanciful re-creation of a 19th-century seaside resort complete with grand Victorian cottages, picket fences and colorful public buildings, Seaside's neo-traditionalist approach has found many fans.

►► Marianna/Florida Caverns State Park *236 C2*

3345 Caverns Road (off S.R. 167, north of Marianna); tel: 850/482-9598, www.floridastateparks.org
Open: daily 8–dusk, cave tours 9–4.30 Mar–Sep; 9–4 Oct–Feb. Admission: inexpensive

The Florida peninsula is a vast limestone plateau, honeycombed with underground caverns, rivers and sinkholes. Most of the caverns are permanently flooded because they are below the water-table level, but at Marianna the Chipola River has cut deep into the limestone, reducing water levels and revealing a superb network of caves.

The upper-level caverns are permanently dry; the lower levels, around 65ft (19.5m) below ground, fill with water during the flood season, in winter. Within the caverns, stalactites, stalagmites, rimstones, flowstones and ribbon formations continue to develop all the time—very slowly. It takes roughly 100 years to grow a single cubic inch (16 cubic centimeters) of solid calcite. The formations are caused by precipitation: rainwater collects carbon dioxide from the air to create a weak carbonic solution that filters through the limestone to the dry cave. There, it evaporates into a concentrated limestone solution, and speleotherms (cave formations) gradually develop. At Marianna, the formations come in two different colors: Brilliant white, formed by calcium carbonate, and an orange-yellow tint, from iron oxide in the soil. Above ground, the 1,280-acre (512ha) park offers two good nature trails, picnicking areas, horseback-riding, canoeing (see page 244), fishing and a swimming hole.

PUCKER UP
Jefferson County celebrates its status as a watermelon growing region with an annual festival held during the last week of June. Activities include a beauty pageant, a canoe race, a parade, a golf tournament and a mess of good ol' country cookin'. The highlights are the sock hop, melon run and horseshoe tournament

▶ Monticello *237 D2*

Named after Thomas Jefferson's Virginia mansion, Monticello was founded in 1827 at one of the highest points in the state—235ft (70m) above sea level. Today, it is a quiet country town and an important agricultural center, with historical roots that can be traced back to the cotton plantations established in the area before the town itself. In the early days, the citizens of Monticello were prosperous, reactionary and influential. Noted politicians, judges and the state's first elected governor, William D. Moseley, came from the district, and local

(Continued on on page 246)

The courthouse in Monticello

There is no better way to explore the quiet backwaters of Florida than by paddling your own canoe. The state has 36 designated canoe trails along miles of scenic waterways. The Panhandle offers plenty of waterborne opportunities, from a gentle novice meander or family style inner-tube rides to more challenging creek runs for experienced canoeists.

CANOE TRAILS
Officially designated canoe trails are managed as part of the Florida Recreational Trail System. For further details, contact the Office of Greenways and Trails, 3900 Commonwealth, Mail Station 795, Tallahassee, FL 32399–3000, tel: 850/245-2052.

Canoe Capital of Florida **Milton**, north of Pensacola, is the Panhandle's chief canoeing center and is a good base for exploring the tannin-stained **Blackwater River** as it winds its way through the dense woodlands of the Blackwater River State Forest. Local canoe-rental operations provide equipment and shuttle services for visitors to the Blackwater, considered one of the purest sand-bottom rivers in the world, and to **Coldwater Creek**, a pretty, freshwater stream running through the forest, 12 miles (19km) north of Milton. For real back-to-nature adventurers, there is camping in the state park.

Farther east Holmes Creek, which rises in Georgia and eventually empties into Choctawhatchee Bay (sheltered by the Emerald Coast), makes for a lazy day's paddling. There is good fishing along its sandy banks and lush swamplands. The 52-mile (84km) **Chipola River Trail** starts in Florida Caverns State Park, north of Marianna. There the river flows through high limestone bluffs and caves and around a series of small rapids and shoals.

The going is rougher on the top section of narrow, twisting **Econfina Creek**, northeast of Panama City Beach, but this 22-mile (35.5km) trail also offers beautiful springs and gentler waters along its lower reaches.

State park facilities Four state parks and canoeing facilities abut the **Suwannee River** and its tributary, the Sante Fe. At the **Suwannee River State Park**, 20 miles (32km) east of Madison, where the much-sung-about Suwannee is joined by the Withlacoochee River, there is great canoeing country. Otters, beavers and gopher tortoises bustle around the river swamp and hardwood hammock habitats. **Ichetucknee Springs State Park**, one of the most beautiful riverfront parks in Florida, is good for tubing (floating in an inner tube), as well as for canoeing, and **O'Leno State Park** marks the point where the Santa Fe resurfaces after a 3-mile (5km) journey underground. Both are close to U.S. 441, south of Lake City.

Manatee Springs State Park, 23 miles (37km) from the Gulf of Mexico, has canoeing, fishing, swimming, scuba diving and manatees.

Canoeing camp

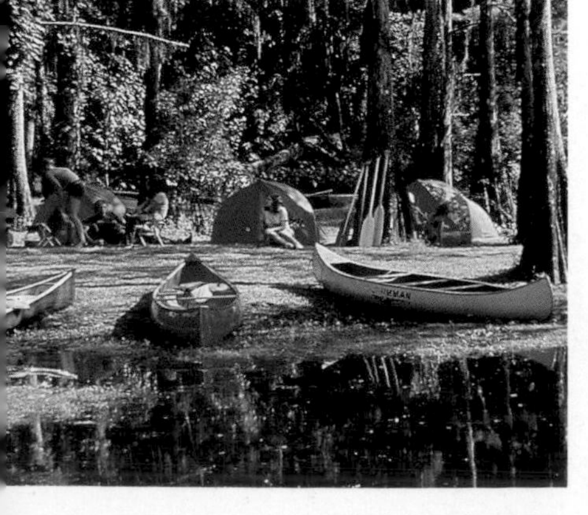

The Gulf Islands National Seashore stretches for across the top of the Gulf of Mexico, from Florida's Santa Rosa Island in the east to West Ship Island off the coast of Mississippi. Abundant plant and animal communities flourish in this magnificent natural preserve, and the three main habitats—dunes, marsh and woodlands—are all represented within the six areas of the Florida district: Santa Rosa, Okaloosa, Naval Live Oaks, Fort Pickens, Pensacola Forts and Perdido Key.

Naval Live Oaks Just across the bay from Pensacola, Naval Live Oaks, at Gulf Breeze (U.S. 98), is the National Park Service headquarters and visitor center. Natural history and historical exhibits, together with an audio-visual presentation, give an overview of the preserve and there is plenty of helpful information.

Santa Rosa This glorious stretch of beach preserve lies east of Pensacola Beach along S.R. 399. Here there are miles of incredibly white sand, with not a condominium in sight.

To protect the fragile dunes, it is strictly boardwalk access only to the shore from designated parking areas. Once on the beach, there is a day use facility at the Navarre Beach end, with picnic shelters, restrooms and a concession stand.

What else is there? The other preserve areas offer several pleasant nature trails, such as the marsh, forest and sandhill trail at **Johnson Beach** on Perdido Key. **Fort Pickens** (see page 249) offers two short and remarkably diverse trails: a 0.25-mile (400m) dune walk, and the 0.5-mile (800m) Blackbird Marsh circuit in the maritime forest. On the mainland, the **Fort Barrancas** trail explores woodlands near the naval air station.

AWESOME OAKS

The 1,378-acre (551ha) woodland park that surrounds Naval Live Oaks is dominated by majestic live oaks. It is so called because in 1828 the U.S. government reserved great tracts of southern oak forest to be managed exclusively for shipbuilding. The heaviest of all the oaks, weighing up to 75 lbs (33.5kg) per cubic foot (0.3 cubic meters), live oaks are also remarkably resistant to disease and decay. There are several nature trails through the forest, which is a haven for foxes, bobcats and raccoons as well as reptiles, from skinks to coral snakes.

MOVING ALONG

The Panhandle's barrier islands are on the move. Littoral currents erode the fine quartz sand from the eastern tip of the islands and deposit it at the western end. Constant winds and storms rearrange the dunes ceaselessly, and the dunes' only protection are the hardy stems and elaborate root systems of the salt-spray-loving sea oats. Sea oats are a protected species along the coast: disturbing them or picking them is against the law.

DIVERS' DELIGHTS
The Gulf of Mexico's crystal-clear waters offer great diving opportunities off Panama City Beach, where wreck dive sites include the tanker *Empire Mica*, the *Grey Ghost* and the 220ft (66m) *Chippewa*. There are several natural coral reefs, and they teem with fish, lobsters and shellfish. Snorkelers and divers can explore the St. Andrews State Park jetties, which range in depth from just 1ft (0.3m) to 50ft (15m). For details of dive and snorkeling trips, contact Hydrospace, Hathaway Marina, tel: 850/234-3063.

(Continued from page 243)

lobbyists were at the forefront of Florida's 1861 secession from the Union. During the mid-19th century, Monticello acquired a wealth of elegant Greek and Classical Revival mansions, pretty stick-style homes with gingerbread detail and needle-spired churches. Several pre-Civil War buildings have survived, and there are more than 40 registered buildings in the Historic District. At the center of town, traffic is routed around the 1909 **Jefferson County Courthouse**, and on the southwest corner of Washington Street is the red-brick 1890 **Perkins Opera House**, which is the focus of a lively arts scene. The ornate Operatic Chamber is an ideal showcase for musical and dramatic performances. Drivers heading west on U.S. 90 can make a pleasant backroad detour to the village of Miccosukee (12 miles/19km west of C.R. 59, then 5 miles/8km north), and follow **Miccosukee Road**, one of thc old, live oak-canopied "cotton trail" roads back to Tallahassee.

►► Panama City Beach *236 B2*

Fun-loving Panama City Beach is typified by its "Miracle Strip" of neon, concrete and cotton candy, which extends for almost 27 miles (43.5km) along the gleaming white Gulf beaches. Love it or loathe it, there is no disputing its distinctive flavor and broad-ranging family appeal. With 18,000 hotel rooms offering everything from secluded luxury resort accommodations to beachside motels and R.V. parks, there is plenty to choose.

The beach is the city's pride and joy, and has recently been the beneficiary of the largest beach nourishment project in Florida's history. Additional sand has extended the shore to a width of 100ft (30m), and dune systems have been created. Here watersports are at the top of the activities list: snorkeling, diving, jet skiing, windsurfing, sailing and parasailing. Fishermen can go for "the big

Panama City Beach

one" on single or party charter boats, or just take it easy and hang a line off one of the numerous piers and jetties. Golf is increasingly popular: There are over 20 excellent courses within a 40-mile (64.5km) radius. Several sports clubs have added top-class hard-surface and clay tennis court facilities as well.

Meanwhile, back on "The Strip," miniature golf courses, featuring model shipwrecks, moated castles and gaping monsters, are open from early to floodlit late, late night. Restaurants, bars, boutiques and video arcades abound, and as the sun goes down, the neon snaps into action and the serious fun begins. Entertainment runs the gamut from comedy to Broadway-style musicals, from fairground thrills to beachclub discos. A notable favorite is the 1,000-seat family oriented Ocean Opry theater (for information and reservations, tel: 850/234-5464) and its crowd-pleasing program of country and western classics, old-time rock 'n' roll, bluegrass and gospel music as well as comedy shows.

Although Panama City Beach is turning into a year-round vacation destination, the main season runs from April through September; the spring break is also busy. Hotel rates are bargains during the winter months, but many attractions are closed off-season.

Gulf World Marine Park, *15412 W. Front Beach Road* (*Open* daily Jun–Aug 9–7. *Admission: expensive*; tel: 850/234-5271, www.gulfworldmarinepark.com) Now expanded with the addition of a climate-controlled tropical garden and 2,000-seat Tropical Garden Theater, this popular marine showcase occupies a prime location in the main beach area. Take in the parrot show, an informative underwater show and scuba demonstration, and the stingray petting pool where visitors are encouraged to feed the rays with slivers of fish held between their fingers. The rays have had their barbs removed and are, therefore, "safe"; visitors may have their own views about the moral issues raised. The dolphins can be stroked, the sharks are fed and there is lots of splashing around in the sea lion and dolphin show. After dark, the new Dolphin Stadium is the setting for a spectacular laser light show, Splash Magic, complete with music, fireworks and a dramatic patriotic salute.

St. Andrews State Recreation Area, *4607 State Park Lane* (*Open* daily 8–dusk. *Admission: inexpensive*; tel: 850/233-5140, www.floridastateparks.org) On the eastern tip of Panama City Beach, this park is one of Florida's most popular. It's also regularly included on the University of Maryland's prestigious "best beach in the U.S." list. Nature trails through the woodlands and dunes offer opportunities to spot wild deer, raccoons, alligators and seabirds, and there is a re-created turpentine still among the pine trees, near the Grand Lagoon fishing pier. Guided hiking tours are available (call for schedules), and there are summer season campfire programs. From the bayside fishing piers you can try to hook speckled trout, red fish and flounder, while bonita, pompano and Spanish and king mackerel are on the Gulf side. There are picnic areas, a campground and boat rentals, and the park is an excellent place for young children.

SUBMARINE MAN
The small and unusual Museum of Man in the Sea, 17314 Back Beach Road (*Open* daily 9–5. *Admission: inexpensive*; tel: 850/235-4101), traces the definitive history of diving, from the earliest records to the miracles of modern science, including marine salvage and construction, archeology and oil drilling. There are lots of dioramas, models and equipment, plus a landmark orange Sealab deep-diving capsule anchored in the parking lot.

Acrobatic dolphins and sea lion shows at Gulf World

Try out the rides in Shipwreck Island Water Park, then recover in the sun

Shell Island, *ferry access from St. Andrews S.R.A.* (*Open* Apr–Oct, daily in summer, weekends only low season. *Admission: moderate*; tel: 850/233-5140) Scheduled to become a state park in the near future, this sheller's paradise lies just off Panama City Beach. Also known as Hurricane Island, it has 7 miles (11km) of untouched shoreline shaded by a smattering of pines. Three-hour shell safaris leave from **Captain Anderson's Marina**, *5550 North Lagoon Drive* (tel: 850/234-3435 or 800/874-2415, www.captainansersonsmarina.com), and **Treasure Island Marina**, *3605 Thomas Drive* (tel: 850/234-7245, www.treasureislandmarine.com), from April through early October. There are also glass-bottom boat trips and dolphin-feeding excursions.

Shipwreck Island Water Park, *12201 Middle Beach Road* (*Open* 10–4.30 mid-Apr to May; 10.30–5.30 Jun–Labor Day. *Admission: expensive;* tel: 850/234-333, www.miraclestrippark.com) Shipwreck Island is the answer to what you can do during the day. There are six exotically landscaped acres of watery fun park, fully equipped with lifeguards, restaurant facilities, snack bars, sundecks, shops and free parking. Meander down the 1,600ft (480m) Lazy River on an inner tube; check out the Ocean Motion wave pool; or try out the flumes, speed slides and 370ft (111m) White Water Tube Ride for thrills and spills. Then settle down under a sun umbrella while the kids splash about in the thoughtfully miniaturized Tadpole Hole.

ZooWorld, *9008 Front Beach Road* (*Open* daily 9–dusk. *Admission: moderate;* tel: 850/230-4839, www.zoo-world.us) A small zoo set in 7.5 acres (3ha) of tropical gardens, ZooWorld has a full complement of around 350 animals, among them monkeys, bears, big cats, exotic birds, giraffes, camels, reptiles and Florida alligators. You can meet baby goats and other farm animals in the petting zoo. The zoo also takes care of 15 rare and endangered species as part of its commitment to the internationally recognized Species Survival Plan (SSP).

TEEPEES FOR TOTS
A fun outing for young children is Bay County's Junior Museum, 1731 N. Jenks Avenue, in Panama City (*Open* Tue–Fri 9–4.30, Sat 10–4. *Admission: inexpensive*; tel: 850/769-6128). It adopts a hands-on approach to its science, art and nature exhibits. Children can play Native American games and explore a life-size teepee, feed chickens and ducks in a recreated pioneer homestead and investigate the nature trail.

►►► Pensacola *236 A2*

The second oldest city in Florida, Pensacola is proud of its history and has three fine historical districts to prove it: The **Seville Historic District**, where the first stockade was erected in 1752; **Palafox Street**, leading down to the waterfront; and 19th-century **North Hill**, with its elegant houses built by wealthy lumber merchants. Sightseeing also includes sophisticated state-of-the-art technology on display at the **National Museum of Naval Aviation**.

Across the bay, Pensacola's beaches are responsible for turning the city into a major resort—40 miles (64.5km) of 99 percent pure quartz sand. **Pensacola Beach**, on Santa Rosa Island, is lined with hotels, boutiques and cafés and is popular for watersports. To the west is **Perdido Key**, part of the Gulf Islands National Seashore; it has free showers and changing facilities in the Johnson Beach area. Or head east along S.R. 399 for the fabulous undeveloped dunes of the **Santa Rosa** and **Navarre beaches**.

Fort Pickens, *W. Santa Rosa Island* (*Open* daily 8.30–dusk. *Admission: moderate* per car; tel: 850/934-2635, www.nps.gov) Strategically sited at the entrance to Pensacola Bay, Fort Pickens was the largest of four defensive fortresses constructed to protect the harbor in the 1800s. More than 21 million locally made bricks were transported out to the island on barges to reinforce the massive five-sided earthworks.

Originally, the fortress was surrounded by a 10ft-deep (3m) moat, but this has since been filled. Bastions with a broad range of firepower anchor the corners, and heavy cannon once lined the wall. To the left of the sallyport (entrance) are the officers' quarters, which were used to house the captured Apache chief Geronimo. Geronimo's enforced stay (1886–1888) generated the beginnings of Pensacola's tourist industry, when curious folk came to ogle at his humiliating downfall. Today, there are historic and natural history displays, beach access and a ranger station.

CITY OF FIVE FLAGS

In 1559, 500 Spanish soldiers and 1,000 colonists sailed into Pensacola Bay and established a settlement. It lasted just two years. But the Europeans were back to stay in the late 17th century, and in less than 100 years the area was controlled by Spanish, French and British interests. Those three, plus the Confederate forces of the 19th century and the forces of post-Civil War America, add up to Pensacola's nickname, the "City of Five Flags."

Marine life exhibits capture the imagination of a visitor to Pensacola's Fort Pickens

Historic Pensacola Village, *Zaragoza and Tarragona Streets* (*Open* museums and restored historic homes Mon–Sat 10–4. *Guided tours* Mon–Sat 11–1. *Admission: inexpensive* combination tickets with the T T Wentworth Florida State Museum; tel: 850/595-5985, ext. 110) Also known as the **Seville Historic District** (www.sevilledistrict.com), this is one of three exceptional preservation districts found in Pensacola. The original street plans were laid out by the British in the mid-18th century, and were later retained by the Spanish, although the names of the streets were changed. Today, the area looks much as it would have appeared in the late 1880s. First stop is the ticket and tour office located in the **Tivoli House**, 205 E. Zaragoza Street. Accompanied tours visit a selection of immaculately restored historic homes, while other village properties are open for self-guided tours.

A good place to begin a visit is at the **Museum of Commerce**, Zaragoza and Tarragona streets. A short video presentation covers Pensacola's history, and a re-created late 19th-century shopping street features a print shop and a pharmacy; and hardware, music and toy stores. Across the street, exhibits in the **Museum of Industry** illustrate Pensacola's two founding strengths, the maritime and lumber industries.

Opposite the Tivoli House are two prime examples of early architecture. **Julee Cottage**, built in 1805, was owned by renowned Pensacolan Julee Panton, a "free woman of color." Its companion, the **Lavalle House** (pronounced La-va-lay), is an eye-catching affair dating from the same year. It was built by one Charles Lavalle with the intention of attracting French Creole lodgers—who might prefer the bright color scheme.

Florida's oldest Protestant church, **Old Christ Church**, faces pretty, tree-shaded Seville Square. Across the street is the **Dorr House**, a beautifully restored 1870 Greek Revival building. The last of the village's official properties, **Quina House**, which was constructed in 1821, is a cosmopolitan mixture of Spanish-French Creole architecture. Lear-Richeblave Historic House, 214 East Zaragoza Street, was built for a shipping magnate and now hosts exhibits charting the development of modern Pensacola and the families who helped make it happen.

There is plenty more to see with the help of the self-guided *Historical Guide to Pensacola* leaflet (obtainable from Tivoli House). Many houses have been converted into folksy law offices, and the local boutique and restaurant owners are usually delighted to regale visitors with tales of their historic surroundings.

Other local museums worth visiting are the **Pensacola Historical Museum**, housed in the Arbona Building, 115 East Zaragoza Street, www.pensacolahistory.org; the **Pensacola Museum of Art**, 407 S. Jefferson Street, in the former city jail; and the **T. T. Wentworth Florida State Museum**, on Jefferson between Government and Zaragoza streets, where local history exhibits introduce visitors to Pensacola's Colonial Archeological Trail.

SLAVES AND SCALPELS
Tucked behind a shopfront in the downtown business district, the Civil War Soldiers Museum, 108 S. Palafox Street (*Open* Tue–Sat 10–4. *Admission: inexpensive*; tel: 850/469-1900) gives a vivid account of the origins of slavery in the U.S. and the Civil War. A range of artifacts and photographs follows the main characters, actions and campaigns, and there is a particularly comprehensive (and gory) selection of medical equipment—the collection was established by a doctor.

National Museum of Naval Aviation, *N.A.S. Pensacola, 1750 Radford Boulevard (via U.S. 98)* (*Open* daily 9–5. *Admission free*; tel: 850/452-3606) "Top Gun fun" shrieks the slogan, and visitors are greeted at the entrance by an F14 Tom

Cat—one of 160 planes, all with a tale to tell. This is indeed an amazing attraction—one of the largest air and space museums in the world. For sheer scale, check out the full-size reconstruction of a World War II aircraft carrier, the USS *Cabot* in the West Wing. The model displays Corsair, Avenger and Hellcat fighters on its wooden decking, while examples of Wildcat, Dauntless and Kingfisher aircraft are locked in stationary flight overhead. The collection features aircraft from the earliest wood-and-canvas prototypes to sophisticated space gadgetry. Flying boats, supersonic jets, moon buggies and naval-aviation memorabilia all earn a place in the Hall of Fame. Video presentations deliver the excitement of flight secondhand; getting closer to the action, there is an IMAX theater (tel: 850/453-2002), and F-4 and A-7 jet cockpit simulators, plus a chance to take the controls of a TH-57 helicopter trainer. Tours with former pilots add special insight to tales of derring-do, and a visit to the Hanger Bay restoration facility provides a opportunity to watch volunteers refurbish historical aircraft.

EARLY DEFENSES

Long before the US Air Force arrived to protect Pensacola Bay, Spanish colonists fortified a strategic bluff (*barranca*) overlooking the harbor entrance and later built a sunken mini-fortress. Visitors to the air station are free to explore 18th- to 19th-century Fort Barrancas, and the forward artillery defenses of the Advance Redoubt, signposted from the aviation museum.

Inside the National Museum of Naval Aviation

ARTISTIC LICENSE
One of America's best-loved musical storytellers, Stephen C. Foster, never saw the Suwannee, or even visited Florida. Looking for a good ol' Southern name for one of his compositions, he had no compunction about tailoring the Suwannee to "S'wanee" to fit the two-syllable cadence he needed. A prolific composer, Foster has about 200 songs to his credit, including singalong favorite *Oh Susannah* and the lilting *Jeannie with the Light-brown Hair.*

►► Ponce de León Springs S.R.A. *236 B2*

2860 Ponce de León Springs Road (off U.S. 90, north of I–10); tel: 850/836-4281, www.floridastateparks.org
Open: daily 8–dusk. Admission: inexpensive

When you drive across the Panhandle on a baking hot day, this is a great place to stop for a picnic and cooling swim. The main spring produces millions of gallons of crystal-clear water daily, and some find its constant 68°F (20°C) temperature a lot more refreshing than the lukewarm waters of the Gulf. There are picnic benches and barbecue grills (bring charcoal) in the shade of pine and cypress trees; canoe rentals and fishing; two self-guided nature trails, and ranger-led seasonal guided walks.

►► Suwannee River *237 E1*

White Springs (U.S. 41)

In 1851, composer Stephen C. Foster immortalized the state's second largest river in his melody *Old Folks at Home*, better known as *Way Down upon the Swanee River*. It was adopted as Florida's official state song in 1935. A former spa resort 10 miles (16km) northwest of Lake City, White Springs has cashed in on the free promotion with its annual **Florida Folk Festival**, held here each May.

Nearby, the **Stephen Foster State Park Museum** (*Open daily 9–5. Admission: inexpensive*; tel: 904/397-2733, www.floridastateparks.org) contains the remnants of the original Victorian spa, a collection of rare musical instruments and a 93-bell carillon that runs through a medley of Foster compositions. There are also summer season paddlewheel boat excursions.

►► The ZOO *236 A2*

5701 Gulf Breeze Parkway (12 miles /19km east of Gulf Breeze, on U.S. 98); tel: 850/932-2229
Open: summer, daily 9–4. Admission: moderate

There is plenty to do at this 30-acre (12ha) zoo, with more than 600 animals, botanical gardens, a children's petting corner and a safari train that rides around "natural habitat" enclosures. Take a ride on an elephant or hand feed giraffes from a purpose-built high-rise feeding station, and catch a show at the amphitheater.

On the Suwannee River, Florida's most famous waterway

More than three-quarters of the Panhandle's state parks offer short nature walks within their preserves, but for something a little more exacting there are several longer routes. In 1979, the Florida Recreational Trails Act authorized the establishment of a network of scenic and historic trails, and there are plans to create a series of hiking routes from Pensacola across to Lake Okeechobee and from Big Cypress Swamp in southwest Florida up to the Gulf Islands National Seashore.

Rails to trails One way to create routes is to convert abandoned railroad tracks into multi-use trails, and the first of these to open was the **Tallahassee–St. Marks Historic Railroad State Trail** in the eastern Panhandle. Once a transportation corridor for cotton and other goods, the 16-mile (25.5km) trail starts south of Tallahassee (off S.R. 363), and is open to hikers, horseback riders and bicyclists—it is the most popular biking trail in Florida.

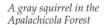

St. Marks National Wildlife Refuge Within St. Mark's National Wildlife Refuge on Apalachee Bay, there is a great choice of trails, from the half-day Ridge Trail (4.5 miles/7km) and Stoney Bayou Trail (6 miles/9.5km), to the longer Otter Lake Trail (8 miles/13km) and Deep Creek Trail (12 miles/19km). The 45-mile (72.5km) St. Marks Trail winds into some of the more remote areas of this coastal marsh and swampland preserve. It ends east of Sopchoppy, where the Apalachicola Trail begins its 22-mile (35.5km) hike across four rivers into the wilderness regions of the Apalachicola National Forest.

Other trails For a shorter introduction to the forest, take the circular Camel Lake Trail (4 miles/6.5km) from the Camel Lake Recreation Area off S.R. 12 north of Wilma. West of Apalachicola, **St. Joseph Peninsula State Park** is the start of the 18-mile/29km St. Joseph Peninsula Trail, which loops through the wilderness preserve via the beach, pine woods and marshlands. It is an excellent birdwatching area, with more than 209 species recorded. In the western Panhandle region, hikers can venture across the Blackwater State Forest on the Jackson Red Ground Trail (21 miles/34km) or sample the Sweetwater Hiking Trail, a short 4.5-mile (7km) walk from the Krul Recreation Area in the middle of the forest near Munson.

A gray squirrel in the Apalachicola Forest

CEREMONIAL CENTER
The name Tallahassee comes from the Apalachee word for "land of the old fields" or "abandoned villages." Archeological surveys of the Lake Jackson area, north of the city, have revealed evidence of a Mississippi Native American ceremonial center dating back more than eight centuries. Spanish explorer Hernando de Soto celebrated the first Christmas Mass on the continent here in 1539.

▶▶▶ Tallahassee

237 D2

By the 1820s, the hunt was on for a government seat where Florida's newly elected state legislature could meet, somewhere between the two historic centers of St. Augustine and Pensacola. A scout was sent out from each city, and the two met on the hill called Tallahassee. Suggestions that the capital should shift to the growing urban and business centers in the southeast have met with rebuff, and present-day Tallahassians guard their position and history jealously.

Surrounded by gently rolling hills, forests and lakes, old plantations and the accents of America's Deep South, Tallahassee seems a world away from the crowded southern tourist trails. Quiet streets lined with trees draped with Spanish moss exude old-fashioned charm, even though they're just minutes from the bustling **Capitol Complex** at the center of downtown.

Two major universities are based here: Florida State (F.S.U.), with its mighty Seminoles football team, and Florida Agricultural and Mechanical (F.A.M.U.), founded in 1887. Florida's "Sunshine Act" made it one of the first states to insist that legislative sessions be open to the public, so a visit to the New Capitol building during the March through May sessions is a popular excursion. The nearby elegant **Governor's Mansion**, 700 N. Adams Street, modeled on General Andrew Jackson's Tennessee plantation home, is open to view at the same time.

A good way to get around downtown is on the **Old Town Trolley**, which provides free services and makes frequent stops (weekdays 8–5, weekends 9–3; tel: 850/413-8200). Shopping in Tallahassee is focused on the malls along Apalachee Parkway. **Governor's Square** offers the best range of boutiques and department stores, with the bonus of an unrivaled view of the Old and New Capitol buildings from the top of the parkway heading back into town. Springtime visitors will find Tallahassee in a festive mood, with a four-week (March through April) jamboree of arts, crafts, entertainment and parades.

The Fourth of July parade in Tallahassee

Walk

Downtown Tallahassee

Start from the Old Capitol on Monroe Street at Apalachee Parkway.

Across the street, the twin granite slabs of the **Vietnam Veteran's Memorial** commemorate the 1,942 known Floridian casualties of the conflict. The **Union Bank Building**, facing Apalachee Parkway, is Florida's oldest surviving bank. This restored 1841 Federal-style edifice now houses Florida A&M's Black Archives Extension and displays.

Walk back up to Monroe; turn right.

The **Exchange Building**, 201 Monroe, is a fine example of art deco office architecture, built in 1927 and decorated with reliefs and stone griffins.

Turn left on College, then turn left again on Adams.

This attractive restored area, with its old Southern-style, neoclassical buildings, is known as the **Adams Street Commons**.

Turn right on Jefferson for two blocks to Bronough.

The **Museum of Florida History**, 500 S. Bronough, is situated just across the intersection (see page 257).

Continue along Bronough to Madison, and turn left.

On the corner of Madison and Monroe, the **Jackson Square Marker** indicates the original site of downtown Tallahassee circa 1824, a village of wooden cottages and stores that stretched from Call Street to the south wing of the Old Capitol.

CRADLE-AND-GRAVE BRIGADE

One of Florida's Civil War actions is celebrated every spring with a reenactment of the Battle of Natural Bridge. At the Natural Bridge Battlefield State Historic Site, 15 miles (24km) southeast of Tallahassee, volunteers dressed as Confederate and Union troops set up encampments at the site near the St. Marks River and honor the Confederate victory of March 3–7, 1865. The victory preserved Tallahassee as the only Confederate capital east of the Mississippi never to fall into Union hands during the Civil War. The victory was quite an accomplishment since the Confederate troops were largely old men and boys facing seasoned Union soldiers. For information, tel: 850/922-6007.

The Capitol Complex in Tallahassee

A. B. Maclay State Gardens, *3540 Thomasville Road* (*Open* daily 8–dusk. Maclay House Jan–Apr, daily 9–5. *Admission: inexpensive*; tel: 850/487-4556, www.floridastateparks.org) Just north of I–10, this is one of the loveliest gardens in Florida, founded by New York financier Alfred B. Maclay in 1923. Maclay's creative landscaping combined native pines and oaks with a diverse selection of exotic imported species, all incorporated into a network of walks, paths, pools and lawns surrounding his house and stretching down to Lake Hall. The camellias (around 100 varieties) commence their flowering season in December, and the gardens are at the height of their beauty from January through April, when the furnished house is also open to the public. Big Pine Nature Trail winds through the woodlands around the lake, where visitors can picnic, boat and fish. Alligators and turtles have been spotted in the lake and more than 150 species of birds and animals inhabit the woodlands.

Capitol Complex, *S. Monroe (at Apalachee Parkway)* (*Open* Mon–Fri 9–4.30, Sat 10–4.30, Sun noon–4.30. *Admission free*; tel: 850/487-1902) The towering 22-story New Capitol building (see panel opposite) may dominate Tallahassee's modest skyline, but the **Old Capitol** remains the curator of Florida's early legislative history. Time was of the essence when the original Capitol was constructed on this site in 1845. A half-century later it had to be completely remodeled by architect Frank P. Milburn. Milburn's classical designs incorporated triangular tympana above the columned porticoes of the east and west entrances, which are embossed with pressed-metal reliefs of details from the state seal. Crowning the creation is a 136ft (41m) dome with a colorful stained-glass decoration. The distinctive candy-striped awnings also date from Milburn's day.

The building was further enlarged in 1923, housing the Senate Chamber at one end and the House of Representatives at the other, with the Supreme Court downstairs. The restored chambers have been furnished with authentic reproductions of the original wicker-seat armchairs, arranged in wide semicircles. In between, former offices house an excellent permanent history exhibit, illustrated with memorabilia, photographs and fascinating tales of early legislators and their times.

Edward Ball Wakulla Springs State Park, *550 Wakulla Park Drive, S.R. 267 at S.R. 61, 15 miles (24km) south of Tallahassee* (*Open* daily 8–dusk. *Admission: inexpensive*; tel: 850/224-5950, www.floridastateparks.org) At Wakulla, the freshwater springs are among the world's largest and deepest. The centerpiece of the 2,860-acre (1,144ha) park is a pool above the main spring, which Native Americans called "mysteries of strange water." Some 600,000 gallons (2.7 million liters) of water per minute flow from an underground river into the pool, which is so astonishingly clear that even its deepest point (185ft/55.5m below) is visible, as is the entrance to a subterranean cavern where mastodon bones have been discovered.

A glass-bottom boat makes regular trips around the pool, and there are ample opportunties to see wildlife—another boat ferries passengers down the scenic Wakulla River, where deer, turtles, alligators and the abundant bird life along the riverbanks can be spotted. Nine species of herons and egrets, plus vultures, anhingas, kites and osprey nest and feed here all year—though the population swells dramatically during the winter migration. There is a swimming hole, nature trails, plus shady picnic tables and barbecue grills, as well as accommodations and a restaurant

Museum of Florida History, *500 S. Bronough Street* (*Open* Mon–Fri 9–4.30, Sat 10–4.30, Sun noon–4.30. *Admission free*; tel: 850/245-6400) Interesting and informative, this user-friendly jaunt through Florida history starts with geological relics and the skeleton of a giant prehistoric mastodon, then runs through sunken treasures salvaged from Spanish galleons and Civil War battle flags right through to the Roaring Twenties. You can go "all aboard" a reconstructed steamboat for a 19th century riverside view, or, in contrast, take a look at how an earlier generation set up "tin can" vacation campgrounds in the first great tourist boom of the 1920s.

Park Avenue and Calhoun Street Historic Districts These gracious tree-shaded streets are lined with the homes and churches of Tallahassee's prominent 19th-century citizens. Walking tour brochures are available from the information center in the New Capitol. Notable stops along the way include the 1830s Greek Revival-style **Columns**, *100 N. Duval (at Park)*, the city's oldest surviving structure, moved from the site where it was put up by a Georgian banker, William "Money" Wiliams. **Knott House Museum**, *301 East Park Street* (*Open* for guided

GOVERNMENT IN ACTION
The State Legislature in the New Capitol building is in session from March through May, and visitors can watch the proceedings in both chambers from viewing galleries on the sixth floor (*Open* Mon–Fri 9–11, 1–3, Sat–Sun 9–3. *Guided tours* on the hour. *Admission free*; tel: 850/413-9200). The 22nd-floor Observatory affords a panoramic view of the city, plus an exhibition gallery for mainly contemporary Floridian artists.

The Old Town Trolley

PICTORIAL HISTORY
One of 72 buildings across the United States constructed under the Works Progress Administration during the 1930s Depression years, the Old U.S. Courthouse, 110 W. Park Avenue, is well worth a quick stop for the humorous murals in its foyer. Laced with amusing detail, a series of gentle, tongue-in-cheek scenes illustrates the development of the state, from the Native Americans through the muskets and flags of the Spanish explorers and Civil War to the emancipated women golfers and sunseekers of the 1920s and 1930s.

tours Wed–Fri 1, 2, 3; Sat 10–3 on the hour. *Admission: donation*; tel: 850/922-2459) is also known as "The House that Rhymes" after its eccentric 1920s occupant Luella Knott, who decorated the antique furnishings with examples of her poetry, which she tied on with ribbons. It was on the steps of this house on May 20 1865 that Gen. Edward McCook of the Union Army read out the Emancipation Proclamation. Look out also for the Brokaw-McDougall House, Virginia Street.

San Luis de Apalachee Archeological and Historic Site, *2020 Mission Road (at Ocala Road)* (*Open* Tue–Sun 10–4. *Admission free*; tel: 850/487-3711) This site, located on a hillside west of the downtown district, has a history as a Spanish mission and an Apalachee Native American village. So far, the digs have uncovered a wealth of archeological relics, and excavation work is still in progress. Objects include pottery, weapons and jewelry.

The Spanish settlement was in existence in 1656 and contained a religious complex. There were also houses built alongside a large Native American council house. The entire village was deliberately burned to the ground in 1704 to prevent it falling into British hands. There are special guided tours and events on Saturday.

Tallahassee Museum of History and Natural Science, *3945 Museum Drive (off Lake Bradford Road)* (*Open* Mon–Sat 9–5, Sun 12.30–5. *Admission: moderate*; tel: 850/575-8684, www.tallahasseemuseum.org) This excellent outdoor museum has a wide range of exhibits, from an 1880s-style Big Bend Farm to bobcats and brown bears. In a shady glade, the main farmhouse is surrounded by outbuildings, including a smithy, smokehouse and barn where farmyard animals are tended by staff in period costume. Cotton and cane grow in the garden, and mules munch away in the stables.

A boardwalk trail spans a cypress swamp area on Lake Bradford and then continues around natural-habitat enclosures for basking alligators, Florida panthers, red foxes, skunks and white-tailed deer. The walk-through aviary provides interesting birdspotting. A group of historic buildings includes an 1890s schoolroom, the 1850 Bellevue Plantation house and the Bethlehem Missionary Baptist Church, built in 1937 by one of Florida's first black Baptist congregations. There are picnic and play areas as well as a gift shop.

Farming 1880s-style at the Tallahassee Museum of History and Natural Science

Drive

Into the Panhandle

See map on page 236.

This drive west into the central Panhandle from Tallahassee makes an equally good day trip or an off-interstate route halfway to Pensacola. Along the way there are opportunities for antiques shopping, discovering beautifully preserved antebellum houses, some underground exploration, picnicking and a cooling swim.

Leave Tallahassee on N. Monroe Street (U.S. 27) and cross I–10. In Havana (11 miles/17.5km), continue one block from the intersection with S.R. 12 and park on Seventh Avenue.

Havana's tiny but attractive antiques district is a popular spot for browsers. Start at the Cannery, an old factory building given over to antiques dealers, and artists' studios and galleries. Stores and indoor markets on Main Street offer easily portable mementos, such as vintage posters and *Time* magazines.

Retrace your route to S.R. 12 at Ninth Avenue; turn right (west). At the first traffic light in Quincy (11 miles/17.5km), turn left on Madison. The red-brick Chamber of Commerce is on the corner.

Explore **Quincy**'s elegant antebellum heritage on foot with the Chamber of Commerce's excellent brochure *A Tour of Historic Quincy*. Founded in 1828, Quincy's fortunes were built on tobacco and on the Quincy State Bank's farsighted investment in the fledgling Coca-Cola Company.

By the courthouse, turn right on U.S. 90 (west) for 20 miles (32km).

The next landmark is **Chattahoochee**, which has a panoramic view of the central region's pine and oakwood forests. The **Apalachicola River** marks the change to Central Time (turn your watch back one hour).

On **Victory Bridge**, look north for a view of the 6,130ft (1,839m) **Jim Woodruff Hydroelectric Dam**, built in the late 1950s. This is a great fishing spot and a watersports center. For a closer look, there is an observation point off to the right (2 miles/3km) from Chattahoochee).

In Marianna (25 miles/40km from Chattahoochee), follow signs for the Florida Caverns.

Florida Caverns State Park reveals the very foundations of the state in a series of magnificent limestone caves cut into the plateau (see page 242).

Back at U.S. 90, day trippers can head back to Tallahassee via the fast I–10 (turn left on U.S. 90 and follow signs to the interstate). For Pensacola, turn right on U.S. 90.

One last stop en route to Pensacola is a refreshing swim at **Ponce de León Springs State Recreation Area** (47 miles/75.5km). (See page 252.)

I–10 is just one mile (1.6km) from Ponce de León.

On the Apalachicola River

Arriving

Air routes
Most major American airlines schedule regular flights into Florida including Delta (www.delta .com), Continental (www.continental .com), Southwest (www.southwest.com), Northwest (www.nwa.com), and U.S. Airways (www.usairways.com). The smaller airports are usually accessible through the commuter flights of major domestic carriers.

Scheduled flights by major European airlines including British Airways (www.ba.com) fly direct to Miami, Orlando International and Tampa.

Packages that combine airfare and vacation activities at special rates are available through American airline companies and specialist travel agents.

From the UK, companies such as Virgin Atlantic (www.virgin-atlantic .com) and Thomas Cook (www.thomascook.co.uk) offer packages and holidays.

Specialist reservation websites will allow you to compare prices for flights (and hotels) before you book. Try www.expedia .com, www.lastminute.com or www.ebookers.com.

The price you pay for a flight will depend on a number of factors, such as how many stops or transfers you make, or how far in advance you make a reservation.

Smoking All flights in U.S. air space are non-smoking with heavy fines if the rule is broken. Airport smoking is confined to designated areas.

Ground transportation Some hotels provide airport transfers, while car rental companies operate shuttle services to their parking lots. Otherwise there are local bus services and a plentiful supply of taxis. Taxis are often worth the added expense for speed and convenience, and fares to downtown areas are usually reasonable. (For fuller details of transportation into Miami, see page 84.)

Major Florida airports
Daytona Beach, tel: 904/248-8030
Fort Lauderdale, tel: 954/359-6100
Jacksonville, tel: 904/741-2000
Key West, tel: 305/296-5439
Miami, tel: 305/876-7000
Orlando International, tel: 407/825-3887
Palm Beach, tel: 561/471-7420
Panama City–Bay County, tel: 850/763-6751
St. Petersburg/Clearwater, tel: 727/453-7800
Tampa, tel: 813/870-8700.

Beaches

No point in Florida is more than 60 miles (96.5km) from salt water. This long, lean peninsula is bordered by a 526-mile (847km) Atlantic coast from Fernandina Beach to Key West and a 792-mile (1,275km) coast along the Gulf of Mexico and Florida Bay from Pensacola to Key West. If you were to stretch Florida's coast into a straight line, it would extend for about 1,800 miles (2,892km). What's more, if you add in the perimeter of all islands surrounded by salt water, Florida has about 8,500 miles (13,685km) of tidal shoreline. Florida's coastline comprises about 1,016 miles (1,636km) of sand beaches.

Visitors unaccustomed to strong subtropical sun run a risk of sunburn and heat prostration on Florida beaches, even in winter. Many natives go to the beach early in the day or in the late afternoon; follow their lead. If you must be out in direct sun at midday, limit your sun exposure and strenuous exercise, drink plenty of liquids and wear a hat. Swim only in guarded areas.

The state owns all beaches below the median high-tide line, even in front of hotels and private resorts, but gaining access to the public beach can be a problem along much of Florida's coastline. You must pay to enter and/or park at most state, county and local beachfront parks. Where hotels dominate the beach frontage, public parking may be limited or nonexistent.

Along the Atlantic coast from the Georgia border through the Daytona Beach area, the beaches are broad and firm, and some can be driven on. Some beachfront communities in this area charge for that; others provide free beach access for vehicles.

Travel Facts

Beaches *(continued)*

From the Treasure Coast south, erosion has affected the beaches. Major beach rehabilitation projects have been completed in Fort Lauderdale, the Sunny Isles area of Miami-Dade County, Miami Beach and Key Biscayne. In the Florida Keys, coral reefs and prevailing currents prevent sand from building up to form beaches. The few Keys beaches are small, narrow and generally have little or no sandy bottom.

On the Gulf Coast, Captiva Island is losing sand to neighboring Sanibel Island, where a stroll beside the water at sunrise or sunset can be a truly sensual experience. Currents bring all sorts of unusual shells onto Sanibel's beach and scatter sharks' teeth across Venice and Caspersen beaches in south Sarasota County. Siesta Beach in Sarasota County claims to have Florida's softest white sand. At the north end of Longboat Key in Manatee County, accretion has built a magnificent beach in the vicinity of Beer Can Island. Much of that sand came from Coquina Beach and Bradenton Beach. Caladesi Island State Park, in Pinellas County, is one of Florida's few undeveloped barrier islands.

In Florida's Panhandle, the Gulf Island National Seashore maintains 150 miles (241km) of beach noted for its sugarlike sand and the impressive dune formations near Fort Walton Beach. Expect the beaches outside Panama City and Pensacola to be crowded on summer weekends.

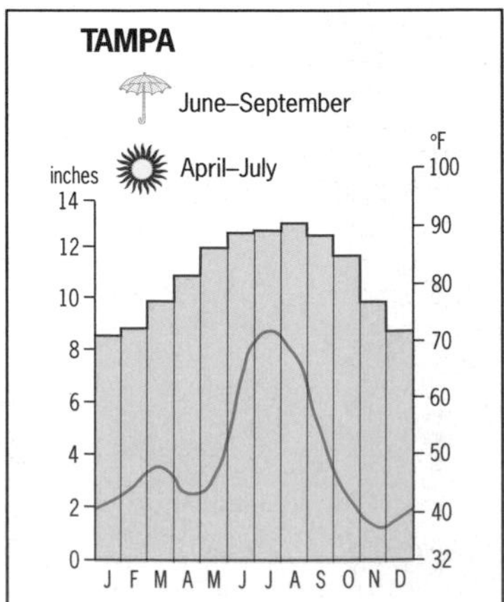

Camping

Camping is popular in Florida. There are privately run campgrounds, plus resorts and national and state parks throughout the state. Facilities range from elaborate "pull thru's" designed for RVs to rustic backwoods campsites for hikers. Many campgrounds offer on-site trailer and tent rentals, but it is advisable to make reservations in advance, particularly during the winter months.

The *Florida Camping Directory* lists some 200 member campgrounds around the state with information about their RV and camping facilities, and on-site amenities such as pools, convenience shops, and children's playgrounds. For a copy of the directory, contact the **Florida Association of R.V. Parks &**

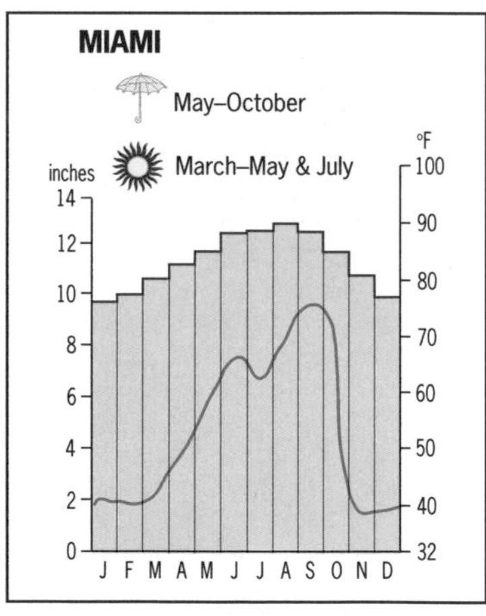

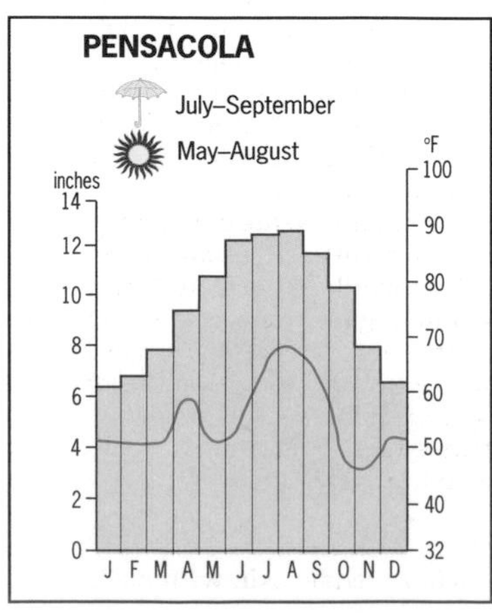

Campgrounds, 1340 Vickers Road, Tallahassee, FL 32303, tel: 850/562-7151, www.floridacamping.com.

For information about camping in the state's parks, contact the **Florida Department of Environmental Protection**, Division of Recreation and Parks, Mail Station 535, 3900 Commonwealth Boulevard, Tallahassee, FL 32399-3000, tel: 850/242-2118.

A popular option is to rent an R.V. from a local rental company. **Cruise America**, 2915 North Orange Blossom Trail, Kissimmee, tel: 407/931-1409 or 800/671-8042 rents out motorhomes and vans. Services include airport transfers.

Children

Many Florida resorts cater specifically to families and hotels in every price bracket often offer free lodging for children up to 18 sharing a room with their parents.

Most larger theme parks provide a range of children's facilities, from changing rooms with all the requisite toiletries to strollers. However, parents of small children should take into consideration how overwhelming the theme park experience can be. Re-entry hand stamps allow guests to take a break from the park during the day, perhaps returning to the hotel for lunch and a swim then revisiting the park in the late afternoon. While on the subject of theme parks, parents should also take advantage of the children's name tags that are often available at park information offices. Lost children can be speedily reunited with their families if the authorities know whom to contact.

Beyond the theme parks, Florida's numerous attractions are generally child-friendly, from state parks with swimming and canoeing, to excellent science and natural history museums with a strong interactive element. Museum stores are a good source of semi-educational games and books with a Florida theme.

Perhaps the greatest danger to young children is the sun. Its rays can burn tender skin within a few minutes. If children are going to be exposed to the sunlight for any length of time, and that includes sightseeing, not just swimming and sunbathing, be sure to cover them liberally with sunscreen with a high SPF. Hats are essential for small children, while older, fashion-conscious children can generally be induced to wear baseball caps. Keep children hydrated throughout the day. (See also **Health** section.)

Climate (see charts on opposite page) Florida winters, especially in the southern part of the state, are mild. Except in the northern regions, winter temperatures seldom drop below freezing; snow is a rare event anywhere in Florida. The shoulder seasons of spring and fall generally provide the best weather, ideal for sightseeing and sports. Summer days can be real scorchers. The early part of summer is typically hot and dry. As summer progresses, high humidity and a pattern of almost daily afternoon thunderstorms sets in.

Crime

For the most part, Florida is as safe as anywhere in the world. Its notorious reputation is based largely on a few incidents which have resulted in additional safety measures being introduced, such as tourist routes signposted with a sun symbol to guide visitors from the airport to

Hollywood Boulevard, W.D.W.

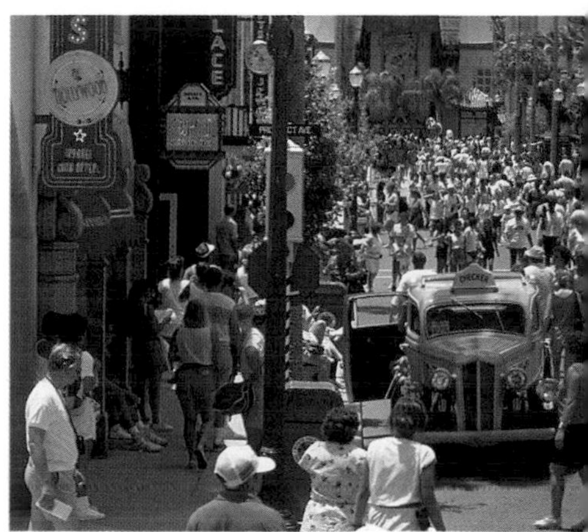

main roads, and rental cars no longer carry identifying license plates. As elsewhere in the U.S., there are certain urban areas that may be unsuitable for lone travelers, particularly women, and especially at night. When visiting cities, check on your destination and route in advance with the staff at your hotel or motel and follow their advice.

When in doubt about an area, do not explore alone, or take a cab instead of walking.

Drivers should take a few simple precautions that should prevent most problems.

- Consider a cell phone rental if you are renting a car. Most of the national operators offer this option.
- Keep the doors locked when driving through unfamiliar areas.
- Don't stop for or pick up anyone.
- Lock all the doors and the trunk when you park the car and make sure that packages, cameras and other valuables are out of sight.

In the event of an accident, find a well-lit telephone booth—gas stations, stores, or diners are recommended—and dial 911.

Drinking

The sale and consumption of alcohol in bars, restaurants, stores and other public places is restricted to adults age 21 and over. It is also illegal to drink or have an open can or bottle of an alcoholic beverage in a car.

Sunshine Skyway, Tampa

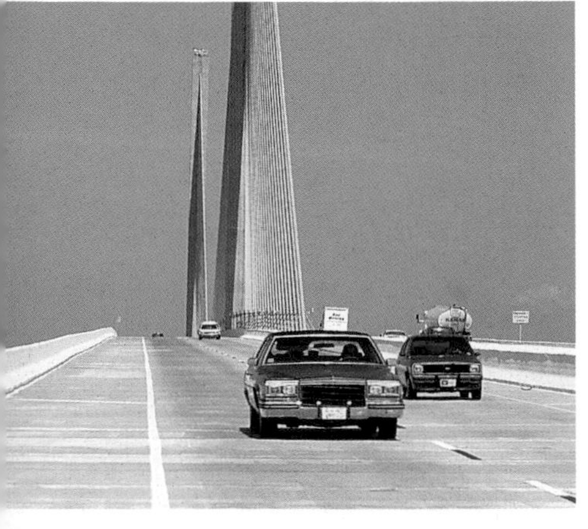

Driving

Renting a car It's relatively inexpensive to rent a car in Florida. Rental companies operating in Florida include:

Alamo, tel: 800/462-5266, www.alamo.com
Avis, tel: 800/230-4898, www.avis.com
Budget, tel: 800/527-0700, www.budget.com
Dollar, tel: 800/800-3665, www.dollar.com
Hertz, tel: 800/654-3131, www.hertz.com
National, tel: 800/CAR-RENT, www.nationalcar.com
Thrifty, tel: 800/847-4389, www.thrifty.com.

These companies maintain airport and city locations throughout Florida.

Local firms offer good deals in major Florida cities. These include First Class Rent-A-Car, tel: 800/729-0053; Enterprise Car Rental, tel: 305/636-0377; and Payless, tel: 800/729-5255. Down in Key West, try Tropical Rent-a-Car, tel: 305/294-8136.

Car rental can often be cheaper to organize before you leave for Florida. You can make arrangements through a package company or through a discount travel company, such as Expedia (www.expedia.com).

Wheelchair Getaways Inc., tel: 561/748-8414 or 800/637-7577 in south Florida; tel: 407/281-8369 or 800/424-4990 in north Florida rent full-size and minivans equipped with wheelchair lifts and tie-downs from Miami, Fort Lauderdale, West Palm Beach, Jacksonville, Orlando, Daytona Beach, Sarasota, St. Petersburg, Tampa and Ft. Myers/Naples.

It's always best to know a few essentials *before* you arrive at the car-rental counter. The minimum age for renting a car is 21; some companies surcharge drivers under 25.

Find out what the collision damage waiver (C.D.W.) costs; there's usually a $20–$30 daily surcharge. Also find out if your corporate or personal insurance already covers damage to a rental car (if so, bring along a photocopy of the benefits section). More and more companies are now holding renters responsible for theft and vandalism if they don't buy the C.D.W.; in response, some credit card and insurance companies are extending *their* coverage to rental cars. It is generally more cost effective to fill up the tank with gas just before returning the vehicle to the rental car office. Child seats should be reserved in advance.

Emergencies

Dial: 911

An operator or dispatcher will connect calls to the appropriate emergency service, including the police and fire departments, ambulance, and medical services. To ensure that the emergency services arrive as quickly as possible, give accurate directions, including the street name and nearest cross-street together with any further details to assist them. On interstate highways, call boxes have been installed every quarter to half mile (400–800m). These boxes allow callers to alert police, ambulance, and mechanical services without dialing 911.

Health

Drugstores are plentiful and usually open 9–9; most larger towns and cities have walk-in medical and dental clinics listed in the telephone directory.

Sunburn is a common affliction, and a chronic case of it is agonizing and dangerous. So do not underestimate the sun's power reflected off the sand and sea.

- Use plenty of sunscreen with a high SPF—at least 15 even if you don't burn easily.
- Wear a hat.
- Restrict the time you spend in the sun, at least during the first few days of your visit.
- Drink plenty of fluids (not including alcohol, which is dehydrating).

Hitchhiking

The best advice is not to do it, and do not pick up hitchhikers either. Hitchhiking is against the law on toll roads and interstates, and throughout the Florida Keys.

Lost property

For lost property in hotels, check with the front desk or hotel security. Taxi companies and public transportation telephone numbers are listed in local telephone directories. Lost or stolen travelers' checks and credit cards should be reported to the issuing companies immediately (keep a list of the numbers on the checks) and to the police. The police should also be informed of lost travel documents, and it is advisable to obtain a police report about valuable items for insurance purposes.

Maps

Car rental companies supply basic maps, but for extensive touring it is a good idea to pick up large-scale maps, such as the Rand McNally series, from a bookstore. (If you are lost in a city, it may help to remember that most cities' **avenues** run north–south and **streets** east–west.)

Chambers of Commerce and local visitor information centers publish and distribute local maps, walking tour brochures and information on bicycle routes. State and national parks issue maps of scenic drives, hiking routes and interpretive trails on admission.

Visit Florida will provide state maps on application to its head office in Tallahassee or at its offices abroad (see **Tourist information**, page 268).

Media

Newspapers Most Florida communities publish weekly newspapers, while larger cities support daily publications. The *Miami Herald*, *Orlando Sentinel*, *Tampa Tribune* and Jacksonville's *Florida Times-Union* are some of the better ones. *USA Today* is widely available from self-service news bins in every town; the *New York Times* and *Wall Street Journal* can be found at newsstands.

Television and radio There is hardly a motel or hotel room in the state without a television, though chi chi

CONVERSION CHARTS

FROM	TO	MULTIPLY BY
Inches	Centimeters	2.54
Centimeters	Inches	0.3937
Feet	Meters	0.3048
Meters	Feet	3.2810
Yards	Meters	0.9144
Meters	Yards	1.0940
Miles	Kilometers	1.6090
Kilometers	Miles	0.6214
Acres	Hectares	0.4047
Hectares	Acres	2.4710
Gallons	Liters	3.7854
Liters	Gallons	0.2641
Ounces	Grams	28.35
Grams	Ounces	0.0353
Pounds	Grams	453.6
Grams	Pounds	0.0022
Pounds	Kilograms	0.4536
Kilograms	Pounds	2.205
Tons	Metric tons	0.907
Metric tons	Tons	1.102

MEN'S SUITS

UK	36	38	40	42	44	46	48
Rest of Europe	46	48	50	52	54	56	58
US	36	38	40	42	44	46	48

DRESS SIZES

UK	8	10	12	14	16	18
France	36	38	40	42	44	46
Italy	38	40	42	44	46	48
Rest of Europe	34	36	38	40	42	44
US	6	8	10	12	14	16

MEN'S SHIRTS

UK	14	14.5	15	15.5	16	16.5	17
Rest of Europe	36	37	38	39/40	41	42	43
US	14	14.5	15	15.5	16	16.5	17

MEN'S SHOES

UK	7	7.5	8.5	9.5	10.5	11
Rest of Europe	41	42	43	44	45	46
US	8	8.5	9.5	10.5	11.5	12

WOMEN'S SHOES

UK	4.5	5	5.5	6	6.5	7
Rest of Europe	38	38	39	39	40	41
US	6	6.5	7	7.5	8	8.5

bed-and-breakfasts tend not to permit them among the Victoriana. Even the least sophisticated accommodations offer no less than six to eight channels; if a hotel offers cable stations such as H.B.O. or Cinemax, the choice increases dramatically.

Money matters/cash machines

Virtually all banks nowadays have ATMs. There are some eight major ATM networks, the largest of which are **Cirrus**, owned by MasterCard, and **Plus**, affiliated with Visa. Some banks belong to more than one network. These cards are not automatically issued; you have to ask for them. Cards issued by American Express, Visa and MasterCard may also be used in the ATMs, but the fees are usually higher than the fees on bank cards, and there is a daily interest charge on the "loan," even if monthly bills are paid on time. **Express Cash** lets American Express cardholders withdraw cash. American Express also issues a Traveler's Cheque Card, a prepaid reloadable ATM card, that isn't linked to your bank account. You don't need to be an existing account holder. For details contact www.americanexpress.com. Express Cash is not a cash advance service; only money already in the linked checking account can be withdrawn. Apply for a PIN (Personal Identification Number) and link your accounts at least two or three weeks before departure.

Each network has a toll-free number you can call to locate machines in a given city: Cirrus, 800/424-7787; Plus, 800/843-7587; Express Cash, 800/227-4669. Check with your bank for fees and for the amount of cash you can withdraw per day.

Opening hours

The following opening hours are a guideline only:
Banks: Monday to Thursday 9am–4pm, Friday 9am–5pm.
Drugstores: daily 9am–9pm; some are open 24 hours.
Offices: Monday to Friday 8 or 9am–5 or 6pm.

Stores: Supermarkets, Monday to Saturday 8am–9pm, Sunday 8am–7pm; some are open 24 hours; downtown, Monday to Friday 10am–6pm, Saturday 10am–1pm or 6pm; malls, Monday to Saturday 10am–9pm, Sunday 10am–6pm.

Organized tours

With Florida's many miles of coastline and proximity to offshore islands, the most obvious opportunity for touring is to take a cruise. These range from two-hour cruises to week-long (or longer) trips to the Bahamas, the Caribbean and beyond.

Many of these longer trips depart from Miami, but shorter excursions—one-day, half-day or evening cruises—depart from many places in the state. A few of the shorter trips offer casino gambling on board. For information about local cruises, contact the Convention and Visitors Bureau where you are staying.

Police

Law enforcement is divided into three main jurisdictions: **city police** within the urban areas; the **sheriff** outside the city limits; and the **highway patrol**, which handles traffic accidents and offenses beyond the city limits. Other agencies also deal with specific areas of law enforcement, such as drugs and major criminal investigations.

In an emergency dial **911** for all services. Nonemergency police numbers are listed in local telephone directories.

Post offices

Post office hours vary, but in most places are 9am–4.30 or 5pm on weekdays. Some are open on Saturday mornings. Stamps may be purchased at hotels and drugstores, as well as at post offices. Remember to keep small change handy for stamp machines.

Public transportation

The most popular method of transportation on the ground is, without doubt, the car (see **Driving**). For alternative, though less-convenient travel options, check out **Greyhound**

Street bar, Miami

which connects with more than 100 Florida destinations. **Amtrak** serves Miami, Jacksonville, Orlando, Tallahassee, Tampa and 35 other stops.

Amtrak, 60 N.E. Massachusetts Avenue, Washington, DC 20002, tel: 202/906-3000 or 800/872-7245, www.amtrak.com. Greyhound Lines Inc., PO Box 660606, Dallas, TX 75248, tel: 972/789-7000 or 800/231-222. www.greyhound.com.

Taxi cabs can be picked up at airports, bus and train stations, or from major hotels. They tend not to cruise the streets looking for fares so you'll have to call for one.

Senior citizens

Many hotels, resorts, restaurants, and attractions offer senior citizens discounts or special rates. Be sure to ask if no information is on display.

Sports and recreation

Regional visitor information bureaus can provide a wealth of information about sporting and recreational opportunities in their areas. For statewide information, contact the **Florida Sports Foundation**, 2930 Kerry Forst parkway, Tallahassee, FL 32309, tel: 850/488-8347; www.flasports.com. For information about state park facilities, contact the Department of Environmental Protection, Division of Recreation and Parks, Mail Station 535, 3900 Commonwealth Boulevard, Tallahassee, FL 32399-3000, tel: 850/245-2157; www.dep.state.fl.us/parks.

Interstate bus

Student and youth travel
Florida has a limited number of youth hostels in prime locations, such as Miami Beach, Key West, Clearwater Beach, and Orlando.

For information on affiliated properties, contact Hosteling International, 8401 Colesville Road, Suite 600, Silver Spring, MD, tel: 301/495-1240, www.hiusa.org, or overseas branches of the Youth Hostel Association.

Time
Florida has two time zones. Most of the state operates on Eastern Standard Time, while the Panhandle region west of the Apalachicola River keeps Central Standard Time.

Tipping
The standard tip for a restaurant bill or a taxi ride is 20 percent; 15–20 percent for full-service wait staff; and $1 per bag for bellhops, airport porters and doormen.

Tourist information
Most towns throughout Florida have a Chamber of Commerce. Major cities have Convention and Visitors Bureaus that will answer inquiries.

For more information in advance of traveling, you should contact Visit Florida or any of the main regional offices whose addresses and websites follow:

Visit Florida, 661 E. Jefferson Street, Suite 300, Tallahassee, FL 32301, tel: 850/488-5607 or 888/7FLAUSA, www.flausa.com; (Canada) Taurus House, 512 Duplex Avenue, Toronto, Ontario M4R 2E3, tel: 416/485-2573; e-mail: hgroenindijk@thermgroup.ca; (UK/Europe) KBC-PR, Suite 3, Falmers Court, London Road, Uckfield, East Sussex, TH22 1HN , tel: 01825 763636, e-mail: esther.williamson@kbc-pr.com

Daytona Beach Area Convention & Visitors Bureau, 126 E. Orange Avenue, PO Box 910, Daytona Beach, FL 32114, tel: 386/255-0415 or 800/544-0415, www.daytonabeach.com

Emerald Coast Convention & Visitors Bureau, 1540 Miracle Strip parkway, Fort Walton Beach, FL 32548, tel: 850/651-7131 or 800/322-3319; www.destin-fwb.com

Florida Keys and Key West, 1201 White Street, #102, Key West, FL 33041-0866, tel: 305/296-1552 or 800/FLA KEYS; www.fla-keys.com

Florida's Space Coast Office of Tourism, 2725 Judge Fran Jamieson Way #B-105, Viera, FL 32910, tel: 321/637-5483 or 800/936-2326; www.space-coast.com

Greater Fort Lauderdale Convention & Visitors Bureau, 100 East Broward Boulevard, Suite 200, Fort Lauderdale, FL33301, tel: 954/765-4466 or 800/22-SUNNY; www.sunny.org

Greater Miami Convention & Visitors Bureau, 701 Brickell Avenue, Suite 2700, Miami, FL 33131, tel: 305/539-3000 or 800/993-8448; www.miamiandbeaches.com

Jacksonville and The Beaches Convention & Visitors Bureau, 500 Water Street, Suite 1000, Jacksonville, FL 32202, tel: 904/798-9111 or 800/733-2668; www.jaxcvb.com

The Beaches of Fort Myers & Sanibel, 12800 University Drive, Suite 550, Fort Myers, FL 33907, tel: 239/383-3500 or 800/237-6444; www.fortmyers-sanibel.com

Naples – Marco Island – Everglades (Paradise Coast), 3050 North Horsehsoe Drive, Suite 218, Naples, FL 34104, tel: 239/403-2425 or 800/688-3600, www.paradisecoast.com

Orlando/Orange County Convention & Visitors Bureau, 6700 Forum Drive, Suite 100, Orlando, FL 32821-8087, tel: 407/363-5872 or 800/257-0060; www.orlandoinfo.com

Palm Beach County Convention & Visitors Bureau, 1555 Palm Beach Lakes Boulevard, Suite 800, West Palm Beach, FL 33401, tel: 561/233-3000 or 800/833-5733; www.palmbeachfl.com

Panama City Beach Convention & Visitors Bureau, P.O. Box 9473, Panama City Beach, FL 32417, tel: 850/233-5070 or 800/PCBEACH; www.thebeachloversbeach.com

Pensacola Convention & Visitors Information Center, 1401 E. Gregory Street, Pensacola, FL 32501, tel: 850/434-1234 or 800/874-1234; www.visitpensacola.com

St Augustine, Ponte Vedra & The Beaches Convention & Visitors Bureau, 88 Riberia Street, Suite 400, St. Augustine, FL 32084, tel: 904/829-1711 or 800/653-2489; www.visitoldcity.com

St. Petersburg/Clearwater Area Convention & Visitors Bureau, 13805 58th Street, Suite 2-200, Clearwatrer, FL 33760, tel: 727/464-7200; www.floridasbeach.com

Sarasota Convention & Visitors Bureau, 655 N. Tamiami Trail, Sarasota, FL 34236, tel: 941/957-1877 or 800/552-9799; www.sarasotafl.com

Tampa/Hillsborough Convention & Visitors Association, 400 N. Tampa Street, Suite 2800, Tampa, FL 33602, tel: 813/223-1111; www.visittampabay.com

Travelers with disabilities
Facilities for people with disabilities are widespread in Florida. Public buildings are required to have some form of access for wheelchair users, and many public buses are now supplied with wheelchair lifts.

The Florida Governor's Alliance operate in conjunction with The Able Trust , 106 East College Avenue, Suite 820, Tallahassee, FL 32301, tel: 850/224-4493 (voice and TDD) or 888/838-ABLE, www.ablestrust.org.

People with visual impairments traveling with guide dogs will find it relatively easy to take their dogs into attractions.

At some attractions, viewing may be somewhat restricted and access to certain rides impossible or forbidden for safety reasons. Generally, efforts are made to provide assistance, and wheelchairs, for those with disabilities.

Walt Disney World offers a useful *Guidebook for Guests with Disabilities*, available from Guest Letters, PO Box 10040, Lake Buena Vista, FL 32830-10040, tel: 407/824-4321. Information for Universal Orlando can be obtained from 1000 Universal Studios Drive, Orlando, FL 32816, tel: 407/393-8080. W.D.W. and transportation services are equipped with motorized platforms.

Tours and specially equipped hotel rooms are also available and should be booked well in advance. Avis, Hertz and National car rentals have a limited number of hand-controlled cars. Be sure to make an early reservation. (See also **Renting a car**.)

Useful contacts Information about individual and group tours for travelers with disabilities is available from the Society for the Society for Accessible Travel and Hospitality (tel: 212/447-7284, www.sath.org); the Travel Information Service (tel: 215/456-9600); and members of Mobility International U.S.A. (tel: 541/343-1284 (tel and TTY), www.miusa.org). Travel agencies experienced in arranging vacations for physically or mentally disabled people include Access Adventures (tel: 716/889-9096); Flying Wheels Travel (tel: 507/451-5005, ww.flyingwheelstravel.com); and New Directions (tel: 805/967-2841).

ACCOMMODATIONS

The choice of accommodations in Florida is enormous, varied, and well-priced. You can save money by visiting Florida out of season (April through December) when prices plummet by as much as half. The exception is the Panhandle region and the northern East Coast, the only bit of Florida to feel the cold in winter, where prices are lower in October to May. Florida accommodations are generally spacious, with room for up to four people in some double rooms. There is often no charge for children under 18 staying with their parents.

Another popular option is suite accommodations. Efficiencies can be found in most budget or moderately priced hotels and motels. Apartments and condos are an excellent solution for families, though most require a minimum stay of three to seven days. Families should also look for hotel resorts. Many resorts now offer special children's programs.

MIAMI

Expensive

Biltmore Hotel
1200 Anastasia Avenue, Coral Gables
tel: 305/445-1926 or 800/727-1926; www.biltmorehotel.com
279 spacious rooms in a luxurious Mediterranean Revival landmark. Elegant restaurants, tennis, golf, pool, fitness center.

Conrad Miami
Espirito Santo Plaza, 1395 Brickell Avenue
tel: 305/503-6500;
www.conradhotels.hilton.com
This freestanding steel-and-glass edifice sits in the heart of downtown Miami overlooking Bayside and the financial district. With 203 rooms, suites and multi-bedroom residences, this is the height of luxury. Excellent dining and fitness spa.

Delano Hotel
1685 Collins Avenue, Miami Beach
tel: 305/672-2000 or 800/555-5001; www.delanohotelmiamibeach.com
208 rooms on the beach in one of Miami's coolest hotels; a popular haunt of visiting celebs. Restaurant, pool, fitness, women's rooftop bathhouse.

Doral Golf Resort and Spa
4400 N.W. 87th Avenue tel: 305/592-2000 or 800/713-6725; www.doralgolf.com
Superb complex with 694 rooms and suites, five golf courses, and Golf Learning Center, tennis, swimming pool, restaurants, nightclub, child care.

Loews Miami Beach
1601 Collins Avenue, Miami Beach
tel: 305/604-1601; www.loewshotel.com
800 rooms in an elegant Mediterranean beachfront property with an art deco annex in the adjacent St. Moritz Hotel, and exemplary service.

Sonesta Beach Resort
350 Ocean Drive, Key Biscayne
tel: 305/361-2021 or 800/SONESTA; www.sonesta.com
304 rooms and suites in luxurious beachfront resort; tennis, watersports, free children's entertainment program.

The Tides
1220 Ocean Drive, Miami Beach
tel: 305/604-5070 or 800/439-4095; www.thetideshotel.com
Ultra-chic showcase of the art deco boutique hotel group, Island Outpost. 45 rooms/suites with ocean views. Restaurants, pool and a fitness center.

Moderate

Avalon/Majestic Hotel
700 Ocean Drive, Miami Beach
tel: 305/538-0133 or 800/933-3306
108 rooms in the heart of the Art Deco District in a deco building with modern amenities and restaurant facing the beach.

The Clinton Hotel
825 Washington Avenue, South Beach
tel: 303/938-4040;
www.clintonsouthbeach.com
One of a number of exceptionally styled contemporary hotels in South Beach, The Clinton features well-furnished modern rooms, a great French restaurant, Aïgo, and a salon/spa/fitness center with wellness treatments. Ths is good value for the product and location.

Governor Hotel
435 21st Street, Miami Beach
tel: 305/532-2100 or 800/542-0444; www.sunshinehotels.com
125 attractive, well-priced rooms one block from the ocean near the Convention Center. Pool; dining; walking distance to Lincoln Road shops.

Hotel Place St. Michel
162 Alcazar Avenue, Coral Gables
tel: 305/444-1666 or 800/848-HOTEL; www.hotelplacestmichel.com
Charming 27-room hotel on the expensive side of moderate. Ceiling fans, antiques, award-winning restaurant. Sundeck, pool, fitness.

Miami River Inn
118 S.W. South River Drive
tel: 305/325-0045 or 800/HOTEL-89; www.miamiriverinn.com
Historic B&B complex with 40 individual, antique-furnished rooms close to downtown. Gardens and pool.

Budget

Bay Harbor Inn & Suites
9660 E. Bay Harbor Drive, Bay Harbor Islands/Miami Beach tel: 305/868-4141; www.bayharborinn.com
46 attractive rooms and suites on Indian Creek waterfront; pool, good restaurants, complimentary breakfast served on a yacht.

Best Western South Beach
1020–1050 Washington Avenue, Miami Beach
tel: 305/674-1930 or 800/343-1930; www.bestwestern.com
Four art deco hotels offering 150 rooms (some with kitchen) two blocks from the ocean. Gardens, pool, bike rentals; significant gay clientele.

Clay Hotel and International Hostel
1438 Washington Avenue, Miami Beach
tel: 305/534-2988 or 800/379-CLAY; www.clayhotel.com
Beach bargain, 80 rooms in the Art Deco District.

Accommodations & Restaurants

The Creek and Banana Beach Bungalows
2360 Collins Avenue, Miami Beach
tel: 305/538-1951 or 800/746-7835;
www.bananabungalow.com
85 budget dorms and rooms in tropical gardens across from the beach. Restaurants, bar and kitchen; pool, fitness.
Essex House Hotel
1001 Collins Avenue, Miami Beach
tel: 305/534-2700 or 800/553-7739;
www.essexhotel.com
79 pastel-painted and refurbished rooms in a notable art deco hotel a block from the beach. Close to shopping and dining.
Ocean Surf Hotel
7436 Ocean Terrace, Miami Beach
tel: 305/866-1648 or 800/555-0411;
www.theoceansurfhotel.com
49 rooms in a charming family operated art deco hotel modeled after an ocean liner with porthole windows out to sea. Close to shopping and dining.

THE KEYS AND EVERGLADES

Expensive

Cheeca Lodge
MM 82.5, Islamorada tel: 305/664-4651
or 800/327-2888; www.cheeca.com
203 units in famous resort complex. Golf, tennis, fishing, watersports, fine dining and kids' activities.
LaMer Hotel
504–506 South Street, Key West
tel: 305/296-6577 or 800/354-4455;
www.lamerhotel.com
On the beachfront in the heart of Key West, this wooden, balconied mansion surrounded by palm trees is furnished in English Colonial style.
Marquesa Hotel
600 Fleming Street, Key West
tel: 305/292-1919 or 800/869-4631;
www.marquesa.com
27 rooms in a collection of beautifully restored and furnished old Key West houses set in lovely gardens. Two pools; excellent casual restaurant.
The Moorings
123 Beach Road, Islamorada
tel: 305/664-4708
18 traditional Keys-style apartments (and a three-bedroom house) in charming, small, quiet grounds with gardens, beach, pool and tennis.
Sheraton Beach Resort
MM 97, Key Largo tel: 305/852-5553;
www.starwoodhotels.com
Private beach, watersports, pools, tennis, four restaurants, children's activities; 200 rooms/suites.

Moderate

Banana Bay Resort & Marina
2319 N. Roosevelt Boulevard, Key West (MM2)
tel: 305/296-6925 or 800/226-2621;
www.bananabay.com
50 spacious rooms/suites in small resort north of town. Excellent watersports facilities, dive shop, private beach, pool, fitness and spa.
Faro Blanco Marine Resort
MM 48.2, Marathon tel: 305/743-9018 or
800/759-3276; www.spottswood.com
Ocean and bayfront hotel-marina complex with 60-plus units from houseboats and cottages to condos. Pool, dive shop, dining.
Key Lime Inn
725 Truman Avenue, Key West
tel: 305/294-5229 or 800/549-4430;
www.keylimeinn.com
Appealing Bahama-style cottage complex with 37 well-equipped rooms two blocks from Duval; pool.
Largo Lodge Motel
MM 101.5, Key Largo tel: 305/451-0424
or 800/IN THE SUN; www.largolodge.com
Seven efficiencies set in a tropical garden; air-conditioning, screened porches (minimum age 16).
Lime Tree Bay Resort
MM 68.5, Long Key tel: 305/664-4740 or
800/723-4519; www.limetreebayresort.com
30 units (some with kitchens) in attractive bayside gardens. Watersports, barbeque grills, hammocks.
Marina del Mar Resort and Marina
MM 100, Key Largo tel: 305/451-4107 or
800/451-3483; www.marinadelmar.com
76 rooms, suites and villas in bayside resort and oceanside marina. Dive packages, watersports, tennis, dining and dancing.
Southernmost Hotel
1319 Duval Street, Key West
tel: 305/296-5611 or 800/354-4455;
www.oldtownresorts.com
127 rooms in tropical setting. Pool-side tiki bar; near restaurants and nightlife.

Budget

Accommodations Key West by Greg O'Berry
701 Caroline Street, Key West
tel: 305/294-6639 or 800/654-2781
Vacation rentals from Key West through Big Pine Key. Condos, cottages and family houses.
The Grand
1116 Grinnell Street, Key West
tel: 305/294-0590 or 888/947-2630;
www.thegrandguesthouse.com
Ten rooms/suites (with kitchenettes) in spruce and friendly guesthouse. Terrific value.
Island Bay Resort
MM 92.5, Tavernier tel: 305/852-4087 or
800/654-5397; www.islandfun.com/islandbay
Ten small guesthouse/efficiencies in complex; dive boat and dock.
Parmer's Place Cottages
MM 29, Little Torch Key tel: 305/872-2157
44 spotless units (rooms, efficiencies, and apartments); family friendly atmosphere and staff; pool.
Ragged Edge Resort & Marina
MM 86.5, 243 Treasure Harbor Road,
Islamorada tel: 305/852-5389 or
800/436-2023; www.ragged-edge.com
Ten wood-paneled units with decks or porches in two-story buildings in oceanfront position. Pool; kitchens.

CENTRAL FLORIDA

Expensive

Hyatt Regency Grand Cypress
1 Grand Cypress Boulevard, Orlando
tel: 407/239-1234 or 800/233-1234;
www.hyatt.com
725 rooms, with tennis, golf, equestrian and fitness centers, nature reserve.

Peabody Orlando
9810 International Drive, Orlando
tel: 407/352-4000 or 800/PEABODY;
www.peabodyorlando.com
Plush, high-rise Peabody has a choice of upscale restaurants, plus the twice-daily "march of the Peabody ducks."

Portfino Bay
Universal Orlando, 5600 Universal Boulevard, Orlando tel: 407/503-1000 or 1/800-LOEWS;
www.loewshotels.com
795 luxurious rooms and suites in a pretty pastel Italian-themed resort. Pools, dining, health club.

W.D.W., Grand Floridian Beach Resort, Polynesian Resort (Magic Kingdom), **Dolphin, Swan, Yacht** and **Beach Club Resorts** (Epcot), **Wilderness Lodge**
Central Reservations, Box 10100, Lake Buena Vista, Fl 32830 tel: 407/939-6244
Spacious family rooms, excellent facilities, dining and transportation to parks.

Moderate

Best Western Maingate East Hotel and Suites
4018 West Vine Street, Kissimmee
tel: 3407/870-2000 or 877/444-2407;
www.bestwestern.com
Only 7 miles (11km) from Disney and close to downtown Kissimmee, the hotel offers 223 upgraded rooms. Facilities range from heated pool, spa and fitness room to guest laundry.

Cabot Lodge Hotel
3726 S.W. 40th Boulevard, Gainesville
tel: 352/375-2400 or 800/843-8735;
www.cabotlodgegainesville.com
208 modern rooms off I–75; pool, fitness center, complimentary breakfast.

Chalet Suzanne
3800 Chalet Suzanne Drive (off C.R. 17A), 4.5 miles (7km) north of Lake Wales
tel: 941/676-6011 or 800/433-6011;
www.chaletsuzanne.com
30 rooms in country inn on lake. Good restaurant.

Crowne Plaza Universal
7800 Universal Boulevard, Orlando
tel: 407/355-0550 or 1-800/294-0946
www.crowneplazauniversal.com
A tourist and business hotel with a pool, fitness room and guest laundry facilities. Just one block from International Drive, the hotel has a shuttle service to Disney and Universal.

Herlong Mansion
Cholokka Boulevard, Micanopy
tel: 352/466-3322 or 800/437-5664
12 B&B rooms in antebellum mansion. Home-cooked breakfasts; charming historic village.

Seven Sisters
820 S.E. Fort King Street, Ocala
tel: 352/867-1170 or 800/250-3496
Eight antiques-filled B&B rooms in a delightful Queen Anne-style house.

W.D.W. Caribbean Beach Resort, Port Orleans, Dixie Landings
Central Reservations, Box 10100, Lake Buena Vista, FL 32830 tel: 407/939-6244;
www.disneyworld.com
Caribbean/Deep South themed resort hotels; great Disney facilities at moderate prices.

Budget

Econo Lodge Maingate Hawaiian Resort
7514 W. Irlo Bronson Memorial Highway, Kissimmee tel: 407/396-2000 or 800/365-6935; www.econolodge.com
445 rooms with tropical theme; close to W.D.W.; heated pool and whirlpool; dining, car rental.

Hojo Inn Maingate East
6051 W. Irlo Bronson Memorial Highway, Kissimmee tel: 407/396-1748 or 800/288-4678; www.hojomge.com
367 rooms in sprawling chain hotel with swimming pools, free transportation to W.D.W., close to shops and restaurants.

Sleep Inn Universal
5606 Major Boulevard, orlando
tel: 407/363-1333; www.choicehotels.com
Close to the Universal parks, this modern hotel has a restaurant and a pool.

Unicorn Inn
8 S. Orlando Avenue, Kissimmee
tel: 407/846-1200 or 800/865-7212;
www.touristguide.com/b&b/florida/unicorn
Ten rooms in friendly English B&B. Restored historic home downtown.

W.D.W. All-Star Sports Movies and Music Resorts
Central Reservations, Box 10100, Lake Buena Vista, FL 32830 tel: 407/939-6244;
www.disneyworld.com
5,760 rooms in Disney's three budget-priced resorts. Family friendly; good facilities.

W.D.W. Fort Wilderness Resort and Campground
Central Reservations, Box 10100, Lake Buena Vista, FL 32830 tel: 407/939-6244;
www.disneyworld.com
784 campgrounds and 408 one-bedroom cabins (sleep 4–6). Woodland setting; great facilities.

THE GOLD COAST

Expensive

Boca Raton Resort & Club
501 E. Camino Real, Boca Raton
tel: 561/447-3000 or 800/491-BOCA;
www.bocaresort.com
963 deluxe rooms in superb Mizner/modern creation; golf, pools, tennis, health club, restaurants.

The Breakers
1 S. County Road, Palm Beach
tel: 561/655-6611 or 888/273-2537;
www.thebreakers.com
572-room landmark on the ocean; golf, tennis, croquet, fine dining.

Colony Hotel
155 Hammon Avenue, Palm Beach
tel: 561/655-5430 or 800/521-5525;
www.thecolonypalmbeach.com
100 classy rooms between the beach and Worth Avenue; pool, fitness, restaurant.

Hyatt Regency Pier 66
2301 S.E. 17th Street, Fort Lauderdale
tel: 954/525-6666 or 800/327-3796;
www.hyatt.com
388 rooms and suites downtown. Pool, fitness room; California Café dining room.

The Pillars
111 N. Birch Road, Fort Lauderdale
tel: 954/467-9639 or 800/800-7666; www.pillarshotel.com
Elegantly appointed 23-room property a block from the ocean on New River Sound. Pool; charming service.

Moderate

Hibiscus House
501 West 30th Street, West Palm Beach
tel: 501/863-5633 or 800/203-4927; www.hisbicushouse.com
Built in 1922, this mansion has been painstakingly renovated. Rooms have terraces or balconies, the public spaces are sumptuous and the house is surrounded by verdant gardens.

Hotel Biba
320 Belvedere Road, West Palm Beach
tel: 501/832-0094; www.hotelbiba.com
This 430-room hotel has been fashioned by designer Barbara Hulanicki and landscape architect Donald Murakami in the shell of a landmark building in central West Palm Beach.

Lago Mar Resort Hotel & Club
1700 S. Ocean Lane, Fort Lauderdale
tel: 954/523-6511 or 800/LAGOMAR; www.lagomar.com
Attractive beachfront complex with 212 rooms and suites; pools, tennis, mini-golf, restaurant.

Palm Beach Historic Inn
365 S. County Road, Palm Beach
tel: 561/832-4009; www.palmbeachhistoricinn.com
Nine rooms and four suites in B&B that is in walking distance from Worth Avenue and the beach.

Ramada Inn Hollywood Beach
101 N. Ocean Drive, Hollywood
tel: 954/921-0990 or 800/331-6103; www.ramada.com
360 rooms and studios with art deco touches; pool, tennis, fitness, restaurants, shopping, child care.

Budget

A Little Inn by the Sea
4546 El Mar Drive, Lauderdale-by-the-Sea
tel: 954/772-2450 or 800/492-0311; www.alittleinn.com
Delightful 37-unit B&B on the ocean with views, pool, some efficiencies, and cosmopolitan clientele.

Beachcomber Apartment Motel
3024 S. Ocean Boulevard, Palm Beach
tel: 561/585-4646 or 800/833-7122
Oceanfront location for 45 spacious units; some kitchens and balconies.

Manta Ray Inn
1715 S. Surf Road, Hollywood
tel: 954/921-9666 or 800/255-0595; www.mantarayinn.com
12 spacious, fully equipped apartments right on the beach and close to Hollywood's stores, restaurants and sports facilities.

Riverside Hotel
620 E. Las Olas Boulevard, Fort Lauderdale
tel: 954/467-0671 or 800/325-3280; www.riversidehotel.com
109 spacious rooms in attractive, central, old hotel; pool, restaurant.

Riviera Palms Motel
3960 N. Ocean Boulevard, Delray Beach
tel: 561/276-3032
Rooms and efficiencies near beach; pool.

Sailfish Marina & Resort
98 Lake Drive, Palm Beach Shores
tel: 561/844-1724 or 800/446-4577; www.sailfishmarina.com
23 rooms two blocks from beach; pool, sportfishing charters, restaurant, bar and barbecue.

Sea Chateau Resort
555 N. Birch Road, Fort Lauderdale
tel: 954/566-8331 or 800/726-3732
17 pretty rooms and efficiencies 200 yards (180m) from beach; pool, coffee, pastries.

Tropic Cay Beach Resort Hotel
529 N. Atlantic Boulevard, Fort Lauderdale
tel: 954/564-5900 or 800/463-2333
45 beachfront efficiencies and units. Close to watersports, tennis, shopping.

Villas-by-the-Sea Resort & Beach Club
4456 El Mar Drive, Lauderdale-by-the-Sea
tel: 954/772-3550 or 800/247-8963
141 smart rooms and efficiencies in landscaped grounds; pool, tennis, barbecue grills.

EAST COAST

Expensive

Adam's Mark Daytona Beach Resort
100 N. Atlantic Avenue, Daytona Beach
tel: 904/254-8200 or 800/444-2326; www.adamsmark.com
437 rooms in a prime oceanfront location. Pools and fitness, dining, children's facilities.

Amelia Island Plantation
3000 First Coast Highway, Amelia Island
tel: 904/261-6161; www.aipfl.com
Superb resort set in a nature preserve; beach, pools, tennis, golf, fishing, riding, fine dining.

Amelia Island Williams House
103 S. 9th Street, Fernandina Beach
tel: 904/277-2328 or 800/414-9258; www.williamshouse.com
One of Fernandina's finest historic B&B homes. Oriental art and antiques. Four rooms.
Other historic B&B options include: Hoyt House (tel: 904/277-4300; www.hoythouse.com), and The Bailey House (tel: 904/261-5390; www.bailey-house.com).

Casablanca Inn
24 Avenida Menendez, St. Augustine
tel: 904/829-0928; www.casablancainn.com
20 rooms in gracious old town-center B&B. River views, whirlpool, bicycles.

Casa Monica Hotel
95 Cordova Street, St. Augustine
tel: 904/827-1888; www.casamonica.com
Superbly restored 137-room Flagler-era hotel. Handsome Spanish-Revival decor; pool.

Disney's Vero Beach Resort
9250 Island Grove Terrace, Vero Beach
tel: 561/234-2000 or 800/359-8000; www.dvcresorts.com
Rooms and one- and two-bedroom cottages in themed Old Florida beachfront timeshare complex, open to all. Pools, boating, tennis, fitness, fishing and golf.

Omni Hotel
245 Water Street, Jacksonville
tel: 904/355-6664 or 800/843-6664; www.omnihotels.com
354 classy rooms/suites around luxuriant atrium; pool, health club, excellent restaurant.

Ponte Vedra Inn & Club
200 Ponte Vedra Boulevard, Ponte Vedra Beach tel: 904/285-1111 or 800/234-7842; www.pvresorts.com
222 rooms and suites in luxurious old-style oceanfront country club resort. Golf, tennis, spa. Fine dining.

Moderate

Bahama House
2001 S. Atlantic Avenue, Daytona Beach Shores tel: 386/248-2001 or 800/571-2001; www.daytonabahamahouse.com
87 tropically themed and well-equipped efficiencies. Right on the beach; pool, helpful staff.

Castillo Real
530 A1A Beach Boulevard, St Augustine Beach
tel: 904/471-3505 or 800/762-5311; www.castilloreal.com
Clarion boutique hotel opened in 2004. Rooms and suites are around a Moorish-style atrium. Shuttle bus to old St Augustine (3 miles/5km).

Driftwood Inn
3150 Ocean Drive, Vero Beach
tel: 727/231-0550; www.driftwoodinn.com
A 1930s inn made of driftwood and beachcombing finds, with 100 rooms and efficiencies.

Fawlty Towers Resort
100 E. Cocoa Beach Causeway, Cocoa Beach
tel: 321/784-3870 or 800/887-3870
32 spacious and attractive rooms in shocking pink complex one block from the beach. Pool and pretty garden with bar.

Hutchinson Inn Seaside Resort
9750 S. Ocean Drive, Jensen Beach, Fort Pierce tel: 561/229-2000
21 units on ocean; pool, tennis, free barbecue on Saturday nights.

Sea Turtle Inn
1 Ocean Boulevard, Atlantic Beach
tel: 904/249-7402 or 800/874-6000; www.seaturtle.com
194 rooms by the ocean north of Jacksonville Beach. Pool; restaurant.

Sun Viking Lodge
2411 S. Atlantic Avenue, Daytona Beach Shores tel: 368/252-6252 or 800/815-2846; www.sunviking.com
91 rooms and efficiencies in friendly family resort; activity program, beachfront, pools, water slide, spa, café.

Budget

Bayfront Inn
138 Avenida Menendez, St. Augustine
tel: 904/824-1681 or 800/558-3455; www.bayfrontinn.com
33 Spanish-style units around poolr.

Beachside Motel
3172 S. Fletcher Avenue, Fernandina Beach
tel: 904/261-4236; www.beachsidemotel.com
Beachfront bargain with 20 spotless and spacious rooms and efficiencies. Pool deck.

Best Western Aku Tiki
2225 S. Atlantic Avenue, Daytona Beach Shores tel: 386/252-9631 or 800/258-8454; www.bestwestern.com
132 rooms and efficiencies on oceanfront; pool, restaurant.

Best Western Oceanfront
305 1st Street North, Jacksonville Beach
tel: 904/249-4949 or 800/897-8131; www.bestwestern.com
A small Best Western property with just 51 rooms, the Oceanfront sits at the heart of Jacksonville Beach and its swathe of sand. The hotel has a small heated pool and breakfast area. Updated rooms feature fridge and microwave.

Days Inn Oceanfront
1031 S. First Street, Jacksonville Beach
tel: 904/249-7231 or 800/321-2037
155 rooms at some of the best prices on the beach. Pool; restaurant.

Dockside Inn & Resort
1160 Seaway Drive, Fort Pierce
tel: 772/468-3555 or 800/286-1745; www.docksideinn.com
65 units, some with kitchens and/or balconies on inlet; pool, barbecue, fishing.

Dream Inn
3217 S. Atlantic Avenue, Daytona Beach Shores tel: 386/767-2821 or 800/767-9738; www.dreaminn.com
26 rooms in family-run oceanfront property. Balconies, pool, fishing pier, barbecue.

House on Cherry Street
1844 Cherry Street, Jacksonville
tel: 904/384-1999
Four-room B&B in beautiful old house down leafy Riverside lane.

WEST COAST

Expensive

Don CeSar Beach Resort & Spa
3400 Gulf Boulevard, St. Petersburg Beach
tel: 727/360-1881 or 866/728-2206; www.doncesar.com
Pink palace on beach with 226 rooms and 51 suites; pool, watersports, children's programs.

Edgewater Beach Hotel
1901 Gulf Shore Boulevard, Naples
tel: 239/403-2000 or 800/821-0196; www.edgewaternaples.com
124 attractive suites with kitchenette and balcony; friendly atmosphere; beach, pool, fitness, chic dining room.

Marco Island Marriott Resort, Golf Club and Spa
400 S. Collier Boulevard, Marco Island
tel: 239/394-2511 or 800/438-4373; www.marriott.com
One of America's best resorts: beachfront spread with great golf, watersports, gourmet dining and children's entertainment.

Resort at Longboat Key Club
301 Gulf of Mexico Drive, Longboat Key, Sarasota
tel: 239/383-8821 or 888/237-3300; www.longboatkeyclub.com

232 fine suites, 45 holes of golf, 38 tennis courts, and a beachfront location, plus fine dining, fitness center and children's programs.

Ritz-Carlton Naples
280 Vanderbilt Beach Road, Naples
tel: 239/598-3300; www.ritzcarlton.com
One of Florida's top resorts, with 463 rooms, and grand public rooms, fine restaurants, golf, tennis, kids' programs.

Saddlebrook Resort—Tampa
5700 Saddlebrook Way, Wesley Chapel
tel: 813/973-1111 or 800/729-8383; www.saddlebrook.com
790 rooms and suites in countryside 15 miles (24km) north of Tampa; golf course, tennis, fitness, award-winning dining. Good-value packages.

Song of the Sea
863 E. Gulf Drive, Sanibel
tel: 239/472-2220 or 800/965-7772; www.southseas.com
30 efficiencies in seaside B&B with pool. Alfresco breakfasts; close to tennis and golf.

Moderate

Beach View Cottages
3325 W. Gulf Drive, Sanibel Island
tel: 239/472-1202 or 800/860-0532; www.beachviewcottages.com
Efficiencies in relaxed family style complex right on the beach.

Best Western Beach Resort
275 Estero Boulevard, Fort Myers Beach
tel: 941/463-6181 or 800/449-1830; www.southseas.com
180 family-style rooms/condos/cottages in landscaped surroundings; with pool, tennis, watersports, fishing, boat dock, dining.

Diplomat Resort
3155 Gulf of Mexico Drive, Longboat Key, Sarasota tel: 941/383-3791 or 800/344-5418; www.diplomatresort.net
50 spacious units in beachfront apartment complex (two-day minimum stay), with pool.

The Inn by the Sea
287 S. Eleventh Avenue, Naples
tel: 941/649-4124 or 800/584-1268; www.innbythesea-bb.com
Five pretty guest rooms in a 1927 B&B surrounded by tropical palms two blocks from the beach. Near shops and restaurants; bicycles to borrow.

Island's End Resort
1 Pass-a-Grille Way, St. Petersburg Beach
tel: 727/360-5023; www.islandsend.com
Six quiet and charming one- to three-bedroom B&B cottages on the Gulf. Fishing, barbeque grills.

Outrigger Beach Resort
6200 Estero Boulevard, Fort Myers Beach
tel: 239/463-3131 or 800/655-8997; www.outriggerfmb.com;
144 rooms and efficiences on Gulf; pool, tiki bar, dining, bike rental, children's programs.

Island Grand
5500 Gulf Boulevard, St. Petersburg Beach
tel: 727/562-1212 or 800/360-4016; www.tradewindsresort.com
577 (moderate to expensive) rooms and efficiencies in excellent resort, with pools, tennis, sailing and children's activities.

Budget

Beach House
4960 Estero Boulevard, Fort Myers Beach
tel: 941/463-4004; www.travelbase.com/destinations/ft-myers/beach-house
14 rooms and apartments in delightful house amid condos.

Comfort Inn & Marina Downtown Naples
1221 5th Avenue South, Naples
tel: 239/649-5800; www.choicehotels.com
The perfect budget waterfront option. Comfort Cruise Sightseeing boat for trips around the harbor. Heated pool and bar on site.

Econo Lodge Beachfront Resort
6 South Gulfview Boulevard, Clearwater Beach
tel: 272/446-3400 or 877/424-6423; www.econolodge.com
Good budget choice directly on Clearwater Beach. Attracts the young crowd during holiday seasons.

Holiday Inn Busch Gardens
2701 E. Fowler Avenue, Tampa
tel: 813/971-4710 or 800/315-2664
Sprawling family friendly complex with 400-plus rooms/suites; pool, dining, and shopping nearby.

Lido Beach Palms
148 Cleveland Drive, Lido Key, Sarasota
tel: 941/383-9505 or 800/237-9505; www.longboatkey.com
One- and two-bedroom apartments. Pool, barbecue, near shops and restaurants.

Olde Naples Inn
801 S. Third Street, Naples
tel: 941/262-5194 or 800/637-6036; www.bestof.net/naples/hotels/oldenaplesinn
60 rooms and efficiencies in pleasant motel with pool, a short walk from the beach.

Palm Pavilion Inn
18 Bay Esplanade, Clearwater Beach
tel: 727/446-6777 or 800/123-7256; www.palmpavilioninn.com
Smartly restored deco hotel by the beach. 27 rooms/efficiencies; pool, rooftop sundeck.

THE PANHANDLE

Expensive

Bay Point Marriott Resort
4200 Marriott Drive, Panama City Beach
tel: 850/236-6000 or 800/874-7105; www.marriott.com
355 elegant rooms, suites and villas; beach, woods, golf, tennis, watersports, children's activities.

Edgewater Beach Resort
11212 Front Beach Road, Panama City Beach
tel: 850/235-4044 or 800/874-8686; www.edgewaterbeachresort.com
464 deluxe units and villas by beach or golf course in good central location; pools, tennis, watersports.

Henderson Park Inn
2700 U.S. 98 East, Destin
tel: 850/837-4853 or 800/336-4853
Romantic B&B escape, with antique furnishings, beach views, pool; 35 rooms with patio/balcony.

Pelican Walk Condominiums
6905 Thomas Drive, Panama City Beach
tel: 850/233-0076 or 800/543-3307
Attractive beachside condo development with one-, two-, and three-bed apartments.

Seaside Cottage Rental Agency
P.O. Box 4730, Seaside, FL 32459
tel: 850/231-2222 or 888/277-8696;
www.seasidefl.com
Vacation rentals in the Old Floridian-style beach resort of Seaside.

Moderate

Cedar Key Bed & Breakfast
3rd and F Streets, Cedar Key
tel: 352/543-9000 or 877/453-5051;
www.cedarkeybandb.com
Pretty rooms in an 1880s gingerbread-trimmed residence.

Coombs House Inn
80 6th Street, Apalachicola tel: 850/653-9199; www.combshouseinn.com
Grand Victorian B&B with 10 rooms; plus eight more in a quiet cottage across the street.

Four Points Hotel by Sheraton
1325 Miracle Strip Parkway, Fort Walton Beach
tel: 850/243-8116 or 800/874-8104;
www.sheraton4pts.com
229 oversize rooms, some efficiencies. Beachfront, pools, dining and fitness center.

Gibson Inn
51 Avenue C, Apalachicola
tel: 850/653-2191; www.gibsoninn.com
30 rooms in fine restored building; dining.

Governor's Inn
209 S. Adams Street, Tallahassee
tel: 850/681-6855 or 800/342-7717;
www.thegovinn.com
40 luxurious rooms and suites; V.I.P. treatment, elegant dining room, breakfast, airport shuttle.

Inn at Killearn Country Club
100 Tyron Circle, Tallahassee
tel: 850/893-2186 or 800/476-4101
39 units in relaxing woodland setting; pool, city's finest golf course, tennis, fitness, fine dining.

New World Inn
600 S. Palafox Street, Pensacola
tel: 850/432-4111;
www.newworldlanding.com
15 deluxe rooms and suites with antique furnishings; excellent restaurant; airport shuttle.

Sandestin Golf and Beach Resort
9300 U.S. 98 West, Destin
tel: 850/267-8150 or 800/622-1038
Huge sports-orientated complex offering rooms, condos and villas. Beachfront position, golf, pools.

Budget

Days Inn
710 N. Palafox Street, Pensacola
tel: 850/438-4922; www.daysinn.com
150 rooms and efficiencies near historic district; pool, coffee shop, Continental breakfast.

Flamingo Motel and Tower
15525 Front Beach Road (U.S. 98), Panama City Beach tel: 850/234-2232 or 800/828-0400;
www.flamingohotel.com
67 efficiencies around garden on the beach.

Georgian Terrace
14415 Front Beach Road (U.S. 98), Panama City Beach
tel: 850/234-2144 or 888/882-2144
30 efficiencies on beach, with pool.

La Quinta Inn Tallahassee South
2850 Apalachee Parkway
tel: 850/878-5099; www.lq.com
Well-designed and furnished rooms make this national chain a good option for tourers. This hotel is only 3 miles (5km) from the city center yet close to shopping and eateries. Small pool on site.

Leeside Inn & Marina
1350 U.S. 98, Okaloosa Island E. Fort Walton Beach
tel: 850/243-7359 or 800/824-2747;
www.leesideinn.com
106 rooms and efficiencies adjoining National Seashore; pool, watersports, fishing, restaurant.

Mermaid's Landing
12685 S.R. 24, Cedar Key
tel: 352/543-5949 or 877/543-5949;
www.mermaidslanding.com
Eight spotless wooden cottages (sleep 2–6) with kitchens in a small property on the back bayou.

The Smokehouse Ranch
Rural Route 1 (PO Box 518), Branford (Hatchbend)
tel: 386/935-2662 or 877/258-9686;
www.smokehouseranch.com
Family-owned working ranch in rural Florida offering B&B in rustic lodge suites, cottages and cabins. Some self-catering options. Just enjoy the peace and quiet and the surrounding parkland.

RESTAURANTS

Florida's cuisine, like its culture, is diverse. The basic ingredients—seafood, fresh vegetables and exotic fruits, like the yellow Key lime used in Key lime pie—may be produced locally, but cooking styles can be worlds apart. Caribbean cooking has inspired the tasty new local "Floribbean" style; Cuban cuisine, based in Miami and Tampa, has outposts throughout the state; and European cuisines from French to Greek all find a niche in Florida's numerous eateries. There is *nouvelle cuisine*, New American-style, spicy Cajun food, and down-home country cooking with a distinctive Southern flavor. It will not cost a fortune to try out any of them.

Dining out in Florida is a casual affair. Families are welcome just about everywhere; special children's portions and money-saving "early bird" specials (usually served between 5 and 7) are standard.

MIAMI

Expensive

Astor Place Bar & Grill
Astor Hotel, 956 Washington Avenue, Miami Beach tel: 305/672-7217
Stunning atrium setting for sophisticated fusion fare.

Blue Door
Delano Hotel, 1685 Collins Avenue, Miami Beach tel: 305/674-6400;
www.delanohotelmiamibeach.com
Fashionable dining room with a clientele and exotic French-Floribbean menu to match.

Chef Allen's
19088 N.E. 29th Avenue, Aventura
tel: 305/935-2900; www.chefallens.com
New American contemporary cuisine at its best; elegant decoesque furnishings.
Nemo
100 Collins Avenue, Miami Beach
tel: 305/532-4550; www.nemorestaurant.com
Gourmet magnet way down in SoBe. Amazing metalwork decor, and delicious Asian-influenced cuisine, plus Hedy Goldsmith's *pâtisseries*.
Norman's
21 Almeria Avenue, Coral Gables
tel: 305/446-6767; www.normans.com
High profile chef Norman Van Aken's New World shrine has a casual-elegant clientele to match his rum-and-pepper-painted grouper and other adventurous concoctions.
Pacific Time
915 Lincoln Road, Miami Beach
tel: 305/534-5979; www.pacifictime.biz
Artfully casual and enormously popular eatery offering an enticing Pacific Rim menu with a Floridian twist, from the soft-shell crab tempura to baked Alaska Key West with tangy lime.

Restaurant St. Michel
Hotel Place St. Michel, 162 Alcazar Avenue, Coral Gables tel: 305/446-6572
Old World dining room; delicious French/American cuisine from Long Island duck to spring lamb.
Yuca
501 Lincoln Road, Miami Beach
tel: 305/532-9822; www.yuca.com
Airy, glass-wrapped pastel and blonde wood setting for fans of imaginative Cuban food, with the occasional Asian influence. Try the guava-barbecued baby back ribs and three-bean terrine.

Moderate

A Fish Called Avalon
Avalon Hotel, 700 Ocean Drive, Miami Beach
tel: 305/522-1727; www.avalonhotels.com
New American cuisine and local seafood in a sleek Art Deco District setting.
Bangkok Bangkok
157 Giralda Avenue, Coral Gables
tel: 305/444-2397
Popular local Thai restaurant, with excellent curries.
Café Med
CocoWalk, 3015 Grand Avenue, Coconut Grove
tel: 305/443-1770
Mediterranean dishes and tasty thin-crust pizzas cooked in the wood-burning oven.
Café Prima Pasta
414 71st Street, North Miami Beach
tel: 305/867-0106
One of the best pasta cafés in town. Handmade pasta, fresh sauces. Always busy.
Joe's Stone Crab Restaurant
11 Washington Avenue, Miami Beach
tel: 305/673-0365; www.joesstonecrab.com
Closed: Jun–early Oct
Seafood institution; informal, but expect lines.
Larios on the Beach
820 Ocean Drive, Miami Beach
tel: 305/532-9577
Cuban restaurant/sidewalk café brings Little Havana to the beach—has the best black beans in town.

Monty's Stone Crab Seafood House and Raw Bar
2550 S. Bayshore Drive, Coconut Grove
tel: 305/856-3992; and 300 Alton Road, Miami Beach tel: 305/673-3444; www.montysstonecrab.com
Seafood, steaks, snacks and entertainment. Coconut Grove outlet is just a raw bar.
NOA (Noodles of Asia)
801 Lincoln Road, Miami Beach
tel: 305/925-0050
Very stylish, very SoBe noodle shop where you can also tuck in to Thai beef salad and wild desserts.
Spiga
1228 Collins Avenue, Miami Beach
tel: 305/534-0079; www.hotelimpalamiamibeach.com
Welcoming neighborhood Italian specializing in fresh homemade pastas, meat and dessert flans.
Van Dyke Café
846 Lincoln Road, Miami Beach
tel: 305/534-3600
Trendy corner spot with sidewalk seating and an eclectic café menu throughout the day. Salads, omelets, eggplant parmigiana and jazz.

Budget

Balans
1022 Lincoln Road, Miami Beach
tel: 305/534-9191; www.balans.com
Astonishingly good value sidewalk bistro on fun Lincoln Road Mall. Mediterranean-Asian cooking plus sticky toffee pudding from English owners.
Café Tu Tu Tango
CocoWalk, 3015 Grand Avenue, Coconut Grove
tel: 305/529-2222; www.cafetututango.com
Funky-artsy tapas café serving up designer pizza, chicken wings, tortillas, kebabs and more.
La Carreta
3632 S.W. 8th Street, Little Havana
tel: 305/444-7501
Cuban specials served in casual, family atmosphere.
Casa Larios
7705 West Flagler Street, Miami
tel: 305/266-5494
Great Cuban staples including delicious roast meats, rice and beans at this budget eatery, voted one of Florida's Top 500 by *Florida Trend Magazine*.
Daily Bread
2400 S.W. 27th Street, Coral Gables
tel: 305/856-0363
Sandwich shop with seating. Middle Eastern salads and dips, and spinach pastries. Very generous.
Jake's Bar and Grill
6901 Red Road, Coral Gables
tel: 305/662-8632
At the upper end of the budget price range, this restaurant has won *Wine Spectator* magazine awards. Contemporary American cuisine.
News Café
800 Ocean Drive, Miami Beach
tel: 305/538-6397
Hip hangout; great brunches; open 24 hours.
Oasis South Beach Restaurant and Lounge
840 First Street, Miami Beach
tel: 305/266-5494
For a change, try this Lebanese retaurant. They have live belly dancing at weekends.

Orlando Seafood Restaurant & Fish Market
501 N.W. 37th Avenue tel: 305/642-6767
A stand-up affair: fresh swordfish, snapper, kingfish, and delicious fish *croquetas* (deep-fried fish cakes).
San Loco
235 14th Street, Miami Beach
tel: 305/538-3009
Witheringly hot chili and hearty tacos, burritos and enchiladas. Open late.

KEYS AND EVERGLADES

Expensive
Café Marquesa
600 Fleming Street, Key West
tel: 305/292-1919; www.marquesa.com
New American fare, fresh Florida ingredients and a dash of the Oriental. Pretty surroundings.
Louie's Backyard
700 Waddell Avenue, Key West
tel: 305/294-1061; www.louiesbackyard.com
Innovative menu with local specialties featuring a Caribbean twist; has lovely waterfront views.
Marker 88
MM 88, Plantation Key tel: 305/852-9315
Spectacular sunset views accompany adventurous seafood and regional dishes (even alligator).
Morada Bay
MM 81, Islamorada tel: 305/664-0604
Delectable bayside dining room with an eclectic Caribbean-American menu, particularly seafood.

Moderate
Alice's Key West
1114 Duval Street, key West
tel: 305/292-5733; www.aliceskeywest.com
Alice Weingarten runs this funky Caribbean eatery serving excellent spicy cuisine she calls "New World Fusion Confusion."
Bagatelle
115 Duval Street, Key West
tel: 305/296-6609;
www.bagatelle-keywest.com
Historic "conch" architecture and interesting Caribbean specials.
Fish House Restaurant & Seafood Market
MM 102.4, Key Largo tel: 305/451-4665;
www.fishhouse.com
Homemade conch specialties and a singing waiter.
Frank Keys Café
MM 100, Key Largo tel: 305/453-0310;
www.frankkeyscafe.com
Cottage in the woods serving Floribbean-Mediterranean seafood, pasta and Key lime pie.
Mangoes
700 Duval Street, Key West
tel: 305/292-4606;
www.mangoeskeywest.com
Floribbean dishes—wraps, pasta and seafood.
Pepe's
806 Caroline Street, Key West
tel: 305/294-7192
Small diner with pine furnishings and garden seating. Big breakfasts, daily specials, barbecues.
Rick's Blue Heaven
729 Thomas Street, Key West
tel: 305/296-8666; www.blueheavenkw.com
Funky old house with outdoor trestles and beer served from a bathtub. Great barbecue, vegetarian Caribbean menu.
Rod & Gun Club
200 Riverside Drive, Everglades City
tel: 941/695-2101
Hunting and fishing lodge by the water. Dine on the veranda from small but well-prepared menu.

Budget
El Siboney
900 Catherine Street (at Margaret), Key West
tel: 305/296-4184
No frills Cuban neighborhood spot. Generous piles of chicken and beans, paella, and spicy picadillo.
Half Shell Raw Bar
Land's End Village, Key West
tel: 305/294-7496; www.halfshellrawbar.com
Oysters, fish sandwiches and seasonal specials; overlooking the docks.
Herbie's
MM 50.5, Marathon tel: 305/743-6373
Informal and friendly; serves great spicy chowder.
Islamorada Fish Company
MM 81.5, Islamorada tel: 305/6644-5071 or 800/258-2559; www.ifcstonecrab.com
No-nonsense fresh fish shop and restaurant. Freshest fish available, shrimp, scallops and stone crab claws in season.
Mrs Mac's Kitchen
MM 99.8, Key Largo tel: 305/451-3722
Home-cooked specials, such as meatloaf and chili.
Num Thai
MM 103.2, Key Largo tel: 305/451-5955
Authentic Thai cuisine including hot curries and soups. Also has a sushi bar.
Shuckers Raw Bar & Grill
MM 48.5, 1415 15th Street, Marathon
tel: 305/743-8686
Nautical decor to match fishy menu; great-value fish baskets.
Sloppy Joe's
201 Duval Street, Key West
tel: 305/294-5717; www.sloppyjoes.com
A Key West institution since 1933 when Ernest Hemingway came daily for company and cocktails. Visit for the atmosphere and the sandwiches and finger food to accompany your cocktail.
Turtle Kraals
Land's End Village, Key West
tel: 305/294-2640; www.turtlekraaals.com
Noisy, popular dockside bar-restaurant; turtles for viewing only.

CENTRAL FLORIDA

Expensive
Chalet Suzanne
3800 Chalet Suzanne Drive (off C.R. 17A), 4.5 miles (7km) north of Lake Wales
tel: 941/676-6011; www.chaletsuzanne.com
Charming country inn with an award-winning small menu of American-Continental chef's specials.
Chefs de France
Epcot, Walt Disney World tel: 407/939-3463; www.disney.go.com
French menu devised by three of France's top chefs: Verge, Bocuse and Lenôtre. Elegant surroundings in the French pavilion; a real treat.

Chef Justin's Park Plaza Gardens
319 Park Avenue South, Winter Park
tel: 407/645-2475;
www.parkplazagardens.com
Creative Florida cuisine in a pretty covered courtyard. Local favorite with a long wine list.
Dux
Peabody Hotel, 9801 International Drive, Orlando tel: 407/352-4000;
www.peabodyorlando.com
Sumptuous restaurant with innovative menu and fine cellar. Jackets requested.
Manuel's on the 28th
390 N. Orange Avenue, Orlando
tel: 407/246-6580;
www.manuelsonthe28th.com
Sophisticated Floribbean cuisine on the 28th floor of the downtown Bank of America building.
Portobello Yacht Club
Downtown Disney Pleasure Island
tel: 407/939-3463; www.disney.go.com
On the lagoon; serves great Northern Italian dishes, homemade pastas, pizzas, seafood.

Moderate
Bongo's Cuban Café
Downtown Disney West Side
tel: 407/934-7639;
www.bongoscubancafe.com
Fun atmosphere, live music and hearty Cuban cooking from chicken and rice to black beans.
Clewiston Inn
108 Royal Palm Avenue (at U.S. 27), Clewiston
tel: 863/983-8151; www.clewistoninn.com
Fine old Southern-style dining room in historic inn.
Ming Court
9188 International Drive, Orlando
tel: 407/351-9988; www.ming-court.com
Serves Chinese food, regional favorites, and seafood in attractive surroundings; dancing.
Pebbles
12551 S.R. 535, Lake Buena Vista
tel: 407/827-1111;
www.pebblesworldwide.com
New American menu, seafood and salads.
Race Rock
8986 International Drive, Orlando
tel: 407/248-9876; www.racerock.com
Restaurant with motor racing theme. Serves American cooking, pizzas, pasta.
Rainforest Café
Downtown Disney Marketplace
tel: 407/827-8500; www.rainforestcafe.com
Landmark mini-volcano with computer-animated wildlife. American menu with a Caribbean twist.
Steve's Café Americain
12 W. University Avenue, Gainesville
tel: 352/377-9337
New American cooking in an open kitchen; smart and casual. Dinner only.
Teppankaki Dining Room
Epcot, Walt Disney World tel: 407/939-3463;
www.disney.go.com
Sample traditional Japanese cuisine.
Texas de Brazil
5259 International Drive, Orlando
tel: 407/355-0355; www.texasdebrazil.com
This authentic Brazilian churrascaria specializes in steaks grilled to perfection. However, the signature dish is a huge skewer of your favorite meat served up with aplomb at your table.

Budget
Café Tu Tu Tango
8625 International Drive, Orlando
tel: 407/248-2222; www.cafetututango.com
World cuisine (from Cajun to Greek) and cocktails served in a re-created artist's loft.
Hard Rock Café
Universal Orlando, CityWalk, Orlando
tel: 407/351-7625; www.hardrockcafe.com
Hamburgers, barbecue, salads and memorabilia in the world's biggest Hard Rock.
Jimmy Buffett's Margaritaville
Universal Orlando, CityWalk, Orlando
tel: 407/244-0420;
www.margaritavilleorlando.com
Laid-back Florida Keys-themed joint specializing in cheeseburgers and namesake margaritas.
Olive Garden
7653 International Drive, Orlando
tel: 407/264-0420; www.ollivegarden.com
Good-value, friendly Italian restaurant chain.
Panache at the Wine & Cheese Gallery
113 N. Main Street, Gainesville tel: 352/372-8446
Innovative bistro-cum-sandwich shop behind a deli-wine store. Lunch only. Patio dining.
Wolfgang Puck Express
Downtown Disney Marketplace
tel: 407/939-3463; www.wolfgangpuck.com
Exotic pizza toppings, focaccia sandwiches and salads. Also try the excellent **Wolfgang Puck Café** at Downtown Disney West Side.

THE GOLD COAST

Expensive
Darrel & Oliver's Café Maxx
2601 E. Atlantic Boulevard, Pompano Beach
tel: 954/782-0606
Innovative New World-Floribbean cuisine; fresh seafood specialties and art deco styling.
Eduardo de San Angel
2822 E. Commercial Boulevard, Fort Lauderdale tel: 954/772-4731;
www.eduardodesanangel.com
Try gourmet Mexican cuisine at this upscale venue, voted one of the Top 500 restaurants in the state by *Florida Trend* magazine.
Johannes
47 E. Palmetto Park Road, Boca Raton
tel: 561/394-0007
This Austrian-born chef mixes classics like *foie gras* with national dishes such as Kobe beef to produce eclectic and ever-changing menus. He also holds theme evenings.
Mark's Las Olas
1032 E. Las Olas Boulevard, Fort Lauderdale
tel: 954/463-1000; www.chefmark.com
Owner/chef Mark Militello's blend of creative contemporary cuisine made with fresh local ingredients is all the rage. Reservations a must.
La Vieille Maison
770 E. Palmetto Park Road, Boca Raton
tel: 561/391-6701
Mizner-era setting for fine French cuisine.

Moderate

15th Street Fisheries
1900 S.E. 15th Street, Fort Lauderdale
tel: 954/763-2777;
www.15streetfisheries.com
Award-winning seafood and waterfront views.

Blue Anchor
804 E. Atlantic Avenue, Delray Beach
tel: 561/272-7272
Great British pub grub, from steak-and-kidney pie to Stilton cheese, plus beers and Sunday breakfast.

Café Protégé
2400 Metrocenter Boulevard, West Palm Beach tel: 561/687-2433
Restaurant showcase for master chefs and students from the Florida Culinary Institute.

Chuck & Harold's
207 Royal Poinciana Way, Palm Beach
tel: 561/659-1440; www.muer.com
Tropical decor, tiles and beams; varied Californian menu. Live entertainment.

Las Olas Café
922 E. Las Olas Boulevard, Fort Lauderdale
tel: 954/524-4300; www.lasolascafe.com
Pretty courtyard and dining room off main drag. Tasty homemade soups, pastas and dairy specials.

Mark's at the Park
344 Plaza Real, Mizner Park, Boca Raton
tel: 561/395-0770; www.chefmark.com
Lunch from the tempting Mediterranean-inspired menu is a reasonably priced experience; dinner is a little more expensive.

Martha's
6024 N.Ocean Drive, Hollywood
tel: 954/923-5444
Nouvelle American with plenty of seafood. Waterside setting; live music at weekends.

No Anchovies
12650 PGA Boulevard, West Palm Beach
tel: 561/622-7855
Jolly, family friendly Italian with a long menu of pastas, pizzas, salads and meats from the oak-fired grill.

Sushi Blues Café
2009 Harrison Street, Hollywood
tel: 954/929-9560; www.sushiblues.com
Sushi and live jazz (Thu–Sun) make a great pairing at this small but popular venue.

Budget

Banana Boat
739 E. Ocean Avenue, Boynton Beach
tel: 561/732-9400
Casual waterfront spot; mostly seafood, dockside bar, entertainment.

Cheeburger, Cheeburger
708 E. Las Olas Boulevard, Fort Lauderdale
tel: 954/524-8824; www.cheeburger.com
Mega cheeseburgers, onion loaf, malts and low, low prices for this classy neighborhood.

John G's
10 S. Ocean Boulevard, Lake Worth
tel: 561/585-9860; www.johngs.com
Busy, informal and on the beach; burgers, omelets, pasta. Closed evenings.

Lighthouse Restaurant
1510 U.S. 1, Jupiter tel: 561/746-4811
Good home cooking from beef stew to crab cakes, and scrumptious desserts.

Tom's Place
7251 N. Federal Highway, Boca Raton
tel: 561/997-0920
Barbecued ribs and chicken favored by N.F.L. players.

EAST COAST

Expensive

Beech Street Grill
801 Beech Street, Fernandina Beach
tel: 904/277-3662; www.beechstreetgrill.com
A series of small modish dining rooms in an 1889 historic district house. New American cuisine, local seafood and good wine list.

Dolphin Depot
704 N. First Street, Jacksonville Beach
tel: 904/270 1424
Popular seafood joint with daily specials.

Mango Tree
118 N. Atlantic Avenue, Cocoa Beach
tel: 321/799-0513;
www.mangotreerestaurant.com
Elegant tropical decor; delicious light, fresh American cuisine.

Matthew's
2107 Hendricks Avenue, Jacksonville
tel: 904/396-9922;
www.matthewsrestaurant.com
Smart chic San Marco district showcase for Matthew Madure's stunning cuisine marrying New American-Asian-Mediterranean influences.

95 Cordova
Casa Monica Hotel, 95 Cordova Street, St. Augustine tel: 904/810-6810;
www.95cordova.com
Sumptuous decor, antique furnishings, and an eclectic, innovative Mediterranean-American south-western menu.

Moderate

A1A Aleworks
1 King Street, St. Augustine
tel: 904/829-2977; a1aaleworks.com
Restaurant and micro-brewery with a New World menu and outdoor seating.

The Back Marlin
53 West Osceola Street, Stuart
tel: 772/286-3126; www.pawnbroker.com
Entrées concentrate on seafood, but you can also enjoy salads, pizzas and pastas.

Black Tulip
207 Brevard Avenue, Historic Cocoa Village
tel: 321/631-1133
Continental fare in the historic district.

Columbia
98 St. George Street, St. Augustine
tel: 904/824-3341;
www.columbiarestaruant.com
Spanish, Cuban and Continental dishes.

Down Under Restaurant
AIA at Intracoastal Waterway, Fernandina Beach tel: 904/261-1001
Alaskan king crab, grouper, oysters and steaks.

Mangrove Matties
1640 Seaway Drive, Fort Pierce
tel: 772/466-1044
Great waterfront views as well as sumptuous Sunday brunch.

Max's Restaurant
1312 Beach Boulevard, Jacksonville Beach
tel: 904/247-6820; www.maxsrestaurant.us
Characterful eatery overlooking a courtyard. Fresh seafood and Mediterranean influences.
Ocean Grill
1050 Sexton Plaza (Beachland Boulevard), Vero Beach tel: 772/231-5409; www.ocean-grill.com
Local favorite; seafood, steaks, with ocean view.
Raintree
102 San Marco Avenue, St. Augustine
tel: 904/829-5953; www.raintreerestaurant.com
Beautifully restored old house; seasonal menu with plenty of seafood and marvelous desserts.
Riverside Café
1 Beachland Boulevard, Vero Beach
tel: 772/234-5550
Riverfront restaurant serving Continental fare. Outdoor seating, bar, entertainment.

Budget

Bubba's FishCamp
421 S. Federal Highway, Stuart
tel: 561/220-3747
Rustic fish camp style and great Southern cooking: fried chicken, hush puppies.

Cruisin' Café
2 S. Atlantic Avenue, Daytona Beach
tel: 386/253-5522
Motorsports-theme restaurant. Burgers, steaks and seafood.
Florida Cracker Café
81 St. George Street, St. Augustine
tel: 904/829-0397
Busy café serving up shrimp, tuna, po'boy sandwiches and gator tail fritters.
Florida House Inn
20 S. 3rd Street, Fernandina Beach
tel: 904/261-3300 or 800/258-3301
All-you-can-eat Southern cooking, served boarding house fashion in Florida's oldest lodging.
Philly's Finest Cheese Steak and Pizza
1527 3rd Street, Jacksonville Beach
tel: 904/241-7188
Busy sports bar with varied snack menu, though it's famed locally for its cheese steak sandwiches.
Rusty's Seafood & Oyster Bar
628 Glen Cheek Drive, Port Canaveral
tel: 321/783-2033; www.rustysseafood.com
Also at 2 S. Atlantic Avenue, Cocoa Beach (tel: 321/783-2401)
Waterfront views and generous seafood specials.
Santa Maria
135 Avenida Menendez, St. Augustine
tel: 904/829-6578
Seafood, steaks and chicken in family-run landmark by the marina.

WEST COAST

Expensive

Armani's
Grand Hyatt Tampa Bay, 2900 Bayport Drive Tampa tel: 813/207-6800
Stylish Northern Italian restaurant garlanded with awards. Amazing antipasti; grand rooftop views.
Bern's Steak House
1208 S. Howard Avenue, Tampa
tel: 813/251-2421; www.bernsteakhouse.com
Clubby decor, exemplary service, prime steaks and organic vegetables. Huge wine list.
Café L'Europe
431 St. Armands Circle, Sarasota
tel: 941/388-4415; www.cafeleurope.com
Fashionably elegant, arty setting; delicate French *nouvelle cuisine* seafood, veal and beef dishes.
Marchand's Grill
Renaissance Vinoy Resort, 501 5th Avenue N.E., St. Petersburg tel: 727/894-1000; www.marriott.com
Elegant dining room, bay views and sophisticated New American-Floribbean menu. Long wine list.
Marek's Collier House
112 Bald Eagle Drive, Marco Island
tel: 239/642-9948
American-international cuisine in gracious historic home. Smart-casual.
Mise en Place—An American Bistro
442 W. Kennedy Boulevard, Tampa
tel: 813/254-5373; www.miseonline.com
Inventive New American cuisine with French-Italian-Japanese influences.
Veranda
2122 Second Street, Fort Myers
tel: 239/332-2065; www.theverandarestaurant.com
Historical buildings with garden court; innovative regional Southern menu.

Moderate

Bob Heilman's Beachcomber
447 Mandalay Avenue, Clearwater Beach
tel: 727/442-4144; www.heilmansbeachcomber.com
Popular casual welcoming restaurant with a broad American menu and local art on the walls.
Bubble Room
15001 Captiva Drive, Captiva
tel: 239/472-5558; www.bubbleroomrestaurant.com
Wacky 1940s kitsch decor; monster platters.
Columbia
2117 7th Avenue, Ybor City, Tampa
tel: 813/248-4961; www.columbiarestaurant.com
Landmark Spanish restaurant; rustic decor and traditional menu.
Louis Pappas' Riverside
10 W. Dodecanese Boulevard, Tarpon Springs
tel: 727/937-5101; www.pappasriverside.com
Busy tourist spot that serves great Greek food.
Prawnbroker
13451 McGregor Boulevard, Fort Myers
tel: 941/489-2226; www.pawnbroker.com
Local favorite; mainly fish menu, steak and poultry.
Riverwalk Fish & Ale House
1200 S. Fifth Avenue, Naples
tel: 941/263-2734
Dockside dining in the Old Marine Marketplace.
Wine Cellar
17307 N. Gulf Boulevard, Redington Beach
tel: 727/393-3491; www.thewinecellar.com
Warm atmosphere, plus award-winning American and Middle-European menu.

Budget

California Pizza Kitchen
5555 U.S. 41 N., Naples
tel: 239/566-1900; www.ckp.com
Dandy find in an upscale mall. Designer pizzas and world cooking, salads, sandwiches and more.

Lighthouse Café
362 Periwinkle Way, Sanibel
tel: 941/472-0303; www.lighthousecafe.com
Cosy café dishing up wonderful home-style meals. Breakfast, steak sandwiches and seafood.

Roger's Real Pit Bar-B-Que
6851 66th Street, Pinellas Park
tel: 727/544-6671
Baby-back ribs, franks and beans plus wonderful salad bar.

Seafood & Sunsets at Julie's
351 S. Gulf Boulevard, Clearwater Beach
tel: 727/441-2548
Beach shack with good seafood and sunset views.

Turtles on Little Sarasota Bay
8875 Midnight Pass Road, Siesta Key, Sarasota tel: 941/346-2207
Central bayfront seafood joint with outdoor seating. Local favorite; child-friendly.

THE PANHANDLE

Expensive

Andrews 228
228 S. Adams Street, Tallahassee
tel: 850/222-3444;
www.andrewsdowntown.com
Political district favorite serving small, elegant New American menu in a Frenchified setting.

Criolla's
170 Scenic 30A, Grayton Beach
tel: 850/267-1267; www.criollas.com
Creative cuisine with a tropical New World flavor. Smart-casual dress; notable wine cellar.

Jamie's Wine Bar & Restaurant
424 E. Zaragoza Street, Pensacola
tel: 850/434-2911
Lovely historic district cottage setting for Floribbean-Mediterranean-Asian fusion cuisine, plus a huge and varied wine list.

Magnolia Grill
99 11th Street, Apalachicola
tel: 850/653-8000;
www.chefeddiesatmagnoliagrill.com
Sophisticated seafood from chef Eddie Cass, served up in a charming historic cottage.

Moderate

Boar's Head
17290 Front Beach Road, Panama City Beach
tel: 850/234-6628;
www.boarsheadrestaurant.com
Woodsy interior; generous prime rib and seafood platters.

Capt. Anderson's
5551 N. Lagoon Drive, Panama City Beach
tel: 850/234-2225; www.captandersons.com
Top seafood restaurant.

Chez Pierre
1215 Thomasville Road, Tallahassee
tel: 850/222-0936; www.chezpierre.com
French café with broad menu, light lunches, pastries.

Flamingo Café
414 E. U.S. 98, Destin tel: 850/837-0961
Chic decor, harbor views and a more casual patio area. Floribbean and fish specialties.

Flounders Chowder & Ale House
800 Quietwater Beach Road, Pensacola Beach
tel: 850/932-2003
Lively pub-restaurant on Santa Rosa Sound serving a broad American menu with seafood specials. Entertainment and dance floor.

Gibson Inn
51 Avenue C, Apalachicola tel: 850/653-2191; www.gibsoninn.com
Historic inn serving varied menu of classic dishes and plenty of seafood. Semiformal.

Island Hotel
273 2nd Street, Cedar Key tel: 352/543-5111; www.islandhotel-cedarkey.com
Historic wood-built inn with a seafood restaurant specializing in local crabs, clams and oysters.

Mesquite Charlie's
5901 N. "W" Street, Pensacola
tel: 850/434-0498
Famous charcoal-grilled steaks and seafood. Western decor; Little Cowpokes menu.

Staff's Seafood
24 S.W. Miracle Strip Parkway, Fort Walton
tel: 850/243-3482
Cross to the mainland for heaped mixed seafood skillets, gumbo, Florida lobster or steaks.

Budget

Andrew's Capital Bar & Grill
228 S. Adams Street, Tallahassee
tel: 850/222-3444;
www.andrewsdowntown.com
New York-style deli and grill with outdoor seating.

Barnacle Bill's
1830 N. Monroe Street, Tallahassee
tel: 850/385-8734; www.barnaclebills.com
Pasta, poultry, seafood; kids eat free on Sundays.

Billy's Oyster Bar I
3000 Thomas Drive, Panama City Beach
tel: 850/235-2349
Oysters every which way; lobster, crawfish, crab and shrimp.

Blue Desert Café
12518 S.R. 44, Cedar Key tel: 352/543-9111
Sandwiches, pastas, pizzas and home-cooked desserts dished up in a shotgun cottage.

Captain Dave's
3796 Old Highway 98, Destin
tel: 850/837-2627
Family style seafood spot overlooking the Gulf; dancing and entertainment.

The Hut
U.S. 98, Apalachicola tel: 850/653-9410
Rustic seafood and steak joint; a popular bar.

McGuire's Irish Pub
600 E. Gregory Street, Pensacola
tel: 850/433-6789; www.mcguirespub.com
Ribs, burgers, sandwiches, seafood.

Magnolia Grill
Brooks Bridge 98 Center, 255 Miracle Strip Parkway, Fort Walton tel: 850/302-0266; www.magnoliagrillfwb.com
Nostalgia-packed diner and good Cajun, Italian and seafood dining.

A

B

C

D

E

F

T

U

V

Y

Z

Acknowledgments

The Automobile Association wishes to thank the following photographers, libraries and associations for their assistance in the preparation of this book.

ALACHUA COUNTY VISITORS & CONVENTION BUREAU 26a, 27; **BABCOCK WILDERNESS ADVENTURES** 20a, 32; **BUSCH GARDENS** 24/5, 226b, 227; **DACS/© SALVADOR DALI, GALA-SALVADOR DALI FOUNDATION, DACS, LONDON 2005** 217; **DAYTONA INTERNATIONAL SPEEDWAY** 174a; **©DISNEY ENTERPRISES, INC.** 28, 29, 123, 124, 127, 128, 131, 133, 263; **MARY EVANS PICTURE LIBRARY** 37, 39; **HENRY FLAGLER MUSEUM** 160a; **FLORIDA DEPARTMENT OF COMMERCE** 23, 41, 64a, 64b, 83a, 83b, 164b, 183b, 184a, 190, 191, 225, 244b, 245, 246, 248, 251, 255; **GEIGER & ASSOCIATES** 15, 18/19, 197, 214; **GETTY IMAGES** 36/7; **GRAND ROMANCE** 185; **JIM GUND** 173a; **KISSIMMEE ST CLOUD CONVENTION & VISITORS BUREAU** 184b; **LEE COUNTY VISITORS & CONVENTION BUREAU** 200, 202, 205, 209; **NATURE PHOTOGRAPHERS LTD** 95b, 157 (P R Sterry), 159 (W S Paton), 211b P R Sterry); **HENRY PLANT MUSEUM** 226; **POPPERFOTO** 42b; **ROYAL GEOGRAPHIC SOCIETY** 32; **ST AUGUSTINE/ST JOHNS COUNTY CHAMBER OF COMMERCE** 26b, 43; **SARASOTA CONVENTION & VISITORS BUREAU** 222a, 222b, 223, 224a, 224b; **SPECTRUM COLOUR LIBRARY** 170b, 171; **EMMA STANFORD** 34t, 113; **TAMPA/HILLSBOROUGH CONVENTION & VISITORS BUREAU** 228; **UNIVERSAL STUDIOS** 118, 119, 120, 121; **ZIMMERMAN AGENCY** 257.

The remaining pictures are from the Association's own library (**AA WORLD TRAVEL LIBRARY**) and were taken by **Pete Bennett**, with the exception of the following pages: **Kirk Lee Aeder** 195; **Jon Davison** 4b, 10, 25, 51, 58a, 72, 74, 78, 99, 102/3, 107, 163, 241, 242; **Larry Dunmire** 165a; **David Lyons** 154b, 155; Larry Provo 14, 16, 17, 19, 21, 22, 33a, 33b, 38a, 38b, 44, 45, 47, 48a, 50/1, 52, 53, 54, 58b, 61, 65b, 70, 79, 80, 81a, 81b, 87, 88, 91, 92, 93, 95a, 98, 100, 101, 102, 107a, 138, 139, 140, 141, 142, 148, 149b, 150, 152, 153, 156, 160b, 161, 162, 166, 167, 168, 169, 194a, 244a, 245a, 250, 253a, 261; **Tony Souter** 116, 196; **James A Tims** 3, 4a, 5a, 5b, 6, 6/7, 7, 8a, 9a, 9b, 49, 63a, 71, 94, 97, 105, 106, 109b,144, 145, 149a, 154a, 173b, 199, 210, 211a, 213, 218, 220, 237.

Contributors

Original copy editor: Audrey Horne Revision verifier: Lindsay Bennett
Revision copy editor: Marilynne Lanng